The
King of the Jews

A Verse-by-Verse Commentary on

The Gospel According
to Matthew

by

John R. Rice, D.D., Litt.D.

www.solidchristianbooks.com

2015

Contents

5

AUTHOR'S PREFACE

May eternal praises rise to God for His Word, the Bible. If every reader and student of this commentary on the Gospel According to Matthew receives one-tenth of the spiritual light and blessing received in preparing this commentary, the results will be beyond calculation.

This commentary grew out of a series of correspondence lessons I gave to some five hundred students in 1937-38. Before that time I had, with five years' toil, prepared written notes on every chapter of every book in the Bible. As pastor of the Galilean Baptist Church in Dallas, Texas, I had systematically led the Sunday School through a study of the Bible, chapter by chapter. But in the midst of the heavy labors and responsibilities of the ministry, with the duties of pastor, with regular radio services, with frequent revival campaigns, the author felt himself harried and rushed too much for the joyful devotional study of the Bible which he desired. The preparing of from five to ten messages each week became burdensome. I was determined to force myself to give the time to Bible study which was needed, so I deliberately undertook to give a correspondence course of lessons through the Gospel of Matthew, preparing and mailing the lessons on one chapter each week. There followed twenty-eight of the happiest weeks I have ever spent. Now sermon topics and themes and texts crowded to my mind so that I was never able to preach often enough to use the material God gave me. Those Bible lessons were the basis for this commentary.

Again in recent years the enormous editorial and administrative burdens, in addition to my evangelistic ministry, led me to again seek a refreshing in Bible study by going back to a thorough verse-by-verse study of Matthew and the enlarging and rewriting of the chapters on Matthew. So blessed has been the result that I have solemnly vowed that whenever again the Lord's work gets burdensome and I am tempted to neglect that wonderful fount of blessings, the Bible, and find it difficult to take time for the constant study and meditation in the Word itself, which should be the Christian's joy as well as his food, I will prepare a commentary on another book in the Bible.

It is only fair that in the beginning every student should understand the viewpoint of this commentary. It agrees with the inspired statement of the Psalmist, "For ever, O Lord, thy word is settled in heaven" (Ps. 119:89). And again, "Thy word is true from the beginning: and every one of thy righteous judgments endureth forever" (Ps. 119:160). I agree with the inspired prophet who said, "The grass withereth, the flower fadeth: but the word of our God shall stand for ever" (Isa. 40:8). And we believe With the dear Lord Jesus our Saviour, the mighty Son of God, that "Man shall not live by bread alone, but by every word that proceeded out of the mouth of God" (Matt. 4:4). And He said, "For verily I say unto you, Till heaven and earth pass, one jot or one tittle shall in no wise pass from the law, till all be fulfilled" (Matt. 5:18). I believe in the verbal inspiration of the original manuscripts of the Bible. While I do not claim there have been no mistakes of copying and translating, yet I believe that we have at hand substantially, without any material or serious variation, the eternal and infallible Word of God. And the author has come to this conclusion through many years of, intensive study, as a university and seminary student, a college teacher, an author whose books and pamphlets have reached some fourteen million copies circulated in twenty-two languages, an editor for twenty years, an evangelist of wide-spread experience, and as a Christian who has tried the promises of God and found them all true! I am convinced that the only people who do not believe the Bible are those who have not studied it devoutly and tried it thoroughly, and do not know the evidence in its favor, or who have a deliberate and wicked bias against God and the truth.

Thus I believe all the great fundamentals of the Christian faith. The Bible is the infallible Word of God. Christ is the pre-existent Creator, the virgin-born Saviour who died for our sins and rose bodily from the grave for our justification. Believing the Bible, I have no trouble in believing all the historic Christian faith clearly taught therein.

I believe in the premillennial second coming of Christ. Although that position is not what we were taught in college and seminary, it is the position to which we have been forced by a believing, childlike study and faith in the Word of God.

But let it be noted that I do not endorse every speculation and heresy which some would attach to the premillennial position. I do not believe that the rapture of the saints will be secret. I believe it is imminent, will be sudden, unexpected. I do not believe that one can, by reading the newspapers, find signs that will indicate when Christ's return is approaching. I believe that Christ will return, may return at any moment, because He said so. I do not believe that anybody can tell even approximately when Christ will return.

I believe that Christ did offer Himself as King to the Jews. But let it be clearly understood that I believe all the things foretold in the Old Testament would come to pass. The crucifixion of Christ, His resurrection from the dead, the tribulation time, the rise of the Man of Sin, etc, were plainly foretold in the Old Testament. Daniel's seventieth week must transpire as prophesied.

Let it be understood also that I do not believe God has ever had more than one plan of salvation nor that He ever will have any other. Unsaved Jews who died without Christ are lost without remedy, just as is every other person who has died without Christ. The plan of salvation to be offered Jews through the tribulation time and afterward will be exactly the same as offered Jews and Gentiles today.

It is unfortunate that the plain truth that Jesus is coming again literally, bodily, personally, should have been brought into reproach by so many heresies. But heresies concerning great doctrines do not invalidate true doctrines.

The reader will find this commentary on Matthew to be really a very earnest Bible study. You will not find a compilation of what all the other commentaries have said. You will not find the pages cluttered with speculation and guesses. We have studied many authors but our primary study has been the Word of God itself, and the reader will find that again and again we interpret Scripture by Scripture. Thousands of references to other parts of the Bible will help to make clear the meaning of the Scriptures as one studies the Gospel According to Matthew.

We tremble to send the book forth. It is not a fraction as good as it ought to be to tell of the mighty King of the Jews, the Saviour of sinners. Doubtless many faults and omissions will appear. Yet it is my constant prayer that God will use these comments to shed light upon the Blessed Book and that fires of evangelism will burn warm in the hearts of those who study it. Oh, to win more of the precious souls for whom Christ died! We believe that God has given some

15

help here for those who would be soul winners and those who would preach the Word of God with power. If so, may His name be praised.

JOHN R. RICE

April, 1955

Introduction to the Gospel of Matthew

THE AUTHOR: From earliest times it has been agreed that this first Gospel was written by "Matthew the publican," as he calls himself (Matt. 10:3). In the note on the Gospel of Matthew, the International Standard Bible Encyclopedia says, "The Gospel... was unanimously ascribed by the testimony of the ancient church to the Apostle Matthew..." (p. 2009). The story of his call to follow Jesus is given in Matthew 9:9, Mark 2:14, and Luke 5:27-29. Notice that Mark and Luke call him Levi. Mark gives the name of his father, Alphaeus. The publicans were tax collectors, usually dishonest extortioners, often rich and always hated by the Jews. It is remarkable that Matthew, even after the death and resurrection of Christ, still called himself "Matthew the publican." There is no more reason for calling Matthew "Saint Matthew" than to say "Saint Isaiah," or "Saint Moses." All Christians are saints (Rom. 1:7; I Cor. 1:2).

DATE: The Gospel According to Matthew was evidently written between 50 and 70 A.D. It seems certain that the solemn warning of Jesus in Matthew 23:33-39, which certainly looked forward to the utter destruction of Jerusalem, would not have been given with no further comment if that destruction had already happened. Again in Matthew 24:1-3 the coming destruction of the temple was foretold, and concerning all these things, the Apostle Matthew says, "Whoso readeth [Matthew's Gospel], let him understand" (Matt. 24:15). It seems impossible that these things could have been written after the destruction of Jerusalem and after the dispersion of Jews to the whole world, with a slaughter of many thousands, without those matters being referred to in the Gospel of Matthew discussing these things.

THE GOSPEL: It is called "The Gospel According to Matthew." The "Gospel" means good news of Christ's life, death, and resurrection. See Paul's definition of the Gospel in I Corinthians 15:1-7, and you will understand why the book of Matthew is a "Gospel" and the book of Romans or of Acts is not. All books of the Bible are the Word of God, but these four which tell of the life, death, and resurrection of Jesus are particularly called "the Gospels." Let the beginner learn now to compare Matthew, Mark, Luke, and John to find the same events. The first three are called the "Synoptic Gospels" because they follow about the same chronological order and give many of the same events. The book of John differs more widely. Each separate Gospel gives many events and teachings that the others do not give. Each one is a divinely inspired and accurate account of events as far as it goes.

HUMAN SOURCES OF MATTHEW'S GOSPEL: Endless and needless speculation has concerned itself with so- called sources of Matthew's Gospel. Actually, the historic Christian position, fully credible, is that Matthew's Gospel was inspired of God, word for word in the original manuscript, as were all the books of the Bible. Matthew was but the willing, believing agent of the Holy Spirit. Divine inspiration can account perfectly for similarities and differences between Matthew and the other Gospels. Some have supposed that the Gospel of Matthew was first written in Hebrew by Matthew. Jamieson, Fausset, and Brown's *Critical, Experimental and Practical Commentary* in the introduction to the Gospels, says, "*Papias... is* reported by Irenaeus, Eusebius, &c,, to have stated, in a lost work of his, that 'Matthew drew up the oracles (meaning his Gospel) in the Hebrew dialect (or tongue), and every one interpreted them as he was able' " (p. xxviii). Others of the church fathers thought the same. But this commentary says, "There is the strongest reason to suspect that most of the preceding testimonies are, after all, but one testimony – that of Papias – repeated from hand to hand" (p. xxix). Again, "We have not a tittle of historical evidence that it is a *Translation,* either by Matthew himself or any one else" (p. xxxi). And "Further, not a trace can be discovered in this Gospel itself of its being a Translation (p. xxxi). Still again, this great commentary said, "It remains, then, that our Greek Matthew is the original of that Gospel, and that no other original ever existed... The following among others hold to this view, of the sole originality of the Greek Matthew: *Erasmus, Calvin, Beza, Lightfoot, Wetstein, Lardner, Hug, Fritzsche, Credner, de Wette, Stuart, da Costa, Fairbairn, Roberts*" (p. xxxii). Dean Alford (in later writings), James Orr, E. Y. Mullins, agree. It is only third-hand, inconsequential hearsay, that the Gospel of Matthew was ever written in Aramaic or Hebrew before written in Greek.

Some have imagined that Matthew was copied largely from Mark simply because of similar synoptic material. However, there is no evidence except an unbelieving determination to find a human explanation for the book of Matthew, aside from divine inspiration. Unbelieving scholars have manufactured also an imaginary manuscript, "Q," from which they think the Synoptic Gospels quoted largely. There is no such manuscript now, and there is no real evidence that anybody ever saw such a manuscript or that it ever existed. It is a creature of the imagination of unbelieving scholarship. We agree with Dr. Henry C. Thiessen: "We feel that Matthew and Luke are not mere human adaptations of the materials in Mark, together with some more or less reliable supplementary materials derived from other sources; but that they are equally inspired with Mark, divinely originated to give specific pictures of the wonderful life and work of our Lord" (Introduction to the New Testament, p. 117).

If Matthew copied anything, he did it only under the clear instruction of the Holy Spirit, and we have not a hint in the Scriptures themselves that Matthew copied. The Holy Spirit gave the matter; the Holy Spirit gave the words, so Matthew did not need to rely upon his own judgment, his memory, the testimony of eyewitnesses, upon manuscripts before him, or any other human source. If he used any human source, he did it only by divine inspiration which would correct all the mistakes and make a perfect, infallibly accurate part of the divine revelation, the Word of God.

MATTHEW I

Verse 1 The Special Emphasis of Matthew's Gospel

This verse shows the viewpoint and emphasis of the book of Matthew as it differs from the other Gospels. Compare it with Mark 1:1, "the gospel of Jesus Christ, the Son of God," with no genealogy, since Christ, in Mark, is pictured as a servant, though the Son of God. Luke begins with human events, then in Luke 3:28-38 the genealogy begins with Jesus and traces Him back to Adam. So Luke is primarily the Gospel of Jesus as the "Son of man," the God in human form, with human temptations which He overcame, human compassion for all men, the Christ of the Gentiles as well as of the Jews. In Luke, Jesus repeatedly calls Himself "the Son of Man." Compare this also with John 1:1-5. The book of John was written to prove that Jesus is the Son of God (John 20:31), and His human ancestry is not discussed, but the inspired Word leaps back to the ages before the creation when Christ was with the Father and equal with God, "in the beginning."

Now the Gospel of Matthew is the story of "Jesus Christ, the son of David, the son of Abraham" (Matt. 1:1).

Jesus to Inherit David's Throne

"THE SON OF DAVID." Jesus Christ is descended from David and so inherits the eternal covenant to David's seed. Read that covenant in II Samuel 7:4-16:

"And it came to pass that night that the word of the Lord came unto Nathan, saying, Go and tell my servant David, Thus saith the Lord, Shalt thou build me an house for me to dwell in? Whereas I have not dwelt in any house since the time that I brought up the children of Israel out of Egypt, even to this day, but have walked in a tent and in a tabernacle. In all the places wherein I have walked with all the children of Israel spake I a word with any of the tribes of Israel, whom I commanded to feed my people Israel, saying, Why build ye

not me an house of cedar? Now therefore so shalt thou say unto my servant David, Thus saith the Lord of hosts, I took thee from the sheepcoie, from following the sheep, to be ruler over my people, over Israel: And I was with thee whithersoever thou wentest, and have cut off all thine enemies out of thy sight, and have made thee a great name, like unto the name of the great men that are in the earth. Moreover I will appoint a place for my people Israel, and will plant them, that they may dwell in a place of their own, and move n neither shall the children of wickedness afflict them any more, as beforetime, And as since the time that I commanded judges to be over my people Israel, and have caused thee to rest from all thine enemies. Also the Lord telleth thee that he will make thee an house. And when thy days be fulfilled, and thou shaltt sleep with thy fathers, I will set up thy seed after thee, which shall proceed out of thy bowels, and I will establish his kingdom. He shall build an house for my name, and I will stablish the throne of his kingdom for ever. I will be his father, and he shall be my son. If he commit iniquity, I will chasten him with the rod of and with the stripes of the children of men: But my mercy shall not depart away from him, as I took it from Saul, whom I put away before thee. And thine house and thy kingdom shall be established for ever before thee: thy throne shall be established for ever."

Also read the same covenant in I Chronicles 17:7-14:

"Now therefore thus shalt thou say unto my servant David, Thus saith the Lord of hosts, took thee from the sheep- cote, even from following the sheep, that thou shouldest be ruler over my people Israel: And I have been with thee whithersoever thou has walked, and have cut off all thine enemies from before thee, and have made thee a name like the name of the great men that are in the earth. Also I will ordain a place for my people Israel, and will plant them, and they shall dwell in their place, and shall be moved no more; neither shall the children of wickedness waste them any more, as at the beginning, And since the time that I commanded judges to be over my people Israel. Moreover I will subdue all thine enemies. Furthermore I tell thee that the Lord will build thee an house. And it shall come to pass, when thy days be expired that thou must go to be with thy fathers, that I will raise up thy seed after thee, which shall be of thy sons; and I will establish his kingdom. He shall build me an house, and I will stablish his throne for ever. I will be his father, and he shall be my son: and I will not take my mercy away

from him, as I took it from him that was before thee: But I will settle him in mine house and in my kingdom for ever: and his throne shall be established for evermore."

God promised David that in the future He would establish David's throne at Jerusalem, with David's seed upon that throne *"for ever"* The only way that can possibly be will be for Jesus to come back and reign on David's throne, and for that promised millennial reign to be merged into the everlasting reign of God.

See also the promise of Isaiah 9:6, 7, particularly verse 7:

"For unto us a child is born, unto us a son is given: and the government shall be upon his shoulder: and his name shall be called Wonderful, Counsellor, The mighty God, The everlasting Father, The Prince of Peace. Of the increase of his government and peace there shall be no end, upon the throne of David, and upon his kingdom, to order it, and to establish it with judgment and with justice from henceforth even for ever. The zeal of the Lord of hosts will perform this."

See Isaiah, chapter 11; also see Psalm 89:3, 4, 34-37.

Notice the promise of the Angel Gabriel to Mary in Luke 1:32, 33:

"He shall be great, and shall be called the Son of the Highest: and the Lord God shall give unto him the throne of his father David: And he shall reign over the house of Jacob for ever; and of his kingdom there shall be no end."

So Matthew tells the story of Jesus as the Son of David who will return to the earth and reign on David's throne, restoring His kingdom forever. Jesus is THE SEED, long promised to David.

Jesus, the Seed of Abraham, Inherits His Covenant

"THE SON OF ABRAHAM." To understand this, you must read God's covenant to Abraham in Genesis, chapters 13, 14 and 15, and in Genesis 17:6-8:

"And I will make thee exceeding fruitful, and I will make nations of thee, and kings shall come out of thee. And I will establish my covenant between me and thee and thy seed after thee in their

22

generations for an everlasting covenant, to be a God unto thee, an after thee. And I will give unto thee, and to thy seed after thee, the land wherein thou art a stranger, all the land of Canaan, for an everlasting possession; and I will be their God."

Abraham's seed is to inherit all the land of Canaan "for an everlasting possession." The only possession Jews have ever had of Canaan has been temporary thus far, but their possession of the land will be eternally established forever. The same thing is promised in many other places. See II Samuel 7:10, Jeremiah 23:3-8, Jeremiah 33:14-26, and Ezekiel 37:15-28. Notice that many other passages tell of the regathering of Israel under one king, the seed of David, in the land of Palestine. Christ will inherit this land promised to Abraham together with Abraham and others of his seed. Read carefully Galatians 3:16-18, particularly verse 16. To Abraham and his seed the promises were made, not to many "seeds," but primarily to one "SEED," that is, Christ.

Matthew is written, then, about Jesus as the King of the Jews.

The terms, then, "King of the Jews" and "the Son of David" will be used a number of times in the book of Matthew and the Gospel will tell how Jesus was born "King of the Jews," how the wise men of the East sought the "King of the Jews" (Matt. 2:2), how Jesus was crucified as "THE KING OF THE JEWS" (Matt. 27:37).

Verses 2-16 The Official Genealogy of Jesus

This is the ancestry of Joseph, the husband of Mary, and not literally the ancestry of Christ. This is the *official* record of Christ through His foster father, Joseph. The *literal* genealogy of Christ through His mother, Mary, is given in Luke 3:23-38. A prayerful notice will prove that they are not the same. The father of Joseph here (vs. 16) is Jacob. Joseph was evidently son-in-law of Heli, the father of Mary (Luke 3:23). Notice the words printed in italics which were not in the original manuscripts but inserted by the trans-lators to make sense, and rightly so. The two genealogies are not the same. The Scofield Reference Bible properly says:

In Matthew, where unquestionably we have the genealogy of Joseph, we are told (I. 16) that Joseph was the son of Jacob. In what sense, then, could he be called in Luke "the son of Heli"? He could not be by natural generation the son both of Jacob and of Heli. But in Luke it is not said that Heli *begat* Joseph, so that the natural explanation is that Joseph was the son-in-law of Heli, who was, like himself, a descendant of David. That he should in that case be called "son of Heli" ("son" is not in the Greek, but rightly supplied by the translators) would be in accord with Jewish usage (cf. I Sam. 24. 16). The conclusion is therefore inevitable that in Luke we have Mary's genealogy; and Joseph was "son of Heli" because espoused to Heli's daughter. The genealogy in Luke is Mary's, whose father, Heli, was descended from David.

Notice that the *official* genealogy here in Matthew runs back through the line of reigning kings from Jechonias (vs. 12), otherwise called Jehoiachin, or Coniah, back to Solomon and David (vss. 6, 7), but the   genealogy of

Mary goes back outside the reigning line to Nathan, the brother of Solomon, another son of David. Study this very carefully. The difference in these two genealogies explains Jeremiah 22:28-30:

"Is this man Coniah a despised broken is he a vessel wherein is no pleasure? wherefore are they cast out, he and his seed, and are cast into a land which they earth, earth, earth, hear the word of the Lord. Thus the Lord, Write ye this man childless, a man that shall not prosper in his days: for no man of his seed shall prosper, sitting upon the throne of David, and ruling ruling any more in Judah."

Coniah, another name for Jehoiachin or Jechonias, was, with his brother, Zedekiah, the last of the reigning line of kings on David's throne. That is, his son did not sit upon the throne of David. And God said that he was to be written down as childless since no descendant of his WOULD EVER reign on David's throne. This man, Coniah, or Jechonias, is in the genealogy of Joseph (Matt. 1:12). So while it is the *official* genealogy of Jesus, it is not His literal genealogy, *could not be!* No person descended from Jechonias could ever reign on David's throne. Joseph was descended from Coniah, so could not be the father of Jesus, if Jesus is to reign on David's throne as promised. This shows how both Old and New Testaments teach that Jesus was born of a virgin, without a human father, and that Joseph could not have been the real father of Jesus.

From Abraham to David are included in both genealogies. Both Mary and Joseph were descended from David. And Jesus was both officially and literally of the seed of David and of Abraham; officially through His foster father, Joseph, and literally through His real mother, Mary.

Do not fail to prayerfully meditate on this wonderful genealogy in Matthew 1:2-16. Notice the following points of blessing – (1) Gentiles are included in the ancestry of Christ: Rahab of Jericho (Rachab, vs. 5), Ruth the Moabitess (vs. 5), and the wives of others of these men. (2) Certain women are called by name: Tamar (Thamar, vs. 3), Rahab, Ruth, Bath-sheba, "her that had been the wife of Urias" (vs. 6). (3) Of these women three were harlots or adulteresses: Tamar (Gen. 38), Rahab (Josh. 6), and Bath-sheba (II Sam. 11). (4) In the genealogy are kings and paupers, saints and the vilest sinners; for instance, study the life of wicked Manasseh (Manasses, II Kings 21:1-18 and II Chron. 33:1-20). The lesson from these things is that Christ is the Saviour of Gentiles as well as of Jews, the Saviour of harlots and idolaters as well as of moral people, the Saviour of poor as well as of rich. "For he hath made him to be sin for us, who knew no sin; that we might be made the righteousness of God in him" (II Cor. 5:21). "...God sending his own Son in the likeness of sinful flesh, and for sin, condemned sin in the flesh" (Rom. 8:3).

Verse 17 Three Times Fourteen Generations

For convenience and memory the genealogy is divided into three series of fourteen. Generations are counted according to the Jewish custom and may skip from father to son or from grandfather to grandson. Actually three men in the line are left out as you see by comparing this genealogy in Matthew with the stricter genealogy given in I Chronicles 3:10-16. Those omitted are Ahaziah, Joash, and Amaziah (I Chron. 3:11, 12). Matthew Henry suggests that they may have been omitted because they were of the wicked seed of Queen Athaliah, the daughter of Ahab and Jezebel of the Northern Kingdom. Read the story of them in II Chronicles, chapters 22 to 25, and in II Kings 8:24 and II Kings 14:20. Read God's estimate of Ahab and Jezebel in I Kings 16:29-33 which may explain why these three of their descendants on the throne of Judah were omitted from the official genealogy of the King.

Remember this is the official genealogy. Possibly it was identical with that kept in the temple records. It might have been used here by God's choice because it is the same as the official Jewish record. It would therefore follow their custom of counting the genealogy of the king of Judah.

Verses 18,19 Joseph's Heartbreaking Dilemma

Compare this with Luke 1:26-35 where the details of the annunciation and conception are related. The word *espoused* means engaged, but was much stronger than present-day engagements. We suppose it involved a contract of marriage, but they had not actually come together as man and wife. This engagement would need to be broken by divorce, such as was permitted Jews in Deuteronomy 24:1. Consider Joseph's heartbreaking predicament. He knew Mary as a virtuous and devout woman, his promised bride, yet apparently she had played the harlot and so according to Mosaic Law, if publicly exposed, should be stoned according to Leviticus 20:10 and especially Deuteronomy 22:23, 24. Since Joseph could not know for sure the circumstances, whether her supposed sin was in the city or in the country (according to Deut. 22:25-27), then Joseph was not obligated to expose her. Being a tender-hearted and merciful good man, he chose to put her away privily, evidently with a broken heart.

Verses 20-25 The Virtue of Joseph

In these verses Joseph stands out as a man of the finest Christian character. First, he was just and merciful. Second, he was thoughtful, anxiously and prayerfully seeking to do right ("while he thought on these things..." vs. 20). Third, he was a man of deep faith, immediately believing the angel. Fourth, he willingly obeyed the command of God to take Mary as his wife and he named the baby *Jesus,* according to command. Fifth, Joseph must have been a man of great restraint and strength of character since he "knew her not till she had brought forth her firstborn son..." Though Mary

26

lived in his home and was legally his wife, he allowed her to remain a virgin according to the prophecy of Isaiah 7:14. One might preach a blessed sermon upon Joseph.

Mary a Normal Wife and Mother After Jesus Was Born

Please note again, "Then Joseph... took unto him his wife: And knew her not till she had brought forth her firstborn son." This Scripture not only indicates that Mary was a virgin when Jesus was conceived, and a virgin when Jesus was born, but it also indicates that after the birth of Jesus, Joseph and Mary had the normal relations of husband and wife. Since never a word of Scripture is wasted, it is fair to assume that if Joseph "knew her not till she had brought forth her firstborn son," he did know her *after* she had brought forth her firstborn son. The Catholic dogma that Mary is a perpetual virgin and was never a wife is not taught in the Bible.

Again, the Scripture names Jesus as her "firstborn son." Jesus is not called simply Mary's son, and certainly not called her only son, but her "firstborn son." The language infers that there were other sons and daughters born to Mary and Joseph after the birth of Jesus. Matthew 13:55, 56 says, "Is not this the carpenter's son? is not his mother called Mary? and his brethren, James, and Joses, and Simon, and Judas? And his sisters, are they not all with us?" The brothers of Jesus are mentioned many times, for example in Matthew 12:46, 47; John 7:3-5. In Galatians 1:19 Paul said, "But other of the apostles saw I none, save James the Lord's brother."

Always in the Bible these brothers of Jesus are called brothers or brethren, and the Bible believer should take these terms at face value.

But the strongest proof that Mary had other children is Psalm 69:8, "I am become a stranger to my brethren and an alien unto my mother's children." John 2:17 quotes the preceding verse as referring to Jesus, as verse 21 clearly does.

The Catholic idea that these men were cousins of Jesus, and that Mary was a perpetual virgin, never having other children, is not borne out by the Scriptures.

In Luke 1:36 the angel of God told Mary, "And, behold, thy cousin Elisabeth…" So there is a Greek word for cousin, but it was never used as regarding the brothers of the Lord Jesus.

Besides, no good spiritual and doctrinal end is served by teaching that Mary was born without sin, lived without marriage, was carried bodily to Heaven, is "Queen of Heaven," etc. All that is calculated to take glory from Jesus Christ and put it on Mary. Joseph 'knew not Mary till she brought forth her firstborn son.' After that, they lived normally as godly Christian husband and wife, had other children some of whom, at least, are named in the Bible. Mary was only human, not deity incarnate as was Jesus. She is no mediator, no intercessor for mankind. To pray to Mary is folly; to worship her is idolatry.

The angel here was probably the same Angel Gabriel that appeared to Mary (Luke 1:26-33). The same explanation is made about the child conceived in her womb, that it was done by the Holy Ghost without a human father.

May I suggest certain themes for meditation. (1) The birth of Jesus from the body of a human mother, nursed at her breast, forever glorifies motherhood and childbearing. (2) The name *Jesus* means deliverer, saviour, just as does the Old Testament name, *Joshua.* Joshua, in the New Testament, is called Jesus (Acts 7:45). (3) Consider how Joshua, with the same name, was a type of Christ. Joshua followed Moses; so Christ and grace follow the law; the New Testament follows the Old Testament. Joshua led the children of Israel into the Promised Land out of the wilderness; so Christ will lead us into His kingdom and victory.

As Joshua delivered the children of Israel from all their enemies, so Christ saves us from sin and will eventually deliver His saints from all the power of the Evil One. (4) Consider the blessed ministry of angels in revealing the will of God in connection with the Bible.

In verses 22 and 23 the reference is to Isaiah 7:14. Here it was foretold hundreds of years before that the Saviour should be born of a virgin.

The Virgin Birth of Christ

The virgin birth of Christ is one of the most important doctrines of the Bible. Notice from verse 23 that "a virgin shall be with child," or as it is given in Isaiah 7:14, "a virgin shall conceive." Mary conceived while yet a virgin. She was still a virgin when the Saviour was born: "and shall bring forth a son." That is further stated by verses 24 and 25: "Joseph... knew her not till she had brought forth her firstborn son." The virgin birth is particularly stated in Isaiah, in Matthew, and in Luke. When the angel gave the promise of the birth of Christ to Mary, she said, "How shall this be, seeing I know not a man?" (Luke 1:34). Read the answer of the angel in Luke 1:35. Jesus was conceived in the womb of the virgin by the Holy Ghost, without a human father, and for that reason, says the angel, "therefore also that holy thing which shall be born of thee shall be called the Son of God." Jesus is the Son of God because He was virgin born. If the virgin birth of Christ is not true, then Christ is not the unique Son of God He claims to be. Any teacher or preacher who doubts the virgin birth of Christ is an infidel. This is a cardinal doctrine.

Note how many times the virgin birth is taught explicitly and implicitly in the Bible.

1. Isaiah 7:14 clearly states, "Therefore the Lord himself shall give you a sign; Behold, a virgin shall conceive, and bear a son, and shall call his name Immanuel."

2. Jeremiah 31:22 says, "...for the Lord hath created a new thing in the earth, A woman shall compass a man." Does not this mean that a woman alone, without a man, should have a man-child? That is what Mary did. And that virgin birth is "a new thing in the earth," unique, never to be repeated. Christ alone is virgin born.

3. Matthew 1:20-25 tells us that that which was conceived in the womb of Mary was by the Holy Ghost, fulfilling Isaiah 7:14; that a virgin did conceive, and, still a virgin, did bring forth a son, and that this Son is our Saviour, God's Son come in the flesh by a miraculous birth.

4. Luke 1:26-37 tells how the Angel Gabriel appeared "To a virgin espoused to a man whose name was Joseph, of the house of David; and the virgin's name was Mary." It states Mary's honest question:

"How shall this be, seeing I know not a man?" Then the answer of the Angel Gabriel is given in Luke 1:35. "And the angel answered and said unto her, The Holy Ghost shall come upon thee, and the power of the Highest shall overshadow thee: therefore also that holy thing which shall be born of thee shall be called the Son of God." A miracle? Certainly! But the Angel Gabriel settled that easily for Mary and for all believers in the God of the Bible when he explained to Mary in Luke 1:37, "For with God nothing shall be impossible."

5. Luke 2:48, 49 tells us that Jesus, at the age of twelve, clearly insisted that Joseph was not his father, but that in a peculiar and unique sense God alone was His Father. Mary said to Jesus, referring to Joseph, "thy father and I have sought thee sorrowing." Of course she knew that Joseph was not the father of Jesus, but spoke of him so as a matter of custom. All over the world foster fathers are called "father" by adopted children. My own father taught me to call my stepmother "mama," not meaning that she was my mother, but that she took a mother's place. So Joseph took a father's place, and thus Mary spoke of Joseph as "thy father." But Jesus answered, "How is it that ye sought me? wist ye not that I must be about my Father's business?" (Luke 2:49). His clear meaning is that while He was subject to Joseph, it must not be thought that Joseph was His father. God Himself was literally, physically, His Father. He was virgin born, with no human father!

6. John's Gospel likewise teaches the virgin birth in stating that Jesus is "the only begotten Son" (John 1:14, 18; 3:16, 18). "Only begotten" means the only one begotten physically, directly, and literally, by God, without a human father. That could mean nothing less than the virgin birth!

7. Hebrews 11:17 also speaks of Isaac, who was a type of Christ, as Abraham's "only begotten son." Isaac was not really Abraham's only begotten son, but was counted, so as a type of God's only begotten Son.

8. First John 4:9 has the same expression.

9. But everywhere in the New Testament the virgin birth of Jesus is implied. The bungling, zealous new convert, Philip, trying to win Nathanael, spoke of Jesus as "Jesus of Nazareth, the son of Joseph" (John 1:45), It is not surprising that he, having been

converted probably that very day, spoke of Jesus by accommodation as "the son of Joseph." But there is not any serious statement that Jesus is the son of Joseph in the whole Bible, nor is there a single implication that He was begotten, conceived, and bora of natural generation. Throughout the New Testament the things said about Jesus could only be true if He were supernaturally conceived, the very Son of God literally, as no one else ever was the Son of God.

Again and again Jesus is spoken of as Creator. "All things were made by him; and without him was not any thing made that was made" (John 1:3). See also Hebrews 1:2 and Ephesians 3:9. His pre-existence with God is clearly stated. "In the beginning was the Word, and the Word was with God... The same was in the beginning with God" (John 1:1, 2). "And the Word was made flesh..." (John 1:14). The birth of Jesus simply meant that God's pre-existent Son was put in the womb of a virgin by an incomparable miracle. And so Christ, the pre-existent Christ who had been with the Father from the beginning, came into this world as man by a virgin birth.

In fact, it is repeatedly claimed that Christ is deity, that Christ is God, one with the Father. "...And the Word was God" (John 1:1). "I and my Father are one" (John 10:30). That meant, necessarily, that Jesus was different from other men, essentially different in origin and nature. He really is, as Isaiah 9:6 plainly tells us, not only the child born, the Son given, but "The mighty God, The everlasting Father." Jesus is God in human form! That sets Him apart from every other child born in the world and makes absolutely necessary His supernatural conception and His virgin birth.

In John, chapter 8, this question of Christ's deity and origin came up for discussion between Christ and the Pharisees. Jesus said, "Ye neither know me, nor my Father: if ye had known me, ye should have known my Father also" (John 8:19). Again He said, "Ye are from beneath; I am from above: ye are of this world; l am not of this world. I said therefore unto you, that ye shall die in your sins: for if ye believe not that I am he, ye shall die in your sins" (John 8:23, 24).

Here is a clear statement from Jesus Himself that He was from above and that all others are from beneath. He said, "ye are of this world; I am not of this world." The Jews to whom Jesus spoke were, by natural generation and by natural birth, of this world, born of the flesh. Jesus was, by supernatural conception, the only begotten of the Father, from above. Jesus certainly referred to His origin here. It was the origin of His physical body, too, to which He referred, because He was clearly speaking of the physical generation of the Pharisees to whom He spoke. Jesus meant that these Pharisees were begotten naturally of a tainted, sinful race, with a human father and a human mother and a natural birth. He was begotten supernaturally by the Spirit of God from above, and so was literally (the only one physically begotten) of God. By origin Christ was miraculous; all others are natural. He was born of a virgin without a human father; all others have human fathers.

The virgin birth of Christ is an essential doctrine interwoven with all the Word of God. To deny the virgin birth is to deny the deity of Christ, the inspiration of the Bible, the foundation of Christianity.

Matthew 1:23 Is God's Translation of Isaiah 7:14

Matthew 1:22 and 23 not only says that Jesus was born of a virgin; it says that Isaiah 7:14 says the same thing! "Now all this was done, that it might be fulfilled which was spoken of the Lord by the prophet, saying, Behold, a virgin shall be with child, and shall bring forth a son, and they shall call his name Emmanuel, which being interpreted is, God with us." This Scripture clearly claims to give a translation of Isaiah 7:14. So the new Revised Standard Version of the Bible is mistaken and wrong in translating Isaiah 7:14, "Behold... a young woman shall conceive..." It should be, "Behold, a virgin shall conceive." Isaiah 7:14, then, is a prophecy of the virgin birth of Christ, and only unbelievers who do not accept the Bible as the authoritative Word of God will deny it. The Greek word *parthenos,* translated *virgin* in the King James Version in Matthew 1:23, is also translated the same way in the RSV, the American Standard Version, and practically every other English translation of the Bible. There can be no possible misunderstanding of the word here in Matthew. It expressly claims not only that Jesus was born of a virgin, but that Isaiah 7:14 foretold this virgin birth. It is wonderful, that with all the discussion about what Isaiah 7:14 really means, we have the infallibly inspired answer from God in Matthew 1:23. Isaiah 7:14 says not merely that a young woman should conceive and bear a son, Immanuel, but that this young woman would be a virgin.

In the Septuagint, a translation of the Old Testament into Greek by Hebrew scholars some two hundred years before Christ, Isaiah 7:14 is translated into the Greek, as it is in our Greek New Testament, in Matthew 1 ;23. For the Hebrew word *almah* in Isaiah 7:14, the Septuagint used the Greek word *parthenos*, clearly and indisputably meaning *virgin.*

At the present time all translators of the Old Testament deal with a dead language and must refer to lexicons, or search out the usage of Hebrew words in the Old Testament the best they can. But the translators of the Septuagint translated from their native tongue, the living Hebrew language which they used regularly, into the Greek, then a common language. No modern translator has the advantages in translating Hebrew which the seventy elders translating the Septuagint had. They said that *almah* in Isaiah 7:14 meant *parthenos* just as Matthew 1:23 says in the Greek, or literally *virgin* in English.

The Hebrew word *almah* translated in Isaiah 7:14 in the King James Version and the American Standard Version, the Septuagint, and most other translations, as *virgin* occurs in the Old Testament Hebrew six other times as follows:

In Genesis 24:43 it is used of the virgin bride (Rebekah) which Abraham's servant prayed he might find for Isaac.

In the Song of Solomon 1:3 we read, "Because of the savour of thy good ointments thy name is as ointment poured forth, therefore do the virgins love thee." There is no indication in the context that the term *virgins* here means anything but virgins.

In the same book, the Song of Solomon 6:8, the Hebrew word *almah* is used again, translated *virgin:* "There are threescore queens, and fourscore concubines, and virgins without number." Here the term *virgins* certainly means single girls, not queens, and not concubines, but literally virgin girls.

Maid is a synonym for *virgins,* and twice in the Old Testament *almah* is translated *maid.*

In Exodus 2:8 the word is used about little Miriam, the sister of the baby Moses who watched his little basket boat, and ran to get her mother as a Hebrew nurse to work for Pharaoh's daughter, caring for Moses. All the Hebrew tradition was that Miriam was a small child at the time, and the Scriptures indicate as much. Obviously she would be regarded as a virgin and obviously *young woman* would not be a proper translation for the word *almah* in Exodus 2:8.

In Proverbs 30:18 and 19 three wonderful, beautiful things are mentioned. "Yea, four which I know not." And one of these wonderful, beautiful things is the course of young love, "the way of a man with a maid." The word *maid* is a translation of the Hebrew word *almah* and obviously refers to a virgin girl wooed by a man who falls in love with her.

In Psalm 68:25 the Hebrew word *almah* is translated *damsels,* and refers to girls in a holy procession. "The singers went before, the players on instruments followed after; among them were the damsels playing with timbrels." These young girls worshiping God would be presumed to be virgins.

In not a single case is the Hebrew word *almah* in the Old Testament used to refer clearly to a married woman, or to an impure woman. It means *virgin,* and is properly so translated in most translations of the Bible including the King James and the American Standard Versions, and the Septuagint. Best of all, it is so translated by the Spirit of God Himself in Matthew 1:23.

Critics say that Isaiah 7:14 should have used the Hebrew word *bethulah,* had it meant literally *virgin.* Critics, following the unconverted Jews after the time of Christ, and some lexicons, say that *bethulah* is the proper Hebrew word for *virgin,* A study of the use of *bethulah* in the Old Testament, however, seems clearly to prove them wrong.

In Isaiah 23:12 "O thou oppressed virgin" refers to Zidon, the wicked, idolatrous city, announcing its coming destruction!

In Isaiah 37:22 the word *bethulah* translated *virgin is* used for Jerusalem, "The virgin, the daughter of Zion," when her sins had brought Sennacherib against the city. God here takes the part of Jerusalem, but Jerusalem was not strictly a virgin.

In Jeremiah 18:13 God uses the word *virgin* to represent Israel. "The virgin of Israel hath done a very horrible thing." This sin is described: "Because my people have forgotten me, they have burned incense to vanity, and they have caused them to stumble in their ways from the ancient paths, to walk in paths, in a way not cast up." Therefore because of their idolatry, God will "make their land desolate, and a perpetual hissing" (vs. 16) and will "scatter them as with an east wind before the enemy" (vs. 17). Certainly, wicked, idolatrous Israel, given over to be destroyed for her spiritual harlotry, is not here properly called *virgin*. The word *bethulah* does not necessarily mean *virgin*.

In Jeremiah 14:17 the word *virgin* (bethulah) is similarly used for Israel, being then punished for her iniquities.

Similar use is made of the word in Jeremiah 31:4, Jeremiah 31:21, Lamentation 1:15, and Lamentation 2:13.

In each of the above cases the word *bethulah* is used for wicked cities being punished for their sins, usually for idolatry, and in these cases, the word *bethulah* could not strictly mean *virgin*.

Another case is in Joel 1:8, "Lament like a virgin girded with sackcloth for the husband of her youth." Here a widow is meant by the Hebrew word *bethulah*.

Let our hearts be comforted concerning the ravings of the critics. All the actual evidence goes to reassure Christians not only that Jesus was born of a virgin, but that His virgin birth was foretold, and that Matthew 1:23 properly translates Isaiah 7:14.

MATTHEW II

Verses 1,2 The Wise Men From the East

Bethlehem is about six miles south of Jerusalem, originally called Ephrath. It was the home of Boaz, Naomi, and Ruth (Ruth 1:1, 22). Being the birthplace of David, it is sometimes called "The city of David."

In connection with this chapter you must read carefully Luke, chapter 2. It tells how Joseph and Mary were in Bethlehem to register for the taxation under the Roman Empire. Mary lived in the province of Galilee in the little city of Nazareth (Luke 1:26), and it is presumed that Joseph lived nearby. God brought them to Bethlehem for the birth of the Saviour that the Scripture, Micah 5:2, which is quoted in Matthew 2:6, might be fulfilled: "But thou, Bethlehem Ephratah, though thou be little among the thousands of Judah, yet out of thee shall he come forth unto me that is to be ruler in Israel; whose goings forth have been from of old, from everlasting."

Luke, chapter 2, also tells us that the wise men from the East were not the only visitors to the baby Jesus. Shepherds in the field were visited by the angel of the Lord. (Was it the same angel, Gabriel, that appeared to Mary, Zacharias, and probably Joseph?) He told them that the Saviour was born that day (probably that night), and they went to see the baby Jesus just after His birth (Luke 2:8-20).

"In the days of Herod the king," that is, while King Herod ruled over Judea as a puppet king under the Roman Empire, "came wise men from the east," literally magi or magicians. The term means about the same as the magicians and wise men mentioned in Daniel 1:20; 2:2, 13, 14, 18, 24, 27. Of these wise men, Daniel was the greatest.

The wise men came "from the east." On a Bible map of the Assyrian and Babylonian empires, trace a course east from Jerusalem across the Syrian desert to the first place from which these men could have come and you will find it was evidently the region of ancient Babylon. These men were not fortunetellers, nor sorcerers, but they were spiritually minded, cultured men who sought after God. How would they know about the One who should be born "King of the Jews"? Why should they come to Jerusalem? Here is the evident answer: they were men of ancient Babylon who had found the book of Daniel. They may have had other parts of the Old Testament which- Daniel had left among the wise men of his day long before. However, this does not seem likely, since they did not have Micah's prophecy that Jesus should be born in Bethlehem. From these writings of Daniel, they knew that the Jews looked for a coming Prince descended from David. Likely the particular passage upon which they based their hope was Daniel 9:24-26:

"Seventy weeks are determined upon thy people and upon thy holy city, to finish the transgression, and to make an end of sins, and to make reconciliation for iniquity, and to bring in everlasting righteousness, and to seal up the vision and prophecy, and to anoint the most Holy. Know therefore and understand, that from the going forth of the commandment to restore and to build, Jerusalem unto the Messiah the Prince shall be seven weeks, and threescore and two weeks: the street shall be built again, and the wall, even in troublous times. And after threescore and two weeks shall Messiah be cut off, but not for himself: and the people of the prince that shall come shall destroy the city and the sanctuary; and the end thereof shall be with a flood, and unto the end of the war desolations are determined."

They were looking for "Messiah the Prince" of Daniel's people, the Jews, and therefore the King of the Jews. Study Daniel 9:24-26 carefully and you will see why they expected Jesus at this particular time. It was to be sixty-nine weeks or sevens of years (69 x 7 = 483 years) from the time that the decree sending a remnant of Israelites under Ezra and Nehemiah back to Palestine to restore Jerusalem and the temple until the time the Saviour came. Wise men one generation after another had kept a record and had carefully counted the 483 years. Daniel's prophecy was fulfilled; now they came to seek the King of the Jews.

Do not think that the star led them to Jerusalem. It did not. They said, "We have seen his star in *the east.*" The star seems to have appeared to them as a signal to start, but they already knew from the Scriptures that the coming Saviour would be a King of the Jews, therefore they came to the Jewish capital city seeking Him. They saw the star when they left in the East, but did not see it again until, leaving Jerusalem, they started for Bethlehem.

An important lesson for us here is that the wise men depended first upon the Word of God, then on outward evidences and leadership. Every Christian needs to learn that wisdom. If you want revelation from God, first learn what He has to say in His Word. If you want to know that you are saved, first take the evidence of God's Word. He says that one who trusts in Him is saved and has everlasting life (John 3:16, 18, 36; 5:24; 6:47). Feeling and Christian joy are good, but we should depend first upon the plain statements of God's Word. We need not ask for signs and dreams or human counsel until first we have done all that is commanded in the Word of God. God will make other things confirm His Word. First the wise men believed the Bible about the time of the Saviour's coming. Then a star encouraged them. Next they came to Jerusalem for the King of the Jews, and there finding more Scripture, they found more light.

Verses 3-6 The King of Israel Born at Bethlehem

Herod, king over the province of Judea but subject to the Roman emperor, was naturally excited to hear that someone was born who should be King of the Jews. Herod feared that he might lose his throne. Herod was not a student of the Old Testament Scriptures, but called the chief priests and scribes who were (vs. 4), asking them where the coming Saviour was to be born. Verse 6 is a quotation of Micah 5:2, allowing for the translation of the Old Testament Hebrew into Greek and then into English which gives a slight difference in words. The wise men in the East had the book of Daniel, since Daniel had lived among them and had written his book there, but the Prophet Micah had lived in Palestine (Micah 1:1), and these Eastern magi did not have the prophecy concerning Bethlehem as the birthplace of Christ. Wisely, they followed what light they had until they could get further light from the Scriptures.

Are you not impressed that God foretold not only the time of the Saviour's birth, but the very village in which He should be born? This is strong evidence for the deity of Christ and for the divine authority and inspiration of the Scriptures.

Notice, too, the promise that Jesus "shall rule my people Israel" (vs. 6, quoted from Micah 5:2). That is very similar to the promise the angel gave to Mary before the Saviour's birth in Luke 1:32, 33, "He shall be great, and shall be called the Son of the Highest: and the Lord God shall give unto him the throne of his father David: And he shall reign over the house of Jacob for ever; and of his kingdom there shall be no end." Jesus is going to be literally the King of the Jews and rule over Jews on David's throne in Jerusalem, though He has not yet come into His kingdom. That kingdom will be at the second coming of Christ. "When the Son of man shall come in his glory, and all the holy angels with him, then shall he sit upon the throne of his glory" (Matt. 25:31). Then the apostles will rule on twelve thrones with Him, judging the twelve tribes of Israel (Matt. 19:28). Other saints now in Heaven will then rule with Christ on the earth. "And hast made us unto our God kings and priests: and we shall reign on the earth" (Rev. 5:10). "And I saw thrones, and they sat upon them, and judgment was given unto them: and I saw the souls of them that were beheaded for the witness of Jesus, and for the word of God, and which had not worshipped the beast, neither his image, neither had received his mark upon their foreheads, or in their hands; and they lived and reigned with Christ a thousand years" (Rev. 20:4). Also see Romans 8:17, and II Timothy 2:12. Revelation 2:26, 27 says, "And he that overcometh, and keepeth my works unto the end, to him will I give power over the nations: And he shall rule them with a rod of iron; as the vessels of a potter shall they be broken to shivers: even as I received of my Father."

It is true that God already "hath translated us into the kingdom of his dear Son" (Col. 1:13), so there is a sense in which Christians, those born of God, are in Christ's kingdom. All of us should surrender to Christ as absolute Lord, Dictator, Ruler, King. The kingdom of God the Father into which people are born at the new birth is also "the kingdom of his dear Son." But that certainly is not the kingdom promised Christ as the descendant of David. "And the Lord God shall give unto him the throne of his father David: And he shall reign over the house of Jacob for ever..." (Luke 1:32, 33) certainly means an earthly kingdom not yet established. The prayer, "Thy kingdom come. Thy will be done in earth, as it is in heaven" (Matt. 6:10), has not been fulfilled. But it will be fulfilled in that coming kingdom of Christ.

Verse 3 says that Herod "was troubled, and all Jerusalem with him." How strange and how sad! They should have rung the bells of rejoicing all over the city! Priests should have offered sacrifices of thanksgiving, and the people should have had feasts with laughter and praises – their Saviour was born as promised so many hundreds of years ago! Instead of that, Jerusalem was troubled. So it will be with many about the second coming of Christ. This world is the enemy of Christ and does not want Him to appear, just as Herod and the Jewish leaders did not want Him to appear the first time. Would you be troubled if you knew that Jesus would be here today? Is your business, is your life, are your plans of the kind that you would have no shame nor fear if you knew Jesus would return today? Herod and Jerusalem showed their wickedness when they were troubled about the coming of the Saviour.

Why were not the Jewish leaders and Herod already out at Bethlehem looking for the Saviour? Herod knew there was a Christ who would come, though he had never studied enough of the Bible to learn where He should be born. Why did not they go now and seek the baby Jesus for themselves? Alas! they had other plans to them more important. At His birth, Jesus had the homage of His mother, of Joseph, of poor shepherds from the fields, and of these Gentile wise men from the East. Jewish leaders would not go five or six miles to see the Saviour! Bethlehem had no room in the inn (Luke 2:7). Later the Son of Man had not where to lay His head (Matt. 8:20), then when he died, He was buried in a borrowed tomb (Matt. 27:59, 60). This world has no room nor time for Jesus!

But before you criticize others, do you have time for Him? Have you had time today for a secret time of prayer and meditation and praise? Is He first in your plans and in your life?

Verses 7-11 The Worship and Gifts of the Wise Men

Herod was a wicked hypocrite who wished to harm the baby Jesus, but he told the wise men of the prophecy saying that the Saviour should be born at Bethlehem. Notice verse 9 particularly. They departed for Bethlehem on the authority of the Word of God, and, behold, God then gave them another assurance by sending the star before them! This is the first time they had seen the star since they had left the East; no wonder they were glad! It always pays to go by the Bible. One who claims salvation on the written Word of God can be sure that God will honor his faith. When he starts to obey God, depending on His promises, then he will have other assurances, too. Obey the Word of God, then trust God to give further assurance by feeling or other evidence. These men believed the Bible and acted on what light they had, then God sent them further proof.

Notice the way they worshiped Jesus. They knew that He was God as well as a King. They did not worship Mary, for Mary was not divine. A devoted, blessed, Christian woman, she is worthy of our respect and admiration, but not of our worship. Jesus Himself said, "There is none good but one, that is, God" (Matt. 19:17), and that excluded Mary. Not being God, she was sinful like all mankind. Jesus Himself is God, therefore, is good.

These wise men did not call Mary "the Mother of God," did not ask her to "intercede with her divine Son," as Catholics do. The Catholic adoration of Mary, prayers to Mary, are wholly without Bible foundation. There is neither precept nor example for them in the Word of God. The Bible doctrine is clear that "there is one God, and one mediator between God and men, the man Christ Jesus; Who gave himself a ransom for all, to be testified in due time" (I Tim. 2:5, 6). So the wise men worshiped Jesus. Let us see that we do the same. Not priests, nor saints, nor Mary, nor even angels deserve our worship. That is reserved for deity, and Jesus is God. So the wise men worshiped Jesus.

Notice the gifts: "gold, and frankincense, and myrrh" (vs. 11). Gold may well represent wealth and power for a king. Frankincense represents worship and praise for God. Myrrh, bitter spices, represents suffering for an atoning Saviour. How much these spiritually minded wise men knew of the character of the great Saviour they worshiped! God had surely opened their hearts to understand what Scriptures they read. These gifts indicated that they knew at least something about the second coming and reign of Christ, about His virgin birth and deity, about His crucifixion and death for sinners. Compare the myrrh with the anointing for His burial given Jesus by Mary (John 12:5-7).

Verse 12 Wise Men Warned in a Dream

Notice how God deals with His creatures. When He has instructions in the Word of God, we are expected to follow them. When the wise men had gone as far as the Scriptures could lead them, then God warned them in a dream not to return to Herod (vs. 12). Be sure to go to the Bible first for help, then ask freely for any further light needed.

Verses 13-15 Jesus Taken to Egypt

"The angel of the Lord" in verse 13 must be the same angel as appeared to Joseph before (Matt. 1:20, 24), perhaps the same angel that appeared to Mary in Luke 1:26. If so, he was the Angel Gabriel, the one who also appeared to Zacharias, foretelling the birth of John the Baptist (Luke 1:19). Since no Scripture would give these specific instructions, God revealed His will by an angel in a dream. God can use dreams and visions, though He rarely does. Let us always remember to take first the Word of God.

Before Joseph took Mary and the baby Jesus down into Egypt, other things occurred which are revealed in Luke 2:21-38. Jesus was circumcised when He was eight days old and formally named JESUS (Luke 2:21). The circumcision was according to the plain command of the Mosaic Law in Leviticus 12:2, 3. God had first given this command to Abraham (Gen. 17:12). Then Mary was kept separate, ceremonially unclean, for thirty-three days before she could go to the temple, according to the command in Leviticus 12:4. Then Jesus was brought to the temple to be presented to the Lord. Every firstborn male among the Jews was so offered (Exod. 13:12-16; Num. 8:17). Then they offered a sacrifice which by the law was required to be a lamb and a pigeon or turtledove (Lev. 12:6). But if one were too poor to bring a lamb, then he should bring two turtledoves or two young pigeons, one for a burnt-offering and one for a sin-offering (Lev. 12:8). Since Joseph and Mary were very poor and had no lamb, it appears, they brought the birds (Luke 2:24).

Study in Luke 2:25-35 the story of Simeon, a Spirit-filled man to whom God had revealed that he would live until this time when the Saviour was born. He knew the promises of God. Read his glorious testimony. There also appeared Anna the prophetess (Luke 2:36-38) to praise God for the birth of the Saviour. The few spiritually minded people who understood and believed the Old Testament were looking for the coming of the Saviour at the time appointed in Daniel 9:25.

How careful the Holy Spirit is always to remind us of the infallible inspiration of the Scripture! Verse 15 says that the baby Jesus was taken into Egypt, "that it might be fulfilled which was spoken of the Lord by the prophet, saying, Out of Egypt have I called my son." The Scripture is quoted from Hosea 11:1. The meaning was originally twofold. First, God called the nation Israel out of Egypt under Moses, and Israel is called "my son." But the more important meaning is prophetic. God would call this baby Son, Jesus, out of Egypt; so Joseph took Him there, by divine instructions.

Let us learn, then, that the Word of God is God's own writing; that it has richer meanings than the casual eye sees; and most important, let us learn that all the Bible is about Jesus Christ. Old Testament and New have Him as their subject. We should expect to find references to Christ, therefore, in every type and sacrifice, in all historical narratives, and in all prophetic portions as well, of the Word of God. "...he [Moses] wrote of me," said Jesus (John 5:46). After His resurrection, Jesus showed the two on the road to Emmaus, "beginning at Moses and all the prophets... in all the scriptures the things concerning himself" (Luke 24:27).

How old was Jesus when He went to Egypt? Perhaps less than two years old. The wise men found Jesus in "the house" (vs. 11), not the stable. Then Herod inquired diligently "what time the star appeared" which marked his birth (vs. 7). Later Herod killed all the children "from two years old and under, according to the time which he had diligently enquired of the wise men." That indicates that Jesus was possibly nearly two years old when he was carried to Egypt.

Yet, since he seems to have killed girl babies as well as boys, Herod would have killed children somewhat older than he thought Jesus to be at the time, in order to make sure, if he could, to kill the baby Jesus. So we cannot say Jesus was two, nor even nearly two, with any surety. We only know that there had been time for the wise men to come from the East, time for the circumcision and offering in the temple of the baby Jesus, and for related events. So Jesus was a baby, perhaps a year old, more or less, when the wise men came, and when He was carried to Egypt by Joseph.

Verses 16-18 Herod's Murder of Bethlehem Babies

Notice the Scripture fulfilled here from Jeremiah 31:15. Many such Old Testament Scriptures have a double meaning. How much sin is done by those who hate Jesus! Reading carefully Jeremiah 31, you will see that the innocent children killed by Herod are a type of all the Jews who have been persecuted and slain by wicked Gentile rulers, as they will be by the Antichrist during the tribulation.

Verses 19-23 Jesus Brought to Nazareth Where He Grew Up

Joseph and Mary returned from Egypt, first thinking to settle in the province of Judea about Jerusalem. Then, fearful for the child Jesus, they returned to the little city Nazareth, and there Jesus grew up. Here the story of the childhood of Jesus ends in Matthew and no more is heard until Jesus is about thirty years old and begins His ministry. (Compare Matthew 3:13-17 with Luke 3:21-23). Luke, however, gives an added glimpse of the Saviour. Luke 2:40 tells of His growth and development in body and spirit and in the grace of God, and Luke 2:41-52 tells of a most interesting incident when Jesus was twelve years old.

How we would love to read the full life story of the dear Lord Jesus as a child and young man! But God's purpose in this account is to show His deity, show how His birth fulfilled all prophecies on the subject to the letter. The Bible authenticates Jesus, and Jesus authenticates the Bible. The deity of Christ and the divine inspiration of the Bible stand or fall together. No one will long believe in Christ's deity who denies the infallible accuracy of the Word which so clearly foretells His coming.

But the childhood of Jesus is not to be dwelt on. He fulfilled all the law perfectly. He lived a perfect life, subject to proper human as well as divine authority.

In your mind distinguish carefully between these periods in the life of Christ on earth. 1. His childhood and manhood till thirty years old, sinless, but working no miracles, doing no public ministry. 2. His active ministry after being filled with the Spirit at His baptism, till Gethsemane. 3. His atoning suffering and death. 4. His resurrected life, teaching the disciples forty days till His ascension.

MATTHEW III

Verses 1-4 The Ministry of John the Baptist

The birth of John the Baptist is related in Luke 1. Zacharias and Elisabeth, his mother and father, were old; he was born in answer to prayer, the aged mother being given supernatural strength to conceive, as in the case of Sarah who bore Isaac (Luke 1:7). Compare with Genesis 17:15-17; Genesis 18:9-14; Genesis 21:1-7. Elisabeth, the mother of John the Baptist, was a cousin of Mary, the mother of Jesus (Luke 1:36). John the Baptist was a Nazarite. It was foretold by the angel who announced his birth that John "shall drink neither wine nor strong drink" (Luke 1:15). Compare this with Numbers 6:1-21. Read the wonderful announcement about John the Baptist in Luke 1:13-17. He was filled with the Holy Ghost from his mother's womb (Luke 1:15), the only man of whom that is said in the Bible.

We must not underestimate the greatness of John the Baptist. His ministry was foretold by the Prophet Isaiah in Isaiah 40:3-5:

"The voice of him that crieth in the wilderness Prepare ye the way of the Lord ,make straight in the desert a highway for our God. Every valley shall be exalted, and every mountain and hill shall be made low: and the crooked shall be made straight, and the rough places plain: And the glory of the Lord shall be revealed, and all flesh shall see it together: for the mouth of the Lord hath spoken it."

Jesus said that there was never a greater born of woman (Luke 7:28). Read the commendation of Jesus in Luke 7:24-28:

"And when the messengers of John were departed, he began to speak unto the people concerning John, What went ye out into the wilderness for to see? A reed shaken with the wind? But what went ye out for to see? A man clothed in soft raiment? Behold, they which are gorgeously apparelled, and live delicately, are in kings' courts. But what went ye out for to see? A prophet? Yea, I say unto you, and much more than a prophet. This is he, of whom it is written, Behold, I send my messenger before thy face, which skull prepare thy way before thee. For I say unto you, Among those that are born

of women there is not a greater prophet than John the Baptist: but he that is least in the kingdom of God is greater than he."

See also what Jesus said in Matthew 11:7-14:

"And as they departed, Jesus began to say unto the multitudes concerning John, What went ye out into the wilderness to see? A reed shaken with the wind? But what went ye out for to see? A man clothed in soft raiment? behold, they that wear soft clothing are in kings' houses. But what went ye out for to see? A prophet? yea, I say unto you, and more than a prophet. For this is he, of whom it is written, Behold, I send my messenger before thy face, which shall prepare thy way before thee. Verily I say unto you, Among them that are born of women there hath not risen a than John the Baptist: notwithstanding he that is least in the kingdom of heaven is greater than he. And from the days of John the Baptist until now the kingdom of heaven suffereth violence, and the violent take it by force. For all the prophets and the law prophesied until John. And if ye will receive it, this is Elias, which was for to come."

Do not be misled by a false interpretation of Matthew 11:11 and Luke 7:28, "He that is least in the kingdom of heaven is greater than he." That does not mean that John will not be in the kingdom of Heaven, nor that other Christians will be greater than he will then be. It means that in the kingdom of Heaven, all will then be greater than John the Baptist was in his human ministry, but John also will be greater then.

Mark 1:1 dates "the beginning of the gospel of Jesus Christ," with the ministry of John the Baptist. The angel said that John the Baptist "shall go before him [Jesus] in the spirit and power of Elias, to turn the hearts of the fathers to the children, and the disobedient to the wisdom of the just; to make ready a people prepared for the Lord" (Luke 1:17).

Notice the humility of John. He grew up in the wilderness (Luke 1:80). It was there that "the word of God came unto John" (Luke 3:2). His ministry was in the wilderness (pasture land and uncultivated land). Luke 3:3 says he preached in "all the country about Jordan." Notice his country dress: raiment of camel's hair with a leather belt. Notice his simple food: locusts and wild honey. Preachers need more of what John the Baptist had – the power of the Holy Spirit, a separated life, and absolute boldness in calling people to repentance for sin. Schools, language, manner, personality, clothes do not make powerful preachers. People do not hear a preacher because he dresses like a fop or talks like a scholar, but they will hear a man with the fire of God and the message of God, with absolute sincerity and conviction, with life-transforming power.

Notice the message, "Repent ye: for the kingdom of heaven is at hand." "The kingdom of heaven" is a term used only in Matthew and nowhere else in the Bible. It evidently refers in some measure to the kingdom of Christ on earth, that kingdom spoken of in Daniel 2:44 which 'the God of Heaven shall set up,' the heavenly kingdom under the rule of Christ. Remember that Matthew is writing about Jesus particularly as "the son of David, the son of Abraham" (Matt. 1:1). That kingdom of Heaven, John the Baptist says, was "at hand," that is, very near. The Jews could have had their kingdom if they would, but only after the crucifixion and resurrection and the prophecied seventieth week of Daniel, etc. John did not say it had begun. Jesus preached the same message when He began His ministry, "Repent: for the kingdom of heaven is at hand" (Matt. 4:17). The twelve disciples sent out over Israel were instructed also to preach, "The kingdom of heaven is at hand" (Matt. 10:7). But the kingdom of Christ was rejected by the Jews and thereafter He preached only individual repentance since the nation itself did not accept the King. Never any more did Jesus or His apostles, or any New Testament preacher preach that the kingdom of Heaven was "at hand." The kingdom is coming, but now it waits until the King returns. In the tribulation period, just before Christ returns to reign, then again the kingdom will be at hand and the good news or Gospel of the kingdom will be preached (Matt 24:14).

However, one must not think that John preached a different plan of salvation than that preached by Jesus or Paul. There is only one Gospel, "the everlasting gospel" (Rev. 14:6). Paul said by divine inspiration, "But though we, or an angel from heaven, preach any other gospel unto you than that which we have preached unto you, let him be accursed" (Gal. 1:8). The Gospel which John the Baptist preached is made clear by his divinely inspired and recorded words in John 3:36: "He that believeth on the Son hath everlasting life: and he that believeth not the Son shall not see life; but the wrath of God abideth on him." It was the same Gospel which Paul preached of a crucified, buried, and risen Saviour in whose atoning death a sinner may trust for pardon.

Although the kingdom was at hand and that fact was used as an incentive to get people to accept the Gospel, that did not mean that it was a different plan of salvation at all. The kingdom of Heaven parables (Matthew, chapters 13 and 25) all look forward to the postponed reign at the second coming of Christ.

New Testament preachers all preached repentance later, but they did not preach that the kingdom was "at hand." Now we are taught to pray for the coming of the kingdom, "Thy kingdom come" (Matt. 6:10).

Verses 5-10 The Baptism of John

Notice the amazing number who heard John preach and were baptized of him: "Jerusalem, and all Judea, and all the region round about Jordan." Were these all truly converted? Possibly some were not, but certainly multitudes were, for the angel foretelling his birth said, "And many of the children of Israel shall he turn to the Lord their God" (Luke 1:16). See also the inspired words of John's father, Zacharias, in Luke 1:67-79. John really prepared the whole nation for the coming of the Saviour. Do not minimize this marvelous revival, one of the greatest in human history, led by the only man who was filled with the Holy Ghost from birth. The repentance of most of the people was genuine.

The Pharisees and Sadducees (vss. 7, 8) wanted to be baptized (Luke 3:7), but did not repent. John preached the same doctrine of the new birth that Jesus gave Nicodemus (John 3:3, 5, 7). See also Deuteronomy 30:6 and Ezekiel 36:26. Baptism is never in order until a person has genuinely repented and really has a new heart. One who has not been converted by faith in Christ lies to the public and to God when he is baptized, for baptism professes a change of heart, professes that the old sinner is counted dead and that one has a new life to live. "Generation of vipers" means people with unchanged, sinful hearts, with all the natural wickedness. Satan himself appeared in the Garden of Eden as a serpent. He is called "that old serpent, which is the Devil, and Satan..." (Rev. 20:2). To unconverted Pharisees Jesus said, "Ye are of your father the devil, and the lusts of your father ye will do" (John 8:44). So John the

Baptist called unconverted people "generation of vipers." Every preacher ought to preach so to any who wish to be baptized without first repenting and trusting Christ for salvation. In doubtful cases, preachers should, like John the Baptist, refuse to baptize those who show no evidence of repentance, who bring forth no fruits meet, that is fit, for repentance.

Preachers are not required to baptize all who apply for baptism. Either the preacher himself, in unusual cases, as did John the Baptist and as did Philip in the case of the eunuch (Acts 8:37), should pass on whether the man shows evidence of having trusted Christ, or a group of Christians assembled should pass on that matter as did the Jewish Christians who came with Peter to the house of Cornelius (Acts 10:47). The custom of having a congregation approve the converts for baptism is thus scriptural. Baptism does not save, and should only be given where people are already saved.

Preachers need more holy boldness together with tenderness in demanding that people sincerely turn from their sins and trust Christ.

Verse 9, "God is able of these stones to raise up children..." indicates the miraculous character of conversion. Salvation is a miracle, a supernatural work of God in the heart. Just as if God would take a stone and make a man, so He takes a sinner and makes a child of God.

Verse 10, "the axe is laid unto the root of the trees," referred particularly to the Jews. God had dealt long with them, with every type and shadow, every sacrifice and ceremonial worship picturing the coming Messiah. The fruit demanded was repentance, and those who would not repent would come to judgment and the fires of Hell. But God's axe is always laid at the root of the tree for those warned but unrepentant.

Notice more of John's preaching given not here but in Luke 3:10-16. Read carefully John 1:15-36 concerning John the Baptist. You will see that some Jews thought John the Baptist was the long promised Christ, the Saviour, which he denied plainly. Others thought that he was Elijah, here called Elias. They believed this from Malachi 4:5, 6 which tells that Elijah must come again. Compare that passage with Luke 1:17 and you will see that John truly did in part fulfill that prophecy, but not in whole. Elijah will truly come (Matt. 17:11) and probably will be one of the two witnesses in the Great Tribulation time mentioned in Revelation 11:3-12. Some Jews also thought Jesus was Elijah (Matt 16:14).

Verses 11,12 Baptism "With the Holy Ghost and Fire"

Compare this statement of John with that of Jesus (Acts 1:5). It there refers to the filling of the Spirit which occurred at Pentecost (Acts 2:4). The baptism with fire (vs. 11) seems to be eternal punishment of the unsaved as explained in verse 12, "he will burn up the chaff with unquenchable fire." These verses do not mean that baptism with the Holy Spirit would do away with baptism in water. The Lord simply used the occasion of John's baptizing to give the promise through him of baptism of the Holy Spirit to come later. Long after Pentecost the apostles continued to baptize, and there is not a hint in the New Testament that God's plan ever changed. Rather, the Great Commission (Matt. 28:19, 20) expressly states that converts in all nations were to be baptized even "unto the end of the world." Baptism of the Holy Spirit was never intended as a substitute for baptism in water.

In this connection, get the correct interpretation of Ephesians 4:5. The baptism there referred to, "One Lord, one faith, one baptism," is evidently baptism in water. The simple term *baptism* in the New Testament, when not modified by the clear meaning of the context, means literal baptism, that is, immersion in water. For instance, the term *water baptism* as used today among some Christians is not the way baptism is mentioned in the Scripture. *Baptism* in the Bible means immersion in water. That was the usual and well-understood designation. Thousands were baptized in water, and the term was used commonly referring only to baptism in water before the term was ever used concerning baptism with the Spirit. Baptism is literal immersion, a burial, and the literal use of the term refers to immersion in water. "Baptism with the Holy Spirit" is an unusual and figurative use of the term *baptism*. Many other terms such as "filled with the Spirit," "anointed," "the gift of the Holy Ghost," "after that the Holy Ghost is come upon you" are used for the same event which happened at Pentecost. "Filled with the Holy Ghost" is the most usual term, and the term used in Acts 2:4.

51

People may still be filled with the Spirit (a few times figuratively called "the baptism of the Spirit") and every Christian is commanded to be baptized, that is, immersed in water, as a symbol of his faith in the Christ who died, was buried and rose again.

"I indeed baptize you with water unto repentance" John says in verse 11. But *unto* here is a translation of the Greek *eis,* an indefinite preposition of reference. It is sometimes translated *to, into, unto, against, among, at, for, towards,* etc. So baptized "unto repentance" simply means baptized pointing to repentance or referring to repentance already passed. Baptism is not in order to repentance, not before repentance, just as baptism is not in order to salvation or before salvation.

The word *for* in Acts 2:38, "baptized… for the remission of sins" is this same word *eis.* People are baptized pointing to or for the remission of sins already received. So here in Matthew 3:11, John the Baptist baptized, pointing to repentance which had already taken place in the heart.

Verses 13-17 The Baptism of Jesus

Jesus came from Galilee, from the town of Nazareth (Mark 1:9) to the River Jordan not far from Jerusalem. We suppose He walked. He made that journey just to be baptized, an estimated distance of ninety miles or more. That emphasizes the importance of baptism. Baptism does not save, and Jesus needed no saving. He acted as our Example. Every newborn Christian should be baptized. Notice the word "us" in verse 15. In my Bible I have drawn a line from that word to the margin and written, "Jesus and me." It is a righteous act of obedience for a Christian to be baptized as Jesus was.

Notice the form of baptism. He was baptized "in Jordan" (vs. 6). After baptism, He "went up straightway out of the water" (vs. 16). Jesus was immersed in the River Jordan. The form of baptism is also shown in Acts 8:38, "And he commanded the chariot to stand still: and they went down both into the water, both Philip and the eunuch; and he baptized him." Romans 6:3-5 teaches that baptism pictures the death of Christ and His burial, that one raised out of the water pictures the resurrection of Christ. In baptism, the Christian publicly claims to be identified with Christ through the new birth and publicly professes his faith in the death and resurrection of Christ. Colossians 2:12 teaches the same thing.

The Scofield note on this subject seems misleading to me. There is no baptism in the Old Testament. Penitent sinners were never commanded to be baptized in Old Testament times, and the word *baptism* is never even mentioned. There were "divers washings" or immersions (Heb. 9:10) in the ceremonial law, but these were never like New Testament baptism. They were never intended as a public profession of faith in Christ by a new convert. They were not a public confession of repentance of sin and a turning of the heart of God. Again we say emphatically that there was nothing in the ceremonial law of the Old Testament even remotely akin to New Testament baptism, the immersion of a believer in water as a public profession of faith, as a public object lesson of the burial and resurrection of Jesus Christ and one's own personal participation in that sacrifice. One looks in vain for any Old Testament Scripture that will affect or explain the New Testament ordinance of baptism.

Baptism is a New Testament rite, a symbol whereby newborn Christians can proclaim themselves to be Christians. Jesus was baptized as our Example. A careful study shows that Jesus meant the various events concerning His baptism to be an example to all Christians. Before this time Jesus had never preached a sermon nor worked a miracle nor taught a congregation. (1) The baptism was the beginning of Christ's public ministry, as it ought to be the beginning of every happy Christian life. (2) Jesus was anointed with the Holy Spirit for service at His baptism (vs. 16). Luke says that Jesus was praying after His baptism when the Holy Ghost descended upon Him (Luke 3:21, 22). In Luke, notice the emphasis put upon Jesus' being full of the Holy Ghost (Luke 4:1, 14-22, etc.). In that, He is our Example, also. See Acts 2:38, 39 as evidence that Christians should be filled with the Holy Ghost after obedience in baptism. Also see Acts 5:32. Jesus, in submitting to baptism and in praying, fulfilled the two conditions of Holy Spirit power, obedience and prayer, mentioned in Acts 5:32 and Luke 11:13. (3) The voice from Heaven indicates that every Christian should have sweet assurance of salvation after baptism, and thousands of Christians have known their highest joy as they came out of the baptismal waters. I have known many Christians to shout with joy when baptized. If the regenerated reader has not followed Christ in this blessed example, then let me urge you to do so as soon as possible to His glory.

Some Bible teachers mistakenly try to show a difference between the baptism of John and Christian baptism, but the Bible mentions no difference. The baptism of John was the only baptism Jesus had, the only baptism the apostles had, and was no different either in form or meaning from the baptism commanded in the Great Commission and practiced by converts among both Jews and Gentiles. The rebaptism of the disciples at Ephesus (Acts 19:1-6) was not because their baptism was John's baptism. Nothing was wrong with their baptism except that they had not understood the full import of their baptism. They should have been filled with the Holy Spirit when they were baptized, or immediately following their baptism. Baptism should have begun with them a victorious, powerful life of service, but it did not. Apollos had only known of Christian events and Christian teaching up to and including the baptism by John (Acts 18:25). He was right on the plan of salvation as John preached it, but knew nothing of the events of Pentecost, nor of the promise of Jesus of Holy Spirit power to those who tarried in Jerusalem.

My pamphlet, *Bible Baptism*, nine chapters, 64 pages, same publishers, may be found most interesting and helpful.

MATTHEW IV

Verse 1 Jesus Filled, Led by Holy Spirit, Tempted

The third chapter of Matthew (vs. 16) ended with Jesus' being anointed with the Holy Spirit from Heaven. Do not think of that coming of the Holy Spirit upon Christ as a temporary matter. It was the time when He was "anointed... to preach the gospel... to heal the brokenhearted," deliver captives, give sight to the blind (Luke 4:18). From this time forth, Jesus will be led and empowered in every detail by the Holy Spirit. Before, He was a perfect and sinless Man, but now He is a Spirit-filled Man. Do not think that the works of Jesus were done with His supernatural power as Creator, the power with which He made the worlds as the Son of God. No, when Christ came to earth, He came as the Son of God, it is true, but He emptied Himself of His glory and took on Him the form of sinful flesh (Rom. 8:3), Read particularly Philippians 2:5-8. Therefore Jesus could say, "the words that I speak unto you I speak not of myself: but the Father that dwelleth in me, he doeth the works" (John 14:10). Jesus was the, the *Messiah.* The Greek and Hebrew names both mean *the Anointed One.*

Jesus worked in the power of the Holy Spirit until His death on the cross. And then afterward as He gave instructions to His disciples, it was through the power of the Holy Ghost (Acts 1:2). Peter told Cornelius and his household that all the ministry of Jesus – healing, miracles, etc. – was because He was anointed with the Holy Ghost (Acts 10:38). Jesus never needed to be filled again with the Holy Spirit. The Holy Spirit was given to Him without measure (John 3:34), that is, in limitless degree. Did Jesus exercise in His earthly ministry more power than Christians may? Only in that the power of the Spirit in Him was never limited by sin. He never grieved the Spirit nor quenched the Spirit, but always walked in the Spirit. Jesus never again needed to have a "crisis-filling" with the Spirit, for the simple reason that He was always filled and being filled. He was the perfect Vessel for the Spirit with never any loss of power. We are imperfect and sinful and must be cleansed again and filled again repeatedly. Consider Jesus as a perfect Vessel with no leaks, filled continually and completely with the Spirit of God, with no self-will or sin. Consider us Christians as vessels with many leaks and partly filled with our own will and way and desires. Aside from this distinction, every Christian needs to be filled with the Spirit of God just as Jesus was, and he can be. In fact, Jesus was filled with the Holy Spirit at His baptism in answer to prayer, just as we should be (Luke 3:21, 22). See how Acts 10:38 speaks: "How God anointed Jesus of Nazareth with the Holy Ghost and with power."

He is our Example about being filled with the Spirit just as He is our Example about baptism. All the terms used in the Bible about Jesus' being "anointed" (Luke 4:18), "led by the Spirit" (Luke 4:1), "full of the Holy Ghost" (Luke 4:1), etc., are likewise used about Christians in the Bible (II Cor. 1:21; I John 2:27; Rom. 8:14; Gal. 5:18; Acts 6:5).

Compare this account of the temptation of Jesus with Mark 1:12, 13; Luke 4:1-13. Compare the temptation of Jesus also with that of Eve and Adam (Gen. 3:1-6). Both temptations began with food, appealed to pride, put a question mark about God's Word or promises, and offered a substitute for God's plan. See also Scofield Bible note on this subject.

Jesus was "led by the Spirit..." to be "tempted of the devil." It seems strange that the Holy Spirit should lead Jesus directly into temptation. Compare with Matthew 6: 13 where Christians are taught to pray, "Lead us not into temptation, but deliver us from evil," and with "Watch and pray, that ye enter not into temptation" (Matt. 26:41). Christ was led into temptation to take our place. In some sense, He was our Substitute and must go farther than we ever need to go. Sometimes, in the very will of God, we are most sorely tempted. But anywhere the Spirit clearly leads, He will give grace and victory over temptation. If we watch and pray as we ought, we will not be tempted more than we are able to bear. Suppose you memorize the wonderful promise in I Corinthians 10:13, "There hath no temptation taken you but such as is common to man: but God is faithful, who will not suffer you to be tempted above that ye are able; but will with the temptation also make a way to escape, that ye may be able to bear it." Sin is never necessary for a Christian. While none of us is sinless and perfect, it is always our fault and not God's.

Verse 2 Genuinely Tempted

Why did Jesus fast forty days? So that He might be as weak as any man ever would be when tempted. He was as hungry, as frail; the temptation was as overpowering as any human being ever faced! He "was in all points tempted like as we are" (Heb. 4:15). Psalm 103:14, "For he knoweth our frame; he remembereth that we are dust," is especially true since Jesus Himself had the same kind of a frame and was made also of dust and that by choice. Praise His name! Read Hebrews 2:14-18; 4:14-16; 10:19-23. No wonder a Christian is urged, "Let us therefore come boldly unto the throne of grace, that we may obtain mercy, and find grace to help in time of need" (Heb. 4:16), when we have such a High Priest to intercede for us, to be our Advocate.

Was Jesus really tempted? Did He feel the tug and pull of desire? The answer is that He most certainly was tempted. The Scripture says so. He was hungry, tormentingly, fiercely hungry! His poor stomach gnawed with desire. His weakened body cried out for food and He doubtless felt all the lightheadedness and perhaps delirium that men who go long days without food feel. Certainly this was a real and definite temptation, as definite and real as any man ever faced. Jesus never one time gave way to it, but He felt the pull of it just as He felt the pull of every other temptation that men are ever tempted with. His body was like our bodies. He put Himself in our place, and yet never sinned.

Verses 3,4 The First Temptation of Jesus: Bread

Why did not Jesus make bread out of stones? He certainly had power to do so. But it would have been wrong (1) because it would be putting self first when God had Him there for another purpose. (2) It is always wrong to listen to any suggestion of Satan. If Satan tells you to do something that seems all right, still you had better flee. (3) What man needs, any man, in the most desperate time of temptation, is not bread first, but the will of God. I do not agree with those who say you must first give poor people bread and then the Gospel. The Gospel is always more important than bread, and to be in the will of God is better than any human prosperity. If

57

Jesus had chosen bread here, then He could not have later given in Matthew 6:33 the command, "Seek ye first the kingdom of God, and his righteousness; and all these things shall be added unto you." If the poor have Christ first, then they can get daily bread. The heathen do not need civilization first, with higher standards of living; they need the Gospel first, then other needed things follow.

Jesus defeated the Devil with Scripture. Any Christian who follows the example of Jesus (1) in being led by the Spirit, and (2) in relying upon and using the perfect Word of God under the Spirit's leadership, can defeat Satan every time. Jesus in this matter acted as our Example. With His supernatural power as the Son of God, the Creator of the heavens and earth (Heb. 1:2; John 1:3), with all power in Heaven and in earth (Matt. 28:18), Jesus could have rebuked Satan and sent him to Hell without even considering his proposition. But in this matter Jesus was acting not only for Himself, but as an example for all mankind. He must deal with Satan just as we poor, weak mortals have to deal with him. If His temptation was to be of any help to us, then He must use methods available to the weakest of God's children, and this He did. We can have the same Holy Spirit to fill us and guide us, and can have the same Word of God to answer Satan and deliver us from temptation.

The Scripture Jesus quoted in verse 4 is from Deuteronomy 8:3. There are several wonderful things about this *verse.* (1) It is for *man,* all mankind. Jesus, by using this verse, put Himself on the same basis as every human being and claimed this Scripture, not as the Son of God, but as the Son of man. The author's sermon, "Behold the Man," in the book, *"And God Remembered..."* will give help on this subject. (2) This Scripture teaches verbal or word-for-word inspiration of the Bible. The Bible is not only the Word of God but the very words are the words of God. In the original manuscripts, "every word... proceedeth out of the mouth of God" (Matt. 4:4). That kind of Bible is so infallibly perfect that a Christian may rely on it. (3) Notice that it teaches that the Bible is just as important as daily bread, yea, more so. A Christian ought to spend as much time feeding on the Word as he does feeding on bread. No Christian can be spiritually prosperous and successful without meditating day and night on the Word of God. The Word of God helps to give victory over sin. Psalm 119:11 says, "Thy word have I hid in mine heart, that I might not sin against thee." Study carefully the contrast in the first Psalm between the sinful man and the man who meditates in the Word of God day and night. Notice also the promise to Joshua in Joshua 1:7, 8 depending on the way he observed and followed the Bible and meditated in it day and night.

Verses 5-7 The Second Temptation of Jesus: Spectacular Signs

Notice the term "holy city," Jerusalem. Jerusalem is also called "the city of the great King" (Matt. 5:55). Jerusalem will be the seat of Christ's reign on earth (Mic. 4:2). God has eternal promises about this city (I Kings 9:3; II Chron. 7:16),

This time the Devil quotes Scripture. What he quotes in verse 6 is from Psalm 91:11, 12. Many false doctrines and "isms" in the world quote Scripture. Spiritualists, Mormons, those who teach salvation by works, salvation by the church, etc., quote Scripture. Remember that false apostles were transformed into the apostles of Christ; Satan is transformed into an angel of light and his ministers into ministers of righteousness (II Cor. 11:13-15). Do not be deceived by Satan's false use of Scripture. Evidently the heart of Satan's temptation was that if Jesus would show His miraculous power, people would follow Him quicker. This would be much easier than demanding that people repent as Jesus demanded (vs. 17). Jesus did not seek to have the applause of worldly-minded and wicked men or He would have done what Satan suggested.

Notice the answer of Jesus in verse 7, quoting from Deuteronomy 6:16. We ought to believe all the promises of God and rest safely in them. The promise of angels bearing us up and caring for us (Ps. 91:11, 12), which Satan quoted, is a blessed promise, but it ought not to be used as the basis for presumption to tempt God. Notice the promise to Christians in Mark 16:18 about serpents and deadly poison. Yet it would be presumptuous and wicked and tempting God to pick up a serpent deliberately to be bitten or to drink poison to prove how spiritual or full of faith one is. That would not be faith but presumption, tempting God. "Whatsoever is not of faith is sin" (Rom. 14:23). God only gives faith for wonders when they are done under His leading and for His glory. It would have been a sin for Jesus to work a miracle that would do no one good but simply glorify Himself in a carnal sense to receive the applause and admiration of fleshly men without causing anyone to love God better.

Notice again how Jesus defeated Satan by Scripture. Sometimes you cannot overcome temptations unless you have 'hid in the heart' many Scriptures so the Spirit can help you choose one that will answer every quibble of Satan.

Notice the armour of a Christian (Eph. 6:11-17), particularly the reference to "the sword of the Spirit, which is the word of God." See also Hebrews 4:12 and Jeremiah 23:29. None of us knows enough and relies enough on the marvelous power in the living, eternal Word of God.

Verses 8-11 Third Temptation of Jesus: Kingdom Without Crucifixion

In the last temptation here Satan comes to the heart of the matter. Satan knows that Christ is to reign over all the kingdoms of this world, from the throne of His father David. On this matter, Satan is wiser than some preachers. The kingdoms of this world are now in the hands of Satan, else there would have been no real temptation in this case. Satan is "the god of this world" II Cor. 4:4). While God rightly owns the kingdoms of the world and deals with the rulers, and "the powers that be are ordained of God" (Rom. 13:1), yet no nation on the earth is now a Christian nation. Satan has the pre-eminence in present world affairs. This temptation is an offer from Satan to give Jesus the kingdom which is promised Him for the future, but to obtain it by sin instead of by the cross. Satan would have Jesus take the world as it is without any Second Coming, without any purging, without any judgment on sin, without any destruction of the Gentile powers. In this matter Satan was like many amillennialists who do not believe in a literal reign of Christ. In verse 9 Satan has in mind the same sinful plan which caused him to fall from Heaven (Isa. 14:12-14). He wants to put himself above God. This illustrates that the heart of Self-Ish-Ness is SIN and the heart of sin is "I" which is back of every opposition to God and all rebellion against Jesus Christ. This is the only reason anybody rejects Christ as Saviour as you see from John 3:19-21. See Isaiah 53:6. Christ rejectors deliberately hold on to sin and self-will.

Satan hates the cross and this temptation is a bold bid to get Jesus to detour around the cross. This temptation faced Jesus every day of His life. It is the same temptation which Peter brought Him (Matt. 16:22), and the rebuke of Jesus to Peter was similar to His rebuke of Satan here. Compare "Get thee behind me, Satan" (Matt. 16:23), and "Get thee hence, Satan" (Matt. 4:10). On the cross Jesus was urged by the mob, "If thou be the Son of God, come down from the cross" (Matt. 27:40; Mark 15:29-32), by the chief priests and scribes (Matt. 27:41, 42), and "the thieves also, which were crucified with him, cast the same in his teeth" (Matt. 27:44; Luke 23:39). In the Garden of Gethsemane, Satan tried to kill Jesus before He could go to the cross. His soul was "exceeding sorrowful, EVEN UNTO DEATH" (Matt. 26:38). Only by praying through did Jesus escape death in the Garden that night as you will see from Hebrews 5:7. Death in the Garden, missing the cross, was the cup that Jesus begged might pass from Him, and His prayer was answered. An angel came and ministered to Jesus and strengthened Him (Luke 22:43) that He might go to the cross. Satan hates the cross above all things. God grant that every Christian may glory continually in that which is our victory (Gal. 6:14). Our victory is in a crucified Saviour and our testimony to the cross (Rev. 12:11). Compare the testing of Jesus in the wilderness and in Gethsemane in Matthew 4:11 with Luke 22:43. Jesus received strength for His poor, frail, fainting body in both cases when He resisted temptation. So every one of us may have all we need if we faithfully resist Satan. What a glorious Example for us poor sinners. Hallelujah!

Verses 12-17 Jesus Removes to Capernaum; Preaches Repentance

The public ministry of Jesus in Galilee from His new home in Capernaum here discussed is mentioned also in Mark 1:14 and Luke 4:14, 15. Verse 12 indicates that Jesus was careful not to take away from the credit and fame of John the Baptist. Compare this with John 4:1-3, where He left Judea to avoid overshadowing John too much. See your Bible map of Palestine. Judea is the section around about Jerusalem. North of that is Samaria, and further north, around the west and south coast of the little Sea of Galilee, is the little province of Galilee. Nazareth is a small town.

The seacoast mentioned in verse 13 is of the Sea of Galilee, a small sea, often called a lake (Luke 5:1), about thirteen miles long and seven or eight miles wide. Capernaum was a larger city and on the seacoast. Remember that Palestine originally was divided among the twelve tribes and this ministry in the edge of Naphtali and Zebulun was foretold by Isaiah in Isaiah 9:1, 2, quoted by Matthew in verses 13 to 16. Notice that in verse 16 Jesus is called "great light." Compare this with the words of Zacharias in Luke 1:78, 79. See also John 8:12 and John 9:5 where Jesus calls Himself "the light of the world."

The preaching of Jesus, "Repent: for the kingdom of heaven is at hand," (vs. 17) is the same message as John the Baptist preached (Matt. 3:2), discussed in notes on chapter 3.

Verses 18-22 The Call of Peter, Andrew, James, and John

The conversion of Peter and Andrew is told in John 1:40-42. Andrew was first converted and won his brother, Peter. This call is evidently after that conversion. See also Mark 1:16-20 and Luke 5:1-11 where much more detail is given. Compare this call of Peter also with the second call after he had lapsed into sin and gone back to fishing (John 21:1-19, especially verse 19).

"Fishers of men," Jesus made them. Everyone who really follows Jesus becomes a soul winner; Jesus *makes* him a soul winner. Peter gave up income from fishing; what did he gain? See Matthew 19:27-29 and Daniel 12:3. Have you "left all" to follow Jesus? If you do not win souls, it is because you do not follow Jesus, verse 19 says.

It is remarkable that the three greatest of the apostles were fishermen. Perhaps Zebedee was very prosperous, owning a ship (vs. 22) and having hired servants (Mark 1:20). These four, Peter, Andrew, James, and John, were partners (Mark 1:16, Luke 5:10). And we suppose that all four were vigorous and successful men with ships and equipment, making a good living.

Verses 23-25 Jesus Preaching the Gospel of the Kingdom

The fame of Jesus was very great, reaching north into Syria (vs. 24), and drawing people from Decapolis (across the little Sea of Galilee), from Jerusalem, and even across the lower Jordan River (vs. 25). People must have come on foot as far as one hundred miles to hear His preaching and to see His miracles. The healings in verses 23 and 24 must have been many.

Notice "the gospel of the kingdom" which Jesus preached (vs. 23). It was simply the one, unchanging Gospel, an offer of salvation through an atoning Saviour, but preached with special urgency, since the kingdom was "at hand" (vs. 17). The pressing imminence of the kingdom, with the King Himself present, justified calling that Gospel "the gospel of the kingdom." However Jewish leaders and the Jewish people as a whole rejected the King, and the succeeding events which must be fulfilled (Christ's sufferings, crucifixion, death, and resurrection) did not lead at once into the overthrow of Gentile kingdoms, the restoration of David's throne and Christ's reign over Israel as one supposes it might have done, had the Jews as a nation repented and turned to Him in saving faith. It is not profitable to speculate as to what might have been. Certainly what did occur was foreknown to God.

This "gospel of the kingdom" will be preached again in the tribulation time just before Christ returns to reign (Matt. 24:14). After the twelve disciples preached this Gospel with the emphasis on the coming kingdom (Matt. 10:7) and were persecuted, and the Gospel was largely rejected over the whole area occupied by Jews, we do not find this terminology used. Preachers preach the same Gospel, the good news of the same salvation, but it was not necessarily or primarily in view of a kingdom immediately at hand.

We note in Acts 1:3 that Jesus, after His resurrection, spent forty days with the disciples, "speaking of the things pertaining to the kingdom of God," and the term *kingdom of God* is frequently used in the New Testament, and sometimes, at least, refers to the present Lordship of Christ and salvation (John 3:3, 5). However, the terms *kingdom of Heaven* and *the gospel of the kingdom* seem to be used in the Gospel of Matthew because of a peculiar Jewish cast of this Gospel. The Jews were more immediately interested in the restoration of David's throne and the regathering of scattered Israel and their delivery from Roman rule than Gentiles would be. So the Gospel according to Matthew, which is more clearly Jewish in color than those written by Mark, Luke and John, uses these terms looking toward the reign of Christ.

MATTHEW V

Verses 1,2 Beginning the Sermon on the Mount

Remember that this is in Galilee on a mountain not far from Capernaum, on the Sea of Galilee. Capernaum was now His home (Matt. 4:13). There were multitudes of people present, many thousands, we suppose, from a wide territory (Matt. 4:24, 25).

Jesus, perfectly filled with the Spirit, the Son of God, launched into His ministry immediately after His anointing with the Spirit at His baptism (Matt. 3:16; Luke 3:22; Luke 4:18, 19). Do not count this Sermon on the Mount as the halting effort of a young preacher. It is the perfect, glorious work of the Spirit-filled Son of God.

Matthew, chapters 5, 6 and 7, contain this famous Sermon on the Mount. It is regarded as the most marvelous sermon on human conduct ever preached, in the Bible or out, inspired or uninspired. There are many, many verses which ought to be memorized, and the entire three chapters are worth memorizing. We hope that every student will memorize the first twelve verses of this chapter – "The Beatitudes" or "The Blesseds."

Verse 3 The Blessed Poor

Compare this with Luke 6:20. Notice that Luke says "poor" while Matthew says "poor in spirit." The meaning is the same, with Matthew going into more detail. Luke says "kingdom of God," while Matthew says "kingdom of heaven." It is blessed to be poor, particularly if the poverty is felt in the spirit. Compare this with "Woe unto you that are rich!" (Luke 6:24). The Saviour did not mean it is good to be poor without any spiritual riches or spiritual virtues. Rather, He meant that in dealing with God it is a blessed thing to have the humility of the poor, the broken heart of the poor. If a man feels his need, his poverty, so that he can pray as a poor and needy creature begging for help, then blessed is that man, for he will be heard. The poor in spirit are those who see their helplessness and see how valueless are temporal things – wealth, houses, land, fame. A rich man can be "poor in spirit." A poor man can be proud and haughty and so have none of the virtues of the poor, and miss the blessing God means for the poor. See Revelation 3:17, 18 where God describes those who do not feel poor but really are wretchedly poor in His sight. These miss God's blessing. Compare this with James 2:1-6. James 2:5 speaks of the poor as "heirs of the kingdom" as does Matthew 5:3.

God particularly loves the poor. He will not hear the prayers of those who do not help the poor (Prov. 21:13; Isa. 58:7, 10; Prov. 14:31; Ps. 41:1; Prov. 19:17). God forbids moneylenders to keep as security the garment of the poor (Exod. 22:25-27). Jesus preached the Gospel especially to the poor (Matt. 11:5). And in winning souls, we are especially enjoined to "bring in hither the poor, and the maimed, and the halt, and the blind" (Luke 14:21). The poor have many blessings that the rich do not have: usually better health, happier marriages, more children, less worries, fewer suicides, and are easier to reach with the Gospel (Luke 18:23-25; Mark 12:37). Lazarus, the poor beggar, was saved, while the rich man was lost (Luke 16:22, 23). Jesus is "the poor man's Friend." O Christian, do not strive to be rich; rather, "be content with such things as ye have" (Heb. 13:5; I Tim. 6:6-11). Seek first the kingdom of God (Matt. 6:33) and trust the Saviour who loves the poor!

Jesus Himself, "though he was rich, yet for your sakes he became poor, that ye through his poverty might be rich" (II Cor. 8:9). What infinite grace! He was born in a stable and laid in a borrowed manger when there was no room for Him in the inn. Though the foxes had holes and the birds of the air had nests, yet the Son of man had not where to lay His head (Matt. 8:20). And when He died, He left only a seamless garment and was buried in a borrowed grave (John 19:23, 24; Matt. 27:60). Every poor man ought to love Jesus Christ.

Verse 4 The Blessed Mourners

Here is a paradox. Jesus seems to say that it is happy to be sad; it is fortunate to be unfortunate; that we are to rejoice over weeping. Indeed, that is true, though it does not seem so to human wisdom. But it means what it says, and Jesus said more about it which is told in Luke 6:21. He said, "Blessed are ye that hunger now: for ye shall be filled. Blessed are ye that weep now: for ye shall laugh." Joy comes out of sorrow, and blessing out of trouble. Notice some of the blessings the Bible says come from sorrow: (1) God is near to the brokenhearted (Ps. 34:18); (2) God hears the prayer of the brokenhearted (Ps. 51:17); (3) Tribulation worketh patience, develops character (Rom. 5:3); (4) "For our light affliction, which is but for a moment, worketh for us a far more exceeding and eternal weight of glory" (II Cor. 4:17), that is, wonderful reward in Heaven. Compare this verse with Revelation 7:17 and 21:4. Every sorrow of a Christian will be rewarded many fold in Heaven. How sad to miss joys in Heaven because we never mourned here!

Mourning and sorrow sometimes bring revival (Isa. 66:8; Jonah 2:5-10; Ps. 126:5, 6). Compare this verse also with the blessed promise, "Weeping may endure for a night, but joy cometh in the morning" (Ps. 30:5). Laughter oftentimes goes with pride, indifference and worldly-mindedness. Mourning goes with prayer, contrition, penitence and humility. Only those who know sorrow can be near the Saviour and understand the Saviour, for He was "a man of sorrows, and acquainted with grief" (Isa. 53:3; Matt. 26:37, 38). See James 4:9, 10. The great men of the Bible were men of tears: *Jeremiah* (Lam. 1:12; Jer. 9:1); *David* (Ps. 6:6; 42:3); *Paul* (Acts 20:31; Rom. 9:2, 3; II Cor. 2:4; II Cor. 4:8-10; Phil. 3:18).

Sorrow often leads sinners to be saved. The death of Lazarus was for the glory of God (John 11:4, 14, 15) and led others to be saved (John 12:10, 11).

God is nearer to the widow and orphan than to the married wife or protected child; nearer to the poor than the rich; nearer to the hungry than the full. Better have evil things and sorrow here, like Lazarus the beggar, and be comforted later, than to have riches here and to be tormented later, like the rich man (Luke 16:25). Thank God for sorrow! Blessed are those who mourn! Thank God for the comfort.

Verse 5 The Blessed Meek

Jesus is quoting from Psalm 37:11. See also Psalm 25:9. Meekness is another word for humility. See James 4:10; I Peter 5:6; Luke 14:11. The inheritance promised to the meek will come when Christ rules on the earth. Now the proud, the haughty, the rich, the warlike, the selfish, the brutal, too largely rule on earth. Verse 5 here is a promise of the coming kingdom of Christ. Notice that it is on "earth." We are taught to pray, "Thy kingdom come. Thy will be done *in earth*, as it is in heaven" (Matt. 6:10). The reign of Christ will be on earth with His throne at Jerusalem (Isa. 2:1-4; 11:9; Rev. 5:10). Notice many of these promises plainly say the kingdom will be on "the earth." See also Micah 4:1-8 and Luke 19:17-19. The meek will not fully inherit the earth until Jesus returns to reign.

Verse 6 Hunger for Christ Our Righteousness

Many invitations are given in the Bible for those who are thirsty. See Isaiah 55:1, 2; John 4:10-14; Revelation 21:6; 22:17. Spiritual thirst is a great virtue. The psalmist said, "As the hart panteth after the water brooks, so panteth my soul after thee, O God. My soul thirsteth for God, for the living God: when shall I come and appear before God?" (Ps. 42:1, 2). God sees the longing of the soul as well as hears the spoken cry.

A kindred promise is Isaiah 44:3, "For I will pour water upon him that is thirsty, and floods upon the dry ground: I will pour my spirit upon thy seed, and my blessing upon thine offspring."

The blessed thing about hungering and thirsting after righteousness is that one "shall be filled." Eventually, of course, all Christians will be filled with righteousness, will be all they aspire to be, and without sin. If people long to be righteous, they will be righteous, and that is a blessed thought. But that is not the primary meaning here. Those who hunger and thirst after righteousness will be filled with righteousness far better than any of their own, for Christ is the righteousness of God. Those who hunger after righteousness must turn to Christ and in receiving Him are tilled with righteousness. Much of the book of Romans is written to tell of that righteousness of Jesus which a poor, undeserving sinner may claim for his own and be tilled. The righteousness of God is manifest in the death of Christ on the cross paying for sin (Rom. 3:21-26). Read that passage carefully. This righteousness is received "by faith of Jesus Christ." "Abraham believed God, and it was counted unto him for righteousness" (Rom. 4:3). So every one "that worketh not, [has no righteousness of his own] but believeth on him that justifieth the ungodly, his faith is counted for righteousness" (Rom. 4:5). Paul quotes David as describing "the blessedness of the man, unto whom God imputeth righteousness without works" (Rom. 4:6-8). Compare with Psalm 32:1, 2. Romans 4:6 uses similar language to Matthew 5:6, both speaking of the blessed man who hungers and thirsts after righteousness and receives it, but not human righteousness; rather the righteousness of Christ imputed to him.

Read Romans 10:1-13. Go through that passage underlining *righteousness*. Verse 10 shows it is received by faith. Romans 10:4 sums up the whole thing, "For Christ is the end of the law for righteousness to every one that believeth." All who really hunger after righteousness will gladly receive Christ. Those who do not want Christ do not want righteousness. The Sermon on the Mount is not all law. Much of it is Gospel, as is verse 6.

Remember that Christ calls Himself the Bread from Heaven (John 6:33-58). This bread is received by trusting Him. There is no true righteousness and no salvation without eating and drinking of Christ by faith. Speaking of works and righteousness, Jesus said, "This is the *work* of God, that ye believe on him whom he hath sent" (John 6:29). Praise God that those who are thirsty and hungry are freely invited to be filled with Christ, who is the righteousness of God.

Verse 7 The Blessing of Being Merciful

In Matthew 18:23-35 Jesus gave a parable with this exact lesson, 'Forgive if you would be forgiven.' He even taught us to remember this when we pray, and to forgive all (Matt. 6:12, 14, 15; Mark 11:25, 26). Our showing mercy to others is a condition of God's showing mercy to us and answering our prayers. The other side of the story is pictured in James 2:13. If we judge harshly, we shall be judged harshly. These verses are of great importance. I suggest particularly that you memorize Ephesians 4:32. Notice how many times one is to forgive the same person – 490 times! (Matt. 18:21, 22). To forgive means to have a spirit like Christ, and nothing can please the Father better or make surer your own forgiveness. An especially strong promise on this is Luke 6:36, 37: "Be ye therefore merciful, as your Father also is merciful. Judge not, and ye shall not be judged: condemn not, and ye shall not be condemned: forgive, and ye shall be forgiven."

If one reads this who has in his heart some grudge, unforgiveness against anybody in the world, then I beg you this moment, before you leave this page, forgive it, blot it out and remove that stumbling block between you and God. Forgive and be forgiven of God!

This beatitude surely refers primarily to Christians. However, genuine repentance in a sinner's heart would seem to tend to merry for others. Yet a lost sinner immediately receives salvation, forgiveness from all sins, instantly upon penitent faith. Here the forgiveness refers to restored fellowship with God, the cleansing which Christians daily need and are taught to pray for (Matt. 6:12-14).

Verse 8 The Blessed Pure in Heart

Two meanings are possible here:

1. One who has been cleansed in heart, that is, born again, will see God, that is, will be saved. God purifies the hearts of sinners by faith (Acts 15:9). Again the Scripture says that people 'purify their hearts in obeying the truth' (that is the Gospel message to repent and believe); this purification is a work through the Spirit and one so purified is born again (I Pet. 1:22, 23). See also Titus 2:14. Every converted person becomes a partaker of the divine nature (II Pet. 1:4) and God's seed remains in the Christian so that a certain part of every Christian cannot sin (I John 3:9). Notice that the beatitude here says, "Blessed are the pure IN HEART." That is another way of saying, 'Blessed are those who have received a new heart from God when they were born again.'

2. A second meaning is, that as one is pure in his thoughts and life and puts the Lord first and turns away from worldliness and sin, he will feel the presence of God more and more, know the will of God, come face to face with God. Jesus promised the disciples He and the Father would manifest themselves (through the Holy Spirit) to those who love Him and keep His commandments (John 14:15-26). The Holy Spirit reveals the Father to us and particularly to Christians who so love Christ as to keep His commandments and live for Him. With this in mind, the Apostle Paul by divine inspiration commanded Timothy, "Keep thyself pure" (I Tim, 5:22). Second Timothy 2:19-22 is on the same subject. He was to "flee also youthful lusts... out of a pure heart." Timothy was to be an

example in purity (I Tim. 4:12) and was to treat Christian women "with all purity" (I Tim. 5:2). The cry of David in Psalm 51, especially verses 2, T, 10, is for a pure heart. May our dear Heavenly Father wash and cleanse the heart of every reader and make it pure in His holy sight that we, too, may see God, having Him revealed to us day by day through the Holy Spirit and through the Word.

Verse 9 The Blessed Peacemaker

Jesus, God's Son Himself, is the greatest Peacemaker. How fitting, then, that other peacemakers should be thought like Jesus and be called the children of God. Peacemaking is another term for brotherly love. The outside world does not recognize many Christian virtues, but it does recognize the virtue of brotherly love. "By this shall all men know that ye are my disciples, if ye have love one to another" (John 13:35). Love is a coin good in every market, a badge of godliness recognized by the vilest sinners. How many Christians lose all their influence for God because they are not peaceable, but quarrelsome; not kindly and forgiving, but bitter and hateful! The Bible has many warnings about tattlers, busybodies in other men's affairs and talebearers. See especially Proverbs 26:20, I Timothy 5:13, II Thessalonians 3:11 and I Peter 4:15.

Peacemaking involves all the Christian virtues, brotherly love, unselfishness, humility, forgiveness. See Romans 12:18; Romans 14:19; I Thessalonians 5:13; II Timothy 2:22; Hebrews 12:14; James 3:17, 18. Famous examples of peacemaking in the Old Testament are those of Abraham (Genesis 13:8, 9) of Isaac (Genesis 26:17-22) of Jacob (Genesis 32:13 to 33:4). Remember that peacemakers will be called the children of God. How happy, how blessed is the peacemaker!

Verse 10-12 Blessed Are the Persecuted

Notice that this beatitude has the same blessing as that in verse 3, "...their's is the kingdom of heaven" (vs. 10), and "great is your reward in heaven" (vs. 12). Compare this passage with Luke 6:22, 23. These verses say you are blessed and happy if you should be persecuted, but Luke 6:26 gives the other side of this truth, "Woe unto you, when all men shall speak well of you! for so did their fathers to the false prophets." The mark of a true prophet is persecution for righteousness' sake. The mark of a false prophet is popularity. Christians ought to be like Jesus, and the world hated Him and persecuted Him (John 15:18-21; John 17:14). Many times the true Christian must suffer if he is true to Christ. Notice that one of the hardest things is that he must suffer evil talk and slander. People "shall say all manner of evil against you falsely, for my sake" (vs. 11) and shall "cast out your name as evil" (Luke 6:22). This is the last beatitude, and the burden which seems harder than all others has yet the greater blessing than all others. While the other beatitudes for the poor in spirit, the mourning, the meek, the hungering and thirsting after righteousness, the merciful, the pure in heart and the peacemakers are all simply called blessed, in one verse each, this beatitude is given three verses, restated and with the express command, "Rejoice, and be exceeding glad"! And in Luke we are even commanded, "Rejoice ye in that day, and *leap for joy"!* The highest blessedness of a Christian is to suffer as Jesus suffered, and for His sweet name's sake and for no sins of our own.

There is no blessing in suffering for our own sins (I Pet. 2:19, 20), but when we suffer for Jesus' sake, what wonderful reward is to be ours. We ought to rejoice openly, happily, gloriously if we are sometimes allowed to suffer for Jesus' sake. The same thing is told in I Peter 4:16. The true Christian ought to expect persecution for he will get it. See II Timothy. 5:12. The example of Christ and all the apostles, particularly Paul, ought to teach us to expect persecutions. Spurgeon was despised by the Baptists of his day, withdrew from the Baptist Union of England because of its modernism. Finney was feared and slandered as a sensationalist, accused of various religious excesses and heresies. Moody was called "Crazy Moody." Torrey was counted a fanatic on the Holy Spirit and prayer, misunderstood and hurt even by good Christian men in his old age. Yes, God's truest saints have suffered persecution. The apostles were "rejoicing that they were counted worthy to suffer shame for his name" (Acts 5:41).

This blessing of persecution, the greatest blessing about which we are commanded to have the greatest joy, has its reward primarily in Heaven and in the reign of Christ on earth, just as the poor will have their reward in that blessed kingdom, too. One can be happy that he is poor and willingly consent to stay poor for Christ's sake.

Just so, a Christian ought to be willing to be misunderstood, persecuted and unrewarded until death, rejoicing in the blessed hope set before him. So Jesus did as you see in Hebrews 12:2. Comfort your hearts by the blessed promise of Romans 8:17, 18 and II Corinthians 4:8-18.

Verse 13 Christians Are Saving Salt

Christians are the salt of the earth. Just as salt saves meat from spoiling, Christians are a preservative. We may be sure that long ago terrible calamities would have depopulated the earth but for the saving influence of Christians. God could not destroy Sodom with Lot in it, and if there had been ten Christians, they would have been salt enough to have spared the whole city (Gen. 18:23-32; Gen. 19:22). The intercession of Moses saved the nation Israel from destruction (Exod. 32:31-34). The Holy Spirit working through Christians now so preserves civilization that the terrible Man of Sin cannot be revealed and take control of the world until Christians and the Holy Spirit are caught out at the rapture (II Thess. 2:1-8).

The salt in Bible times was not pure and refined salt as we have now. It was made of rock salt or gathered from evaporated sea water, so it would contain earth and some other minerals. Such salt, if exposed to water and air, might lose its saltiness and Only the trashy part remain. All Christians are partly salt and partly earth, with two natures, the new man and the old man, the child of God with the old fleshly nature (Rom. 7:14-25). If the carnal nature wins out in a Christian's life, then the salt has lost its saltiness, or savor; that is, the Christian has lost his influence to bless and preserve the world, and his Christianity becomes a matter of scorn, trodden under feet of men.

Verses 14-16 Christians Are the Light of the World

Christ Himself is the light of the world (John 1:4-9; John 8:12; John 9:5). Here He says, "YE are the light of the world." Christians should shine with the light and power of Christ in this world. He is our example. We are called to the same mission as Christ (John

73

14:12; John 20:21; I John 4:17). The Christian is salt, light, and a river of water, that Is, of spiritual blessing (John 7:37-39). A Christian is the channel for Christ's light and power, the only way it can reach the lost world about us. Compare this passage with Mark 4:21 and Luke 8:16. Christians need to be burning and shining lights like John the Baptist (John 5:35), getting out the Gospel of Christ to sinners.

A light under a bushel measure would do no good; so a Christian who gives no testimony for Christ would do no good. The candle should be "on a candlestick" (vs. 15), so a Christian ought to be in a church. The candlestick stands for a local church in Revelation 1:20. Christians should let their lights shine by a public profession of faith, baptism, public testimony, soul winning, preaching the Gospel and good works.

A Christian life ought not to be kept secret. Do not believe Satan's lie that men can live just as good outside the church as in it, or please God just as well without public testimonies. Compare this with Matthew 10:32, 33; Romans 10:9, 10; Hebrews 10:25. A Christian's good deeds ought not to be just for show, yet his good life and works ought to shine before men (vs. 16) so that they will glorify God.

Verses 17-22 The Christian and the Old Testament

The Old Testament (the law and prophets) is still the Word of God and profitable for Christians just like the New Testament. Jesus did not do away with the Old Testament. Some of the ceremonial commandments have been fulfilled, but as a whole, the Old Testament is full of rich meaning and blessed commands for Christians. Too many Christians try to evade their duties about tithing, etc., by saying that they are "law." The law is not done away with, but has still spiritual meaning for the Christian. Christians are not under obligation to keep such ceremonial matters as circumcision (I Cor. 7:18-20), the Jewish Sabbath on Saturday (Col. 2:14-17) or the Jewish diet forbidding pork, fish without scales, etc. (I Tim. 4:4, 5). But all the moral laws involved in others of the Ten Commandments and in other parts of the Old Testament are still the standard by which Christians ought to try to live.

Verse 20 explains the duty of Christians. Pharisees kept the letter of the law outwardly, but were inwardly hypocrites (Matt. 23; Luke 18:9-14). But Christians should have the law written in their hearts (Jer. 31:83), that is, a desire to please God and keep the spirit of the commandments. Love fulfills all the law (Matt. 22:37-40; Rom. 13:8-10; Gal. 5:14). In other words, verse 20 means that without a new heart, a heart with the righteousness of Christ and with a divinely implanted love for the will of God, no person can be saved. The righteousness we need is the righteousness obtained in being born again, so different from human morality.

Verses 21 and 22 show how a Christian should interpret the law. Not only those who actually and literally kill are guilty, but one who is "angry with his brother without a cause," or one who calls his brother "Raca" (or dunce) or "Thou fool" is also guilty. An unregenerate man who scorns his brother enough to call him a fool will be punished in Hell as a murderer, guilty of breaking the law! Compare this with Christ's interpretation of the command about adultery in verses 27 and 28. And hatred equals murder (I John 3:15).

The Ten Commandments say, "Thou shalt not kill," but one who hates in his heart is guilty of murder (I John 3:15), and one who even despises his brother enough to call him a fool is in danger of Hell-fire.

Jesus Did Not Contradict nor Countermand the Old Testament

It is of utmost importance to see that Jesus is here endorsing and authenticating all the Old Testament. The term, "the law," in verse 17, refers to the Pentateuch. The term, "the prophets," refers to the major and minor prophets of the Old Testament, but in general the two terms here meant the whole Old Testament, and Jesus came not to destroy but to fulfill the Old Testament Scripture. Those who would reject the creation account in Genesis, the story of the flood, or the miracles of Exodus must deal with Jesus Christ who declared that not one jot or tittle, the smallest letter and part of a letter in the Hebrew language, would pass away till all be fulfilled.

After Christ's resurrection He again declared that one was a fool even to be slow in heart to believe all that the prophets have spoken. "And beginning at Moses and all the prophets, he expounded unto them in all the scriptures the things concerning himself" (Luke 24:25-27). The Lord Jesus meant "all the scriptures"; the whole Old Testament is the inspired, infallible Word of God. Some modernists teach a "progressive revelation," by which they mean that some parts of the Bible are perfect and some less perfect, that the Bible is simply a record of religious thoughts and growth of the Jewish people, containing some revelation from God. Such modernists claim that the Old Testament does not give a true picture of God and they further set themselves up as judges of the moral standards of the Old Testament. But such teaching contradicts the plain statements of Jesus Christ.

Revelation in the Bible is progressive only in the sense that God revealed more about Himself and His will in additional revelations. But the first sentence in Genesis is as infallibly and perfectly the very Word of God as is John 3:16.

Some shallow students would try to make the Lord Jesus contradict Himself in this same fifth chapter of Matthew. They foolishly think that Jesus condemned certain Old Testament teachings after He had plainly said that the law and the prophets were imperishable and that He did not come to destroy the Old Testament. Such students call attention to the six times in this chapter in which Jesus said, "It was said... But I say unto you..." or similar terms, as if Jesus contradicted the Old Testament. But this He did not do as you will see.

1. In verses 21 and 22 Jesus endorses the plain Old Testament command, "Thou shall not kill..." But He adds His own interpretation that even anger and despising one's brother are sins that will bring judgment. Not a hint here that Jesus contradicts the Old Testament!

2. In verses 27, 28 Jesus not only endorses the Old Testament law about adultery, but says that God even judges the heart of man in regard to this sin.

3. In verses 31, 32 Jesus not only endorsed the Mosaic restriction on divorce, but He added even further restrictions.

4. In verses 33, 34 Jesus not only endorsed the Old Testament command that one should not break his oath, but added that we should "swear not at all."

5. In verses 38, 39 Jesus not only endorses the Old Testament command "an eye for an eye," but says that the Christian should immediately offer to make double restitution. If he deserves to be smitten on one cheek, he shall offer two. If he is sued at the law for his coat, he shall give his cloak also. If he is compelled by just law to go a mile in fulfilling the Old Testament command, he shall go two miles.

6. In verses 43 and 44 Jesus not only endorses the plain Old Testament command, "Thou shalt love thy neighbor," but He openly destroys the addition of the scribes, teaching that they should "hate thine enemy," which contradicted the Old. Testament law. See Leviticus 19:17, 18. The Old Testament nowhere commanded people to hate their enemies. That was a contradiction Jewish teachers had added.

In every single case Jesus not only verified the Old Testament law, but gave it wider spiritual application.

Verses 23-26 Making Restitution to One Wronged or Offended

These verses are important to show why prayers are not answered. As a Jew would bring his sacrifice to the altar, so a Christian offers his prayer to God, and God will not hear the prayer of one who has unforgiveness against his brother (Matt. 6:15; 18:35; Mark 11:25, 26). According to these verses, peace among Christian brethren is a most important consideration. Man cannot be right with God without being right with man (I John 2:9; I John 4:20). Every Christian should "agree with thine adversary quickly." Go not only half way, but all the way to make peace, no matter who is to blame. In connection with these verses, see verses 38 to 42 which also refer to restitution. Love, forgiveness, humility, the soft answer which "turneth away wrath" (Prov. 15:1), and the returning of good for evil will make peace, save expense and not cause the Christian to lose anything. I suggest the reader see the two long chapters on

"Hindered Prayer" in this author's book, *PRAYER – Asking and Receiving.*

In this connection, Proverbs 16:7 was once a great blessing to me in bringing peace with some wicked, unsaved people.

Verses 27-30 Sin Is in the Heart Where God Sees

Man judges by the outward appearance, but God looks on the heart (I Sam. 16:7). So all sin really originates in the heart (Matt. 12:34, 35; 15:18, 19; Luke 6:45). So the "respectable" man or woman may be a terrible adulterer or adulteress in the heart. The eye looking lustfully (vs. 29) ought to be judged by the Christian, and the hand that might be itching to take what does not belong to one (vs. 30) ought to make every man realize the wickedness of his heart. See how Jesus always strengthened the Old Testament commands.

These verses mean that being saved is more important than having your eye or having your hand or having your foot; that if it were necessary to keep out of Hell one should be willing to pluck out his eye, to cut off his hand, or cut off his foot. Actually, of course, it is never necessary to pluck out your eye; of course it is never necessary to cut off your hand or foot in order to be saved. But sometimes a lost sinner, in turning to the Lord, has to give up something that he loves better than hi? right eye or his hand or his foot. So whatever it costs when one must give up things to turn to Jesus and get converted and saved, being saved is worth all it costs and more. In other words, people should let nothing in the world jeopardize their souls' safety.

All of us are sinful. Therefore the only hope for any of us is mercy. All must plead guilty to terrible sin in the heart. Remember that the law is a schoolmaster to bring us to Christ (Gal. 3:24), so these verses show us our desperate need of a Saviour.

Verses 29 and 30 mean that the whole body shall be cast into Hell, There is no body but a physical body. Jesus said the same thing in Matthew 10:28, "And fear not them which kill the body, but are not able to kill the soul: but rather fear him which is able to destroy both soul and body in hell." Of course this casting of the body into

Hell will come after the resurrection of the unsaved. The resurrection and judgment of lost people is described in Revelation 20:11-15. Now the spirits of dead sinners are in Hell, but their bodies are in the graves, or in the sea, perhaps. But when the body is raised up and they will be judged, then both soul and body will be cast into Hell, as Jesus said.

Verses 31,32 Fornication, Continued Adultery, Only Reason Allowed for Divorce

Compare this with Matthew 19:3-12 which is fuller. See also Mark 10:2-12; I Corinthians 7:2-16. Verse 31 refers to Deuteronomy 24:1-4, which one ought to read very carefully. It becomes apparent that divorce includes the right to remarry. Notice with special care Deuteronomy 24:3, 4. A woman divorced from one husband and married to another must not go back to the first husband. He is called "her FORMER husband" and is not really her husband any more. People who have done wrong about divorce ought not to do wrong again by breaking the second marriage, as that cannot please God. According to the teaching of Jesus, divorce, allowed to Old Testament Jews because of the hardness of their hearts, is not now permissible except where one party has been guilty of fornication (which means practically the same as adultery, except that fornication is a little stronger term meaning harlotry or continued adultery). Adultery breaks the marriage. Drunkenness, incompatibility, cruelty, etc., ARE NOT Bible reasons for divorce. However, when one party of a divorced couple commits adultery by remarriage, it evidently breaks the marriage vow and bond. The second marriage should not be broken to restore the first, according to Deuteronomy 24:3, 4. If you have so sinned, confess and get forgiveness. Often sin cannot be undone, but can be forgiven. See my pamphlet on *Divorce, the Wreck of Marriage,* or the book, *The Home: Courtship, Marriage and Children.* See discussion on Matthew 19:3-12.

Some say fornication is the sin of unmarried people, adultery the sin of the married. But is not fornication then forbidden in the seventh commandment? Fornication is from *pornea,* same root as word translated *whoremonger* and *harlot*. So fornication means continued adultery.

Verses 33-37 Oaths Forbidden

A Christian ought to be so careful of the truth that a simple word will be believed (vs. 37). Hear the words of the Son of God: "But I say unto you, *Swear not at all"!* Some Christians believe it wrong to take oaths in court, a judicial oath for government purposes. And because of that the Constitution provides that men may say, "I do solemnly affirm," instead of saying, "I do solemnly swear." Thus the Constitution of our country admits that a Christian is bound in conscience not to take the oaths which are forbidden by Jesus Christ. But the oath in court is simply a solemn assertion that one will tell the truth. If even that legal oath is offensive to some Christians, how can any child of God take the unnecessary, unchristian oath of the secret societies and lodges? Jesus said, "Swear not at all." And He said, "Let your communication be, Yea, yea; Nay, nay: for whatsoever is more than these cometh of evil." A child of God has a right to say, "Yes, yes," and "No, no," and he is expected to be believed. And any Christian who ever goes further than that sins against God. Certainly every Christian who ever took a lodge oath violated the command of Jesus Christ, and sinned.

Again in James 5:12 the command is so plain that it cannot be misunderstood: "But above all things, my brethren, swear not, neither by heaven, neither by the earth, neither by any other oath: but let your yea be yea; and your nay, nay; lest ye fall into condemnation."

"Above all things... swear not," says the Word of God, not by Heaven nor by earth, "neither by any other oath." A Christian is not to swear. And the command says that this is "above all things." What excuse have you, then, Christian man or woman, for taking the ungodly and barbarous oaths of the secret societies? How can you face your Lord and Master whose command is so plain? No Christian, then, can take secret society oaths without sinning against God and violating the command of Jesus Christ and of the Bible.

Verses 38-48 Jesus Goes Even Further Than the Old Testament in Requiring Restitution

The reference in verse 38 is to Exodus 21:23-36; Leviticus 24:20 and Deuteronomy 19:21. Notice from these passages and from verses 22 and 23 of this chapter that the Lord speaks here about restitution, making good some wrong you have done. Verse 39 says that Christians ought not to take advantage of that law to get revenge, but the principal meaning is this: if a man thinks you have mistreated him and you owe him the privilege of smiting your cheek, then let him smite both of them. The same lesson is taught in verses 40 to 42. Settle every case out of court if possible, even by giving more than is required (I Cor. 6:1-8). Do whatever is necessary to gain the good will and friendship of those who believe you have wronged them. And not only meet people halfway, but all the way.

Do not lose sight of the idea of restitution here. Verse 42 does not mean that to the first man who asks me for my car I ought to give it. It does mean that if I owe a man something and cannot pay it without giving up my car, I ought to do it quickly and gladly; or if he thinks I owe him, I ought to satisfy his claim. There are sometimes people to whom we ought not to give, since it would do them harm, and there are people to whom we ought not to loan money since it would lead them to sin, extravagance, and folly. But a Christian should go to any legitimate length to pay what he owes and to make restitution for his sin. However, the general sentiment of this Scripture would lead a Christian to be more liberal in his giving and more sympathetic toward the poor and needy, and many other Scriptures teach that we ought to have that attitude.

Take literally verses 43 to 47, and so be really like your Father in Heaven, fit to be His children, since you partake of His loving attitude toward sinners, toward enemies as well as friends. Remember the Beatitudes, especially verses 5, 7, 9, 10 and 11. Until you can love, forgive, and pray for your enemies and do good to them, as Jesus did, you will not be worthy of the name you bear. By loving your enemies and doing good for their evil, you may heap coals of fire on their heads (Prov. 25:21, 22; Rom. 12:20, 21). Verse

48, "Be ye therefore perfect..." gives the perfect standard, as does this whole chapter. We will never attain this until Jesus comes, but we ought to. God is not to blame when we do wrong. God knows we will sin, yet God must set a perfect standard; then He will not be blamable when we do wrong. At least we can strive toward this standard, even as Paul (Phil. 3:11-15).

God simply set a perfect standard. I have always told my children never to lie, never to do wrong. God could not afford to say that it is all right for a Christian to sin, for it is not all right. It is our own fault, and wickedness and sin always bring trouble. But it is still a fact that we do sin. God's standard is perfect, yet we do not keep it. That is the reason we must have a Saviour. Remember that the Sermon on the Mount is law, explained by Jesus. It does not attempt to set up human righteousness as the way to be saved.

This chapter is so rich that it ought to be meditated over with prayerful earnestness. May the Holy Spirit make it a rich and transforming message to your heart and life.

MATTHEW VI

Verses 1-4 Almsgiving Must Be Done Without Thought of Men's Approval: Secret Prayer

Important phrases in understanding these verses are "to be seen of them" (vs. 1) and "as the hypocrites do" (vs. 2). The important thing about giving is its motive. God looks on the heart. Any religious act, if it is to please God, must not be done with the thought of pleasing men or having their praise. Praying, giving, preaching, singing or living with the purpose of securing the favor and praise of men instead of pleasing God is hypocritical and wrong. This was the special sin of the Pharisees (Matt. 23: 5, 14, 23, 25-28).

"Alms" means particularly gifts to the poor. There would be more reason for keeping such gifts secret, to save embarrassment for those who receive alms. When a Christian gives to the poor, he should give in Jesus' name and when to a Christian, as to a brother. In the nature of the case, the right kind of almsgiving must not make the receiver appear as a pauper or publicly brand him as an object of charity. One who gives to the poor in Christ's name will be rewarded by the Father who sees in secret (vs. 4; Prov. 19:17). God will certainly reward and repay everything given to the poor in His name (Deut. 15:9-11; Prov. 22:9; Prov. 28:27; Isa. 58:7-11; Luke 6:38).

Do not think that public giving is always wrong. Many Bible examples prove otherwise. Christians are to let their light shine before men (Matt. 5:16). Jesus commended the widow who gave two mites in public. Jesus, His disciples, and others present saw the gift and the amount of it (Mark 12:41-44). Barnabas' large gift was known to others and recorded in the Bible (Acts 4:36, 37). The vow by Zacchaeus that he would give half his goods to the poor was made in public and evidently was approved by Christ (Luke 19:8, 9). The gifts of Israelites for the tabernacle seem to have been made publicly (Exod. 35:21-29). Certainly the gifts of the princes were not only public, but evidently there had been general agreement among them so that every one made the same offering

(Num. 7:10-89). It is not necessarily wrong for people to know about our giving, when the giving is to the Lord. Sometimes others will be blessed by our example, and the example ought to be known. But if gifts are directly to the poor, the poor should not be embarrassed by any publicity, and in no case should any Christian give with the motive of pleasing men and receiving the applause of men. Christians oftentimes find public giving a temptation to pride. In such cases particularly they ought not to make much of their giving. Primarily, giving, like other religious activities, should be to God and trusting Him only for reward.

Verses 5-8 Avoid Insincerity of Prayers to Impress Men

It is strange how easy it is to be a hypocrite about prayer. In these verses we are warned to watch about praying "as the hypocrites" (vs. 5) and not to pray in order to "be heard for... much speaking" (vs. 7). Prayer is so important that Satan makes it one of his principal grounds of attacking and misleading the Christian. Since prayerfulness is such a great virtue, all of us would like to be known as faithful men and women of prayer. So almost unconsciously Christians are tempted to increase the eloquence and length of their public prayers while they decrease in sincerity. So public prayer may become a snare. Many people use "vain repetitions," repetitions that are vain because they no longer represent the sincere desire of the heart. It is a sin to fall into forms of prayer while we lose the substance. It is a sin to pray as the hypocrites do, to be heard of and seen of men (vs. 5). Those who pray that way already "have their reward," that is, the only reward they will get – the applause of men. Compare the prayer of the Pharisee in Luke 18:11, 12 and Matthew 23:14. "For every one that exalteth himself shall be abased; and he that humbleth himself shall be exalted" (Luke 18:14). Preachers and Christian workers who are in many services are tempted to let public praying take the place of secret praying, but this will never do. No Christian is safe who does not regularly and often and earnestly pray in secret (vs. 6). Note the blessed promise in verse 6. If you cannot meet some other conditions of answered prayer, surely you can meet this one. I hope you will seize upon it today and claim it.

While secret prayer is absolutely necessary and most praying should be in secret, public praying is not necessarily wrong. Jesus prayed in public when He was anointed with the Holy Spirit at His baptism (Luke 3:21). The words of Jesus as He prayed before others at the grave of Lazarus are given in John 11:41, 42. He prayed publicly in Luke 10:21, 22. He prayed before His disciples in John 17, and urged them to pray with Him in the Garden of Gethsemane (Matt. 26: 40, 41). He prayed audibly before the multitude upon the cross (Matt. 27:46; Luke 23:46). Stephen also prayed at his death (Acts 7:59, 60). Solomon prayed before all Israel at the dedication of the temple (II Chron. 6:12-42). The Lord was pleased and answered the prayer (II Chron. 7:1). New Testament Christians are urged to pray in the congregation so that others may "say Amen at thy giving of thanks" (I Cor. 14:16), and if any prays in a foreign language, it is regrettable that he cannot be understood (I Cor. 14:14, 15). Paul also prayed in the presence of the Ephesian elders (Acts 20:36).

VAIN repetition is wrong in prayer, but sincere repetition itself is not. Jesus prayed three times saying the same words (Matt. 26:39, 42, 44). The poor widow of Luke 18:1-5 was commended by the Saviour for her persistence, and Christians are urged to do likewise in prayer (Luke 18:7). We are told in Luke 11:8 that the friend got the three loaves or more, "because of his importunity." Jacob got victory by his persistence in prayer (Gen. 32:26-29). Words one does not mean are "vain repetitions." As long as the heart calls out to God sincerely, it is proper to repeat a prayer until the answer comes.

Verses 9-11 The Model Prayer

It does not matter whether or not this is called "The Lord's Prayer." The Lord gave it, though it is a model for us. Christians should pray "after this manner." See also Luke 11:2-4. Christians may do well to use these words in prayer, but they do far better to use this spirit in prayer. This prayer should be used repeatedly by Christians to check their own prayers to see if they are according to the will of God.

"Our Father which art in heaven..." Only a born-again Christian can pray this prayer. To such a one God is a real, loving, approachable Father. The Christian has had put in his heart by

the Holy Spirit the cry, "Abba, Father" (Rom. 8:15, 16; Gal. 4:6). And the same Spirit bears witness to the Christian that he is a child of God. *Abba* is a very intimate, personal term, like *Papa* or *Daddy*. It is Aramaic, the language used by the common people to whom Jesus spoke. Our position as born-again sons with a loving Father should make us confident and bold in our praying. A loving God is more likely to answer the prayer of His children than of strangers.

"Hallowed be thy name." This means a reverent approach to God. Prayer is primarily request, but the approach to God should include worship, adoration, and submission.

"Thy kingdom come. Thy will be done in earth, as it is in heaven." This is clearly a prayer for the reign of Christ on earth. That kingdom has not yet come. His will is not yet "done in earth, as it is in heaven." Christ will set up His kingdom at His second coming (Matt. 25:31-46). Then the apostles will reign with Him on twelve thrones over the twelve tribes (Matt. 19:28). Other saints will reign with Him likewise "on the earth" (Rev. 5:10). It is the re-establishment of David's kingdom at Jerusalem with Christ on the throne which is foretold. This prayer, "Thy kingdom come," is the same in meaning as the inspired prayer of John in Revelation 22:20, "Even so, come, Lord Jesus."

Here we see the vital importance of the blessed hope of the premillennial coming of Christ in the prayer life of a Christian. The Christian need not pray for the whole world to be converted, for it will not be. He should pray for Christ to come speedily. Compare this with verse 33.

"Give us this day our daily bread" (vs. 11). We ought to pray for physical needs. God fed Elijah by the ravens (I Kings 17:6), by the widow's oil and meal (I Kings 17:9-16), and by an angel (I Kings 19:5-8). The righteous and faithful are promised, "verily thou shalt be fed" (Ps. 37:3). Prayer should be definite. Praise the Lord, He has many, many times sent us money or food, has answered prayer about cars and all kinds of necessities. It is faithless and wicked to believe that God answers prayer only about spiritual things and not about material needs.

But this prayer asks for bread only "this day" or as given in Luke 11:3, "day by day." In asking for today, we should be able to trust

86

about tomorrow. "And having food and raiment let us be therewith content" (I Tim. 6:8). God's plan is for Christians to walk by faith and not by sight, and be content with what each day brings, yet feeling free to ask for what they need. With this in mind, read verses 25 to 34.

Verses 12-15 Forgive and Be Forgiven!

While the notes in the Scofield Reference Bible are usually reliable, we disagree with the comment on this passage and on Luke 11:1-13. I do not believe that the Lord's prayer is "legal ground" or that to pray for Holy Spirit power, as we are commanded in Luke 11:13, is out of date. Notice the difference in wording between verse 12 and Luke 11:4. Notice the two senses in which one may be forgiven. The Christian who prays this prayer has *already* been forgiven *all* his sins as you see from Ephesians 1:7; 4:32; Colossians 1:14; 2:13. That forgiveness covers every sin of past, present and future, since all those were paid for on the cross of Christ, and after faith in Him one's sins are not imputed or charged up to the Christian (Rom. 4:5-8). That is the meaning of forgiveness as it applies to the salvation of the soul.

In these verses, however, we have the secondary meaning, forgiveness as it affects the person who is already saved, already a child of God. Though all my trespasses are already forgiven me (Col. 2:13) and not one of them can ever be charged against me to the condemnation of my soul, yet God is displeased when I sin and that sin interferes with the communion of the child with his 'Father which is in heaven.' Referring to the salvation of my soul, my sins are already all forgiven. But when fresh sin comes between the happy fellowship of the Father and child, then that sin needs to be removed, that is, forgiven, in the secondary sense. This is what the Scripture has in mind in I John 1:1-9. A Christian needs continual cleansing from sin, even though the debt of sin is already settled so that sin cannot take a Christian to Hell. In one sense the Christian is "clean every whit" as Jesus told Peter in John 13:10, but still the Christian needs his feet washed, that is, needs to be cleansed daily from the defilement of this world. And this daily cleansing and daily restoration of intimate, sweet fellowship with the Father we cannot have unless we forgive others their sins against us!

Again I remind you that this teaching is found many places in the Bible (Matt. 5:7; 18:23-35; Mark 11:25, 26). However wicked, however inexcusable anyone's sin against you has been, it is not a fraction as wicked as your sin against God. Forgive quickly, then, so you may be forgiven and have sweet fellowship with the Father and daily cleansing.

Verses 16-18 Fasting: Proper and Improper

Fasting is certainly proper. Daniel fasted (Dan. 9:3; 10:2, 3). Ezra and the Jews en route back to Palestine from Babylon fasted (Ezra 8:21-23) and God heard them. See also Nehemiah 9:1. Esther and her maidens joined Mordecai in fasting and prayer, and God heard and marvelously delivered the Jews (Esther 4:16; chap. 9). This deliverance is today celebrated by Jews in every nation with the feast of Purim. God heard the Ninevites when they fasted and prayed and He spared the city, though He had planned to destroy them (Jonah 3:7-10). And fasting is just as clearly taught in the New Testament. Jesus fasted forty days before His temptation (Matt. 4:2; Luke 4:2). John the Baptist and his disciples fasted often (Matt. 9:14). The disciples of Jesus evidently fasted before Pentecost while they waited and prayed for the filling of the Holy Spirit after Jesus "the bridegroom" was taken away (Matt. 9:15). Many prayers will never be answered without such earnestness and concern as will cause people to lose desire for food (Matt. 17:21). Paul was "in fastings" (II Cor. 6:5). For all this age Jesus gives encouragement to fasting in verses 17 and 18. Fasting is only out of order when it is formal, ceremonial, and insincere.

Fasting is another matter about which one can easily be a hypocrite, just as in giving (vss. 1-4) and in prayer (vss. 5-8). The Pharisees fasted oft (Matt. 9:14), some of them twice a week (Luke 18:12), but it was the fasting of a hypocrite with no real seeking after God. The real scriptural fasting is when one so earnestly desires to seek God's favor that one does without food, sometimes without water (Esther 4T6; Jonah 3:7) and sometimes without the normal relations of husband and wife (I Cor. 7:5). It does not please God for us to fast as a punishment, a way of doing penance. It does please God when we seek Him so earnestly that we lay aside other and less important matters until we find His face. There is a

88

physical reason, too, for fasting when we pray. The mind is usually clearer when bodily energy is not used in the digestion of food. Often a preacher can preach better without eating or a student may study better; so naturally a Christian can sometimes pray better without food. Fasting is not to pass away until wholehearted, heartbroken prayer disappears.

Some of the happiest days I have ever spent have been with groups of Christians who waited before God and did without a meal or two while we prayed and confessed our sins and sought for the will , of God and His blessing. Following such periods of fasting and prayer, I have seen wonderful times of blessing with many souls saved and remarkable answers from God. One should never fast that one may appear to men to fast, and if one does fast, he should be cheerful about it. Every Christian should experience seasons of fasting and prayer. Verse 18 indicates that there is a special reward from God for those who fast secretly, earnestly seeking His face. Such secret giving, secret praying, and secret fasting as commanded in this chapter have special rewards and these rewards will come openly before the world so that all may see (vss. 4, 6, 18).

Verses 19-24 Treasures to Be Laid Up in Heaven, Not on Earth

It was verse 19 that convinced me years ago that I ought not to have life insurance, since it is a form of savings. On verse 19 and the rest hi the chapter I made a covenant with God to try to put His business first and that I would depend upon Him to care for me and my family. We dropped the $10,000 life insurance and have never regretted it a day.

However, each person must find the best application for himself. Each one who renounces savings or life insurance should be assured in his own mind, act on his own faith. These verses do not teach waste. Many Scriptures prove that thrift pleases God. The ants are commended because "they prepare their meat in the summer" (Prov. 30:25). The wise woman is praised because she earns, saves and buys a field (Prov. 31:16). So earning, investing, and thrift are good virtues. And life insurance is a form of saving that may be justified for some. I was led not to carry it for myself. Each must find leading for himself.

89

But these verses teach a clear doctrine that Christians ought not to pile up treasures for themselves on earth. "Mammon" in verse 24 means money, not primarily the Devil. One cannot serve God and property, money, possessions. The deadly danger of treasure is indicated in verse 21. One who lays up money in this world soon sets his heart on this world instead of Heaven, soon has a money lust which is the root of all evil (I Tim. 6:10). The glorious success a Christian can have in the Lord's work depends upon a single eye, that is, mind and heart set clearly in one direction to please God first in everything. Laying by for old age has ruined the soul-winning fire of many an evangelist. Building a home or laying by an estate for wife and children has taken many a preacher out of the ministry. The love of money is the besetting sin of Christian business men. It is very rare that one can lay by much money and be a real soul-winning, Spirit-filled Christian. Preachers sometimes say that Christians ought to make all the money they can make honestly, but that utterly contradicts these words of Jesus. Christians ought to win all the souls they can and try to make enough money for needs. Money ought to be just incidental with a Christian. May every student of the Bible take to heart the teaching of this passage and decide which master he will serve (vs. 24). Great darkness is in the life of the Christian whose mind is divided, trying to serve both God and money (vs. 23).

Verses 25-34 Trusting in God's Care, the Cure of All Fretting

Compare verses 25 and 34. Jesus commands, "Take no thought... what ye shall eat or what ye shall drink... what ye shall put on." Do you believe Jesus meant what He said? And verse 34 says, "Take therefore no thought for the morrow." Evidently there is a shocking and almost universal sin on the part of Christians who are 30 anxious about food and clothes and about tomorrow that they disgrace their profession of faith. Christians should ask for bread day by day (vs. 11), then be 'content with such things as they have' without any worry about the morrow (Heb. 13:5). Murmuring and worry, anxiety about food and drink and provision were the great sins of the Israelites in the wilderness (Exod. 15:24; 16:2, 3, 8).

Verses 26 to 30 definitely promise that the God who feeds the birds who do not sow nor reap nor save, and clothes the lilies of the field which do not toil nor spin, will certainly provide food and raiment for His own dear children!

Christians should not worry about a better job, but be concerned about serving God better. Christians should not worry about food, clothes, and rent money, but rather weep over lost sinners as Jesus did. It is as certain as the promise of Jesus can make it that He will care for His own who depend upon Him. I thank God here that twenty-eight years ago God led me to give up all regular salary and depend upon Him for living expenses and the care of my family. It is my testimony that He has through these years not only cared for food, clothes, and house rent, but has preserved our health, supplied money for radio services, revivals, and hundreds of thousands of dollars for printing the Gospel and has sent many helpers and supplied their need and ours to this good hour. Some Christians fear to trust the Lord to repay even one-tenth of their income; they dare not tithe. These miss a blessing. But rather they ought to surrender everything to Christ and trust Him day by day. Any Christian who commits himself wholly to the Lord to seek first His kingdom and His righteousness will find God Himself adds the food, clothes, and all necessary things.

I suggest that every reader memorize verse 33, then have a quiet season of prayer with God and enter into a holy covenant to trust that promise and meet God upon it from this time forth.

The word *"Gentiles"* in verse 32 might well be translated *the nations* or *the heathen*. Jesus was speaking to the Jews when all other races were heathen people. If a Christian must be worried about food and clothes and anxiously burdened about the needs of tomorrow, what better is he than the heathen? That is the meaning of verses 31 and 32. If your Christianity does not help you to solve the many problems and banish worry about food, clothes, rent, and the needs of tomorrow, then you have shamed Christ and need to go back to this Sermon on the Mount and learn what faith and surrender are!

This Bible study ought to transform lives. In this matter I beg you to get the victory in your heart before you leave this chapter. This chapter calls for a prayer meeting and I pray that every student will finish the study of this chapter with victory in his heart not only about tithing, but about whether God wants you to lay by money or to worry at all about food and clothes.

The perfect cure for anxiety on these and other matters is found in Philippians 4:6, 7. Better memorize these verses.

MATTHEW VII

Verses 1-6 Judging Others Forbidden

"Judge not, that ye be not judged." Compare this with Luke 6:37, 38. That is, one is not to pass judgment on people's motives and hearts, since one does not know them. We can never tell definitely what people think, how they feel, or the desires of their hearts. We cannot tell whether or not people are saved. Only God who knows the heart can do so.

The particular reason given here for not judging others is "that ye be not judged." Do you want others judging your heart, your motives, your deeds, condemning you when they cannot have all the evidence? Luke 6:37 throws further light on this. Judging not is part of being merciful (Luke 6:36) and has the same promise. "Judge not, and ye shall not be judged: condemn not, and ye shall not be condemned: forgive, and ye shall be forgiven: Give, and it shall be given unto you." One who judges others is not merciful and will not receive mercy. If he condemns, he will be condemned. If he will not forgive, then he shall not be forgiven. If he does not give, he shall not receive. This is the law of God.

Compare verse 1 with verses 16 and 20. "Beware of false prophets... Ye shall know them by their fruits." People often think these contradict each other. They do not. We cannot judge people, but we can judge doctrine. I cannot tell whether a man is saved, but I can tell whether his doctrine is true or false, by comparing it with the Bible. A man may be a false prophet (vs. 15) in doctrine, and you can so judge by the fruit, that is, by his teaching. But you cannot certainly know by one's actions whether he is saved or not saved, and you cannot read the motives of the heart. Be merciful about passing judgment or you may be judged without mercy yourself.

Notice "Thou hypocrite" (vs. 5). The term is several times used in this Sermon on the Mount (Matt. 6:2, 5, 16). The sins warned against are the sins of moral church-going people, even of saved people. Christians are often hypocrites about praying, about giving, about fasting, about judging others.

93

Verses 3 to 5 indicate that those most critical of others have the biggest sins. So says Romans 2:1 also. Those really closest to God are charitable, willing to forgive rather than to criticize, anxious to lift up instead of tear down. Here we are told that the ordinary critic has a beam or plank in his own eye when he wants to get the mote or dust out of his brother's eye. The best Christians may have motes or dust in their eyes, since all of us are sinful and weak and live in the midst of a wicked world. They need these motes removed, but we should not listen to the criticisms of those who are in worse sin than the ones they criticize. Verse 3 tells of a universal failing among human beings. It is easier to see the other man's sins than our own. In Luke 6:37-42 the same teaching is given.

Often a Christian who has a complaint against another Christian, after a time of repentance and confession of his own sins will find that his grievance against a brother or sister has completely disappeared. In dozens of cases I have known of backsliders or lost sinners who despised and criticized preachers and their sermons, but when the sinner was saved or the backslider got right with God, he found his criticisms had all disappeared.

"Give not that which is holy unto the dogs, neither cast ye your pearls before swine..." This verse indicates there are some people with whom we ought not to associate and persons sometimes reach a state where we should not even give them the Gospel. The Lord even warns us that when people commit a certain sin ᴧee should not pray for it (I John 5:16). There are times when Christians should shake the dust off their feet and go out of certain homes or even out of certain towns (Matt. 10:14; Luke 10:11). After repeated trainings, Moses said to Pharaoh, "...I will see thy face again no more" (Exod. 10:29). There are times when you can do more to win a lost sinner by giving him some plain, honest words and leaving him for the Holy Spirit to teach. Verse 6 certainly means that there are some people so set in sin that we should not associate with them. On some occasions Christians can fall into such sin that they ought to be excluded from churches (I Cor. 5:1-5) and when they should be treated by Christian people as publicans, that is, avoided as lost sinners are (Matt. 18:17).

However, you must remember that in actual practice the example of Jesus indicates that the self-righteous Pharisees would be the ones to avoid while He gave the Gospel to publicans and harlots and was often gladly received by them.

Remember that those who judge others – people who think they know so much that they feel perfectly free to criticize anybody – are more likely to be the dogs and swine of verse 6 than drunkards and criminals. Often the vilest sinners hear the Gospel most gladly, when self- righteous, critical hypocrites will not.

Beware of the great sin of judging others. Compare it with James 4:11. See also I Timothy 5:19 and Isaiah 65:5. A sermon on this subject by the author is printed in the book, *The Ruin of a Christian,* with the same publisher as this volume. It has helped many.

Verses 7-11 Wonderful Promises About Prayer

Compare this passage with Luke 11:1-13. Great lessons are to be learned by the similarities and the differences. Especially compare verse 11 here with Luke 11:13. One verse promises "GOOD THINGS to them that ask him" and the other promises "THE HOLY SPIRIT to them that ask him." The meaning is that to be anointed with the Holy Spirit of God is equivalent to getting all good things. The Holy Spirit brings happiness, wisdom, leadership, soul-winning power and even helps one pray for whatever he needs.

Notice also that the promise of verses 7 and 8 is repeated in Luke 11:9, 10, and there the particular emphasis is on soul-winning power. There a man (representing a Christian in prayer), is asking bread from one Friend (God) who has plenty, for another friend (the lost sinner) who has none So every Christian may beg God to help him win a sinner to Christ. With that in mind, the promise about asking, seeking, and knocking is given. The promise stands alone and means what it says here about whatever we are asking or seeking or knocking, but the primary meaning in Luke 11 is evidently about soul-winning power, that is, the power of the Holy Spirit as you see in Luke 11:13.

The persistent praying, the 'importunity' mentioned in Luke 11:8, is what is meant by asking, seeking, and knocking in verses 9 and 10 following. The asking is persistent asking; the seeking is continual, earnest, tearful seeking; the knocking is importunate knocking at the door until God opens it. See how a passage in one of the Gospels sheds more light on similar passages in another Gospel. Let the Bible explain itself.

The Scripture says, "For every one that asketh receiveth..." Jesus did not say and did not mean that every person who asks *one time* is always answered. The term *asketh* in the Greek is in the present tense, with the sense of keeping on asking. Here persistent prayer is promised an answer.

If your prayer is wrong, keep on praying and God will show you how to change your prayer to get it answered, as He showed Paul about the thorn in the flesh (II Cor. 12:7-9). See on this the chapter "Just Pray" in my book, *PRAYER – Asking and Receiving.*

What blessed encouragements to pray are given here! Many Bible passages name conditions of answered prayer. God promises to answer the prayer of faith (Matt. 17:20; Mark 9:23; Mark 11:22-24). Elsewhere God promises answered prayer to those who abide in Christ and His will (Ps. 37:4; John 15:7). Again, everything that is asked sincerely in Jesus' name may be had in prayer (John 14:13, 14; John 16:24). Asking according to His will (I John 5:14, 15), obeying His commands (I John 3:22), persistence in prayer (Luke 18:1-8), and agreement in prayer (Matt. 18:19) are all given as definite conditions on which God will answer prayer. Meeting any one of these conditions guarantees the answer to our prayers. God never required that a Christian should meet every condition at once. Knowing our frailty and our sin, He knew that would usually be impossible.

But here, God makes praying even easier. Every one who keeps on asking receives. He who keeps on seeking finds. And to him who keeps on knocking it shall be opened. Do not dodge this plain Word of God. It is true. God answers prayer! Compare it with the promise of Matthew 6:6. The one who sincerely asks will not miss the reward. See also James 4:2. Dear student, possibly you have many sins about prayer. Perhaps you have little faith, or you may not make your requests sincerely in Jesus' name. But the greatest sin you have on the matter of prayer is that *you do not pray!* God wants you to make definite requests and expect definite answers. "Ask, and it shall be given you." God delights to hear and answer prayers. It is one of the marks of His love and His deity. He loves to be called the God who hears prayer (Ps. 65:2). He invites big prayers (Ps. 81:10; Jer. 33:3). He insists that there is nothing too hard for God to do in answer to prayer (Gen. 18:14; Jer. 32:17, 27). He even urges us to pray great prayers like Elijah whose prayers brought drought for three and a half years, and then abundant rain (Jas. 5:14-18).

We are commanded to pray for the kingdom of Christ on earth, for daily bread, for forgiveness, for deliverance from temptation and evil (Matt. 6:10-13), about healing of our bodies (Jas. 5:14, 15), about Holy Spirit, soul-winning power (Luke 11:13), for deliverance from enemies who oppress and misuse us (Luke 18:1-8), about help in trouble (Ps. 34:17, 18; Ps. 50:15). Really, one should pray for anything in the world that one wants (Ps. 37:4; Mark 11:24; John 15:7). Big prayers, many prayers, persistent prayers, believing prayers, greatly honor God. He is more anxious to give than we are to receive, so pray. Happiness depends on answered prayer (John 16:24).

It is a sin not to pray (I Sam. 12:23). Christians should "pray without ceasing" (I Thess. 5:17), should 'pray ALways with ALL prayer, with ALL perseverance for ALL saints,' with begging and watching (Eph. 6:18).

Why not have a new covenant with God now about your prayer life? (1) Write out a list of things that you ought to ask of God. Be definite. Really expect an answer. (2) Set apart a certain time in the day, preferably in the early morning, to watch, pray, meditate and read your Bible. Get things from God. (3) Find what sins in your life displease God and block the answer to your prayers, whether family life (I Pet. 3:1-7), unforgiveness (Matt. 6:14, 15; Mark 11:25, 26), robbing God (Mai. 3:8, 9), rebellion (I Sam. 15:22, 23), or any other sin (Isa. 59:1, 2). Have it out with God. (4) Promise God to openly acknowledge the answers to prayer when they come and give God the glory.

Do you realize how God loves you as a father loves his children? (vs. 11; Ps. 103:13). Do not fail to ask much. We should come boldly to the throne of grace since we have a heavenly High Priest to intercede for us (Heb. 4:16; I John 2:1). If sins have been in the way, a simple heartfelt confession and forsaking of them will remove them (Prov. 28:13; I John 1:9). Take plenty of time on these Scriptures and get them in the heart as well as the head. "But be ye doers of the word, and not hearers only, deceiving your own selves" (Jas. 1:22).

Verse 12 The Golden Rule

This is called the golden rule. This is stated again in Luke 6:31. Notice the connection in Luke, chapter 6, with giving (Luke 6:30), with being merciful (vs. 36), with not judging or condemning, but forgiving (vs. 37), and again giving (vs. 38). Another way of stating this same principle is to "love thy neighbour as thyself" (Matt. 22:39).

It is understood that this golden rule would only be properly applied by those who wish to please God. If I were a wicked drunkard and wanted people to give me liquor or narcotics, that evil wish would not make it proper for me to give to Others these evil things. But we may be sure that any one who earnestly tries to follow the Saviour in this rule would want God's will done. Summed up, this verse means, 'Do good to others as you want them to do good to you.' The last of verse 12 shows that it sums up all of the good of the Mosaic Law and the prophets who interpreted the law in the Old Testament. Compare this with Matthew 22:37-40.

Verses 13,14 More People Lost Than Saved

Compare with this Luke 13:24. The terrible meaning is obvious. The road to Hell is wider than the road to Heaven. More people go to Hell than to Heaven. The gate and the way are Jesus (John 14:6). Any other way in the world by which people try to be saved without being born again by faith in Christ will lead to everlasting destruction. There is only one way of getting to Heaven. See John 10:1; Acts 4:12.

Verses 15-20 Beware of False Prophets

Every Christian ought to be on his guard against false prophets, false teachers. One of the distinctive features of false teachers is that they "come to you in sheep's clothing." They have smooth words, they pretend to believe the Bible, they quote Scriptures. Satan and his ministers come as angels of light and righteousness (II Cor. 11:13-15). One must earnestly try the spirits whether they be of God (I John 4:1). One needs constantly to study the Scriptures to see whether these things are so (Acts 17:11). The good fruits mentioned in verses 16 to 20 are the true Gospel, true Bible teaching. However persuasive or gentlemanly or cultured or kindly a teacher is, if he is not true to the Bible, then beware!

Modernists, preachers, and college teachers who deny the inspiration of the Bible, the deity of Christ and blood redemption, are often very agreeable. They are friendly; they speak kindly; they have culture, personality. A man may quote Scriptures and yet not believe the Bible. He may claim to be a preacher and yet be an infidel. False prophets come in sheep's clothing. Christian Scientists, for instance, seem to have prayers answered for healing and are often cultured people, yet they deny the blood atonement, the need for a new birth, and even the fact of sin.

Your duty about false teachers is 1. Beware (vs. 15). 2. Check their fruits carefully (vss. 16, 20), check them by the Bible. 3. Try the spirits and see whether they be of God (I John 4:1). Some heresies are not so important, but teachers or preachers denying the deity of Christ and blood atonement should not even be received in your church or in your home (II John 7-11). You should not even bid them Godspeed!

Verses 21-23 Religious But Lost!

Compare this with Luke 13:25-30. The sad, sad fact is that many who expect to go to Heaven will be disappointed. Some who think they are saved are not. Millions depend on their morals, their good deeds, depend on their baptism, or church membership, or even on their feelings, and so will go to Hell. Notice that this follows the teaching about false prophets. Many will follow false prophets. Some think they are saved by various rites and ceremonies, by their good deeds, etc. Every preacher deals with the destiny of immortal souls and must beware lest he mislead. There is no salvation except when one definitely trusts in Christ for forgiveness and so has his sins forgiven and his heart changed. The most virtuous woman, the most moral man will awake in torment, perhaps surprised, but certainly condemned forever, if he does not get born again (John 3:3, 5, 7, 18, 36). See my sermon on *Religious – But Lost* on these verses – in pamphlet form, same publisher as this volume.

Notice verse 23 very carefully, "I NEVER knew you." Jesus is not talking to people who were once saved and then fell away. No, He is talking to people whom He never did know in salvation. Notice the sad warning of the five foolish virgins who did not have the oil, which represents being born of the Spirit and so having the Holy Spirit living within as all Christians do (Matt. 25:1-13; Rom. 8:9). Verse 22 indicates that many preachers will not be saved. What about multitudes of Catholic priests and other preachers who teach salvation by works, or salvation by the church? Remember Judas who evidently worked miracles in Christ's name, as this verse says. Let every Christian beware and make sure of his salvation. Heed the warnings of Hebrews 4:1, 2, 11; of II Peter 1:10. Claim the promises of John 3:16, 18; Acts 16:31; Romans 10:9, 10.

Verses 24-29 Build on Christ the Rock

Jesus is here reinforcing the teachings of the preceding verses, 13 to 23. Many hear the Gospel and never do anything about it. The words "and doeth them" do not refer to ordinary good deeds by which men sometimes hope to be saved. Rather the Lord means doing the will of God by trusting in Christ for salvation (John 6:29). One who trusts in Christ, turning from his sins, 'obeys the Gospel' (Rom. 10:16). The good deed of a wise man mentioned in verse 24 is that he "built his house upon a rock." The rock is Christ. The wise man depends upon Christ for salvation and rests in Him. Compare the "wise man" here with the "wise virgins" in Matthew 25:4. "The fear of the Lord is the beginning of wisdom" (Prov. 9:10). The rock is Jesus. "For other foundation can no man lay than that is laid, which is Jesus Christ" (I Cor. 3:11). "That Rock was Christ" (I Cor. 10:4). See also Isaiah 28:16; Matthew 16:18; I Peter 2:6-8.

The song rightly says:

> "On Christ, the solid Rock, I stand;
> All other ground is sinking sand."

Is your house built on Christ, the Rock? Then rejoice today that you are a child of God and saved forever.

MATTHEW VIII

Verses 1-4 A Leper Cleansed

The mountain mentioned is the mount upon which the sermon was preached in chapters 5, 6, and 7. It was in Galilee near the Sea of Galilee as you see from Matthew 4:18-25.

Compare this with Mark 1:40-45 and Luke 5:12-16 which tell the same story.

Notice the leper's attitude, calling Jesus "Lord" (vs. 2). See also I Corinthians 12:3. The thief on the cross called Jesus "Lord" (Luke 23:42), so did the woman taken in adultery (John 8:11), both of whom Jesus instantly forgave. The Syrophenician woman also called Jesus "Lord" and got her prayers answered (Mark 7:28, 29). To sincerely call Jesus *Lord* involves surrender to His will, faith in His power, dependence on His mercy. This leper had full confidence in Christ's power, "thou canst make me clean." That kind of approach was pleasing to Jesus who said, "I will; be thou clean" (vs. 3). When faith says, "Lord, I know You can, will You?" it pleases Christ to be able to say, "I will." Leprosy was a type of sin and was used as a brand for sin in the case of Miriam (Num. 12:10), of Gehazi the servant of Elisha (II Kings 5:27) and of King Uzziah (II Chron. 26:16-21). It is still a serious and dangerous disease in the Philippine Islands, China, India, and certain parts of Africa, and there are leper colonies even in the United States.

The Mosaic Law gave plain rules about lepers (Lev., chapters 13, 14). They were counted unclean and should not be touched by those who would be ceremonially clean for the worship (Lev, 13:45, 46). Any garment or house contaminated was to be purified or destroyed (Lev. 13:51, 52; 14:40-45). When a leper was found to be clean, he showed himself to the priest and offered two clean birds and one or two lambs after the eighth day (Lev. 14:1-32). This leper was cleansed, made ceremonially clean as well as healed, when Jesus cured his leprosy. Jesus required the man to fulfill the Mosaic Law, having the priest certify him clean and offer the sacrifices mentioned in the law (vs. 4; Lev. 14:4, 10). Verse 4 says this was as a testimony unto the priests. Jesus did not deliberately encourage any violation of the Mosaic Law. He gave similar commands to the ten lepers (Luke 17:14).

Notice the command of Jesus in verse 4, "See thou tell no man." Mark 1:45 tells how this command of Jesus was disobeyed and such crowds gathered that "Jesus could no more openly enter into the city." We suppose Jesus did not work this miracle to prove He was the Son of God, but rather out of His love for this man whose faith He honored.

Verses 5-13 The Centurion's Servant Healed

This passage should be studied in connection with Luke 7:1-10, which adds a number of facts not mentioned here. (1) This centurion was greatly, beloved by the Jews and had built a synagogue for them. (2) These Jewish friends came to Jesus beseeching Him to heal the centurion's servant. (3) The centurion had sent word, evidently, before he himself saw Jesus, that he was not worthy to have. Jesus enter into his home. See how the four gospels supplement each other. Do not doubt the accuracy of the Scriptures because the Gospels give varying accounts of the same things. Remember the principle stated in John 21:25 that not nearly all Jesus said and did could be written down. Much more occurred which is not mentioned by any of the Gospels. The believing heart will, accept all the statements of the Bible without seeking to make them contradict each other as they never really do when carefully studied. The account in Luke 7:1-10 shows more of the worth, the humility, and the faith of this Gentile so loved by the Jews. Though he felt himself unworthy even to talk with Jesus, much less to have the Saviour come under his roof, all the Jews felt that he was worthy, and Jesus praised him most highly. The humble receive the attention of Jesus the quickest of all (Luke 14:11; Jas. 4:6, 10).

Note the argument of the centurion in verse 9. This centurion was a man under military authority, taking orders from others, yet having authority himself over a hundred soldiers, as the word *centurion* means. He really felt that if he could command soldiers to come and go, or command his servants, how much more could Jesus, the Son of God, drive away the sickness from his servant.

102

Again we see the principle expressed in verses 2 to 4. Jesus is pleased when we believe that He has the power to do whatsoever He will without being handicapped by the circumstances.

Jesus could heal in the presence of the sick, but could heal just as well being absent. Today He can save a sinner who is here, but can just as easily answer the prayer of a mother for her boy who is a thousand miles away if that mother claims His promise and believes Him. Jesus can heal as well without doctors as with them; can heal one who is "ready to die" as this man was (Luke 7:2) just as well as He can heal a slight illness. Jesus is the Master of circumstances, and the faith of the centurion who believed that Jesus could heal being absent as well as being present greatly honored Christ. Thomas believed when sufficient physical evidence was brought that Jesus was raised from the dead (John 20:27, 28). But Jesus promised a special blessing on those who believed, not having seen (John 20:29).

Reader, can you trust God for daily bread as well when you do not have a job as when you do? Can you expect a revival in opposing circumstances as well as in fair circumstances? Blessed is the faith that can believe Jesus being absent as well as being present; can expect miracles that are unlikely as well as things which are likely. God wants Christians to sow the seed without regarding too much the wind or observing the clouds (Eccles. 11:4). The command is to preach the Word "out of season" as well as "in season" (II Tim. 4:2).

Notice the use of the term "the kingdom of heaven" in verses 11 and 12. The kingdom there discussed would need to be a kingdom on earth since it was to be in the land promised to "Abraham, and Isaac, and Jacob," the land of Palestine (Gen. 13:14-17; 17:8; 28:4). It would need to be a Jewish kingdom since the Jews here are called "the children of the kingdom." In Heaven any believing Gentile is promised just as much as any believing Jew, but God has promises about Palestine which are more especially made to the literal descendants of Abraham, and those by race connected historically with Jerusalem and the throne of David there. These verses show that "the kingdom of heaven" refers to the restoration of the Jewish monarchy when Jesus will sit on the throne of David at Jerusalem as is taught in Isaiah 9:6, 7; Isaiah, chapter 11; Zechariah 14:9; Matthew 19:28; 25:31. It will be a heavenly kingdom in that the will of God will be done on earth as it is in

Heaven (Matt. 6:10) and in the sense that it will be a kingdom which "the God of heaven" shall set up on earth, which kingdom shall never be destroyed (Dan. 2:44).

The warning here is that many Jews reject Christ and so will miss that kingdom of Christ on earth while many Gentiles will come from the East and the West to sit down with Abraham, Isaac and Jacob in tire kingdom, having trusted in Christ as this centurion did. There is much evidence that the centurion was a truly converted soul.

Compare the words of Jesus in verse 13, "and as thou hast believed, so be it done unto thee" with "according to your faith be it unto you" (Matt. 9:29), and again, "If thou canst believe, all things are possible to him that believeth" (Mark 9:23).

Does not your heart rejoice to see how pleased Jesus was at the man's faith, as verse 10 tells? Faith is counted for righteousness (Gen. 15:6) and without faith one cannot please God. (Heb. 11:6).

Verses 14-18 Peter's Wife's Mother Healed

Mark 1:29-34 tells the same story and so does Luke 4:38-41. Notice that Mark and Luke call Peter "Simon." Mark 1:29 indicates that Andrew lived in the same house with Peter. Matthew simply tells that Peter's mother-in-law was sick of a fever, but Luke 4:38 says she "was taken with a *great* fever." That verse also says, "and they besought him for her." They begged Jesus to heal her.

Peter was a married man and no fit predecessor for Roman Catholic popes. Actually, of course, Peter was not a pope nor anything of the kind. Neither the doctrines nor the monstrous organization of Rome had been invented. Peter had no authority over the rest of the apostles, but was himself soundly and publicly rebuked by Paul (Gal. 2:11-14). He certainly never claimed infallibility in church matters, and there is no evidence in history or Scripture that he was bishop or pastor of the church at Rome, or even that he was ever there. The Roman Catholic conception of the church is unscriptural; it relies more on tradition than on the Bible, and Rome has usurped an authority not given in the Scriptures when it claims Peter as the first pope.

"The even" (vs. 16) means sundown (Mark 1:32; Luke 4:40). Mark and Luke both tell that Jesus did not allow the devils to speak because they knew Him.

Verse 17 is a clear reference to Isaiah 53:4. It is not a word for word quotation, but a translation, since Isaiah was written in Hebrew and the New Testament was written in Greek. The word *griefs* there was translated *infirmities* here, and *sorrows* in Isaiah was translated *sicknesses* here. That makes it seem certain that we should take Isaiah 53:5 literally, "with his stripes we are healed." The Scripture here says that when Jesus healed the sick He was fulfilling Isaiah 53:4 and that the sufferings of Christ paid for our physical healing. Is healing in the atonement? I agree with Dr. R. A. Torrey that it is. We believe all the good things a Christian is to inherit were paid for on the cross. On this matter see Romans 8:23 where it is plainly said that "we ourselves groan within ourselves, waiting for the adoption, to wit, THE REDEMPTION of our body" and Romans 8:21 promises that "the creature [the created body] itself also shall be delivered from the bondage of corruption into the glorious liberty of the children of God." Our bodies then are to be redeemed, too, and Christ has already atoned for all the sickness and weakness of sinful flesh. As Matthew 8:17 says, "Himself took our infirmities, and bare our sicknesses." But clearly we do not receive all that is purchased for us till the resurrection.

This is a blessed passage on which Christians have a right to pray for healing of the body each according to such faith as God gives, and according to God's will, and is a sweet promise of the future perfect health and glorious freedom from pain and sorrow which every Christian will one day have. But it is important to remember that we are not promised all this until we receive our glorified bodies at the coming of Christ, when the living saints will be changed and those who have fallen asleep will be raised from the dead (I Cor. 15:52; I Thess. 4:16). Those who believe that every Christian can now obtain perfect health are mistaken. God does heal the sick and invites us to pray for the sick (Jas. 5:13-16). "The prayer of faith shall save the sick," but God does not always give faith for healing. It is not always His will to heal. He did not remove Paul's thorn in the flesh (II Cor. 12:7-9). God Himself often chooses that we shall be sick for our own good and His glory (Job 1:6-12; 2:3-7; John 11:4; Heb. 12:6), not necessarily because of sin. In fact, every Christian should expect to die unless Jesus comes soon.

It is true that Jesus has paid for the perfect healing of our bodies, but it is never promised us that we can receive all that perfect health now. We have more redemption coming, the perfect redemption of our bodies in the future.

Incidentally, the Scripture never teaches that it is wrong to use medicine and doctors. God can use means in healing. For the healing of Hezekiah, God had Isaiah use a plaster of figs (II Kings 20:7; Isa. 38:21), and for Timothy's weak stomach, the inspired apostle instructed that he "use a little wine" or grape juice (I Tim. 5:23).

See the author's pamphlet on *Healing in Answer to Prayer.*

"The other side" in verse 18 means the other side of the Sea of Galilee from Capernaum where Jesus was. It would be only a few miles. The *sea* is really a lake some seven or eight miles wide, thirteen or fourteen miles long.

Verses 19-22 Casual Discipleship Discouraged

Jesus here seemed to discourage those who would follow Him. Rather, He insisted on their carefully weighing the facts before announcing their decision. The same incidents are given in Luke 9:57-62, but in verse 62 Jesus gives the explanation for His plain speech. Disciples should decide so clearly when they start to follow Christ that they will not look back after putting the hand to the plough. Jesus gave similar warnings in Luke 9:23 and Luke 14:26-33. It means forsaking much when you really start out to follow Jesus. He wants people to count the cost. Serving Jesus may mean poverty for us as it meant for Jesus Himself (vs. 20).

The disciple in verse 21 evidently meant, 'Let me delay until my father dies and when he is buried, I will follow You.' It seems unlikely that Jesus would have forbidden a man to go to his father's funeral if he were already dead. "The dead" in verse 22 refers to the spiritually dead. One called of God to serve Him must sometimes leave the care of father and mother in the hands of others who are spiritually dead.

Verses 23-27 Jesus Rebukes Wind and Waves

This account is also given in Mark 4:36-41 and Luke 8:22-25. Mark tells us that "there were also with him other little ships" and Luke tells us with interest, "But as they sailed he fell asleep." The Sea of Galilee (also called the Sea of Tiberias in John 6:1 and the Lake of Gennesaret in Luke 5:1) was small, but serious storms arose considering the small size of the ships.

It was evidently a sin for these disciples to be afraid, the sin of little faith. They felt safer with Jesus awake than with Him asleep, not thinking that in all the universe of God nothing is ever out of His control. Let Christians take a lesson here. If you are frightened and worried by wind, rain, lightning, and other such matters, then confess it to God as a sin and ask Him to take the fear out of your heart. Christians ought to take normal precautions for safety, but in every matter a Christian ought to have sweet peace and "be careful for nothing" since the remedy for every worry and care is given us (Phil. 4:6, 7; I Pet. 5:7). He has promised, "Thou wilt keep him in perfect peace, whose mind is stayed on thee: because he trusteth in thee" (Isa. 26:3). It is sweet to know that all the circumstances – whether threatening weather, poverty, angry men, sickness, or any work of Satan – are all subject to the control of the dear Saviour. Let us trust Him and have peace in any circumstance.

Verses 28-34 Two Demoniacs Healed

Again Mark and Luke tell the same story, in Mark 5:1-20 and Luke 8:26-39. Here Matthew says, "the country of Gergesenes." Mark and Luke say "Gadarenes." Study the other accounts carefully since both are longer than this in Matthew. The most important difference is that Matthew mentions two men while Mark and Luke only mention one of the two, evidently the most striking case. Evidently there were many other details which were not given by any of the Gospel writers. The one man told Jesus that his name was "Legion" because he was evidently possessed by many demons.

107

A careful study of this case leads us to believe that many insane people are made so by being possessed of devils. This man seems to have supernatural strength (Mark 5:3, 4; Luke 8:29). He wore no clothes; did not live in a house but in the tombs or caves where they buried the dead (Luke 8:27). Demons in this man knew Jesus as they always did. "The devils also believe, and tremble" (Jas. 2:19).

Verse 30 is particularly interesting. If demons cannot ruin this soul, then they want to cause property damage. Entering the hogs, they caused them to run down a steep place into the sea and drown. Why did Jesus allow these demons to do the harm they wished? Did they deceive Him or out-bargain Him? No, Jesus often allows Satan to do what he wishes, then gets glory from it. He makes the wrath of men to praise Him (Ps. 76:10). All things work together for good to them that love Him (Rom. 8:28). So here what the demons seemed to do for spite, Jesus permitted and used. Actually, Jesus wanted the people to make a choice between Him and property. It is never possible to serve God and mammon, or money (Matt. 6:24). When the inhabitants begged Jesus to leave their country, the outcome showed that they loved their hogs more than a lost soul, more than they loved Christ. When Jesus allowed the hogs to be killed, actually He struck the idol of these wicked people. How fortunate they would have been had they gained salvation and Jesus, and lost their swine! Jesus meant it for good though they did not take it so. How blind is the person who puts property before Christ! So did the owners of the slave girl delivered by Paul (Acts 16:19). Think how people sell liquor or rent property for gambling or sale of liquor or sell advertising for tobacco, liquor, etc., loving money more than men and property more than Christ!

We are told in Mark 5:18-20 and in Luke 8:38, 39 how the poor maniac, who had been possessed of devils but was now clothed and in his right mind, longed to go with Jesus but He sent him back to his friends and his family to tell what great things God had done for him, and this the saved man joyfully did!

MATTHEW IX

Verses 1-8 Four Bring Palsied Man to Jesus for Healing and Forgiveness

Jesus has been in the country of Gadara, among the Gadarenes or Gergesenes (Matt. 8:28) across the little Sea of Galilee from Capernaum in Galilee, and here He returns to Capernaum where He has made His home since Matthew 4:13.

This beautiful story is enlarged upon in Mark 2:3-12 and Luke 5:18-26. Be sure to notice additional details given in the accounts there. Enormous crowds were about Jesus so that one could not even get close to the door of the house where He was (Mark 2:2). The man sick of a palsy (vs. 2) was brought by four friends (Mark 2:3). Not being able to come in at the door, they went on the housetop, broke up the roof and let the man down through the tiling before Jesus! (Mark 2:4; Luke 5:19). "Their faith" (vs, 2) means that of the men who brought the sick man as well as his own. Often our faith needs encouragement. God wants Christians to unite in prayer and in faith (Matt. 18:19, 20). Even Jesus felt the need of others to pray with Him (Matt. 26:40; Mark 14:37).

Jesus first forgave the man's sins (vs. 3) That is always the most important need as you see from the blessings given in proper order in Psalm 103:3-5. Forgiving comes before healing, or any other blessing in importance. This indicates that when we want healing for our body we should first seek forgiveness for our sins. Notice that teaching in James 5:15, 16. We are to confess our faults to each other as well as to God, and to pray one for another in order to be healed. We would have more cases of wonderful healing of the body if this doctrine were clearly taught and insisted upon. There should be definite repentance and turning from sin and getting sin forgiven first.

The "certain of the scribes" mentioned in verse 3 were really "Pharisees and doctors of the law sitting by, which were come *out of every town of and Judea, and Jerusalem*" (Luke 5:17). "And the power of the Lord was present to heal them," whoever needed healing. These critics of Jesus had assembled from all over the nation! The criticism was "within themselves" (vs. 3), thinking evil "in their hearts" (vs. 4). But praise God, Jesus knew their hearts as He knows the hearts of all men (John 2:24, 25). And Jesus always has power to prove His authority. In this particular case He healed the man to show and illustrate His power to forgive sins (vs. 6).

There is a definite connection between sin and disease, likewise between healing and forgiveness. You see that both are referred to in Isaiah 53:4-6, particularly Isaiah 53:4 as quoted in Matthew 8:17. So everyone who has his sins forgiven must eventually have a resurrected, glorified, perfect body, free from the ravages and marks of sin (Rom. 8:19-23). Romans 8:29 refers clearly to the body as well as to the soul. The healing and perfecting of the body at the return of Christ and the rapture of the saints will be the finished work of salvation.

See then how closely connected are healing and forgiveness. Since sin so often causes disease, we who pray for forgiveness have a perfect right to pray for healing and whenever it is God's will and will glorify His name, we should expect Him to give us faith to be healed. Always we should look forward happily to the perfect cleansing from disease which will be ours in perfectly healthy, glorified human bodies after the resurrection (I Cor. 15:42-57; II Cor. 5:2-4).

Jesus proved Himself the Forgiver of sins by healing the sick, and the palsied man "took up the bed, and went forth before them all; insomuch that they were all amazed, and glorified God, saying, We never saw it on this fashion" (Mark 2:12),

Verse 8 has a marvelous ending: they "glorified God, which had given such power unto *men.*" This power was not given to Jesus alone, but was given to *men.* The power was evidently given in answer to the faith of them who bore the man (vs. 2) to him, and to Jesus all together. The power of God is available to faith. "All things are possible to him that believeth" (Mark ,9:23), to others the same as to Jesus (John 14:12; 20;21), since Jesus was living as our human Example, emptied of His heavenly glory but working in the power of the Holy Spirit (Luke 3:21, 22; 4:1, 14, 16-21). See especially Acts 10:38 which specifically states that the miracles of Jesus, healing, etc., were done because Jesus was anointed with the Holy Ghost. Be sure to notice how the perfect healings of Jesus differed from the methods and results in present so-called healing meetings.

Verse 9 The Call of Matthew the Publican

This Matthew is the disciple who wrote the book of Matthew. He had had the shameful position of a publican or tax collector under the Roman government. These tax collectors were usually wicked and were shunned for their sins. (1) They were counted friends of the Roman Empire which had conquered the Jews. (2) They associated with Gentiles which was necessary as they gave account to the Romans. (3) They were often extortioners as you see from the case of Zacchaeus (Luke 19:8) and the publican in the temple who was slurred by the Pharisee (Luke 18:11). In Mark 2:14 and in Luke 5:27-29 we are told also of the call of Matthew.

Luke calls him Levi and Mark calls him "Levi the son of Alphaeus." Many Bible characters had more than one name just as Peter was also called Simon and Cephas.

The modesty and humility of Matthew are great and God lets them shine through this inspired account. Notice these facts: (1) Matthew plainly tells of his former shameful business instead of seeking to cover it. (2) He continues to call himself "Matthew the publican" (Matt. 10:3). (3) Matthew mentions a dinner where many publicans and sinners came to hear Jesus (vs. 10) but does not tell, as Mark and Luke do, that it was *Matthew* himself who gave the dinner and was evidently responsible for many sinners hearing Christ and perhaps being saved (Mark 2:15; Luke 5:27, 29). (4) Matthew says about himself that "he arose, and followed him" (vs. 9), but Luke is inspired of God to say, "*And he left all,* rose up, and followed him" (Luke 5:28). Matthew gave up a business that would probably have made him wealthy, gave it up willingly and gladly and was counted to have paid a real price to follow Jesus, but he himself did not mention it. "Let another man praise thee, and not thine own mouth" (Prov. 27:2). Here the Holy Spirit who inspired the Gospels directed Matthew in modesty and truth.

Matthew (or Levi) was "the son of Alphaeus" (Mark 2:14). But James, another disciple, was also the "son of Alphaeus" (Matt.

10:3). So we suppose that Matthew and this James were brothers. This was "James the less" (Mark 15:40), probably so called because he was shorter or smaller than the other Apostle James, who was a brother of John and son of Zebedee (Matt. 10:2). If so, there were at least three sets of brothers among the apostles – Peter and Andrew, James and John, and Matthew and James the less.

Verses 10-13 Jesus Loves and Seeks Sinners

The dinner mentioned here is described also in Luke 5:29-32 and in Mark 2:15-17. It was in the home of Matthew; doubtless he invited the publicans and sinners who had been his fast friends. What a wonderful example this is! The maniac of Gadara was told to return to his own house and friends and tell what great things God had done for him (Mark 5:19). Andrew brought his own brother Peter to Jesus (John 1:40-42). Philip brought Nathanael (John 1:45). The woman converted at the well of Sychar in Samaria went and told her townsmen about Jesus, then brought them to hear Him (John 4:28-30; 39-42). So Matthew brought his publican friends and others known as "sinners," that is, publicly known as not keeping the Mosaic Law and so in disgrace with the Pharisees and other religious leaders. All these at a supper in his house heard Jesus. Why not gather unsaved people in your home, invite the preacher to eat with you, then read the Bible, pray and talk about Christ? We ought to use our homes and every social contact for Jesus Christ. Some would come for a dinner who would not come to a "prayer meeting."

Compare this occasion and the words of Jesus with Luke 15:1, 2 and the parables which follow. See also the parable of the Pharisee and publican (Luke 18:9-14). Christ's estimate of the Pharisees is plainly given in Matthew, chapter 23. Jesus never condoned sin. But the sin of a publican is no worse in His eyes than the sin of a Pharisee, and a confessed sinner is much better than a secret and self-righteous sinner who professes to be good. In verse 13 Jesus did not mean that the Pharisees were righteous. They were not, though they claimed to be and thought they were. Jesus calls all, but Pharisees would not hear His call as long as they thought themselves righteous. All alike are sinners and Jesus preferred the penitent publicans to the impenitent Pharisees. In verse 13 Jesus says that the Pharisees had never learned the meaning of mercy. They knew nothing of the atoning blood, Christ's substitutionary sacrifice for men. They depended altogether on their own goodness and not on the mercy of God nor on God's Lamb who takes away the sins of the world.

Verses 14,15 Jesus Speaks of Fasting

(See Mark 2:18-20 and Luke 5:33-35). The Pharisees particularly criticized Jesus for not fasting, calling Him a glutton, a winebibber, and an associate of sinners (Matt. 11:19; Luke 7:34). Jesus was not against fasting. The fasting of John and his disciples must have been pleasing to God for it is nowhere criticized. The fasting of the Pharisees, however, was hypocritical (Matt. 6:16; Luke 18:12) like that condemned in Isaiah 58:3-5. However, the disciples of Jesus had not been taught to fast because He, the Bridegroom, was present with them. Their time of suffering, of waiting for spiritual power and their persecution would come after the Bridegroom was taken away, so they would fast then. Verse 15 indicates that the disciples must have fasted during the time of tarrying before Pentecost just after Jesus was taken away (Acts 1:12-14). Paul fasted likewise, praying for the Holy Spirit's power (Acts 9:9, 11, 17). Later Barnabas, Paul, and other preachers and teachers fasted as they prayed and waited before God (Acts 13:1-3).

Verses 16,17 The New Covenant for the Gospel Message

These two illustrations or parables used by Jesus are recorded also in Mark 2:21, 22 and Luke 5:36-39. Surely you must be impressed by this time that three of the Gospels – Matthew, Mark, and Luke – tell very much of the same story, while John tells many different incidents, sermons, and teachings of Jesus not given in these three. For this reason, Matthew, Mark, and Luke are called "the synoptic Gospels," the three Gospels very similar in outline.

The two parables have the same meaning. "The old garment" in verse 16 is ceremonies of the Mosaic Law, together with the traditions and customs built up around the law by the Pharisees. They wanted Jesus to follow their interpretations of the Sabbath, follow their custom of fasting, make much of circumcision, the priesthood, and the sacrifices. Many times they clashed with Jesus because He did not fit His teaching into their traditions or into the ceremonial part of the Mosaic Law. This is true about the Sabbath (Matt. 12:1-14), about the washing of hands, about the custom of "Corban" (Matt 15:1-11; Mark 7:1-13). So Jesus here is explaining that He did not come simply to fit into the Pharisees' customs and to be subject to and a part of the ceremonial law. On the contrary, He came to bring an entirely new covenant. Jesus did not come to patch up the law which failed to save men because of the weakness of sinful flesh (Rom. 7:10-14; 8:3). Rather, He came now to fulfill all the types and ceremonies and bring in the new covenant.

When Christ died, there were no more sacrifices. When He arose and ascended to the right hand of God, there was no more need of priesthood since He is our High Priest (Heb. 4:14-16; 7:25; 9:11-15). Since now the doctrine of the new birth or circumcision of the heart is made clear, circumcision of the flesh is not required of New Testament Christians. The book of Galatians and the book of Hebrews are both written to make clear that ceremonial law has now completed its part in giving object lessons of spiritual truth. Now Christ has come and fulfilled the ceremonial law. The new covenant supercedes the old, and is better. Read particularly Galatians 4:22-31 which shows the two covenants, the two different systems, law and grace. Jesus brought a new garment entirely; it was not a patching up of the traditions of the Pharisees. He discarded the ceremonies, circumcision, sacrifices, etc., of the ceremonial law. He did not put the new wine of the Gospel in that old bottle. See also Hebrews 8:7-13.

You understand, of course, that the Old Testament is inspired just as is the New Testament and teaches salvation by faith, and foretells Christ's death for sinners (Gen. 15:6; Isa. 53; Acts 10:43). But such teaching had been largely ignored by the Pharisees and they conformed to the letter of the law without understanding the meaning (see vs. 13). Jesus brought in an entirely new dispensation. Jesus did not do away with the Mosaic Law, but fulfilled the ceremonies which picture Him. We still should learn the Old Testament (Luke 24:25-27; John 5:39, 46; Rom. 15:4; I Cor. 10:11; II Tim. 3:16). However, we do not need to follow the Old Testament ceremonials concerning circumcision, diet, Sabbaths, etc. (Col. 2:13-17).

The "bottles" in verse 17 were really wineskins or bags, usually goatskins and carefully sewed to hold wine. Newly tanned skins would stretch and not burst if wine fermented, but older leather would break if sealed up with new wine. So the Gospel of Christ and His teaching was too great to be enclosed within the ceremonies and customs and traditions of the Pharisees. He, the divine Author of the law, put off the old garment and the old bottle of the ceremonial law as a vehicle for spiritual truth for a new when He chose and when His purpose was finished with them.

Verses 18-26 The Ruler's Daughter Raised From the Dead

This story is also given in Mark 5:21-43 and Luke 8:40-56. We suggest that a Scofield Bible is the most useful reference Bible, and it gives references to similar passages such as these.

When Jesus left Gadara where He healed the man possessed with a legion of devils (Matt. 8:28-34) and returned to His own city, Capernaum, many were waiting for Him to heal their sick, etc. (Matt. 9:1, 2; Luke 8:40). Among those glad to see Jesus was this "certain ruler," Jairus (Mark 5:22; Luke 8:41), a ruler or officer of the synagogue (Luke 8:41) at Capernaum, an important man in the community. The daughter was twelve years old and "lay a dying" (Luke 8:42) but died before Jesus got there (Luke 8:49). The ruler in verse 18 may have meant, "my daughter is as good as dead." In fact, it is sometimes difficult for one not a trained physician to know exactly when one is dead. However, Jairus, the ruler, had faith that Jesus could heal her if sick or raise her if dead.

As Jesus and His disciples followed the ruler, many other people came along "and thronged him" (Mark 5:24; Luke 8:42). Mark and Luke add that the woman which came behind and touched the hem of Jesus' garment had spent all her living on physicians and was no better but rather worse. What happened in verses 20 and 21 was secret. No one else knew her mind and heart; no one else knew at once that she was healed except Jesus. It is not told here but Jesus turned about and said, "Who touched my clothes?" Again when the disciples insisted there were many people about Him touching Him, He said, "Who touched me?" (Mark 5:30, 31; Luke 8:45, 46). She had evidently been embarrassed to mention her disease, a female complaint. But Jesus insisted on public acknowledgement of the blessing she had received. "But the woman fearing and trembling, knowing what was done in her, came and fell down before him, and told him all the truth" (Mark 5:33). How pleased Jesus was! Notice His comforting words in verse 22. Jesus could heal when all the physicians had failed and that is still true today! Try Jesus in your hour of trouble and extremity (Ps. 50:15).

Just at this point the messenger came to say that the little girl was dead (Mark 5:35; Luke 8:49). Read the other two accounts and you will see that Jesus went into the room where the little dead girl lay, taking only Peter, James, and John, and the father and mother of the child (Luke 8:51). Jesus said, "Maid, arise" (Luke 8:54), and as Jesus said it and took her hand she arose and Jesus had them give her food (Luke 8:55). Notice the fame and publicity mentioned in verse 26. Jesus had commanded that people not tell it (Mark 5:43; Luke 8:56), but it was in vain. Such marvelous things could not be kept secret!

Verses 27-31 Two Blind Men Healed

Jesus healed a number of blind men (Matt. 12:22; 20:29-34; Mark 10:46-52; Luke 18:35-43). These men spoke of Jesus as the "son of David" (vs. 27). This means that they believed He was the Messiah promised in Isaiah 9:6, 7 who should rule upon David's throne, according to God's covenant with David (II Sam. 7:10-16; Ps. 89:20-29, and especially vss. 35-37). The blind men first followed Jesus, calling after Him, then came to Him into the house (vs. 28). Notice the question Jesus asked them. They believed that He was able. Again, note that remarkable statement, "According to your faith be it unto you" (vs. 29). Notice also the remarkable command of Jesus as heretofore that they should *not* tell it (vs. 30) and the equally remarkable fact that they *did* tell it (vs. 31), as did everyone else who was healed! How could they do otherwise? There must be a wonderful lesson for us here. How can you keep it a secret if God has done great things for you? You should let it be known everywhere, for you have certainly not been forbidden to tell it, but rather encouraged.

See that Jesus did not work these miracles to prove His deity. He lovingly healed the sick and raised the dead because of His

116

compassion. But the essential proof of His deity, the one sign given, was to be His resurrection from the dead, as He clearly says in Matthew 12:39, 40. (See also Rom. 1:4).

Verses 32-34 A Demon Cast Out of Dumb Man

This man was dumb because possessed of a devil. If we would only believe it, it is likely true that many of our troubles are caused by evil spirits who surround us. We think we are too scientific, too sophisticated, too educated to believe in evil spirits, but doubtless they cause much of our disease, particularly diseases of the mind, nerves, etc. See the book, *Pastor Hsi,* from Overseas Missionary Fellowship (formerly China Inland Mission), for modem detailed report of demons on the mission field.

Compare the wicked and blasphemous charge in verse 34 with that of the same kind of Pharisees in Matthew 12:24. Notice the contrast between the attitude of the common people and the ecclesiastical leaders as it is shown in verses 33 and 34 here and in Matthew 12:23, 24. Often today denominational leaders do not accept a preacher, anointed of God, when common people hear him gladly. So it was with Moody, Finney, Wesley, and Billy Sunday.

Verses 35-38 The White Harvest Fields: Reapers Needed

We suppose that "the cities and villages" referred to those in the province of Galilee. Each community had a synagogue, usually, or place where congregations gathered and where the law was read and taught. Notice that He preached "the gospel of the kingdom," still saying evidently as He did at the beginning that "the kingdom of heaven is at hand" (Matt. 4:17). Jesus was still appealing to the Jews as a nation to repent of their sins, accept Him as their King and Lord as well as Saviour. If they had done so, then soon the Jews would have had their kingdom after a period of tribulation, and of course after His crucifixion. His crucifixion and some other matters were so clearly foretold in the Old Testament that they would have come in any case (Ps. 22; Isa. 53; Rev. 13:8; etc.).

117

Gradually, however, the nation was turning against Christ as He insisted on repentance and a new heart, and the Pharisees and Jewish leaders particularly were growing to hate Him, so that when we come to the eleventh chapter of Matthew, we will find that Jesus was rejected and He upbraided the great cities where His mighty works were done because they did not repent (Matt. ll:2l0-24). From that time on, the kingdom of Heaven is no more said to be "at hand." After the disciples preached it throughout Palestine (Matt. 10:7) and it was rejected, it is never again said that "the gospel of the kingdom" was preached. The kingdom was postponed and "the gospel of the kingdom," the one everlasting Gospel but with emphasis on an impending kingdom, will not be preached again until in the great tribulation time it is preached by a converted Jewish remnant just before Jesus returns to set up that kingdom (Matt. 24:14).

We should meditate much on the tender love and compassion of Jesus in verse 36. Do you despise sinners? Do you shun them? Or do you weep over them, love them and try to win them to Christ as He Himself did?

Verses 37 and 38 are similar to Luke 10:2 and John 4:35.

Do you keep the command of verse 38? Do you pray for God to send forth laborers, teachers, preachers, personal soul winners? Do you pray for the preachers whom He has already sent forth? (Eph. 6:18, 19). Do you pray for missionaries, radio preachers, and Gospel papers? Do you pray for this writer, your heavily burdened teacher, who is trying so hard to get out the Gospel to the multi-tudes? And as you pray, do you give? As you pray, ask God if He wants you to go.

Statements like that in verses 37 and 38 are repeated in Luke 10:2 and John 4:34, 35. The harvest is always "plenteous," "great" and "white." Great revivals are always possible, soul winning always in order. See the author's book, *We Can Have Revival Now,* for abundant proof and exposition on this matter.

Let me earnestly urge you to take plenty of time for these Bible lessons. Pray for the Holy Spirit to guide you in each case; meditate on the truths you learn. Fix in your mind the great doctrines here taught and look up every reference prayerfully.

MATTHEW X

Verses 1-7 Jesus Sends Out the Twelve

Some of the apostles had been called one by one before this (Matt. 4:18-22; 9:9). As far as we know, they had been converted during the ministry of John the Baptist and were witnesses of the ministry of Jesus from His baptism by John to His death and resurrection (Acts 1:22). Peter seems to have been either the first one called to be an apostle, though not necessarily the first one saved (Matt. 4:18; Mark 1:16-20; Luke 5:2-11) or the first in importance (vs. 2; Matt. 16:18, 19; Gal. 2:7). His name was called Peter, or Simon, or Cephas (John 1:42). The twelve named here are also named in Mark 3:14-19; Luke 6:12-16. Mark 6:7-13 and Luke 9:1-6 tell also of the sending out of these twelve. Besides these twelve, the Bible calls five other men apostles: Matthias (Acts 1:26), Paul and Barnabas (Acts 14:14), James the Lord's brother (Gal. 1:19) and Jesus Himself (Heb. 3:1).

This is no ordinary preaching tour. The twelve disciples are sent on a particular, highly important mission. They are to go and offer the kingdom of Christ on earth to the Jews as a nation. Notice (1) that they were not to go to any of the Gentiles or Samaritans but to Israel only (vss. 5, 6); (2) that they were to preach the Gospel of the kingdom saying, "The kingdom of heaven is at hand" (vs. 7). John the Baptist came preaching, "Repent ye: for the kingdom of heaven is at hand" (Matt. 3:2). Jesus Christ began to preach the same message (Matt. 4:17). In all His marvelous healing and teaching ministry in Galilee He preached "the gospel of the kingdom" (Matt. 4:23), that is, teaching the good news of salvation, that Jews could now have their kingdom, that their promised Messiah, the Seed of David, was come and that after the Jews as a nation should repent and accept Him, Christ would establish and sit upon David's throne and rule.

That may be the reason the kingdom of Heaven was mentioned several times in the Beatitudes in the Sermon on the Mount (Matt. 5:3, 10). And Matthew 5:5 means the same thing, for the meek will only fully inherit the earth in the reign of Christ. They do not really inherit it now. The message to the Jews of the kingdom continued until the whole nation had a chance to hear it. Jesus had preached

119

it just before this time (Matt. 9:35). Now in a last effort to get the good news about the offered kingdom to the whole nation, Jesus sends these twelve apostles to preach, "The kingdom of heaven is at hand" (vs. 7).

Verses 5 and 6 commanding them not to go to Gentiles or Samaritans, but to Israelites, do not mean that Christ loved Gentiles less, or was not just as anxious for Gentiles to be saved as for Jews. As a *Saviour,* Jesus is the same to Gentiles as He is to Jews. But as a *King,* Jesus is of the literal lineage of David and is to sit upon the throne of His father David, ruling over the house of Jacob forever (II Sam. 7:10-16; Luke 1:32, 33). So the Gospel of salvation is good for Gentiles and Jews alike, but the message of the kingdom was primarily and first to the Jews. The kingdom was at hand and so offered to the Jews. However, that kingdom was rejected as you see in Matthew 11:20. They would not repent. Following that, Jesus began stressing the personal message to individuals to come and be saved (Matt. 11:28-30) without regard to the immediate coming of a kingdom.

Later, Jesus told them that the kingdom now rejected "cometh not with observation" or with outward show (Luke 17:20). One cannot see the kingdom approaching. The kingdom of Christ will not slowly grow. It will come in a gigantic climax, in Christ's literal return with saints and angels, when all the present kingdoms will be destroyed as the great stone cut out of the mountains without hands destroyed completely the image in Nebuchadnezzar's dream as explained in Daniel 2:34, 35. There is now a kingdom of God which one enters by the new birth (John 3:3). But the personal reign of Christ on the throne of David, as promised in Luke 1:32, 33, will not be brought in by human means nor will it approach visibly and gradually.

The kingdom of God was Jews, (wrongly translated "within you" in Luke 17:21). After the nation had rejected Christ, some yet looked for the kingdom of God to appear immediately (Luke 19:11), so Jesus illustrated the delayed kingdom by the parable of the ten pounds (Luke 19:11-27). This was just before His crucifixion. Jesus is now in a "far country." When He receives the kingdom from His Father, He will return and reign.

120

Verses 8-16 Instructions for the Preaching Tour of the Twelve

We can learn many lessons from the instructions of Jesus to these disciples, but not all the instructions are meant to be general rules for everybody to follow. The disciples were going rapidly over the country of Israel and were to waste no time since they would not be able to cover the territory adequately before the Saviour Himself would follow them into other parts of Israel (vs. 23). For instance, it is not necessarily wrong for a preacher to have two coats or shoes, or money for traveling expenses (vss. 9, 10). Compare this with Mark 6:7-13. It is not necessarily wrong to carry bread (Mark 6:8). These were particular instructions to fit that particular occasion. See also Luke 9:1-9 and notice that all three accounts say the apostles were given power and authority "over all devils, and to cure diseases" (Matt. 10:1; Mark 6:7; Luke 9:1). Their power extended even to raising the dead (vs. 8). This was a special case and they were given special power and authority for it which is not always granted to Christians since it is not always necessary. It seems remarkable that Judas (vs. 4), the unsaved apostle (John 6:64, 70, 71), was also given this power. See Matthew 7:21-23.

However, these verses show the terrible importance of giving the Gospel and the responsibility of those who hear it. People will be punished who do not hear God's messengers, whoever they are (vss. 14, 15).

Verse 16 shows that Christians need heavenly wisdom, yet ought to be harmless. We go not in our own strength. We need the whole armour of God (Eph. 6:10-19). "For the weapons of our warfare are not carnal, but mighty through God to the pulling down of strong holds" (II Cor. 10:4).

Verses 17-23 Trials of This Tour Foreshadow the Future Tribulation Time

Compare this passage with Matthew, chapter 24, and see that the Lord Jesus is talking about the same thing. See how verses 17 to

21 fit Matthew 24:9-12. Verse 22 and Mathew 24:13 use practically the same words. But chapter 24 is about "the beginning of sorrows" (vs. 8), about the "abomination of desolation" which will be committed by the Antichrist (vs. 15), about the Great Tribulation at the end of this age (vs. 21), all just before the return of Christ to reign on earth (Matt. 24:27-31). That seems to prove conclusively that there is a double meaning in this tenth chapter of Matthew. What Jesus said in these verses, 17 to 23, was partly about those twelve disciples' going then to preach "the gospel of the kingdom," but He also meant it to fit even more the Jews who will go as witnesses in the closing days of the Great Tribulation preaching the same "gospel of the kingdom" to every nation before the end of the tribulation comes (Matt. 24:14). For instance, Matthew 10:22 certainly refers to that time. A Jewish messenger who lives to the end of the tribulation will be "saved," rescued from the persecutions of the Antichrist.

Verse 18 may have referred to these apostles, but we are not told anywhere in the Bible that these twelve on this trip were brought before kings and governors. We are not told in the Bible of any case that on this particular tour of the land of Palestine one brother did rise up against another brother or father against child or children against parents, as foretold in verse 21. None of the twelve was put to death, for they returned and were with Jesus until His crucifixion. We do not know of any case where these disciples on this tour were persecuted from one city to another as foretold in verse 23.

We may be sure then that in the closing days of the future Great Tribulation, converted Jews will go everywhere preaching the Gospel and will use this Scripture and Matthew 24 as instructions and the Scriptures will be more literally fulfilled in their case than in the case of the twelve apostles. It is my belief that the 144,000 Israelites of Revelation 7:1-8 will be converted and begin witnessing for Christ after the Christians are caught up with Christ at the rapture. Several Scriptures show that some Jews then will be greatly hated by the Man of Sin who will try to kill them. See Daniel 7:25, 26; 9:27; 11:36-45; Matthew 24:15-22; Revelation 12:6, 13-7. These Jews will be in some sense firstfruits of the nation Israel (Rev. 14:1-5, especially vs. 4), that is, they will be saved just a little ahead of the marvelous conversion of the whole nation which is promised (Rom. 11:25-27). That matter of the

Jewish remnant who will preach Christ during the tribulation time needs further study, but surely Jesus must have had them in mind here in Matthew 10:17-23. Meantime, let all of us take warning from the solemn message here given. Hatred, persecution, being dragged before courts for our faith in Christ, may be the destiny of those who are true to Christ, and it certainly will be so during the tribulation time for those who will be converted then.

Verses 24-33 The Disciple to Be Persecuted as His Master but Always in God's Care

Compare verses 24 and 25 with John 13:16; John 15:20. Every Christian ought to be identified with Christ, willing to suffer with Christ. See I Peter 2:19-24 and Hebrews 13:10-14. "As he is, so are we in this world" (I John 4:17).

Jesus has been called Beelzebub (vs. 25) and the Pharisees will call Him that again (Matt. 12:24). Christians then should be willing to suffer in His name.

Happily, a Christian, in the will of God, need not be afraid (vss. 28-31). Christians may suffer, ought to be willing to suffer for Jesus, but they will never suffer more than He permits for His own glory and for our good. Compare this precious promise with Romans 8:35-39. A Christian ought to be so concerned about eternal matters, matters concerning the welfare of souls, that he will not be afraid of anybody who is only able to kill the body (vs. 28).

Compare verse 29 with Luke 12:6. Two sparrows are sold for one farthing, five for two farthings. The extra sparrow is thrown in, but even one little sparrow does not fall to the ground without the notice and care of our pitying and loving Heavenly Father. Your hairs are counted (vs. 80); not one can be destroyed without His knowledge and consent. How foolish, then, to worry since He cares for us like that! Compare this with Matthew 6:25-34. The God who cares for sparrows and lilies and counts your hairs will care for you, O ye of little faith!

Compare verse 32 with Romans 10:9, 10. Verse 33 does not say that one who does not confess Christ is lost, and does not mean that. Sometimes people are secret disciples as was Joseph of Arimathea (John 19:38), but truly saved. Sometimes Christians do hide their lights under a bushel (Matt. 5:15) and the Christian's salt does lose its savor (Matt. 5:13). But to confess Christ openly means that Christ will confess us also and we will have the witness of the Holy Spirit, that Christ owns and claims us before the Father, while those who do not confess Christ lose that joy of communion with Him. Those who deny Christ, that is, reject Him, will be denied (vs. 33).

Verses 34-37 We Should Not Shrink From Trouble and Lose to Follow Christ

A Christian need not always expect outward peace as he serves the Lord. "In the world ye shall have tribulation: but be of good cheer; I have overcome the world" (John 16: S3). This world hates Jesus Christ. He is still "despised and rejected of men" (Isa. 53:3). The opposition and the persecution New Testament Christians faced are normal still. Nominal Christians will not suffer persecution but Spirit-filled, soul-winning Christians who openly oppose sin and urgently plead with sinners to be saved will always be called fanatics, troublemakers, radicals. The world is not essentially changed; human nature is not changed. The Lord Jesus still requires that we put Him before father, mother, son or daughter, or life itself.

Verses 38-42 The Price and Reward of Discipleship

Compare these verses with Mark 8:34-38 and Luke 9:23-26, similar passages. The cross in verse 38 means crucifixion, Christians should crucify the flesh and the desires of the flesh, turn their backs on self, deny self. Paul was crucified to the world and the world to him by the cross (Gal. 6:14). See also Galatians 2:20; 5:24. We should mortify the deeds of the flesh (Rom. 8:13). Every Christian should count himself dead, crucified with Christ (Rom. 6:6-11). Read the author's sermon, "Outside the Gate," on Hebrews 13:10-14 in the book, *What It Costs to Be a Good Christian.* We should remember that we are to side with the crucified Saviour. Paul said, "Who now rejoice in my sufferings for you, and fill up that which is behind of the afflictions of Christ in my flesh for his body's sake, which is the church" (Col. 1:24). Baptism pictures that we enter into Christ's death (Rom. 6:3). We should count ourselves crucified to the world, gladly bearing the reproach of Christ.

Everything you ever give up for Jesus you will get back many fold (vs. 39; also Matt. 19:27-29). Everyone who helps a preacher for Jesus' sake will be blessed with a preacher's reward (vss. 40, 41; Phil. 4:17). Even a drink of cold water given in the name of a disciple will be rewarded (vs. 42).

MATTHEW XI

Verse 1 Jesus Tours Palestine

The twelve disciples had just been instructed (chap. 10) and sent among the cities of the Israelites only (Matt. 10:6), preaching "the gospel of the kingdom," that "the kingdom of heaven is at hand" (Matt. 10:7). Before He sent out the twelve, Jesus had already begun the tour over Palestine (Matt. 9:35-38). Notice that the task was greater than the twelve disciples could do (Matt. 9:37, 38; 10:23). So Jesus sent seventy others also about the same business (Luke 10:1-24), giving them similar instructions to those given the twelve (compare Luke 10:3-12 with Matt. 10:1-16). Be sure to keep careful check on Mark and Luke for passages similar to Matthew.

Verses 2-6 John the Baptist, in Prison, Encouraged by Jesus

Compare this with Luke 7:19-23. Luke adds verse 21, telling of miracles done in the presence of the messengers.

John the Baptist had continued preaching after he baptized Jesus and after the Saviour began His public ministry in Judea (John 3:22-24). Then Jesus left Judea and went into Galilee, evidently because He did not wish to take any of the glory from John's marvelous ministry (John 4:1-3). However, just at that time John was cast into prison and that, too, was a reason for Jesus' leaving Judea and going to Galilee (Matt. 4:12). The ministry of Jesus in Galilee has been studied from Matthew 4:12 on down to this chapter. Meantime, John the Baptist had been imprisoned by Herod because of his bold denunciation of Herod's sins, among others that he had taken his brother's wife (Matt. 14:3-5; Luke 3:19, 20).

In prison John the Baptist became discouraged. This is the hardest temptation Christian workers face after the stress of a great revival campaign is over. There is a natural letdown. See the case of Elijah after the Mount Carmel experience (I Kings 19:1-18) and God's tender care of him. Abraham, the great man of faith, doubted and went down into Egypt in time of a famine (Gen. 12:10-20). David,

126

after great deliverances from Saul and great promises, became discouraged and doubted and went down to the Philistines (I Sam. 27:1 and all of chapters 27, 28 and 29). John the Baptist in prison, with no chance to preach, hearing only secondhand rumors and gossip concerning Jesus and His ministry away in Galilee to the North, doubted whether He was the Son of God which he, John, had already proclaimed Him to be (John 1:15-18, 29-34, 36). Do not blame John. Jesus did not. When he doubted, he did exactly right; he sent to Jesus for evidence and got it.

Let every Christian take comfort in the weaknesses of these great men of God. God still mercifully watched over them, encouraged them, proved Himself to them. Discouragement and doubt are often the products of nerve tension and fatigue. But if you ever doubt, just take your doubts to Jesus and give Him a chance to prove He is all He claims to be, all you ever hoped Him to be. Charles H. Spurgeon has a wonderful lecture on "The Minister's Fainting Fits" or "When a Preacher Is Downcast."

The messengers saw the miracles mentioned in verse 5 and departed and told John. John never was released from prison, but we know he died in faith, reassured and comforted by the Saviour's testimony that He was indeed the promised Saviour, and by the testimony of those who heard and saw the marvelous signs accompanying the Lord's ministry.

Remember that the Lord is always willing to prove Himself to honest people troubled by doubts and His word is, "Come and see" (John 1:39; 1:46; 4:29; 7:17).

Verses 7-15 Jesus Praises John the Baptist

It is the fashion among some "Bible teachers" to minimize the position and importance of John the Baptist. They minimize the baptism of John, speaking of it as if it were a continuation of Old Testament ceremonial rites. It is not. There was nothing equivalent to John's baptism in the Old Testament. They speak as if there were a difference in John's baptism and that of the apostles, but there was not, neither in form nor in meaning. John's baptism was the only baptism Jesus and the apostles had. Some teachers and writers leave the impression that those John baptized were not really saved, though the Scripture tells that he refused to baptize those who did not give evidence of genuine repentance (Matt. 3:7, 8), and though the angel foretold about him that "many of the children of Israel shall he turn to the Lord their God" (Luke 1:16). Some teach that the disciples of John were not necessarily saved, holding that those taught and probably baptized by Apollos (Acts 18:25; Acts 19:1-6) were not saved, but this is untrue. John the Baptist had the same baptism commanded in the Great Commission (Matt. 28:19, 20; Mark 16:15, 16), had the same plan of salvation and the same doctrine of Holy Spirit power since he himself was "filled with the Holy Ghost" (Luke 1:15) from his mother's womb, the same thing that the apostles later got at Pentecost (Acts 2:4).

See John the Baptist's plan of salvation in John 3:36, "He that believeth on the Son hath everlasting life..." The words in John, chapter 3, from verse 27 on, are John the Baptist's. He preached exactly the same Gospel as Christ and Paul. There has never been but one true Gospel, preached by all Old Testament prophets and those of the New Testament, as we see in Acts 10:43, "To him give all the prophets witness, that through his name whosoever believeth in him shall receive remission of sins." Whether it be called "gospel of the kingdom" or "gospel of the circumcision" or "gospel of the uncircumcision" (Gal. 2:7), it is still the same "everlasting gospel" (Rev. 14:6), the "gospel of the grace of God," the one Gospel of Galatians 1:6-9, the Gospel defined in I Corinthians 15:3, 4. To every preacher it is "my gospel" as with Paul (Rom. 16:25). Some personal color or emphasis may be given by the preacher, or the need of the hearer, or an impending want, but the plan of salvation, the essential Gospel, is the same with John the Baptist or Paul or you or me.

John properly begins the New Testament dispensation, the "gospel" dispensation as you see from a careful study of verse 13, Mark 1:1, Acts 1:22 and from the fact that John's ministry in each of the Gospels begins the New Testament story. John was a prophet, but more than a prophet, greater than any prophet (vs. 9). He was the forerunner of Christ (vs. 10). Verse 10 quotes from Isaiah 40:3 which see. See also Luke 1:76, 77.

Jesus said that no man ever born was greater than John the Baptist (vs. 11). The last of verse 11 does not mean that John will

128

miss the kingdom of Heaven. Rather, it means that in the heavenly kingdom of Christ on earth when all have resurrected, glorified bodies, each one will be greater than John the Baptist was on earth, even though he was filled with the Holy Ghost from his mother's womb. Concerning the greatness of John the Baptist, see the angel's words in Luke 1:13-17. The reference to Elijah in verse 14 is explained by Luke 1:17 and Matthew 17:10-13. John the Baptist came "in the spirit and power of Elias," who was probably the greatest of the Old Testament prophets. Neither Elijah nor John wrote any books, but compare their sweeping, nation-wide revivals on Mount Carmel (I Kings 18) and by the River Jordan (Matt. 3:5, 6).

On this Scripture the Scofield Reference Bible says:

Positionally greater, not morally. John Baptist was as great, morally, as any man "born of woman," but as to the *kingdom* he but announced it at hand. The kingdom did not then come, but was rejected, and John was martyred, and the King presently crucified. The least in the kingdom when it was set up in glory... will be in the fullness of power and glory. It is not heaven which is in question, but Messiah's kingdom.

So John the Baptist is as great as any other man and when the kingdom comes, he will have his own great place in it. But the kingdom of Christ on earth is not yet set up.

Jesus likened John the Baptist to Elijah because of Malachi 4:5, 6. The last book in the Old Testament closed with a prophecy that Elijah would return to the earth as the forerunner of the *second* coming of Christ, that is, just "before the great and dreadful day of the Lord." So the New Testament properly begins with the story of John the Baptist who came "in the spirit and power of Elijah," the forerunner of Christ's first coming. Elijah truly will come again (Matt. 17:11). Possibly he will be one of the two witnesses in the Great Tribulation (Rev. 11:3-12), just before "the great and dreadful day of the Lord" which begins at the battle of Armageddon, closing the Great Tribulation and ushering in Christ's reign on earth. But in some sense, John the Baptist fulfilled the Scriptures about Elijah's return (vs. 14; Matt. 17:12).

Verse 12 may refer to the violent opposition against Christ's kingdom displayed by those He commanded to repent. This violence resulted in the crucifixion of Christ. The violent would seize from Jesus His earthly reign. Herod wanted to keep for himself the kingdom that is to belong to "the King of the Jews" (Matt. 2:2). Pharisees and chief priests likewise sought by violence to keep Jesus from taking His place as King over the Jewish people. This is illustrated by the parable and teaching of Jesus in Matthew 21:33-46; Mark 12:1-9; Luke 20:9-19. Other unspiritual and impenitent Jews would have taken Jesus to make Him king by force because of His miracles, such as the feeding of the five thousand (John 6:15), not realizing that He must be crucified and that those who take part in His future reign on earth must be born again (John 3:3, 5).

Verses 16-19 The Scornful Critics of John and Jesus

The universal attitude of the wicked who reject Christ is one of excuses (Luke 14:18). Here we learn that wicked Jews who would not heed the preaching of John the Baptist had insisted that he had a devil, was demon possessed. In modern days men would say he was a fanatic or crazy or radical or sensational. The criticism may have been made by those he refused to baptize because they showed no evidence of repentance (Matt. 3:7, 8). The leaders of the Jews would not receive John's ministry (Matt. 21:25). Here also we learn the criticism about Jesus. He was called "a man gluttonous, and a winebibber, a friend of publicans and sinners." It seems shocking that men criticized the Lord Jesus as a glutton and heavy drinker, which we know was not true, and intimated that by being a friend of publicans and sinners he endorsed them and sought bad company. The truest Christians may expect such persecutions (II Tim. 3:12) and should rejoice when they are persecuted for Jesus' sake (Matt. 5:10-12; Luke 6:22, 23). The last part of verse 19, "But wisdom is justified of her children," means that the truly wise will see and understand the truth about those who live as Jesus did. The truth will come out eventually, and those who really live carefully and prayerfully to please Jesus need not fear the slanders of the wicked.

Verses 20-24 Solemn Warnings to Cities Which Rejected Jesus

The cities of Israel had rejected Jesus. The mighty works of verse 20 mean the miracles mentioned in verse 5, those in Matthew 10:1, those in chapters 8 and 9, and those in Matthew 4:23-25. Despite the marvelous miracles they saw and the preaching which Jesus did, the people did not repent. Particularly mentioned here are Chorazin, Bethsaida (vs. 21) and Capernaum (vs. 23) as the places where His principal miracles were wrought. The wickedness of these cities is said to be greater than Tyre and Sidon (vss. 21, 22) and their hearts harder than those of Sodom (vss. 23, 24). "The gospel of the kingdom" is rejected. The kingdom, heretofore said to be "at hand," is at hand no longer. Hereafter Christ was to preach for individual conversions, and during the entire Gospel age we are never to expect whole nations to be converted nor whole cities.

Instead of putting out the fires of wickedness in this world, we can only expect to win individuals, "pulling them out of the fire; hating even the garment spotted by the flesh" (Jude 23). Some of the seed sown will fall by the wayside unheeded, carried away by Satan; some will fall in stony ground, and those professing to be saved will have no real change of heart; other seed will fall among thorns and those really saved will bring no fruit to real perfection, and some seed will fall in good ground and bring forth fruit (Matt. 13:3-8, 18-23). Every teaching of the Bible on this point shows the world as a whole to be unconverted and only individuals being saved. We may "evangelize the world" in the sense that the Gospel may be preached to all the world, but we will never get the whole world converted. Likewise, there is no such thing as a "Christian nation," since in any nation we suppose only a small per cent are truly born-again Christians. Fortunately, America was founded on Christian principles, and in that sense is more nearly Christian than most.

Notice that from this time on the stress is on individual salvation more than before. See verses 28 to 30 where Jesus offers rest of soul to the individual. The plan of salvation had been the same all along, but the offer of the kingdom to the Jews was now postponed.

Incidentally, notice the doctrine in verses 22 and 24 that there will be degrees of punishment in the judgment and therefore in Hell. It will be easier on the people of Sodom, Tyre, and Sidon than on the people of Chorazin, Bethsaida, and Capernaum. Compare that with Revelation 20:12, 13, "according to their works."

Verses 25,26 Hidden Things Revealed Not to Wise but to Babes

Notice the blessed doctrine in verse 25. God deliberately reveals Himself and His plans more to the poor than the rich, more to the humble than the proud, more to the unlearned than to the wise and prudent. Wisdom and prudence are a handicap in knowing the will of God if one thinks about his wisdom and depends upon his knowledge instead of childlike and humble faith in God. Compare this with Isaiah 5:21; Proverbs 3:7; I Corinthians 1:17-29; 2:1, 2. Notice that "God hath *chosen* the foolish things of the world to confound the wise" and the weak to confound the mighty. That is the secret of Paul's thorn in the flesh (II Cor. 12:9, 10).

Verse 27 Jesus to Be First

Verse 27 illustrates again that Jesus is the first of all with the Father. All Judgment is given to the Son (John 5:22). No man comes to the Father except by Jesus Christ (John 14:6; I John 5:12). God has planned that Jesus Christ must have the preeminence in all things (Col. 1:18). Praise His dear name, He is worthy of all honor and praise, world without end, Amen!

Verses 28-30 Soul Rest in Jesus

Here is a sweet personal message to the laboring and burdened. Jesus especially loves the poor (Luke 6:20), the publicans and sinners (vs. 19; Luke 15:1, 2), the burdened. It is silly for laboring men to turn to communism and atheism as they did in Russia and as the labor movement has a tendency to do in America. Jesus Christ is the true Friend of the laboring men. Let those who have burdens take them to the Lord (Ps. 50:15; 55:22). The testimony of David is, "This poor man cried, and the Lord heard him, and saved him out of all his troubles" (Ps. 34:6). There is a blessed promise in I Peter 5:7. What is Christ's invitation? "Come." Some would teach that Christ's main requirement is "Do." They are wrong. Poor sinner, you may be saved by simply coming. See Isaiah 1:18; 55:1; John 6:37; II Peter 3:9; Revelation 22:17. Some think one is saved by "being," but character never won Heaven. We come, He *makes* us. We come, He *gives* us righteousness.

Do not fear to take upon you the yoke of Christ (vs. 29). It is easy and light. "His commandments are not grievous" (I John 5:3). When one seems to lose one's life for Christ's sake and the Gospel's, one really saves it (Matt. 16:25; Mark 8:35; Luke 9:24). The sinner is the servant of sin, and his yoke is a hard, binding yoke (Prov. 13:15; John 8:34). The man who is free to drink becomes a slave to drink. Even so pleasure, money-making, or any sin shackles the sinner. But when one becomes the bondslave of Jesus Christ, one finds His yoke easy and the greatest freedom and joy in His service.

Oh, Jesus, "the meek and lowly in heart"! What sweet rest to the soul He gives!

In your Bible go through these three verses and underline the seven personal pronouns referring to Jesus: *me, I, my, me, I, my, my*. He does not ask one to come to religion or to Christianity or the church or morality or reformation or baptism, but to Jesus Christ Himself. Notice the connection between verses 27 and 29. Only the Son reveals the Father; nobody else can. One who has Christ has salvation, the new birth, a changed heart, a home in Heaven and everlasting life. In the author's book, *Revival Appeals*, see the sermon, "Come Unto Me."

MATTHEW XII

Verses 1-8 Jesus the Lord of the Sabbath

"At that time," says John A. Broadus, simply means at that general period of time, during the ministry of Jesus in Galilee and Capernaum. Some believe that the events described in John, chapter 5, come between Matthew, chapters 11 and 12. Read that chapter carefully and see that the Pharisees in the nation had already been aroused by the healing of the man on the Sabbath who had been sick thirty-eight years (John 5:9-18). Notice the express statement that Jesus "had broken the sabbath" (John 5:18).

"Corn" here means wheat or barley, a simple word meaning grain, not our American corn or Indian corn. As the disciples walked along the path through the fields, they rubbed out some of the grain in their hands and ate it. The Mosaic Law in Deuteronomy 23:25 plainly permitted them to pluck by hand the heads or ears of grain, though the Sabbath was not mentioned there.

Do not confuse the Sabbath and our Sunday, the Lord's day. The Jewish Sabbath was on Saturday, the seventh day of the week (Exod. 20:8-11). It was a part of the ceremonial or Mosaic Law, first made known at Mount Sinai (Neh. 9:13, 14; Exod. 16:23-30). God had sanctified the Sabbath when He created the heavens and earth and rested on the seventh day (Gen. 2:3). However, this was not made known to man until Mount Sinai and was not written down until the law was written in the wilderness by Moses (Exod. 24:4). The Sabbath was given as a special sign to the Jews only (Exod. 31:13-17). See how strictly the Old Testament Sabbath was observed. No fire could be kindled in the houses on the Jewish Sabbath (Exod. 35:2, 3) and a man was put to death by the Lord's command for gathering sticks on that day (Num. 15:32-36). The Pharisees and scribes had added to the divine law of the Old Testament many of their own interpretations and were hypocrites in strictly observing to the smallest letter their rules about the Sabbath as well as the divine commandments, but altogether missed the spiritual significance of the Sabbath. The ceremonial

Jewish Sabbath following six days of labor was a type of salvation by works, if one could perfectly keep the law in every part. Of course no one was ever able to do so; therefore no one ever attained the heavenly rest by work (Acts 15:10; Rom. 3:20; 8:3; Gal. 2:16).

The Lord's Day, our Sunday, the first day of the week, is not a Sabbath and is never called that in the Bible. In fact, there is not a single commandment in the New Testament either to observe the Jewish Sabbath, Saturday, or to observe the first day of the week. In this connection, read Colossians 2:13-17 carefully and see that verse 16 forbids a Christian to be judged by the Old Testament ceremonial law and specifically names "the sabbath days" as part of that ceremonial law which is nailed to the cross of Christ (Col. 2:14) and was simply a shadow or type until Christ should come (Col. 2:17). Christians are not to keep the Jewish Sabbath, just as they were not to keep circumcision and the Jewish dietary laws forbidding the eating of certain meats, etc. The Galatian Christians who were misled by Judaistic teachers into trying to keep again the ceremonial law, circumcision, etc., were rebuked by Paul for returning to "bondage" and trying to observe again the "days" etc., of the ceremonial law (Gal. 4:9,10). New Testament Christians met on the first day of the week to worship and break bread (Acts 20:7). The observance of our Lord's Day is voluntary and pictures salvation by grace, not of works. We enter into spiritual rest by faith without works, so the Lord's Day comes on the first day of the week. Then there should follow six days of labor in the week for the Lord, not in order to gain the Sabbath rest but because we have rested in Christ. See the spiritual meaning taught in Hebrews 4:9. The word *rest* is the Greek *sabbatismos.* Hebrews 4:10 shows that one enters into spiritual rest now and perfect peace by ceasing from his own works and depending on Christ, but "there remaineth therefore a rest [Sabbath] to the people of God" (Heb. 4:9). In the following verse, Hebrews 4:11, change the word *labor* to *hasten* which is a better translation.

All the ceremonial law had a spiritual meaning and to that Jesus calls their attention in verses 3 to 5. When David and his men ate the shewbread (I Sam. 21:1-6), they broke the letter of the law but evidently kept the spirit of the law. The Pharisees did the opposite about many things and were so rebuked by Jesus in Matthew 23:23. They kept the letter about tithing but missed the right spirit of wholehearted surrender to the will of God, love, mercy, judgment, faith, which it ought to symbolize.

"The letter killeth, but the spirit giveth life" (II Cor. 3:6). So priests in the temple did their regular work on the Sabbath day (vs. 5) because it was commanded of God. How much more right had Jesus the Son of God and One with the Father who gave the commandments to break the letter of any one of them or to lay them aside as they were fulfilled. Notice in verses 6 to 8 the authority that Jesus claimed as greater than the temple, or for that matter, greater than all the Mosaic Law. Read what Mark and Luke say about this same incident (Mark 2:23-28; Luke 6:1-5).

For further light on this subject, get the author's pamphlet, *Sunday or Sabbath, Which Should Christians Observe?* a Bible answer to honest Seventh-Day Adventists, twenty-four pages, or the book *Twelve Tremendous themes*.

Verses 9-14 "Lawful to Do Well on the Sabbath"

Here again Jesus violated the Pharisees' conception, at least, of the Sabbath. Verse 9 would make us think it was the same Sabbath day as that mentioned above, except that Luke tells the same story of the two incidents and in Luke 6:6 says, "It came to pass also on *another* sabbath." Jesus seems to have deliberately chosen to force the issue. He claimed to be the Lord of the Sabbath day (vs. 8), the Son of God who had the right to put His own interpretation on His own command. His own authority is one thing that even the Saviour could not compromise. There is no room for compromise or peacemaking on a religious basis with anybody in the world who does not acknowledge the Lord- ship of the Lord Jesus Christ. For this reason, no Christian ought ever to remain in Christian fellowship with a man who is a modernist, that is, who denies the deity of Christ, His blood atonement, and His right to exact obedience of every one. The Lordship of Christ is a fundamental of all the fundamentals. So Jesus called the man out to "stand forth in the midst" and healed him as publicly as possible (Luke 6:8). Jesus must be accepted as the Lord and Master, greater than all their traditions, greater even than the ceremonies of the Mosaic Law, or He would not be accepted at all.

Do not think these Pharisees were praiseworthy. Notice that they had no regard for the man with the withered hand, thinking less of him than of a sheep (vss. 11, 12). They were not really sincere in their devotion to the Mosaic Law. Rather, they liked their own interpretation of it, and the authority which they had in interpreting the law.

Verse 14 shows the Pharisees' intense personal hate against Jesus. They disregarded His miracle which clearly proved Him from God, His tender love for the afflicted, and the obvious good done. Many people care more for their particular doctrinal interpretation than they do for humanity or for Christ Himself. Many people are stronger Baptists or Methodists than they are Christians and care more for some particular tenet which they hold dear than they do about the salvation of a soul. Many a narrow-minded denominationalist despises the greatest soul winners such as Moody, Torrey, Finney, Chapman or Billy Sunday, because he differs with them on some minor point of doctrine, the form of baptism, the form of church government, etc. Every Christian should do all that Jesus commanded, but it is a far greater sin to be wrong in spirit than it is to be wrong in the letter. Jesus was wrong in neither, but the narrow-mindedness which proceeded from the selfish wickedness of the Pharisees is well illustrated here.

The hating Pharisees were seeking an occasion against Christ. Mark 3:2 says, "And they watched him, whether he would heal him on the sabbath day; that they might accuse him." So also Luke 6:7. Their purpose was wicked. Verse 10 here shows that they brought up the subject themselves.

The healing Jesus did was really "lawful," fulfilling the real spirit of all the Mosaic Law (vs. 12). It is always "lawful to do well." It was the deliberate purpose of the Pharisees already to kill Jesus (vs. 14).

Verses 15-21 The Mild and Merciful Saviour

Reading here Mark 3:7-11, we find that Jesus withdrew to the Sea of Galilee. Other beautiful incidents are there told of the great crowds, healings, evil spirits cast out. Why did Jesus charge them not to make Him known (vs. 16)? See also Mark 3:12; 5:43. We believe it is explained by Matthew 16:20, 21; 17:9; Mark 9:30-32 and Luke 9:20-22. Only the resurrection of Christ from the dead after three days and three nights in the grave, pictured by Jonah in the whale's belly, is the proof of Christ's deity. So says Jesus in Matthew 12:39, 40 and Paul in Romans 1:4.

The miracles of Jesus could not possibly have been kept secret (Mark 1:43-45; 7:36, 37). Miracles announce themselves. One thing is clear: Jesus is to be trusted as Saviour, on the basis of His death and resurrection and not primarily on the basis of His other miracles. This sign only He gave to the Pharisees (vss. 38-40). The openhearted needed no further miracles to know that Jesus was what He claimed to be – the Son of God.

Notice the quotation (vss. 17-21) from Isaiah 42:1-4. That passage is given as explanation for His charge to the multitude to "not make him known" (vss. 16, 17). He was to come not seeking publicity but doing His miracles quietly, not striving nor crying and with no man hearing Him proclaim Himself in the streets as King (vs. 19).

The last part of verse 20, "till he send forth judgment unto victory," evidently refers to the second coming of Christ when He will come in flaming fire, taking vengeance, as bold then as He was meek the first time.

"A, bruised reed shall he not break" (vs. 20). Jesus would not condemn the vilest sinner, almost ruined forever, who wanted mercy. A reed (probably used for a musical pipe, or flute, etc.), bruised so it would seem useless, fit only to be broken and thrown away, Jesus could still make perfect and use. Moses was already a failure, eighty years old, herding sheep, when God made him the deliverer of Israel. See what God did with Jerry McCauley the sneak thief and river rat, or Mel Trotter the drunkard, or Matthew the publican, or Mary Magdalene who had seven devils. "The bird with the broken wing" does fly as high again, higher, when Jesus heals it!

"And smoking flax shall he not quench" (vs. 20). This refers to the wick of a lamp, burned down until it gives only smoke and no light. Most people would put it out. That seems to picture a Christian who does not let his light shine, his influence all ruined by worldliness and sin, with no testimony to please God, but rather offensive smoke. But God has given to such people eternal life and Jesus will never cast them away, however worthless or offensive they seem to others (John 5:24; 6:37). What could picture better than these verses the tenderhearted Saviour who loves the sinner, the worthless one, the failure! Here is a glorious Scripture on the eternal salvation of those who trust in Christ, saved without works, undeserving and ungodly (Rom. 4:5-8). Truly "He hath not dealt with us after our sins; nor rewarded us according to our iniquities" (Ps. 103:10), but rather He "is come to seek and to save that which was lost" (Luke 19:10). He does not break a bruised reed nor quench a smoking wick.

Verses 22-32 The Blasphemy Against the Holy Ghost

The message here is discussed in Mark 3:22-30 and in Luke 11:14-23. This was a marvelous healing of one possessed of a devil, blind and dumb. He was literally possessed with a devil and that was admitted. He could not see and he could not speak. Evidently some of our sicknesses, probably much insanity, some nervous breakdowns, and sometimes excessive anger, and slavery to liquor and narcotics, are caused by demon possession. Dictators, like Mussolini, Hitler and Stalin, in their insane rush for power, seemed to be demon possessed. Certainly that will be true in the last days according to Revelation 16:13-16. The locusts coming out of Hell pictured in Revelation, chapter 9, seem to be demons who will possess the armies of the Antichrist.

The Unpardonable Sin

Jesus used this marvelous healing as a background for His teaching about THE UNPARDONABLE SIN (vss. 31, 32). It seems likely these Pharisees committed such a sin. Notice that "Jesus knew their thoughts" (vs. 25). Their principal sin was not in what they said but in what happened in their hearts. Ascribing the works of Christ to the Devil as they did in Verse 24 evidently is NOT the unpardonable sin. "The blasphemy against the Holy Ghost," as it is called in verse 31, this unforgivable sin, is not simply an outward sin of words. Rather, it is inward, a blasphemous attack against the Holy Spirit who presses the

139

question of accepting Christ as Saviour. On the unpardonable sin read also Hebrews 6:4-6; 10:26-29, and I John 5:16.

The following facts are evidently true about the unpardonable sin: (1) There is only one unpardonable sin (vs. 31). It is not murder nor adultery nor cursing, not simply the rejection of Christ. (2) Saved people cannot commit the unpardonable sin since all their sins are already pardoned and they cannot come into condemnation (John 5:24; Col. 2:13). To the saved person, salvation is a finished, present possession. They are "kept by the power of God through faith unto salvation" (John 10:28, 29; I Pet. 1:5). This sin is committed, only by lost people. (3) The unpardonable sin is committed only by sinners of great enlightenment such as these Pharisees here who knew the prophecies and saw marvelous evidence of the power of Christ. See the enlightenment pictured in Hebrews 6:4, 5. In the Bible, Pharaoh in the time of Moses, and Judas Iscariot seem to have committed the unpardonable sin, as the Antichrist will evidently do. (4) The unpardonable sin is connected always with the rejection of Christ by a sinner. Not all who reject Christ as Saviour commit the unpardonable sin, but each one may do so. (5) The unpardonable sin is a complete and final rejection of Christ so definite and blasphemous that it insults and drives away the Holy Spirit forever. Then He no longer moves the heart, brings conviction or arouses desire for salvation. Usually those who feel they have committed the unpardonable sin have not. One who has is unconcerned since the Holy Spirit has withdrawn from him. All true turning to God must be caused by the Holy Spirit's acting on the heart. If He withdraws Himself, God has no other agency with which to convict and save a sinner. This explains why the blasphemy against the Holy Spirit is more dangerous than words against Christ (vs. 52). The Holy Spirit is God's last chance to get a sinner to trust Christ and be saved. (6) The desire to be saved proves that one has not committed the unpardonable sin (Rev. 21:6; 22:17). Every one who takes the mark of the beast in the Great Tribulation time will so commit the unpardonable sin, we suppose, since all will do this except those whose names are written in the book of life (Rev. 13:8; 14:9-11).

For further treatment on the unpardonable sin, see sermon pamphlet, *Crossing the Deadline*, author, 24 pages, same publishers.

If one reads this who is not sure he is saved, then I beg you, beware that you do not drive away the Holy Spirit. If the Holy Spirit deals with you at all, humbly follow His leadership and be saved while you can lest you commit such a sin that has no forgiveness in this world nor in the world to come (vs. 32).

Verses 33-37 By One's Words His Heart Is Revealed

These verses tell what is wrong with the whole world. It is the hearts of men. Wicked thoughts, wicked words, wicked deeds, all proceed from wicked hearts. How can unregenerate, wicked men, called by Jesus a "generation of vipers," poisonous snakes, "speak good things" or do good deeds? Men are wicked by nature just as a rattlesnake is poisonous by nature. Education, culture, reformation will not make a man good nor a poisonous snake safe. You cannot expect good fruit from evil trees, good deeds from unregenerate hearts. Concerning the trees and fruit, notice the words of John the Baptist in Matthew 3:8-10, of Jesus in Matthew 7:16-20 and Luke 6:43, 44. See also Isaiah 57:20; Matthew 15:19 and James 3:12. Any kind of religion that does not change the heart is utterly futile and powerless.

Notice from this passage the importance of words. (1) They are the clearest indication of the state of the heart (vs. 34). (2) Men shall be judged for every idle word which they speak (vs. 36). This helps us to see the importance of public profession of faith in Christ. Compare verse 37 with Matthew 10:32, 33 and Romans 10:9, 10.

Notice how many sins that grieve the Holy Spirit are committed with the tongue according to Ephesians 4:25 to 5:4: (1) Lying, (2) corrupt communication, (3) bitterness, (4) wrath, (5) anger, (6) clamour, (7) evil speaking, (8) foolish talking, (9) jesting.

The third chapter of James tells about the deadly evil of the tongue. It says, 1. Because the tongue is so wicked, not many Christians should try to be "masters," that is, teachers of the; Bible (vs. 1). 2. If one could conquer the tongue, he would be a perfect man (vs. 2). 3. "And the tongue is a fire, a world of iniquity: so is the tongue among our members, that it defileth the whole body, and setteth on fire the course of nature; and it is set on fire of hell" (vs. 6). 4.

The tongue is the one untameable member of the body (vss. 7, 8). 5. It is the member most likely to compromise a Christian's testimony (vss. 9-14). How anxiously Christians ought to watch their tongues and pray the prayers of David, "Set a watch, O Lord, before my mouth; keep the door of my lips" (Ps. 141:3) and, "Let the words of my mouth, and the meditation of my heart, be acceptable in thy sight, O Lord, my strength, and my redeemer" (Ps. 19:14). Notice there again the connection of heart and tongue. The only hope for a Christian to have victory about his tongue is to have daily cleansing of his heart.

Verses 38-42 Jonah, a Type of Christ

Any demand for a sign by these Pharisees was insincere; they had just seen such marvelous healing (vs. 22) as ought to make any sensible man believe whatever Jesus said. It was their insincerity which made Jesus answer as He did in verse 39. Jesus does prove Himself to honest, seeking hearts as He did to doubting Thomas about His resurrection (John 20:24-29). He sent evidence to John the Baptist that He was indeed the Messiah (Matt. 11:4-6). To the perplexed and hungryhearted disciples of John who followed Him, He said, "Come and see" (John 1:39). And to Nathanael who also accepted the invitation to "Come and see," Jesus proved His supernatural knowledge and promised even greater wonders (John 1:46-51). Any heart honestly seeking Jesus will find Him ready to prove Himself as He promised in John 7:17, "If any man will do his will, he shall know of the doctrine, whether it be of God, or whether I speak of myself." Jesus does not care to prove Himself to wicked, malicious hearts who would not serve Him if they knew He is the Saviour, and for this reason, perhaps, He commanded many not to tell it when He healed them. He was not trying to prove Himself to the Pharisees.

"The sign of the prophet Jonas:" these verses are very important. First, Jesus Himself plainly stated that the story about Jonah and the whale is true. Jonah was literally three days and three nights in the fish's belly. The word translated *whale* here in the King James version literally means *a great sea monster*. It may have been a whale or it may have been a certain kind of shark. Certainly, according to Jonah 1:17, it was "a great fish" especially prepared by the Lord "to swallow up Jonah," "and Jonah was in the belly of the fish three days and three nights." Jesus says that that was literally true. If you cannot believe Jonah, then you cannot believe Christ. Modernists who deny the literal accuracy of the book of Jonah are attacking Jesus Christ. If the book of Jonah is not the infallible Word of God, then neither is the book of Matthew, for it says the same thing. And if this account is not true, then Jesus is not what He claimed to be, the Son of God, for Jesus said it was true.

Verse 40 tells how long Jesus was in the grave, "three days and three nights." This is important. It shows that the Catholic tradition that Jesus died on Friday, was buried that night and arose Sunday morning, being in the grave only one day and two nights, is untrue. That mistake of Catholics and others is evidently caused by a wrong interpretation of the "sabbath" mentioned in John 19:31 and other Scriptures. The Sabbath mentioned which began at sundown when Jesus was crucified was the annual Sabbath or rest day which celebrated the passover supper and began the seven day feast of unleavened bread as commanded in Exodus 12:14-19. That Sabbath, an annual day of rest and convocation, came on a set day, the fifteenth day of the month Abib (Lev. 23:6, 7; Deut. 16:1-8). Jesus was crucified, then, on Wednesday, the fourteenth of Abib, the day the passover lamb was killed. He was buried that evening and stayed in the grave three days, Thursday, Friday and Saturday, with the three nights preceding, and arose sometime before day Sunday morning (Matt. 28:1-6). Jesus was in the grave three days and three nights. It could have been more, but could not have been less, I believe, according to Matthew 12:40. So He was in the grave two Sabbaths – one, the annual Sabbath which came always on the fifteenth of Abib at the beginning of the feast of unleavened bread (Exod. 12:14-16), and the regular weekly Jewish Sabbath which came on Saturday, the seventh day of the week. Notice that Jesus ate some passover meals, but did not eat of a passover lamb since the lambs were being killed while Jesus was dying on the cross. When Jesus hung on the cross it was "the preparation of the passover" (John 19:14, 31).

Verses 41 and 42 show that Christians at the great white throne judgment (Rev. 20:12-15) will rise up to testify against the unsaved people. These verses show that Jonah was a type of Christ and makes the event of being swallowed by a whale of great importance as a type of the burial and resurrection of Jesus. The bodily resurrection of Jesus proves His deity. This resurrection, "according to the scriptures" is part of the Gospel (I Cor. 15:4-8) and God took particular pains that there were many witnesses of the resurrected Christ.

Note that one of the principal reasons for apostles was that they should be witnesses of the resurrection (Acts 1:22) and in their preaching the apostles repeatedly referred to this resurrection (Acts 2:24-36; 3:15; 4:10, 33; 5:31, 32; 23:6; 24:15, 21; 25:19). The literal, bodily resurrection of Christ is of utmost importance. Without that all preaching and faith is vain (I Cor. 15:14, 17); the plan of salvation is incomplete, and no one could be saved.

Verses 43-45 Reformed But Not Reborn

Compare this with Luke 11:24-26. There are slight differences.

This is the picture of a lost man who reforms. We learn that an evil spirit may sometimes leave a man without his being converted. Notice that he went out himself; he was not driven out. See also that the evil spirit still speaks of the man as "my house" (vs. 44). The house, when he returns, is "empty." Jesus is not there. The man has never been saved. Many a man's character is "swept, and garnished" but empty of any real salvation, any real comfort, any real living Christ. Reformation will not do. It takes the presence of Christ Himself to save. See I John 5:11-15.

It is important to see that this verse does not picture a saved man who loses salvation, but a lost man out of whom the evil spirit voluntarily goes and then returns.

Verses 46-50 The Mother and Brothers of Jesus Not Better Than Any Who Do the Will of God

This incident is also told in Mark 3:31-35 and Luke 8:19-21. In Luke we learn that the crowd was too great for His mother and brethren to get near (Luke 8:19). The "brethren" of Jesus are His half-brothers whose names were James, Joses, Simon and Judas.

144

He also had half-sisters (Matt. 13:55, 56). These were the children of Mary and Joseph, while Jesus was the Son of Mary and of God. These brethren were evidently not converted at this time and did not believe in Jesus (John 7:5). They were evidently not converted until after Jesus arose from the dead. Jesus sent them a special message (Matt. 28:10). They were converted and were among those tarrying for the Holy Spirit before Pentecost (Acts 1:14). What Jesus commanded others to do in being willing to forsake all (Luke 14:26-33), He Himself did with reference to His own loved ones. See the blessed promise of Jesus to the twelve apostles in Matthew 19:27-29. Verse 29 there shows that for everyone left behind, God will furnish new loved ones. Jesus forsook His own mother and His own brethren that He might be an Elder Brother to everyone who looks to Him, and a Son for every mother to lean upon. Jesus was not only the Son of Mary; He was even more "the Son of man." By doing the will of the Father (vs. 50) one becomes in literal truth related to Jesus as a beloved Brother.

Catholics reason that one should pray to Mary to intercede with her Son Jesus for us. But here we see that any Christian who does the will of God is as acceptable as Mary! Jesus gave no hint that Mary was more than a good Christian woman. Certainly He made it clear that no one should pray to her.

MATTHEW XIII

Verses 1,2 Jesus Preaches From a Ship

You recall that after Jesus was baptized (Matt. 3:13-17), and tempted of Satan (Matt. 4:1-11), and preached some in the region of the lower Jordan River with His disciples baptizing the converts (John 4:1-3), He went back into the province of Galilee where He was brought up. He moved His home, however, from the little town of Nazareth to Capernaum (Matt. 4:12, 13). All that Matthew tells about His public ministry up to this time has taken place in and around the little district of Galilee. With few good roads in that hilly country, the teeming population around the little Sea of Galilee made boats the principal means of communication around its shores. Boats were nearly as important then as automobiles are today. Therefore the very name of the Sea of Galilee has a sweet fragrance of Jesus about it, since so many of the incidents of His ministry happened in connection with that little body of water.

We think of the call of Andrew, Peter, James, and John who were fishermen, to be apostles (Matt. 4:18-22), the stilling of the storm (Matt. 8:24-27), the miraculous draught of fishes on two separate occasions (Luke 5:4-6; John 21:6-8). We do not wonder that beautiful songs have been written about "blue Galilee." Many more people lived around the little sea than now. The land was fertile and on one side was Decapolis (the ten cities) and on the other was Capernaum, a rich city where Jesus made His home. The lake was full of fish and many people evidently made their living by fishing. Crowds gathered on the waterfront and there it was easy for Jesus to preach to them. So He could be seen and heard by many, Jesus sat down in a ship (vs. 2) and "great multitudes" stood on the shore and Jesus taught them. Jesus preached like this at! least one other time, sitting in a ship (Luke 5:3).

Instead of standing, Jesus sat to speak. Jesus was seated when He gave the Sermon on the Mount (Matt. 5:1). The messages were long, and people were moved, not by human eloquence or gesture so much as by the weight of the divine words themselves which they heard in these cases. Jesus "stood up for to read" the Scripture in the synagogue in Nazareth (Luke 4:16) but sat down to begin to speak (Luke 4:20). In some other cases Jesus stood while He spoke

(John 7:37), so did Peter at Pentecost (Acts 2:14) and so did Paul sometimes (Acts 17:22; 21:40; 27:21).

Verses 3-8, 18-23 The Kingdom of Heaven Parables

This thirteenth chapter of Matthew is of exceeding great importance because here in one group are given seven parables, all of which prophesy the course of events during this age. The things taught in the chapter are called by Jesus "the mysteries of the kingdom of heaven" (vs. 11). The last six of the parables all begin with the words, "The kingdom of heaven is likened unto" or "is like unto." Remember that "the kingdom of heaven" is a term used only in this book of Matthew and nowhere else in the Bible.

Remember that the kingdom of Heaven was preached as "at hand" by John the Baptist (Matt. 3:2), by Jesus (Matt. 4:17), by the twelve apostles sent out in their tours to reach all the cities and towns of the Jews (Matt. 10:7). This was called "the gospel of the kingdom" (Matt. 4:23; 9:35). But the Jewish leaders rejected their King (Matt. 9:3, 11, 34). Rejected, Jesus began definite condemnation of the Jewish leaders, predicting judgment on the nation (Matt. 11:20-24). Hereafter Jewish leaders will continually oppose Jesus until finally they put Him to death. So here Jesus begins to reveal for the first time some of the mysteries of the kingdom. The kingdom *was* "at hand" but is at hand no longer. At present, through this entire church age, the kingdom of Heaven does not exist except in the "mystery" form. The literal kingdom of Heaven on earth will be set up at the return of Christ to reign, described in Matthew 25:31 and following.

We understand that sometimes the term "kingdom of heaven" is synonymous with "the kingdom of God." Where Matthew uses the one term, Mark and Luke may use the other in the same context.

In these parables the "kingdom of heaven" seems to refer to what we call Christendom, including the professing Christians, whether saved or lost.

Other parables in Matthew which Jesus said are illustrations of the kingdom of Heaven are of the king who was taking account of his servants (Matt. 18:23-35), of the laborers in the vineyard (Matt.

20:1-16), of the marriage supper (Matt. 22:1-14), and of the ten virgins (Matt. 25:1-13). These parables with many other references to the kingdom and King show that Matthew is especially the kingdom book and that Matthew deals particularly with Jesus as "the King of the Jews." Matthew is therefore of importance in the study of prophecy, revelations concerning future events. The eleven parables in Matthew which Jesus called "the kingdom of heaven" parables give a clear picture of the course of Christianity in this age and of the state of the world at the second coming of Christ.

The testimony of all these parables of Jesus is that the world will grow worse, not better, that not all will be converted, that there will be tares among the wheat; even to "the end of the world" there will be bad fish in the net with the good fish, foolish virgins without oil as well as wise virgins with oil, even when the Saviour comes for His bride (Matt. 25:1-13); there will be many who reject the King's invitation to the marriage of His Son and some even then who will try to get in without the wedding garment (Matt. 22:1-14). There is not a hint of the postmillennial idea that the world is to get better and better until the millennium of universal righteousness and happiness is brought in. Nothing that man can do, not even the Gospel of Christ, will change the present wicked world into a righteous one or the race of Christ-rejectors who crucified the Saviour into a holy generation. Many individuals will be saved throughout this present age, but only the return of Christ, the judgment and destruction of many wicked and other supernatural events which will attend it, will bring in the greatly desired and long promised kingdom of Christ.

The Parable of the Sower

The parable of the sower is given in verses 3 to 8, and explained in verses 18 to 23. The same parable is reported and explained in Mark 4:3-20 and in Luke 8:5-15, which are parallel passages with this. Be careful that you follow closely the interpretation which Jesus Himself gave. Notice the following facts: "The seed is the word of God" (Luke 8:11). The Gospel is represented as being preached to four classes of hearers: (1) the careless or indifferent hearer upon whom it makes no impression, like seed by the wayside or turn row which is picked up by the birds. So Satan takes the Gospel out of the hearts of casual and indifferent hearers (vss. 4, 19). (2) Some who seem to receive the Gospel but have no real change of heart. Jesus says of such an one, "yet hath he not root in himself" (vs. 21). When persecution or trouble arises such a false professor is offended. This certainly pictures people who are interested in religion, perhaps make some claim to be Christians, but never definitely, personally trust Christ for salvation. They have no root in themselves, are unsaved (vss. 5, 21). (3) The seed that fell among thorns (vs. 7) represents those who hear the word and receive it (vs. 22). Such people are evidently saved, but their lives do not bring forth good fruit for the Master. "The care of this world, and the deceitfulness of riches, choke the word, and he becometh unfruitful." People can be really saved who "bring no fruit to perfection" (Luke 8:14). First Corinthians 3:12-15 shows how a Christian can be saved, so as by fire, with his work burned up like wood, hay, and stubble. Many Christians who have been once useful later allow the cares of this world or the deceitfulness of riches to "choke the word" so that they "become unfruitful." (4) Some hear the word, receive it, like seed cast into good, clean ground and bear abundant fruit, thirtyfold, sixtyfold, or a hundredfold.

The first two cases seem to be of unsaved people and the last two cases of Christians. We should notice that some are just as certainly unsaved being friendly toward religion and perhaps in the church as others totally indifferent to the miracles of Christ, while on the other hand we must be sure that some are truly saved whose Christian testimony is choked with the weeds of worldliness and the thorns of covetousness or toil.

Then let every preacher be warned that not all will hear his message. Some who appear to do so are never truly saved. Some who are truly saved will break his heart by failing to bring any fruit to perfection. Some will surprise him gladly, however, with fruit "a hundredfold!"

Verses 9-17 Why Jesus Spoke in Parables

We skipped these verses to consider the explanation of the parable of the sower given by the Saviour. Notice that these parables are to picture or illustrate "the mysteries of the kingdom of heaven" (vs.

11). One would think that they pictured, then, the future literal reign of Christ on earth, but they do not do that except incidentally. Primarily the things illustrated in these parables happen during this present age. They tell about the present mystery form of the postponed kingdom and the events leading up to that kingdom.

These things are "mysteries" because they were not revealed in the Old Testament. As you see from verse 17, none of the prophets and righteous men of the Old Testament foresaw the present, or church, age. They foresaw the first and the second coming of Christ, but the period intervening between them they did not see. It is not foretold in any detail in the Old Testament. There is no clear picture in the Old Testament of the things between the resurrection of Christ and the Great Tribulation period, except that Joel 2:28 and following foretells Pentecost. The Old Testament therefore does not explain the course of this present age. The thirteenth chapter of Matthew in some respects is the most important picture of the tendencies and the course and end of this age in which we live.

As you see from verses 11 and 16, a special blessing is promised to those who understand prophecies. Most of the Jews who heard Christ give these parables did not understand them; the reason is explained in verses 13 to 15. They were spiritually dull of hearing and blind because their heart was gross. Deliberately they had closed their spiritual eyes, not wanting to be converted or changed (vs. 15). Many do not like to believe that the present age must end in disappointment and failure. Most people like to think of our civilization as a great triumph. Men like to hear that they are by nature good and that we have in ourselves the secrets of success, goodness and prosperity.

Men have a natural antagonism to premillennial truth. They do not like to feel that our system of religion, our denominational programs and institutions and leadership, our modern education, civilization, science, and government are all accursed with the leprosy of sin and must utterly fail. This is evidently the reason that not all Bible-believing Christians accept the truth set forth in these verses. Hence, God promises a special blessing for those who in humility accept His verdict concerning the age and understand these spiritual lessons, "the mysteries of the kingdom of heaven," as they are called in verse 11. Compare this also with Revelation 1:3. It is good to study any part of the Bible, but there is a special blessing in studying and understanding the prophecies of the future.

Verses 24-30, 36-43 The Parable of the Tares

Study this parable together with the explanation Jesus Himself gave. It is a parable explaining this present age and how it will end with the beginning of the promised kingdom. Jesus explained the details in verses 38 and 39, "The field is the world; the good seed are the children of the kingdom; but the tares are the children of the wicked one; The enemy that sowed them is the devil; the harvest is the end of the world; and the reapers are the angels." In one glance we have the course of this age. The Devil plants his tares, "children of the wicked one," in the Lord's world among the good seed, "the children of the kingdom." Even at "the end of the world" the field will have many tares. It is not a picture of a converted world. There was no possibility, according to this parable, of the church's converting the world in this age.

The term "the end of the world," used also in Matthew 28:20, means rather the end of this age, this present political world and setup. It has no reference to the end of the earth itself, the planet. Christ will have His heavenly kingdom on this same earth for a thousand years. The coming of Christ will not destroy the ground, but Jesus will destroy the governments of this world. This end of the age is not at the rapture of the saints, when Jesus calls us into the air to meet Him, but later after our honeymoon in Heaven and a thousand years after He returns to the earth as pictured in Revelation 19:11-21. Compare verses 41 and 42 with Matthew 24:27-31. There verses 27 and 30 picture the return of Christ in glory with all the armies of Heaven, coming to fight the battle of Armageddon and set up His kingdom. Verse 28 of Matthew 24 pictures the slaughter of the armies of the Antichrist with the birds of the air to feast on their carcases as told in Revelation 19:17-21. Verse 31 of that 24th chapter of Matthew tells how Christ will send His angels into all parts of the world to gather together His elect, the Jews, who will have been so scattered by their persecution during the tribulation time. So we see that "the reapers are the angels" as verse 39 says. The angels will gather the wicked yet alive on the earth and cast them into Hell (vss. 41, 42). The angels likewise shall gather together the Jews for their kingdom (Matt. 24:31).

In this connection read Matthew 25:31-46 which tells of the same occasion, as a little study will show. In chapter 25, verse 31 tells of the coming of the Son of Man with His angels to reign on the earth. (Remember that is after the rapture of the saints and after the tribulation.) The people of the nations gathered before Him (Matt. 25:32) will be gathered by the angels, we suppose. The kingdom mentioned in Matthew 25:34 is the same kingdom as mentioned in Matthew 13:41, 43 and the punishment in Matthew 25:46 is the same as that of Matthew 13:42. It is important that you study these passages carefully together. The parable of the net in verses 47 to 50 tells the same story and should be studied with this in mind.

A consideration of verses 41 and 43 will show that the kingdom which is here discussed will be upon earth. The angels will "gather out of his kingdom" the unsaved, then the righteous will shine forth in the kingdom without being moved. That indicates that the kingdom must be here on the earth where Jesus will judge the nations and set up His own kingdom.

Verses 31,32 The Parable of the Mustard Seed

Here is another picture of the course of this age, and it is not a good picture. The other parables tell of tares among the wheat, bad fish with the good, much of the sower's seed wasted, etc. The parables do not picture the kingdom of Christ growing, expanding, and developing of itself and taking the world. This parable has often been interpreted as showing a great and blessed growth of the kingdom during this age, but that is evidently not the intention of the Saviour.

Here, I think, is the meaning of the parable. In Bible times the churches started out simply sowing the seed of the Gospel. Preaching, teaching, and in personal work, they went everywhere getting people saved. That is the very heart and essence of New Testament Christianity. But as this wicked age progresses, the emphasis has changed from seed-sowing to tree-growing. Instead of scattering the Gospel, people are now more concerned about building denominational organizations, institutions, and programs. The growth of Roman Catholicism is the best example of that. The great ecclesiastical systems which are now thought to represent Christianity did not appear in the New Testament. The denominational overlordship over preachers and churches, the emphasis on education instead of evangelism and on direction by popes, bishops, denominational secretaries, etc., instead of direction by the Holy Spirit, on character building instead of regeneration – these things are all pictured, I think, by this growth of a tree. And notice the birds which come and lodge in the branches (vs. 32). They may have the same meaning as the fowls in verse 4. The evil one takes the seed out of people's hearts and likewise Satan brings modernism and wickedness into any great denominational system.

A picture of a great denominational system during the tribulation time is given, I think, in Revelation, chapter 17. It seems to be a picture of Roman Catholicism come to its last and highest fruit, probably with other denominations joined in after the saints are called out of the world. Then in chapter 18, read verse 2, where this great evil system which will head up in Rome at that time is accursed by the angel saying, "Babylon the great is fallen, is fallen, and is become the habitation of devils, and the hold of every foul spirit, and a cage of every unclean and hateful BIRD." The great unscriptural, religious system is pictured by the tree in Matthew 13:32, I believe, and the modernism and false doctrine and worldliness, human pride and carnal methods that inevitably accompany such a system are pictured by the birds which come and lodge in the branches thereof. Fundamentalism, in its fight against modernism, must be against the trees that give shelter to the evil birds just as it is against the birds. Study this very prayerfully. Does the Spirit impress you that this is the correct interpretation of this parable?

Remember that more than once in the Bible a human system of civilization or government is pictured by a tree. See Daniel 4:20, 22.

Verses 33 Parable of the Leaven

Again this parable must fit with the other parables in picturing the evil course of this evil age. The leaven here slowly leavening the whole lump does not picture the Gospel conquering the world until the whole world is Christianized. Leaven in the Bible does not picture good, but evil. The bread which was cooked for the angels even in Sodom was unleavened bread (Gen. 19:3). The bread eaten with the passover lamb and in the seven days' feast following must be unleavened bread since it pictured Jesus, our sinless One (Exod. 12:8, 15). Bread offered as an offering picturing Jesus our Sacrifice must be unleavened bread (Lev. 2:4, 5). Jesus commanded the disciples to "beware of the leaven of the Pharisees and of the Sadducees" (Matt. 16:6-12; Mark 8:15). Then the passage in I Corinthians 5:6-8 clearly shows that the Christian ought to be unleavened. The sin of a church member retained in fellowship is likely to lead others astray, and so "a little leaven leaveneth the whole lump." They were commanded to purge out the leaven, to be a new lump unleavened. Notice particularly that leaven is said to represent "malice and wickedness" (I Cor. 5:8). Therefore it is clear that the leaven in Matthew 13:33 does not picture the Gospel. Rather Jesus illustrated this age as being characterized by the slow spreading of wickedness and false doctrine until the whole world would be contaminated with it. With modernism in nearly every denomination, worldliness in the churches, money-love and pride and unbelief in the pulpit, we see the results of the spreading leaven.

It is significant also that woman is used here in picturing the spread of false doctrine and wickedness. Could it refer to the part women have had in the founding of false religions like Christian Science, Spiritism, Unity and the feminizing of the modem church? Dr. Scofield says, "A woman, in the bad ethical sense, always symbolizes something out of place, religiously," and calls attention to Revelation 2:20 and Revelation 17:1-6.

Verses 34,35 The Course of the Age Revealed for First Time

Notice that this was the first time in the history of the world that the course of this present church age was revealed. Jesus uttered things "kept secret from the foundation of the world" (vs. 35). See the importance, then, of this 13th chapter of Matthew.

Verses 44-46 Twin Parables: The Hid Treasure and the Pearl of Great Price

You have probably noticed that the parable of the tares (vss. 24-30) and of the net (vss. 47-50) are very much alike, picturing the separation between saved and lost who will be alive on the earth at the end of the tribulation when Jesus returns with the saints and angels to reign. Both picture the kingdom being begun and the lost people (tares and bad fish) destroyed. You have noticed also that the parable of the mustard seed (vss. 31, 32) and of the leaven (vs. 33) are twin parables with very similar teaching. So the parables of the treasure hid in a field and of the pearl of great price are twin parables with evidently the same meaning. This pairing of the six parables is evidently intentional.

The first parable in the chapter of the sower is a different kind of parable introducing the whole question particularly from the viewpoint of the soul winner. Jesus was there teaching soul winners (particularly the apostles) the reaction to the Gospel which they should expect. Some would be totally indifferent; some would be interested, but not saved; some would be saved but not fruitful; others would be saved and fruitful.

The seven parables together give a complete picture of the course of the age. The last six particularly (six is the human number) tell a persistent story of the decay of civilization and the corruption and adulteration of the Gospel, the mingling of the bad with the good. Remember that the world wants good mixers, but the Lord wants good separators (II Cor. 6:14-18).

The parable of the treasure hid in a field (vs. 44) is often misinterpreted. The treasure is not Christ. Christ is not hidden. Men do not buy Him, and if they find Him, they do not hide Him again. Nor is Christ the pearl of great price, and men do not sell all they have to find Him. People are not saved by works, nor even by sacrifice, but simply by faith in Christ. The Scofield notes on these parables are very helpful. Dr. Scofield thinks that the treasure hid in a field is Israel and the pearl of great price is the church, the body and bride of Christ, including all the saved.

It seems certain that the pearl of great price represents all the saved, foreknown by Christ. Jesus gave up everything that He had, riches, glory, honor, fellowship with the Father, all of Heaven, the plaudits of the angels and His rightful place as Creator and Lord, and humbled Himself to take on Himself the form of a servant, the form of sinful flesh, in poverty, shame, sorrow and hate, temptation and suffering in order to win us. How precious we are in His sight! We are the pearl of great price that Jesus bought at such terrible cost of His own sufferings and blood. It seems to me that the treasure hid in the field has the same meaning. Jesus foreknew who would be saved and loved us enough to purchase us at awful cost. He died for the sins of the whole world (I John 2:2) though He knew the whole world would not be saved. He paid for the whole field, that is the world, in order to get the hid treasure, those who are going to be saved. Differing somewhat with Dr. Scofield, I prefer the interpretation that the hid treasure, like the pearl of great price, represents the souls to be saved by the blood of Christ.

These verses are precious. "Behold, what manner of love the Father hath bestowed upon us"! (I John 3:1).

Verses 47-52 Parable of the Net

In this parable as in that of the tares, the phrase "the end of the world" means the end of this age or dispensation. This age is called in the Scripture "the times of the Gentiles" (Luke 21:24) because Gentiles will have the pre-eminence with a babel of human confusion of war and trouble and sin, until Christ returns and restores again the Jewish throne at Jerusalem. The times of the Gentiles began with Nebuchadnezzar. In a more restricted sense, this parable is talking about the church age. But the end of the age will come, not at the rapture of the saints, but when Christ returns to destroy the kingdoms of this world and to set up His own kingdom at the close of the tribulation. Compare this parable with that of the tares in verses 24 to 30 and you will see that the meaning is almost the same. At the end of the age, this world will still have the tares among the wheat and bad fish not only in the sea, but in the net with the good fish.

Again we are reminded that the angels are the reapers who will "sever the wicked from among the just." Verse 50, like verse 42, tells that Hell is a literal furnace of fire.

Notice the instructions for preachers and teachers in verse 52. Those who understand these parables about the kingdom of Heaven and the course of this age and future events clearly prophesied cannot only preach about the past, "old things," but of the future, "new things." One who does not understand about the coming kingdom of Christ and the course of this age leading toward it, the mysteries of the kingdom of Heaven, is not prepared to preach half of the Bible. Take care, therefore, and "study to shew thyself approved unto God, a workman that needeth not to be ashamed, rightly dividing the word of truth."

Verses 53-58 Jesus' Neighbors Unbelieving and Offended

"His own country" (vss. 54, 57) probably means Nazareth and the small community in which He was reared. They knew by name and work Joseph, and the mother and brothers of Jesus.

Notice "his brethren" in verse 55. Their names are given. They are referred to a good many times. They were evidently not converted before the crucifixion (John 7:5). However, they were Christians after the resurrection, and may have been converted when they received His resurrection message (Matt. 28:10). The brethren of Jesus were among the hundred and twenty who waited and prayed until Pentecost (Acts 1:14). James, one of these brethren, wrote the book of James (James 1:1) and is mentioned in Galatians 1:19 as a leading apostle. Remember that James, the brother of John, was dead (Acts 12:2). Jude, who wrote the book of Jude, may have been another brother of Jesus (Jude 1). Some people believe, particularly Catholics, that Mary was always a virgin, was never in fact Joseph's wife, and had no other children; that these "brethren" are simply cousins of Jesus. But that does not seem to be the meaning of verses 55 and 56 here. Besides, Jesus was only the "firstborn son" (Matt. 1:25) and thereafter she was in fact Joseph's wife. Then Psalm 69:8 clearly pictures Jesus as "a stranger unto my brethren, and an alien unto my mother's children," which would mean that Mary was actually the mother of these others mentioned here, and they therefore were the half-brothers of Jesus. Mary was not a supernatural woman. She was simply a good woman chosen to be the mother of the Saviour. She was a virgin until the Saviour was born, and thereafter was the wife of Joseph and the mother of other children.

Compare verses 57, 58 with Mark 6:1-6 and with Luke 4:16-30 which tell a good deal more of detail and show they even tried to kill Jesus. Mark says that "he *could* there do no mighty work, save that he laid his hands upon a few sick folk, and healed them" (Mark 6:5), while here we are told that "he *did* not many mighty works there because of their unbelief." The unbelief of men can hinder even the hand of God! "All things are possible to him that believeth" (Mark 9:23), but sometimes our unbelief hinders even the working of Christ. God can work in an atmosphere of faith, delights to do so, and honors Himself in doing so. God cannot (without doing wrong and dishonoring Himself) work much in an atmosphere of unbelief and selfishness. Believe, and let Jesus do mighty works!

MATTHEW XIV

Verses 1-14 Herod Murders John the Baptist

Compare this with Mark 6:14-29 and Luke 9:7-9. "Herod the tetrarch" mentioned here in verse 1 is not to be confused with Herod the Great who was ruler in Judea when Christ was born (Matt. 2:1). That King Herod died soon thereafter (Matt. 2:15). The Baby Jesus was not brought back from Egypt until Herod the Great died. Archelaus, son of Herod the Great, "did reign in Judaea in the room of his father Herod" (Matt. 2:22). This Herod the tetrarch was also a son of Herod the Great, but he ruled in the province of Galilee instead of in Judea. This is made clear from Luke 23:6-8. John the Baptist had continued his ministry, we judge, up the Jordan River into Galilee and there came to face Herod and denounce his sin. Josephus says Herod had John imprisoned at Machaerus, east of the Dead Sea. The feast probably took place in the town of Tiberias in Galilee, not far from the southern end of the Sea of Galilee. Here Herod the tetrarch had his palace.

When John the Baptist then sent messengers to Jesus (Matt. 11:2, 3) John was in prison at Herod's castle at Machaerus. Remember that the public ministry of Jesus up to this time had practically all been in Galilee. When the fame of Jesus reached Herod, his conscience was aroused, fearing that Jesus was simply John the Baptist risen from the dead. From Mark 6:20 we find that Herod was afraid of John, "knowing that he was a just man and an holy." When he heard John preach, "He did many things," evidently stirred by the moral teaching of John and fearing his denunciation. Any man who is stirred by great preaching and does not heed it will face an accusing conscience many, many times, as did Herod.

Preachers should heed the example of John the Baptist in boldly denouncing sin. We do not know whether John the Baptist ever preached about Herod to others. But John plainly said to Herod himself, "It is not lawful for thee to have her" (vs. 4). Whether John said this publicly or privately, certainly Herodias, the wicked woman involved, knew about it. John the Baptist was no scandalmonger, but he spoke as plainly to Herod about his sins as he had to the multitudes, including the soldiers, publicans, scribes, and Pharisees in his ministry by the River Jordan (Matt. 3:1-12 and particularly Luke 3:2-17).

The daughter of Herodias (vs. 6) danced. Possibly her dancing was similar to the ballet dancing of today. She danced alone. Her dancing stirred and pleased Herod. Likely she was scantily dressed. It is also likely that Herod and others had been drinking, for it was Herod's birthday (vs. 6) and they "sat... at meat" (vs. 9) at a supper given "to his lords, high captains, and chief estates of Galilee" (Mark 6:21). Dancing usually involves bad company and drinking. Though the girl's name is not given in the Bible, from secular history we learn that it was Salome. It seems likely that several kinds of sin combined to bring about the death of the great prophet, John the Baptist. The hate of a malicious, lewd woman, Herodias; the revelry of a dissolute and lustful king; the vanity of a foolish girl, glad to expose her body before the ribald group of men (just as so many chorus girls, night club entertainers, and dancers continually do) for public applause and profit – all these combined to bring about the death of a noble man of God.

In this connection, it is well to remember that nudity, drinking, dancing, and irreligion go together just as they did in the case of the Israelites who ate and drank and were naked and rose up to play and dance around the golden calf (Exod. 32:6, 19, 25). Anybody who doubts the wickedness of the modern dance should read the author's pamphlet, *What's Wrong With the Dance?* When John was beheaded in prison, it was a time of deep sorrow to Jesus (vs. 13). He felt a need to go apart and pray. Humanly speaking, John the Baptist was a cousin of Jesus, and the two had a great spiritual understanding. Jesus loved him deeply.

Verse 14 shows that the great multitude of people came following Jesus into the desert. Jesus "was moved with compassion toward them and healed their sick." He did not have time for much prayer that day, so He took three- quarters of the night following for prayer (vss. 23, 25).

Verses 15-21 Jesus Feeds the Five Thousand

Here is one of the few events in the life of Christ mentioned by all four of the Gospels. You will find it also in Mark 6:32-44; Luke 9:10-17; John 6:1-14. Read all four accounts carefully. Verse 13 tells us that they departed "by ship into a desert place apart." John tells us this too, and that the feeding of the five thousand took place in a mountain (John 6:1-3). "Desert place" does not mean dry and arid, but simply away from the cities. They had "green grass" there (Mark 6:39). Luke 9:10 tells us that it belonged to a city called Bethsaida.

Of particular interest is John 6:5-9. Jesus asked Philip where they could buy bread to feed that multitude. There, too, we are told that the five loaves and the two fishes belonged to a lad who was found by Andrew, and we are told that Andrew said, "But what are they among so many?" Their unbelief is strange, but no stranger than ours! How little right we have to accuse the apostles! We ask so little and expect so little from God.

Let us learn some lessons from this wonderful miracle when five thousand men besides women and children were fed with five loaves and two fishes.

1. "They need not depart; give ye them to eat." The Christian has at hand the Source who can supply the needs of those around about us. "As thy days, so shall thy strength be" (Deut. 33:25). Claim Psalm 81:10; Jeremiah 32:27; Jeremiah 33:3; Mark 9:23; Mark 11:23, 24. Christians ought not to "pass the buck." We can get heavenly power to face the problems that come to us. We can have the food, the wisdom, the spiritual power required if we really claim the promises.

2. Five loaves and two fishes are few, but they are much when Jesus blesses and breaks them. Remember that God used Moses* rod (Exod. 4:2-5, 29-31; 7:10), pitchers and lamps in Gideon's army (Judg. 7:16-23), the jawbone of an ass in the hand of Samson (Judg. 15:15). "God hath chosen the weak things of the world to confound the things which are mighty" (I Cor. 1:27).

3. Be sure to first bring your talents or supplies to Jesus (vs. 18). He only can make that which would feed one, feed five thousand.

4. The multitude was "commanded" to sit down in orderly groups and ranks by fifties (vs. 19; Luke 9:14). Proper organization, avoiding confusion, is scriptural.

5. Jesus never ate without blessing the meal. We should never eat without returning thanks and asking God to bless the food.

6. Jesus had them save all the fragments left over (John 6:12). There was no waste. Waste would be a sin. The home that wishes Jesus to provide should save the leftovers and carefully use them out of love and gratitude to Christ. Jesus who made food for thousands by a thought commands it be not wasted.

7. There were twelve baskets of fish and bread left, indicating the infinite supply. Jesus could have fed a million as well as five thousand.

8. This was an act of creation, making something from nothing. But it was Jesus who created the universe (John 1:3, 10; Col. 1:16; Heb. 1:2). He holds together the universe, (Col. 1:17). Jesus Christ is "The mighty God" (Isa. 9:6) and all matter is under His control.

Following this wonderful miracle some people would have taken Jesus by force to make Him king as John tells us (John 6:15). They were convinced that He was the Prophet foretold by Moses (Deut. 18:15; John 6:14).

Verses 22-34 Jesus and Peter Walk on the Water

After a feast of bread and fish, Jesus constrained the disciples to get in the ship and go before Him back across the little Sea of Galilee "while he sent the multitudes away." It seems that Jesus wished His disciples to have rest. We suppose He had brought them into the desert place, to rest and pray, but the crowds had thronged them. Other people do not realize the terrible strain on the nerves of Christian workers. Every church should insist that its pastor and other paid workers have vacation time, time to rest, play, pray, and read. If Jesus needed it, and His twelve disciples needed it, so do others.

Then when the twelve had slipped away and He sent the multitude away, Jesus went to keep His secret vigil with His Father. "He went up into a mountain apart to pray" (vs. 23).

He must have stayed there until past three o'clock in the morning when the fourth watch began (vs. 25). The prayer life of Jesus is a wonderful study. What an example and what a rebuke it ought to be to us! Jesus loved to pray; He took time to pray. We may be sure that even Jesus needed to pray. How much more do we!

The disciples had spent most of the night in the boat. The wind was against them and they had not been able to make the few miles back to the other side until Jesus appeared to them. The appearance of Jesus troubled them. How it reveals the depravity of the human heart that we are troubled when Christ or angels draw near. They thought Jesus was a spirit and they were afraid. We have become so earthly and worldly that we look for evil things and not good.

Peter really walked on the water. Do not try to explain away these miracles. It came as other miracles come, by faith. Peter's faith failed "when he saw the wind boisterous" (vs. 30). Any faith that looks much upon outward circumstances will fail. Revivals are not brought by outward , circumstances. A sick person is not healed simply because his is an easy case and God can do it without trouble. No, God is not bound by circumstances. Compare with Ecclesiastes 11:4, "He that observeth the wind shall not sow; and he that regardeth the clouds shall not reap." Remember also Paul's command to Timothy, "Preach the word; be instant in season, out of season" (II Tim. 4:2). Whether it is convenient or not does not have much to do with the success of the Gospel, and the boisterous wind need not have affected Peter's walking on the water. It is wrong to have our faith dependent on circumstances. Rather, we should depend on the God who is above all circumstances. One's salvation does not depend on his feeling. If he trusted Christ, he is saved just as much when he does not feel like it as when he does feel like it. If one has not trusted Christ, he is not saved, no matter how he feels. Let us put our dependence on Christ Himself and His Word. If He said to Peter, "Come," (vs. 29), then Peter had a right to expect Jesus to take care of him.

Jesus said to Peter, "O thou of little faith." Then what did He think of the others who stayed in the boat? Before you criticize Peter, do you have more faith than that? What would Jesus say to you about your faith? Notice the prayer of Peter in three words: "Lord, save me." Long prayers are sometimes necessary in secret but rarely proper in public.

The presence of Jesus made lots of difference (vs. 32). The disciples then worshiped Jesus as the Son of God. Let us thank God for distress, trouble, and fears when they lead us to Jesus and we find comfort in Him.

Verses 35,36 Jesus Heals Many

Jesus has been rejected by the leaders and by most of the people, but crowds of needy, suffering people came to hear Him when He went to a new place. We may well thank God that many are poor, sick, and troubled. Without these things the world would have no time for Jesus. How merciful that He loves us when we are sick, poor, and in trouble, though we are usually ungrateful when we are well, happy, prosperous, and strong.

Some would say that Jesus healed only to prove His deity. Rather, I believe He healed out of His great compassion, as in verse 14 of this chapter Jesus was moved with compassion and so healed in answer to request. We know that it is not always God's will, not always best, to heal the sick. Sometimes one ought to be sick until he learns a lesson God would teach. Sometimes a saint of God is sick to the glory of God. Sometimes God wants to take a Christian on to Heaven "which is far better." But certainly, always, the dear Saviour's compassion for the suffering is the same now as when He was on earth. Always we honor Him to plead for His merciful help in sickness or any trouble.

MATTHEW XV

Verses 1-9 Jesus Denounces the Following of Human Tradition Instead of Scripture

Compare this passage with Mark 7:1-13 which is a little more full. The scribes and Pharisees mentioned in verse 1 were from Jerusalem. These are evidently the same Pharisees who had held a council about how they might destroy Jesus (Matt. 12:14) and had been criticizing Him continually (Matt. 12:2, 38). Certainly they are the same ones who accused Him of casting out devils by the prince of devils (Matt. 12:24) for we are plainly told that it was the scribes who came down from Jerusalem in the companion passage, Mark 3:22, "And the scribes which came down from Jerusalem said, He hath Beelzebub, and by the prince of devils casteth he out devils." They seem to have committed the unpardonable sin.

When the fame of Jesus became widely known, the critical scribes, Pharisees, and Jewish rulers, very jealous of their position of leadership over the people, had many of their number to come and check up on Jesus. They hated Him, feared Him, and soon began to plot His death. They stayed about Jesus in Galilee, constantly criticizing. Matthew 9:3 mentions them as present when Jesus healed the man sick of the palsy, and Luke 5:17 says that there were "Pharisees and doctors of the law sitting by, which were come out of every town of Galilee, and Judaea, and Jerusalem." Many of these wicked, but outwardly moral, hypocrites had evidently committed the unpardonable sin, we suppose, from Matthew 12:24-32. We know their secret purpose was to kill Jesus (Matt. 12:14). Their public criticism here was evidently intended to break down the confidence of the people, to bring to an end His enormous popularity with the common people. They wanted to maintain their authority over, and their income from, the common people, and so would try to break down the influence of Christ before having Him killed.

The question in verse 2 was about the disciples who sometime ate without washing their hands. But they had the same criticism of

Jesus, as Luke 11:38 tells us. Notice the remarkable fact that at this later time Jesus, invited to eat dinner with a Pharisee, deliberately omitted washing His hands! Jesus was determined not to be subject to human traditions and to give no heed to the complaint of these selfish and ungodly men. We should be careful never to do wrong in our independence, but we should be equally careful not to bow down to wicked men in their sins. Ordinarily it would not have been wrong for Jesus to wash before dinner. It would have been wrong for Him to do it in this case if by so doing He would leave the impression that all ought to obey the tradition of the scribes and Pharisees. A great preacher filled a certain pulpit where it was customary for the minister to wear a robe. When asked whether he would do so, he said, "If I need not, I will; but, if I must, I will not."

Is it wrong to follow tradition? Not necessarily. It IS always wrong to take tradition *as authority.* It is proper to please men wherever we can do so in good conscience, pleasing God. It is not proper to bow to the insistence of men that their traditions are the commands of God, as the Pharisees did.

The answer of Jesus was overwhelming. He plainly showed that their traditions ofttimes transgressed the commandment of God (vs. 3). He gave proof in their custom of "Corban" as it is called in Mark 7:11. The commandment of God said, "Honour thy father and thy mother" and 'he that curseth father and mother let him die the death,' quoted from Exodus 20:12 and Leviticus 20:9.

Honoring Father and Mother Means Support by Their Children

Notice the meaning given here to "honour thy father and thy mother." It means to fulfill all the duties of sons or daughters, but PARTICULARLY TO SUPPORT THEM, CARE FOR THEIR NEEDS. For instance, "Honour widows that are widows indeed" (I Tim. 5:3) clearly means financial support, as the context shows. In the same chapter, "Let the elders that rule well be counted worthy of double honour," clearly means that for such ministry, the physical needs of preachers should be provided for. The following verse says, "For the scripture saith, Thou shalt not muzzle the ox that treadeth out the com. And, The labourer is worthy of his reward" (I Tim.

166

5:17,18). In the Bible sense, to honor father and mother includes care for them when they are old or when they need it. And I Timothy, chapter 5, particularly verse 4, shows that the same rule holds for nephews with widowed aunts.

Most old-age pension plans, which would put the support of all old people on the government by taxation, thus clearly violate the command of the Scriptures to honor father and mother.

The importance of this command could hardly be overstressed. For it to be obeyed generally meant that God would prosper the whole nation and preserve them, for the promise was "that thy days may be long upon the land which the Lord thy God giveth thee" (Exod. 20:12). Respect, honor, and provision for parents by their children are such fundamental virtues as to be a background for all morality. To violate them was so serious that the law commanded, as quoted here, "He that curseth father or mother, let him die the death." To put father or mother or dependent widows of the family on the care of the public or of the government is a sin against God, a sin so basic that if widespread it foretells the breakdown of civilization. No nation is safe to dwell long in the land given them by the Lord where children do not honor and provide for their parents. This promise of God leads us to believe that the captivity and later dispersion of Israel were for sins which naturally followed the breakdown in respect for authority in the home and honor for fathers and mothers. Let us learn the important lesson here before we condemn the Pharisees for their sin in the same matter.

Socialism and communism, teaching that the government should tax all to support all, "from each according to his ability, to each according to his need," as Karl Marx taught, is clearly a tradition of men which violates a fundamental of morality. We ought surely to provide for orphans, for helpless old people who have no children to provide for them. There is a place for mercy in caring for those who need and deserve public help. But children should support their own parents, not allowing them to become public charges. "But if any widow have children or nephews, let them learn first to shew piety at home, and to requite their parents: for that is good and acceptable before God" (I Tim. 5:4).

167

Catholics and All Who Put Any Human Authority Equal to the Bible Sin as Did the Pharisees

See here how Jesus puts the Word of God and accepted tradition as opposites. The Roman Catholic church teaches that the traditions of the church are authoritative along with the Bible. Jesus plainly says no. It is a sin to 'make the word of God of no effect by your tradition.' The mass, celibacy required of priests and nuns, confession, prayers to Mary, etc., are all instances of the sin here denounced, following traditions that make the Word of God of none effect.

The Pharisees had a tradition. They called it "the tradition of the elders" (vs. 2). Jesus called it "your tradition" (vs. 3). It was the custom of Corban. If a man should dedicate his property to God or any part of it on which his parents might have a moral claim, then the Pharisees would not allow him to do any more for his father and mother. Suppose a man had a mother or father who were old. Being selfish and hypocritical, he wanted to have the name of being religious, but did not want to fulfill the law by honoring and supporting his father and mother. Such a person would simply say, "It is Corban," that is, in effect, "It is dedicated to God." From that time on he would never give a penny to the support of his father and mother, though they were in poverty and old or reduced to begging. Yet the Pharisees counted such a man a fine, religious man. He might only give to the temple treasury the tithes and such offerings as others were commanded to bring, yet he was counted to have fulfilled his entire duty to his father and mother by dedicating it to God, whether God got the use of it or not.

Actually, our regard for God should be greater even than for our parents, but duties never conflict. God is best honored by those who properly honor their father and mother. Those who properly take care of mother and father from the proper motives will be the ones also who support the Lord's work properly, and God will enable them to do so. To do one good thing is never a proper excuse for failing to do the good thing which the Lord commands in His Word. Jewish leaders, by their traditions, had made of none effect a weighty and vital command of God.

The primary purpose of the Jewish rulers was first to get income for the temple and, therefore, for themselves, for they were covetous (Matt. 23:14, 25). Then as long as they enforced their tradition upon the consciences of men as binding, they were put in the seat of authority and respected and obeyed with great reverence. They had made their tradition about washing the hands before meals so strict that one rabbi, according to the Talmud, declared that to eat with unwashen hands was as bad as adultery. Dr. Broadus thinks that the custom was to immerse the whole body before meals in order that the hands might be clean. The great sin of Jewish leaders was in counting the words of men more important than the Bible.

Here, again, I say, is the sin of Roman Catholics. The words of the church fathers, decrees of church councils, official writings of the pope, etc., are counted as binding, even though they contradict the Bible. Catholics forbid priests and nuns to marry, take away the wine from lay people in the Lord's Supper and, in many other matters, they set the interpretation of the Bible and require people to accept their interpretation. Hence, in most of the world, Catholics are discouraged in studying the Bible for themselves.

When any other writing is put equal with the Bible, the Bible is discredited. This is the sin of Catholics with their teaching about the church and its authority, of Mormons or Latter-day Saints in heeding the Book of Mormon, of Seventh-Day Adventists who believe the writings of Mrs. White inspired, of Christian Science, falsely so-called, in relying on the writings of Mrs. Mary Baker Eddy, etc. In every case where one accepts any other authority as equal with the Bible, the Bible is discredited. So it was with these Jewish leaders.

Verses 1-20 Jesus Explains That Sin Comes From the Heart, not by Failure in Incidental Ceremonies

Compare these verses with Mark 7:14-23. Here Jesus calls the multitude and straightly charges them to listen while He sets out to explain the folly of the tradition of the Pharisees, that it defiles one to eat with unwashen hands. It is hard to break the multitude

169

away from traditions under which they have been born and reared. Remember that any undue honor given to a church or denomination takes honor from Christ. Any people who think preachers can preach only under the authority of a church, whether Catholic, Baptist, or others, will minimize the need for direct leadership and empowering by the Holy Spirit. Any group who listens too carefully to denominational headquarters will sin by not listening carefully enough to the Word of God. This is the terrible danger and harm of most Sunday School literature. It comes to be regarded as essential and authoritative, supplanting the Scriptures in influence. Denominational Sunday School literature, then, usually leads to the same sin as committed by these Pharisees. Let us put the Bible in the hands of all the people and insist that they make it the first and final authority.

The important reason why washing of the hands was not important, and the Pharisees' tradition not to be followed about it, is given in verse 11. Pleasing God and true religion is never primarily a matter of the outward and physical, but it is a matter of the heart. Joining churches, being baptized, attending services, giving money, preaching and praying, legal righteousness – all these may accompany an unconverted and wicked heart, as was the case with the Pharisees. It is true that if the heart is right we will not want to sin in what goes into the mouth, but men cannot be righteous in God's sight through outward acts. God commands men to be baptized, but only when it expresses an obedient, repentant heart. God wants men to give tithes and offerings, but only when it symbolizes truth and love in consecration. God wants people to sing, but only when they sing with the Spirit, and to pray, but only when the heart prays. All sin really comes from the heart. This is the explanation given by Jesus in verses 18 and 19.

The saying, "Cleanliness is next to godliness," is not Scripture. Beware lest you commit the same sin the Pharisees did in making it a part of godliness.

Verse 12 shows the concern of the disciples because the Pharisees were offended. Every preacher must face the temptation to please important men and women. In verse 13 Jesus foretold the breaking of the Pharisees' power. Verse 14 tells how both the blind Pharisees and their people would fall in a ditch. Jesus must have had in mind the destruction of Jerusalem which took place in A.D. 70, with the Jews scattered to all parts of the earth. Since that time the Jews have had no temple and no place of sacrifice. Let us beware lest we be blind leaders of the blind, or follow blind leaders. Morality and following rules are not Christianity.

Do not let anyone use verse 11 as an accuse for using tobacco or whisky. Jesus did not so intend it. He had in mind ceremonial cleanliness. We do have a moral responsibility about what we eat and drink, and there is an immoral act in the heart in connection with the misuse of the body.

The trouble with liquor or tobacco is not just ceremonial defilement such as the Jews had in mind. To literally defile the body morally by association with harlots or by any other such means is strictly counted as a sin in the New Testament (I Cor. 3:16, 17; 6:19, 20), and we are commanded, "Whether therefore ye eat, or drink, or whatsoever ye do, do all to the glory of God" (I Cor. 10:31).

And the most important teaching about Matthew 15:18 and 19 is that men need a change of heart. All sin comes from the heart, and nothing can make a man a Christian except the new birth, a change in the heart.

Verses 21-28 A Canaanite or Syrophenician Woman Prays on Despite Discouragement: Her Daughter Healed

Compare this passage with Mark 7:24-30. Here (vs. 22) the woman is called "a woman of Canaan." In Mark she is called "a Greek, a Syrophenician by nation" (Mark 7:26).

Can you explain the attitude of Jesus toward this woman? Notice the following:

1. Christ would have all know that He has special blessings for the Jews. To the Samaritan woman who hated Jews He said, "salvation is of the Jews" (John 4:22). Paul said there was great advantage in being a Jew (Rom. 3:1, 2), of whom as concerning the flesh, Christ came (Rom. 9:5). Israel, the living remnant of the nation, will yet be saved (Rom. 11:26). And God has not cast away His people whom He foreknew (Rom. 11:1, 2).

171

2. But Jesus here surely pretended an indifference to the woman of Canaan which He did not feel – "He answered her not a word." He had some purpose in that seeming unkindness. Also, He made the extravagant statement, which surely did not reflect His own heart, but the opinion of the apostles, doubtless. He said, "I am not sent but unto the lost sheep of the house of Israel." We know that that is not literally true. "God so loved the world," the whole world, that He sent Jesus (John 3:16). Also, He is the propitiation "for the sins of the whole world" (I John 2:2). So Jesus must have been stating a false Jewish attitude to teach the apostles, and to test this woman. Surely He meant all along to hear her, and she never believed that He was sent only to Jews.

Christ was deliberately testing the faith of this woman. Faith that will not stand testing is poor faith. Abraham's faith was tested when he was commanded to offer Isaac (Gen. 22:2). Israel's faith was tested when the people found themselves facing the Red Sea and Pharaoh's host behind them (Exod. 14:1-12). Elijah prayed for rain seven times before he got even a cloud the size of a man's hand as evidence he was heard (I Kings 18:44). Faith is proven and also grows by testing. God often does not mean "no" when He fails to answer at once. Do not be too easily discouraged by apparent rebuff to your prayers. The fact that you feel no answer and see no evidence need not discourage you. Even when God seems to say "no" to your prayer it may not really mean "no" but may be the testing of your faith for Christ's glory and your own rejoicing. Keep on praying, then.

Importance of Persistent, Bold Praying

Jesus illustrated the proper attitude about persistent prayer in Luke 11:5-8. We are told to keep knocking even when the friend within keeps saying "no." Importunity won him over to arise and give as many loaves as the begging neighbor needed. Remember that the friend who first said "no" represents God. God often says "no" to the first prayer when He will not say "no" to the third or fourth.

Jesus taught the same thing in Luke 18:1-8. We ought always to pray and not to faint even when God seems to answer "no." The widow, asking the unjust judge for justice, got an immediate refusal. She persisted and got her request granted. Jesus said that

172

is the way we are to pray for what we need. If you know that you need what you are asking, as this Canaanite or Syrophenician woman did, then keep on begging even when God seems to say "no!" We must remember that even Christ Himself was not answered when He prayed in the Garden of Gethsemane until He prayed the third time, saying the same words (Matt. 26:44). He prayed with strong crying and tears (Heb. 5:7).

Notice the attitude of this woman of Canaan which so greatly pleased Christ.

1. She accepted the deity of Christ, submitted herself to Him, calling Him Lord. The term means full submission. She worshiped Him (vs. 25). Three times she called Him "Lord." She called Him "thou son of David." She believed the Scriptures, that the Seed of David would come to be the Messiah and that Jesus was this Messiah who should reign on David's throne. It would not be hard for such a Saviour to heal her daughter.

2. She made the burden of her daughter her own burden. She said, "Have mercy on ME" (vs. 22). She prayed, "Lord, help ME" (vs. 25). We can intercede for sinners and others effectively only when we take their burdens upon ourselves. Effective, intercessory prayer without a burdened heart is unusual, if not impossible. Jesus said, "What things soever ye DESIRE, when ye pray, believe that ye receive them, and ye shall have them" (Mark 11:24). Prayer without sincere desire is hypocrisy.

3. Her determination to be heard is shown. She "cried unto him" (vs. 22); "she crieth after us" (vs. 23); she "worshipped him" (vs. 25). She offended the disciples; she made a public spectacle of herself with tears and cries and begging. Though she may have seemed fanatical or beside herself, she got the answer to her prayer!

4. She was humbly submissive. She admitted everything that Jesus said. She was not angry when He said He came first to the Jews (vs. 24). She was not offended when He likened Gentiles to dogs (vs. 26). She said, "Truth, Lord" when He practically told her that she was not worthy of any blessing and deserved nothing at His hands. Yet undeserving, she insisted. How like the prodigal son who said, "I... am no more worthy to be called thy son: make me as one of thy hired servants" (Luke 15:18, 19). People get prayers

173

answered, not because they are worthy, but because they admit their unworthiness, and trust in spite of it.

Faith was her greatest virtue, the thing Jesus commended most (vs. 28). "But without faith it is impossible to please him..." (Heb. 11:6). The woman believed in Christ despite circumstances. She believed He would answer despite the apostles who tried to send her away. She believed He would answer despite His seeming indifference, despite even His own words that first seemed so cold.

Let us say reverently that sometimes Christians ought to argue with God in prayer as this woman did. If the children needed the bread, the dogs could get the crumbs. If she were a dog, then still He was her Master; "the dogs eat of the crumbs which fall from *their* masters' table" (vs. 27). She argued with God. So did Moses in Exodus 32:11-14. He actually caused God to change His plan. So did King Hezekiah when God had planned for him to die (Isa. 38:1-8). Again God changed His avowed intention in answer to prayer. We ought to be more bold in prayer. The Lord is "easy to be in treated," as a Christian is commanded to be (James 3:17). "He will not always chide" (Ps. 103:9). Be more bold in your praying. Be not stubborn about your will but be persistent in asking for what you need when you have the assurance that it is within die promises of God to His dear children. We are taught to pray, "Our Father." If we are only poor dogs, we are His dogs and we have holy claims that He will not deny if we press them.

Verses 29-31 Jesus Preaches to Multitudes and Heals

Mark 7:31-37 is a companion passage and adds more. The place mentioned in verse 29 was near Decapolis (the Greek means ten cities), on the west side of the Sea of Galilee (Mark 7:31). One particular healing is mentioned in Mark 7:32-36, which you should read. It was impossible to keep secret the miracles which Jesus did.

The mercy of Jesus is great as shown here. (1) He sat down before the people. Jesus never withdraws Himself from those who need Him. (2) He healed all that were brought here for healing. The power of Christ is not limited, nor His mercy. He is never tired of doing good, even though these were ungrateful. Doubtless, some of these later hated Him and urged that He be crucified. Many followed Him only for the loaves and fishes and to see the miracles. Matthew Henry calls attention to what curse sin brings on the human race (vs. 30), "lame, blind, dumb, maimed," etc., and also to what works Jesus does (vs. 31). The Pharisees hated Christ but the common people, seeing His miracles, "glorified the God of Israel" (vs. 31). Modernist preachers, unbelieving university professors, the haughty, the greedy, the powerful, the strong among men may dishonor Christ and scorn Him, but common people who bring Him their burdens still praise Him.

Notice the term, "great multitudes," (vs. 30) and "the multitude" (vs. 31). About twenty-three times in Matthew's Gospel, such terms describe the throngs who heard Jesus. Note, then, that the great tent or tabernacle revivals, or crowded city auditoriums or open-air preaching to multitudes more nearly represent the preaching of Jesus than the staid regular church services. Revivals, evangelistic preaching to great crowds, should be the aim as we follow Jesus and try to obey John 14:12, "...the works that I do shall ye do also; and greater works than these shall ye do; because I go unto my Father."

Verses 32-39 Feeding the Four Thousand With Seven Loaves and "a Few Little Fishes"

The feeding of the four thousand is told here and in Mark 8:1-9, while the feeding of the five thousand is mentioned by all four of the Gospels.

This is a separate incident entirely, but very similar to the feeding of the five thousand. In one case there were five loaves and two fishes. In the other case there were seven loaves and a few small fishes. In one case there were about five thousand men, besides women and children (Matt. 14:21), while in the other case there were four thousand men, besides women and children (Matt. 15:38).

The dealing of Jesus with His unbelieving disciples is instructive. The infinite care with which He trained these apostles for about three and a half years suggests that preachers should be thoroughly trained. A bishop, that is, a pastor, should be "not a novice, lest being lifted up with pride he fall into the condemnation of the devil" (I Tim. 3:6). In every event Jesus called the attention of His disciples to the spiritual lesson involved. When He spoke a parable, then privately He interpreted it to them. When He worked a miracle, He first tried to strengthen their faith that they might expect it and learn the secret of power. See verses 32 and 33. In this connection notice that He mentioned the matter afterwards to reinforce the lesson (Matt. 16:8-11). Growing a preacher, a religious leader, is a serious business, requiring time and teaching and care. A man called of God to preach or teach must be willing to learn and grow as these twelve apostles had to do.

Notice the numbers involved in the feeding of the five thousand and four thousand. Five loaves and two fishes makes seven, the perfect number. Then there were seven loaves to feed the four thousand and the number of fishes is omitted. There were twelve baskets full of food taken up after the five thousand were fed (Matt. 14:20), indicating that there was plenty and to spare for the Jews, since twelve is the Jewish number. After the feeding of the four thousand there were seven baskets full taken up, indicating that there was an abundance left for everybody, Gentiles as well as Jews, since seven is the complete number, the perfect number.

In this case, as in feeding the five thousand, Jesus, (1) commanded the multitude to sit down in orderly ranks (vs. 35). (2) He gave thanks and broke the food (vs. 36). (3) He used the disciples to distribute it. How could the Christ, who could do all things alone, choose to use us in His ministry of reconciliation! God allows us to carry to the multitudes the blessing which He so freely offers. (4) Jesus was very careful that their broken bread and fish left unused should be saved. It is a sin to waste even what is given so abundantly.

Verse 39 says that Jesus Came-to⁴the territory of Magdala. This was a small city near the midwestern shore of the little Sea of Galilee. It was south of Bethesda, and was the former home of Mary Magdalene, out of whom Christ cast seven devils (Luke 8:2). Have you been impressed with how many cities and towns there were around this little Sea of Galilee in the time of Christ? Study a map of Palestine in the time of Christ. The country of Galilee must have been teeming with population then. The stone ruins from many cities are found there now. However, the country is now more or less barren and supports a very scanty population, except where modem Jews are now beginning to irrigate and develop it.

A curse is on the land of Palestine, as sin has cursed the whole earth in lesser degree. Palestine is not now the "land flowing with milk and honey" it once was (Exod. 33:3, 13:5). There one would not now find the grapes of Eshcol (Num. 13:23).

MATTHEW XVI

Verses 1-4 Pharisees and Sadducees Tempt Jesus, Asking a Sign From Heaven

See also Mark 8:10-12. Notice that the Scripture says, "The Pharisees also with the Sadducees came." The article *the* indicates that these were the same Pharisees and scribes who came from Jerusalem and have been opposing Jesus all of His ministry in Galilee. Their enmity must have been aroused by the plain condemnation of their lives and teachings and unregenerate hearts given in the Sermon on the Mount (Matt. 5:20; 6:5, 16; 7:15-23). Then, the opposition of the Pharisees has been mentioned in Matthew 9:11; 12:2, 14, 24, 38; 15:1, ff. They hated Jesus, were plotting His death and some had evidently, from what Jesus said, committed the unpardonable sin. There was no sincerity in their request.

Notice that the Sadducees, this time, came with the Pharisees. The Sadducees and the Pharisees were the bitterest enemies, as you see from Acts 23:6-10. Pharisees believed in all the Old Testament, believed in miracles, believed in the resurrection of the dead, and were most careful to keep the outward letter of the law, though they themselves were usually not born again and missed the spiritual meaning of the Scriptures. The Sadducees, on the other hand, were rationalists who did not believe in spirits nor angels, did not believe in the resurrection of the dead. These two parties of religious teachers were in constant opposition among the Jews. Yet here both of them are combined against Jesus. Just so, Herod and Pontius Pilate, bitter enemies, became friends in their opposition to Christ (Luke 23:6-12; Acts 4:25-27). The second Psalm foretells this attitude, that wicked men would all combine against Jesus. There is no hate, no opposition like that against Christ which combines the Sadducees and Pharisees.

They desired a sign from Heaven. Since they claimed to adhere so strictly to the law of Moses, we suppose they were asking for an earthquake, fire, smoke, clouds, and the audible voice of God, such as occurred at Mount Sinai when the law was given (Exod. 19:17-

19; 20:1). That great experience was referred to several times in the Bible, as for example, Deuteronomy 4:11-13; 33:2; Judges 5:5; Psalm 68:8, 17, and Nahum 1:5. It had impressed the whole Jewish race through the years and so is referred to again in Hebrews 12:18-21. However, that passage shows that a New Testament Christian does not face the law on Mount Sinai with its terrible and frightening experiences, but rather, we face the blessed prospect of the heavenly Jerusalem, where the general assembly and church of the firstborn will be gathered with Jesus (Heb. 12:22-24). Such signs as those at Sinai, perhaps, the Pharisees and Sadducees desired.

But their request was utterly insincere. Verse 1 says they came "tempting" Him. They intended to betray Him into some statement that they could condemn. Had He worked such miracles they would have said it was from Satan, as they said He did when He cast out devils (Matt. 12:24). If He refused, they would say they would not believe on Him. They were hypocrites and Jesus plainly told them so (vs. 3). They were a wicked and adulterous generation (vs. 4) and their hypocrisy in asking for a sign continued even to the crucifixion, when Jesus was on the cross, when they said they would believe on Him if He came down from the cross (Matt. 27:42).

They were hypocrites because Jesus had already given every evidence of His power with wonderful miracles, feeding the five thousand, feeding the four thousand, healing the sick, restoring the maimed, walking on the water, etc. Jesus had done literally thousands of miracles, we suppose, from the many references to the multitudes who came to Him with their lame, blind, dumb, maimed, as for example, Matthew 12:15; 14:14, and 15:30. Jesus did not show them any further evidence because they were insincere and would not have believed any that might be given. If we believe the things that God tells us, then we may expect Him to show us more. If we will not be moved by the things already at hand, proving the power of God, the deity of His Son and the authority of His Word, then we would not be moved though one rose from the dead, even as the wicked brothers of the rich man in Hell were not moved (Luke 16:31).

Some would excuse Jews for rejecting Christ, but they had no excuse but their own sinful hearts, just as sinners today never have any logical or good reason for rejecting Christ.

Modernists say they do not believe in Christ's deity because of lack of scientific evidence. They lie. There is overwhelming evidence for every humble and contrite heart that Jesus is all He claimed to be – God, Creator in human form; evidence that the Bible is all Jesus said it is – the infallible Word of God. It is not lack of evidence that makes unbelief, but willfully sinful, biased hearts that are resolutely closed against Christ.

Both formal, self-righteous Pharisees, who do not feel a need for personally coming to Christ for salvation, and infidel Sadducees, who deny the miraculous in Christ and the Bible, will stand without excuse at the judgment as condemned, Christ-rejecting sinners.

The Pharisees claimed to be able to read the signs of the weather. Then how silly for them to say they had not seen sufficient proof that Jesus was the Son of God, the Saviour. The deep sadness of Jesus at their hypocrisy is shown by the way He "sighed deeply in his spirit" over it, as told in Mark 8:12.

But mark that Jesus never claimed that the miracles were the finished proof that He was the Son of God. Other prophets had worked miracles. The deity of Christ was to be proven finally by the one sign, His death and burial and resurrection, particularly His resurrection. It was the sign of Jonah (vs. 4), the same one mentioned in Matthew 12:39,40. Jonah was a type of Christ, and his three days and three nights in the belly of the whale were a type of the burial and resurrection of Jesus from the dead.

Verses 5-12 Jesus Warns Disciples of the Leaven of Pharisees and Sadducees

The little faith of the disciples is shocking. They thought Jesus was rebuking them for not bringing bread. Twice He had displayed His power, feeding five thousand and then four thousand. He had told them to "labour not for the meat which perisheth" (John 6:27), that "man shall not live by bread alone" (Matt. 4:4), that men should seek first the kingdom of God and His righteousness, and that food and clothes would be added (Matt. 6:33). Yet they thought He was concerned about their bringing along bread. But their faith was no less than ours, probably greater than ours.

Let us resolve to fret less about bread and be concerned more about the things of God. That is the way of faith. God does not ask us to go without bread; He rather asks us to trust Him about it. We ought to pray about it, "Give us this day our daily bread," but concerning the future He said, "...Take no thought for your life, what ye shall eat, or what ye shall drink; nor yet for your body, what ye shall put on. Is not the life more than meat, and the body than raiment?" (Matt. 6:25). Our Heavenly Father knows what we need.

Verses 9 and 10 show that if the disciples had meditated as they ought on the blessed experiences of the feeding of the five thousand and the four thousand, they would have had more faith. If we count our blessings, meditate on what God has done for us in the past, recall answers to prayer, we will grow in faith. Ingratitude and thanklessness are the foundation for unbelief. Praise begets faith. The more we thank God for blessings of the past and glorify Him with remembrance of His blessings, the more sure we become that He will never leave us nor forsake us and that His blessings will continue to those who trust Him. Had they dwelt on those blessings of the past, they would not now be fearful about bread, but praising God that He could supply whatever was needed, if necessary.

"The leaven of the Pharisees and of the Sadducees" referred to the doctrine of the Pharisees and Sadducees (vss. 6 and 12). *Leaven* necessarily means *evil*, since yeast is a growth of fungus or microbes. It seems that similar kinds of organisms cause bread to rise, grapejuice to ferment, and meat to spoil. On their visit to Lot, angels ate bread that was unleavened (Gen. 19:3). The feast of the passover was to be accompanied with unleavened bread (Exod. 12:8). Leaven is a picture of "malice and wickedness" (I Cor. 5:8). That passage says that Christians are supposed to be unleavened since Christ represents our Passover. The leaven in the meal pictures the spread of evil doctrine and practice (Matt. 13:33). Notice this: evil spreads naturally, but good never does. A good apple in the midst of rotten apples never makes the bad apples sound. Good never spreads naturally. A rotten apple in the midst of good apples does cause others to rot. Evil spreads naturally, particularly microbes and germs of decay. Since all nature is under a curse like mankind, because of sin, the plants that are pests spread naturally, while useful plants must be cultivated and kept. There is a down-grade tendency in all of nature, particularly in men. The human heart forms a natural seedbed for sin as the human body forms a natural seedbed for disease. Good makes headway among men only by supernatural means, since good is not natural to man and man is not naturally good. But natural men are depraved with an inborn tendency to sin, so that sin spreads among men like leaven or yeast does in dough. Thus the human mind has a natural disposition to pick up false doctrine. So the disciples were warned to beware of the leaven of the Pharisees and Sadducees.

False doctrine, like leaven, has a tendency to come in "privily," "unawares" (II Pet. 2:1; Jude 4). Unbelief creeps in before we know it. We absorb false doctrine unconsciously. No Christian is safe who puts himself where he constantly hears false teaching. Let each student beware of the leaven of false doctrine and realize that he has an inborn tendency toward evil in doctrine as well as in life.

Verses 13-17 Peter's Great Confession

"Coasts" (vs. 13) means borders. Caesarea Philippi was a town some twenty-five or thirty miles north of the Sea of Galilee. Remember that thus far this ministry of Jesus was all in a small territory around the Sea of Galilee.

The question of Jesus (vs. 13) was not because He did not know what men said, but rather, evidently, to test the disciples. Herod, particularly, thought that Jesus was John the Baptist risen from the dead because of Herod's own guilty conscience (Matt. 14:2). John and Jesus had preached the same theme, "Repent ye: for the kingdom of heaven is at hand" (Matt. 3:2; 4:17). Likewise both had disciples baptized. Many were expecting Elias (Elijah) to return to the earth (Matt. 27:47-49; John 1:21). This expectation was based on the plain statement of the prophecy in Malachi 4:5, 6. Elijah will come again, evidently just before the day of the Lord, in the Great Tribulation period. It is thought he will probably be one of the two witnesses mentioned in Revelation 11:3. Practically all admitted that Jesus was a Prophet. Most did not believe He was the Saviour, the Son of God.

"But whom say ye that I am?" Jesus asked. The answer of Peter in verse 16 pleased Jesus greatly. Jesus' words, "Blessed art thou," do not mean, "Peter, you will be rewarded for this statement," but rather they mean, "You have already been blessed in having this revelation made to you." Jesus had not yet died on the cross nor risen from the dead, and the positive conviction which Peter had was not the result of his own wisdom nor of his weighing the evidences, but rather a revelation from God. We must remember that we now have much more evidence that Christ is the Son of God than people then had. The evidence of His resurrection from the dead as given by Paul in I Corinthians 15:1-8 is irresistible. All the evidence has been checked and rechecked repeatedly and the passing centuries continue to prove that Christ is all He claimed to be – the fulfillment of prophecies, the theme of the Bible, the Son of God, the Saviour of the world. The evidence is overwhelming. But still it is true that the trusting conviction that Jesus is the Christ, the Son of God, is given by the Lord Himself (see I John 5:1). No man can come to Christ except the Father draw him (John 6:44. See also John 6:37a). Preachers and Christian workers need to realize that there must be a supernatural work in the heart of a sinner. Conviction is a work of the Holy Spirit, as truly as conversion is. God may allow us to be used in bringing this conviction and decision, but regeneration is a supernatural event. The unaided natural mind that is at enmity with God (Rom. 8:7; I Cor. 2:14) cannot understand the things of God, cannot be trusted to be convinced by the evidence, however strong, that Jesus is the Christ. However, each person is given more light than he follows. Infidels and atheists are often very brainy and intelligent men who become fools on this matter. Pride and other sins often make it so that God turns them over to a reprobate mind that they may believe a lie and be damned (Rom. 1:28; II Thess. 2:10-12). Notice that God gives such a delusion, such a blindness and reprobate mind only to such people "because they received not the love of the truth" (II Thess. 2:10), and because "they did not like to retain God in their knowledge" (Rom. 1:28). People's heads get wrong because their hearts are wrong. It was revealed to Peter's mind that Jesus was the Christ, the Son of the living God, because his heart was seeking to please God.

Verses 18-20 The Church Built on Christ the Rock

On verse 18, the Scofield Bible has this note:

183

There is in the Greek a play upon the words, "thou art Peter (petros – literally, 'a little rock'), and upon this rock (Petra) I will build my church." He does not promise to build His church upon Peter, but upon Himself, as Peter himself is careful to tell us (1 Pet. 2:4-9).

Peter is a loose stone, but Christ Himself is the Bedrock, the Foundation Stone upon which the church is built (I Cor. 3:11).

The church is not built on Peter. The Roman claim that the Catholic church is built on Peter is blasphemous, because it really denies what Christ is here saying, that the church is built on Christ Himself. First Corinthians 3:10 and 11 say, "According to the grace of God which is given unto me, as a wise master builder, I have laid the foundation, and another buildeth thereon. But let every man take heed how he buildeth thereupon. For other foundation can no man lay than that is laid, which is Jesus Christ." There can be no other foundation but Christ, the Rock.

Note these facts. (1) There is absolutely no historical evidence that Peter ever went to Rome. (2) There is no scriptural mention of his being at Rome. He is said, rather, to have been at Babylon, the other direction from Jerusalem (I Pet. 5:13). (3) Paul, writing to Rome, takes all of Romans, chapter 16, to greet many, many Christians by name. Why did he not greet Peter, if Peter were there and were Bishop of Rome, as Catholics claim? (4) When Paul went to Rome as described in Acts 28 his meeting with Christian leaders is told, but no mention is made of Peter! Peter was not at Rome.

Meaning of the Word "Church"

But the best evidence that the Roman Catholic church is not built on Peter is that the Bible never mentions any human organization like the -apostate, worldly Roman church, and it is absolutely unlike the simple New Testament pattern of local, independent churches.

The meaning of the word *church* is important. It never in the Bible means a denomination. Our use of the term *church* in the phrase, "The Roman Catholic Church," or the phrase "The Methodist Church," is thoroughly unscriptural. *Remember, the word "church" never means denomination.* Catholics are not the church of Christ. Baptists are not the church of Christ. The sectarian group that calls itself "the Church of Christ" is not that. The claims of Episcopalians, Greek Catholics, Seventh-Day Adventists, or any other denominational group, that they are "the true church," are untrue. The word *church* as used in the Bible, never one time refers to a denomination. The word means "a called-out assembly." Thus it is used many, many times in the New Testament of local congregations, like the "church at Jerusalem," "the church at Rome," "the church of God at Corinth," "the churches of Galatia," and "the seven churches of Asia." Notice that several local congregations are each called a church, not fractions nor branches of a mother church. Each local assembly was completely and separately a church.

But the assembly of Christ which will be called out to meet Christ at the rapture and will be gathered in the heavenly Jerusalem is also called a church (Heb. 12:22, 23). The church in that sense includes all the saved people. In this sense the word *church* is synonymous with the body of Christ as you will see from Ephesians 1:22, 23 and Colossians 1:18. That is the sense in which the word *church* is used here. It refers to the great assembly of Christians who will be called out to meet Christ, all the firstborn whose names are written in Heaven (Heb. 12:23).

Christ Is Now Building His Church

Again notice the words "I will build." Literally the translation might be better, "I will be building," indicating a continuous process. The Lord is *not* discussing the *origin* or *beginning* of His church, but the process of its growth. Some argue that the church was "founded" during the ministry of Christ when He called out the apostles or others baptized by John the Baptist. But they have in mind an earthly and denominational matter to which the Scripture here surely does not refer at all. Dr. Scofield and other good scholars speak of Pentecost as the birthday of the church. However, the Bible never mentions, not one time, any point as being the time when the church was founded or originated or begun. If the Bible never tells when it began, then it is foolish for us to argue for it. Men who set a time for the beginning of the church usually intend to use it to back up some other pet doctrine or to boost their own particular denomination. It seems clear from I Corinthians 15:51 and I Thessalonians 4:14-17 that all the saved of all ages will be gathered up to meet Christ and will assemble at the heavenly Jerusalem as described in Hebrews 12:22, 23. If so, then the first soul saved (either Adam or Eve, we think), was the beginning of the church, the body of Christ.

At any rate, Christ is now building His church. The growing of this church, or body of Christ, or "household of God" (Eph. 2:19), or "building" (Eph. 2:21), or "holy temple in the Lord" (Eph. 2:21), or "habitation of God through the Spirit" (Eph. 2:22) is now taking place, described in Ephesians 2:19-22, and I Peter 2:5-8. Notice from these passages that the building is now growing or being built. Jesus is building His church or assembly of saved persons, building it on the Rock, Christ Jesus Himself. Each Christian is a 'lively stone.' First Corinthians 12:12-27 discusses this growing of the body of Christ, and verse 13 there says that 'we are all baptized into one body' by the Spirit. Get the meaning clear here. Each one of us is like a brick or stone buried into the wall and becoming a part of the wall. Christ, through the Holy Spirit, puts each new convert into this spiritual building and he is baptized, that is, literally buried, into the body of Christ, becoming a part of it. First Corinthians 12:13 does not speak about one's being baptized with the Holy Spirit for service, covered or surrounded or overwhelmed with the Holy Spirit. Instead, it tells how each Christian is put into the body and buried, and so becomes a part of the body of Christ, the spiritual house which He is building which is His church. The word *baptized* is used figuratively here. One is figuratively buried into the body of Christ and covered as a stone is buried in a wall. One also is figuratively covered with the Holy Spirit when He is poured out upon us in soul-winning power, but that is another matter entirely. Literal baptism, of course, is when one literally, physically, bodily, is buried in water.

The important thing to remember about the word *church* as used here is that every saved person is a part of that church.

We believe in local congregations, New Testament churches, such as they had in Bible times, but that is not what this Scripture is talking about. The gates of Hell do sometimes prevail against local congregations, even against denominations, but they cannot prevail against this body of Christ which He will call out at the rapture.

186

See the author's book, *Twelve Tremendous Themes*, the chapter on " 'Churches' and 'the Church,' " for detailed study here. Also see his book, *The Power of Pentecost*, for detailed evidence that the church did not originate at Pentecost, that it includes Old Testament saints as well as New Testament saints. See discussion there also about I Corinthians 12:13 and various New Testament uses of the term *baptized.*

No Authority Given Peter as Pope

The "keys of the kingdom of heaven" mentioned in verse 19 are difficult to explain. It seems that Peter was given the opportunity of preaching first, at Pentecost, to the Jews, and that he was also given the opportunity of preaching first to the Gentiles (Cornelius and his household) after the resurrection of Christ. At any rate, it means that God intended His apostles, others as well as Peter, to have authority such as other preachers do not have. The Holy Spirit gave to them certain powers and authority which He does not give to others not apostles. Dr. Mantey, well-known Greek scholar, says that "shall be bound" and "shall be loosed" could well be translated "shall have been bound" and "shall have been loosed," indicating that the Holy Spirit would simply reveal to the apostles what had already been bound or loosed in Heaven.

The Roman Catholic claim that the binding and loosing here given to Peter made him a pope, with power to save or to damn, and to rule all Christians, and that this authority was inherited by all popes of Rome, is utterly foreign to the Scripture. Note the following proofs against the papal claim.

1. Peter himself never claimed any authority over the other apostles.

2. At Jerusalem, at a counsel of apostles, James seems to have presided and gave the final verdict (Acts 15:13-21). He said, "my sentence is..."

3. Paul said plainly that Peter taught him nothing new or "added nothing to me" (Gal. 2:6) and that James, Peter, and John, "who seemed to be pillars," (note James is mentioned before Peter, Gal. 2:9) agreed that Paul was as free to go to the Gentiles as they to the Jews.

4. Paul openly rebuked Peter to his face, and was then inspired of God to write it down (Gal. 2:11-14). God seems concerned to prove to us here that Peter was not infallible in faith and morals, had no authority whatever beyond the other apostles.

5. If in Matthew 16:19 Jesus gave Peter special power of binding and loosing, in John 20:21-23 He gave more specifically the same authority to ALL the apostles. He said, "... as my Father hath sent me, even so send I you. And when he had said this, he breathed on them, and saith unto them, Receive ye the Holy Ghost: Whose soever sins ye remit, they are remitted unto them; and whose soever sins ye retain, they are retained." All the apostles were sent as the Father sent Jesus. All had Holy Spirit leading so that they could tell people who had repented that their sins were forgiven, could tell those who had not repented that their sins were unforgiven. But Peter had no special authority more than any other apostle. And none of the apostles ever claimed the powers or authority claimed by the Roman pope.

6. However, the claim of any pope to have inherited any authority from any of the apostles, Peter or others, is without a word of Bible confirmation, Peter was no pope. No pope is foretold as God's vicar on earth. The claim of such authority is an usurpation. Jesus never hinted that there would be an office as prince or pope of the church or that any man would inherit or be elected to that office.

7. But the best answer to the Catholic interpretation of Matthew 16:18 and 19 is in Matthew 18:18 and 19. There Jesus plainly gives exactly the same authority to any two or three Christians meeting in Jesus' name as is here given to Peter! So Matthew 16:18, 19 could not possibly be intended to give papal authority to Peter or popes of the Catholic church.

Verse 20 seems strange. Jesus many times worked miracles and urged that they be kept secret (Matt. 12:16; Mark 1:44; 5:43, etc.). Probably the reason is that Jesus wanted people to be convinced of His deity only by the one particular crowning sign He had given – His bodily resurrection from the dead (Matt. 12:39, 40; 16:4). The primary work of the apostles after Pentecost was bearing witness to the resurrection of Jesus Christ (Acts 1:22). See how many times the resurrection of Christ is mentioned by the apostles in the book of Acts.

Verses 21-26 Jesus Foretells His Crucifixion, Rebukes Peter

Jesus came into this world headed for the cross (vs. 21). Knowing the wickedness of men's hearts (John 2:24), He knew that He would be rejected and slain as foretold in the Old Testament. He had it written of Himself long before that He would die for sinners (Ps. 22; Isa. 53; etc.). Isaiah 50:6, 7 show how Jesus resolutely left Heaven with His face set like a flint toward the cross. See again the connection between the resurrection in verse 21 and the command of verse 20. The resurrection from the dead was necessary for Jesus to save sinners and would prove He was the Son of God.

Peter's answer in verse 22 was human and natural. The flesh shrinks from suffering, shame, and failure. We want success instead of failure, wealth instead of poverty, self-will instead of surrender.

In verse 23 why does Jesus call Peter "Satan"? Because the temptation given through Peter here is from Satan, the very same temptation that Satan brought before in the wilderness. The three temptations in Matthew 4:1-11 climaxed in the offer of Satan to give Jesus the kingdom He desired without going to the cross. If Jesus could be kept from the cross, then Satan would have won every battle against every human soul and eternal doom would have been the fate of all the race. The temptation to avoid the cross is the same temptation that followed Christ to His dying breath. The passers-by said to Jesus, "If thou be the Son of God, come down from the cross" (Matt. 27:40). The chief priests and the elders said, "Let him now come down from the cross, and we will believe him" (Matt. 27:41,42). The thieves "cast the same in his teeth" (Matt. 27:44). In fact, the struggle in the Garden of Gethsemane was over this question. Sorrows were literally killing Jesus that night. "My soul is exceeding sorrowful, even unto death" (Matt. 26:38). Already the blood was bursting through the sweat pores when Jesus prayed, "If it be possible, let this cup pass from me" (Matt. 26:39). The cup He referred to was death that night in the Garden. The burden of the sins of the world and the sorrow were killing Jesus, and it was Satan's plan to cheat the cross by letting the Saviour die before the prophecies could be fulfilled. If Christ had not died "according to the scriptures," and had not been raised from the dead "according to the scriptures" (I Cor. 15:3, 4), then Christ could have saved no one. Hebrews 5:7 makes clear that Jesus prayed to be saved from death *that night,* and His prayer was answered. Jesus was praying WITH the will of God, not against His will. Doubtless His prayers were heard when an angel came and ministered to Him (Luke 22:43). He received supernatural strength to live until the morrow and pay for man's sins as was foretold. However, Satan .lid not let up with his temptations until the end and had many to tempt Jesus to come down from the cross.

Notice that verses 24 to 26 say that every disciple who would follow Jesus must have the same attitude as Jesus had. Consider with this matter Mark 8:31-38 and Luke 9:22-26, similar passages. Notice that Jesus is talking to people already disciples. No man need try to follow Jesus until he is converted, regenerated, born again. But after one is a Christian, if he wants to pattern after Jesus, he must expect a crucifixion of self. Christ is our pattern (John 14:12; 20:21; I Pet. 2:21). If He suffered, we should suffer too. "The servant is not greater than his lord" (John 15:20). "If we suffer, we shall also reign with him" (II Tim. 2:12). If the world hated Jesus, we ought to expect it to hate us (John 15:18). We are urged to go outside the gate with Jesus, bearing His reproach (Heb. 13:13). Paul says, "I am crucified with Christ" (Gal. 2:20).

Baptism pictures not only the death of Christ, but the death of the believer to his own hopes, plans and ambitions, to his own self-will, to his own life (Rom. 6:1-11). We are commanded, "Likewise reckon ye also yourselves to be dead indeed unto sin, but alive unto God through Jesus Christ our Lord" (Rom. 6:11). If you were sincere when you were baptized, you sentenced yourself to death. From that day you should be a new creature, living only in Christ. Paul said, "For to me to live is Christ" (Phil. 1:21).

That is not sad either, not failure but victory. The only true victory and happiness that comes to a Christian comes in surrendering his life and self-will over to Christ. "Whosoever will save his life shall lose it" (vs. 25). But when one loses his life for Christ, he finds it. By becoming bond-slaves of Jesus, with no will of our own, we enter into the fullest freedom, joy and victory that is possible for a human being! Sin enslaves; Christ makes free. Our own will leads to trouble, heartache, and bondage; to surrender our will wholly to Christ means perfect freedom and peace.

190

Verse 24 means that a man who follows Christ must condemn himself to die, then when self is dead on the cross, he can follow Christ. But in Luke 9:23 Jesus said that this self-denial and crucifixion must come "daily." We must give ourselves anew daily, be willing again to have the scorn of the world and to give up our own way. If you did this once, you probably need to do it again now.

Verse 26 shows something of the value of a soul. One soul is worth more than the whole world! What a pitiful loss if one gains fame, wealth, power, and earthly happiness, yet has a poor, lost soul and must spend eternity in Hell, away from God, in torment! God help us to love sinners and win them while we can.

Verses 27,28 Jesus Speaks of His Glorious Coming and the Transfiguration Which Would Picture It

The reward mentioned in verse 27 does not mean salvation. Salvation is free and then besides, we are rewarded for our works. First Corinthians 3:12-15 tells how Christians will be rewarded according to their good works. Those who are saved and have no good works will be "saved; yet so as by fire." The parables of the talents (Matt. 25:14-30) and of the pounds (Luke 19:11-27) give some account of our reward and indicate that we will enter into the rewards during the thousand-year reign on earth after Jesus comes.

The time specified in Matthew 16:27 is not the coming into the air to receive His saints at the rapture, but rather His return with the saints and angels in His glory when every eye shall see Him, the return pictured in Revelation 19:11 and following, when Christ will come to put down all enemies and reign on the earth, the time mentioned in Matthew 24:27-31, 25:31, and in Jude 14. That will occur after the rapture and after the Great Tribulation. When Jesus comes, then His reward will be with Him; the apostles will sit on twelve thrones judging the twelve tribes of Israel (Matt. 19:28). Then some shall rule over five cities, some over ten cities (Luke 19:17, 19).

Talking of His Second Coming in His glory, then Jesus gave verse 28. It has puzzled many people, but it need not. Did some of the disciples standing there see the Son of man coming in His kingdom before their death? Not literally but symbolically they did. The following chapter tells how. They saw Him transfigured before them and in His glory just as He will be at His Second Coming. This is made sure when Peter tells about it by divine inspiration (II Pet. 1:16-18). Read that passage carefully, for it certainly explains Matthew 16:28. The transfiguration was to illustrate "the power and coming of our Lord Jesus Christ." There the disciples "were eyewitnesses of his majesty" (II Pet. 1:16).

Let this illustrate the fact that any Scripture hard to understand may be explained by other Scriptures, if we are prayerful and let the Spirit guide us to them and interpret them.

This lesson has entailed great labor on my part. It is worth days of study on yours, with much prayer. Please look up every reference, review the Scriptures earnestly. Let Psalm 119:16 be your vow.

MATTHEW XVII

Verses 1-8 The Transfiguration

Remember that properly verse 28 of the preceding chapter belongs with this 17th chapter, since it is talking about the same thing. Compare with Mark 9:2-13 and Luke 9:28-36. In those cases the promise is included in the same chapter with the fulfillment. Read carefully those accounts of the transfiguration. The transfiguration is a picture of "the Son of man coming in his kingdom" (Matt. 16:28), and the Apostle Peter, writing by divine inspiration, says that the doctrine of the second coming of Christ does not follow "cunningly devised fables," since he, James and John were "eyewitnesses of his majesty" in the "holy mount" where Jesus was transfigured (II Pet. 1:16-18). The importance of the transfiguration is that it gives a glorious picture of the second coming of Christ in His majesty. Compare these accounts of the transfiguration with Jesus as pictured in Revelation 1:13-16 when "his countenance was as the sun shineth in his strength," when "his feet like unto fine brass, as if they burned in a furnace" and "his eyes were as a flame of fire." Then at His Second Coming, in Revelation 19:11-16, we see a glimpse of His glory again and we believe that is the way He looked on the Mount of Transfiguration. The transfiguration pictured the power and glory of His Second Coming.

The three accounts in Matthew, Mark, and Luke each add to the other. It was six full days after the promise in Matthew 16:28 when they went up into the mount (vs. 1 and Mark 9:2). But Luke says "about an eight days after." Matthew and Mark are counting the full days between. Luke counts the two parts of days, and the phrase used by Luke is an idiom, we believe, often used for week.

Matthew and Mark simply tell that Jesus went up into a mount apart (vs. 1 and Mark 9:2), while Luke tells us He went up to pray and that "as he prayed, the fashion of his countenance was altered," etc. Since Jesus prayed before the Holy Spirit descended upon Him (Luke 3:21, 22), prayed all night before He appointed His twelve apostles (Luke 6:12, 13), prayed in the Garden of Gethsemane before His arrest, trial and crucifixion, it is not strange that He prayed here before He was transfigured.

Peter, James, and John went with Christ to the Mount of Transfiguration. These three were especially chosen as witnesses in this case as they were in other cases (Matt. 26:37; Mark 5:37). "In the mouth of two or three witnesses shall every word be established" (II Cor. 13:1). Peter showed how the apostles used their testimony as eyewitnesses (II Pet. 1:16-18). Possibly the other disciples could have been at the transfiguration but it would have meant climbing a mountain and it would have meant prayer, and doubtless they were not anxious for a prayer meeting. How many Christians have missed transfiguration experiences by avoiding prayer meetings!

The transfigured Jesus must have been the most glorious sight that ever met human eyes. "His face did shine as the sun," the source of the light, and naturally, then, "His raiment was white as the light" (vs. 2). That is how Jesus must appear constantly in Heaven since He really is the Light. Moses, who met Christ there, had come down from Mount Sinai with his face shining so that he put a vail on his face (Exod. 34:29-35). But as Matthew Henry reminds us, Moses' face shone with reflected glory like the moon while Christ Himself shone, the Scripture tells us, "as the sun." Moses had seen God but Christ is God Himself.

Luke says "the fashion of his countenance was altered" (Luke 9:29). This happened while Jesus prayed. Perhaps as Peter, James, and John looked, the sad face of Jesus began to change. Instead of being the Man of Sorrows and acquainted with grief, the suffering Lamb of God, Jesus began to appear as He will when He comes in His glory, "the Lion of the tribe of Juda" (Rev. 5:5), "the Sun of righteousness" (Mai. 4:2), "KING OF KINGS, AND LORD OF LORDS" (Rev. 19:16). What glory it must be to see that changed face of Jesus! We that love Him will see it one day. Peter, James, and John had been accustomed to seeing the Saviour suffering, now they saw Him as He will be when He reigns.

Moses and Elijah at the Transfiguration

Moses and Elijah were present. Why? They were talking with Jesus (vs. 5). Their conversation was about Christ's "decease" (or death) which He should accomplish at Jerusalem (Luke 9:31). The heavenly world knew about the death of Christ for sinners which was coming. It was the absorbing topic of their thoughts and conversation there, and Moses and Elijah were allowed to come and meet Jesus and the apostles on the Mount of Transfiguration there to discuss with Jesus His death! Calvary and the love shown there and the blood spilled there are the themes of Christians' songs, the topics of Christians' praises, the foundation of a Christian's assurance. How grand that in Heaven the saints and angels marveled and longed to discuss that all-surpassing event! The saints will praise Christ forever for redemption by the blood (Rev. 5:8-10).

It is supposed that Moses and Elijah were selected as these heavenly witnesses to represent the law and the prophets. Elijah already had his glorified body since he did not die but was translated (II Kings 2:11). Moses had died and his body was buried by the angels. Was that body preserved that Moses might use it at this time? Or was Moses "clothed upon" with a temporary body till the resurrection? I do not know. Moses and Elijah were here used as heavenly witnesses of the transfiguration of Christ which pictures His Second Coming. It may be, therefore, that Moses and Elijah will be the two witnesses mentioned in Revelation 11:3-12, who will be witnesses just before the return of the Saviour in His glory which was pictured by His transfiguration. Besides, Elijah must return to the earth as foretold in Malachi 4:5, 6 and as Jesus plainly said in this chapter (vs. 11). John the Baptist came in the spirit and power of Elijah (Luke 1:17), and Jesus refers to that here in verse 12, but still Elijah must truly come. Perhaps these two representing the law and the prophets, then, will witness to the ungodly world in the midst of the tribulation preceding the return of Christ in His glory.

By the suggestion of Peter to build three tabernacles (vs. 4), for Jesus, Elijah and Moses, Peter meant well but was not wise. They must go back to the valley of suffering. Christ must go back to be crucified. The father with the poor demon-possessed, lunatic son, was waiting for someone to heal him (vs. 15). That was but a symbol of all the sins, sorrows, and sicknesses of this world that could not be cured except Jesus go on with the Father's plan, to the cross. Crowns do not come before crosses. Reigning does not come before suffering. Blessed is the Christian who learns and becomes reconciled to the thought that this world is not his home. Like Abraham, Isaac, and Jacob, let us be content to be sojourners here, strangers, and pilgrims, seeking the better country when

Jesus shall bring us back to fulfill the promises (Heb. 11:8-16). Christ could not stay with His altered countenance shining as the sun in that transfigured glory and neglect the world for which He came to suffer, die, and save.

Besides, Peter erred in putting Moses and Elijah on a par with Jesus. They were prophets; He is God's only begotten Son. They were frail, sinful men, saved by the blood yet to be shed; He was the Saviour, the sinless One. God seems to have rebuked Peter in speaking from Heaven, "This is my beloved Son... hear ye him." And Jesus stood alone. God will allow no prophet or angel to stand equal with Christ.

Christ's Glory Accompanied by Clouds

Notice the "bright cloud" in verse 5. The manifestation of the divine presence is often accompanied by clouds. God's presence led the Israelites, protected them and rested over them in a pillar of a cloud by day and in a pillar of fire by night (Exod. 13:21, 22; 40:38; Num. 14:14). When the tabernacle was set up, "then a cloud covered the tent of the congregation, and the glory of the Lord filled the tabernacle" (Exod. 40:34). The Lord appeared to Moses "in a thick cloud" (Exod. 19:9). When Jesus ascended to Heaven "a cloud received him out of their sight" (Acts 1:9). When He comes again to reign, "Behold, he cometh with clouds; and every eye shall see him" (Rev. 1:7). Bright clouds ought to be joyful to the Christian, since they are so connected in the Scripture with the glory and the second coming of Christ.

It was a *"bright* cloud" that overshadowed Christ in His transfiguration glory. God manifested Himself on Mount Sinai at the giving of the law in "a thick cloud" (Exod. 19:16), but that terrible sight was not of a bright cloud but of billowing smoke (Exod. 19:18) and "thick darkness" (Exod. 20:21). The darkness of that cloud was an important part of the symbolism which God intended to convey in giving the law.

When Moses told the new generation of Israelites before entering the Promised Land of the giving of the law, he reminded them that it was with "darkness, clouds, and thick darkness" (Deut. 4:11. See also Deut. 5:22; Exod. 20:21). God in the clouds of thick darkness is the God of judgment, the God of the law. Second Samuel 22:10,

12; Psalm 18:11; 97:2 all picture God as revealing Himself in clouds of darkness to destroy His enemies. Evidently God, as pictured in the law, frowned upon a guilty, wicked race from dark clouds of threatening punishment. But in the Lord Jesus Christ God smiles upon sinners from bright clouds, full of mercy and light. How clear it is that by the law shall no flesh be justified in His sight (Rom. 3:20; Gal. 3:11) and that Jesus Himself is the only way to God (John 14:6; Acts 4:12; I John 5:11, 12). Those who reject Him must face the frown of judgment and the dark clouds of retribution. For this reason we are not told whether clouds will be bright or dark at the second coming of Christ when He "cometh with clouds." There will be clouds of judgment for sinners but clouds of glory for saints.

An interesting thought is that the pillar of clouds by day and the fire by night which overshadowed .Israel and led them in the wilderness was the cloud of mercy, not the dark clouds of Mount Sinai and the law. The clouds appeared to them, led them and protected them before they were given the law and after they had broken it, just the same. Just so, God in His mercy blesses us, His people, out of His mercy and not according to our iniquities (Ps. 103:10).

Notice that God spoke on two occasions out of two clouds. "Out of the midst of the fire, of the cloud, and of the thick darkness" (Deut. 5:22), God spoke with an audible voice and gave the Ten Commandments, the law, terrible in its righteousness, commanding death for sinners. But here God spoke with an audible voice out of a bright cloud, saying, "This is my beloved Son, in whom I am well pleased." God speaks in righteousness and in judgment in the law, but in Jesus He smiles with mercy! All who are under the law are under a curse, for it is written, "Cursed is every one that continueth not in all things which are written in the book of law to do them" (Gal. 3:10). But, praise His name, "Christ hath redeemed us from the curse of the law" (Gal. 3:13). God is well pleased in Christ and all of us who are in Him are thereby well pleasing to God. "He hath made us accepted in the beloved. In whom we have redemption through his blood, the forgiveness of sins, according to the riches of his grace" (Eph. 1:6, 7). Notice the words, "IN WHOM I am well pleased" (vs. 5) and 'accepted in the beloved IN WHOM we have redemption through his blood.' Both

Scriptures refer to Christ, the only One whose righteousness pleases the Father!

Here in the presence of Moses through whom the law was given and in the presence of Elijah, a representative of the prophets, the Father, in audible voice, commands us to hear His Son in whom He is well pleased. The fear and prostration of the three apostles (vs. 6) are like that of John the second time when on the Isle of Patmos he saw Jesus again in His glory (Rev. 1:17). Notice the fear that sinners will have at His Second Coming as illustrated by the wailing foretold in Revelation 1:7. Compare the words of verse 5 with those from Heaven when Jesus was baptized (Matt. -3:17). Both times God said, "This is my beloved Son, in whom I am well pleased."

Verses 9-13 Jesus Discusses the Transfiguration With the Disciples

Again Jesus charged them, as He had often done before, not to discuss His miracles, His power, His deity with others (Matt. 16:20; Mark 1:44; 5:43).

The apostles were not to tell of the transfiguration until after Christ rose from the dead (vs. 9). They obeyed this command as we learn in Luke 9:36. Jesus had been rejected by the Jews as their King, the Son of David. To these wicked Jews, then, henceforth He offered only one evidence of His deity and Messiahship, that is, His rising from the dead after the third day, the sign of the prophet Jonas (Matt. 12:39, 40; 16:4).

Having seen Elijah in the transfiguration scene, the apostles asked for an explanation of Malachi 4:5, 6 (See vs. 10). Jesus answered that truly Elijah must literally come. Miracles will be worked and the hearts of the fathers will be turned to the children and the hearts of the children to their fathers, evidently by the testimony and miracles of Elijah as one of the two witnesses just before the great and terrible day of the Lord (Rev. 11:3-12). Compare Revelation 11:6 with the power given Elijah in I Kings 17:1. But verse 12 refers to John the Baptist as verse 13 explains. John was the same kind of prophet as Elijah. Malachi 4:5, 6 will have a double fulfillment. It was figuratively fulfilled in John the Baptist

198

who came "in the spirit and power of Elias" (Luke 1:17). It will literally be fulfilled, however, by Elijah (vs. 12).

There is a most comforting lesson for us in the fact that the disciples knew Moses and Elijah. We will not have to be introduced when we get to Heaven but "then shall I know even as also I am known" (I Cor. 13:12). Likewise, the heavenly visitors knew what was transpiring on earth and of the coming crucifixion of the Saviour, "his decease which he should accomplish at Jerusalem" (Luke 9:31). Our loved ones who have gone on before know what is transpiring on earth. They cannot speak to us but they are a great cloud of witnesses about us (Heb. 12:1). They rejoice in the presence of the angels when a sinner repents (Luke 15:7, 10). The unseen world is not far away and how happy are they who are with the Saviour there! See the author's sermons, "Tears in Heaven," in the book, *"And God Remembered..."* and "Spectators in the Heavenly Grandstand" in the book, *The Scarlet Sin and Other Revival Sermons,* for discussion of the knowledge the saints in Heaven have about us on earth.

Verses 14-21 A Father's Lunatic Son Healed

Jesus must have known how badly He was needed at the foot of the mountain. Here is reason enough why they could not build three tabernacles and stay on the mount.

Notice "the multitude" (vs. 14). It must have been the same great crowd that had followed Him all over Galilee, with some variations. They had followed Him ever since the occasion of Matthew 4:24, 25, and are mentioned after that in Matthew 5:1, 8:1, 18; 9:8, 36; 11:7; 12:15; 13:2, 34, 36; 14:14, 15, 19, 22, 23; 15:30, 32, 33, 35, 36, 39. Sometimes this crowd is spoken of as a "multitude," sometimes as a "great multitude," sometimes in the plural form, "multitudes," or "great multitudes."

Read in Mark 9:14-29 and in Luke 9:37-43, companion passages, about the healing of this boy. The whole multitude was greatly excited (Mark 9:15). The son was a lunatic (vs. 15), possessed of a "dumb spirit" (Mark 9:17). The nine apostles who did not go up on the mount for the transfiguration scene could not heal the boy.

199

Verse 16 is a sad verse. What an indictment of Christians! Compare it with Luke 11:6. The average Christian does not have the bread for sinners, the power to help those in trouble. The man was right in bringing his son to the disciples of Jesus. Those who follow Christ should have the power of Christ. When we, because of our lack of faith and lack of power, would send the people away empty, Jesus would say to us as He did to the twelve, "They need not depart; give ye them to eat" (Matt. 14:16). Later, in such cases, after Jesus was gone, the apostles and other Christians did have the faith to heal (Acts 3:1-8; 5:15, 16; 8:7; 9:32-42; 19:12; 28:8, 9). People have many, many burdens and Christians ought to have power from God to help. Not all the sick will be healed and not all the lost will be saved, but surely we could do more if we had faith in God.

Notice the rebuke of Jesus in verses 17 and 20. Do not excuse these disciples. They could have cast out that devil but for their unbelief. "Without faith it is impossible to please him" (Heb. 11:6). To have faith for wonderful things is a solemn command of Jesus (Mark 11:22). Read the conversation between Jesus and the father given in Mark 9:21-24. There in verse 23 Jesus gave the remarkable promise, "All things are possible to him that believeth." That is a universal promise and not limited there nor anywhere else except by the matter of faith. We ought to pray as the father did, with tears, "Lord, I believe; help thou mine unbelief" (Mark 9:24).

Unbelief here was a sin and indicates that often we could conquer our unbelief, we could have faith, if we did the right thing. "Faith cometh by hearing, and hearing by the word of God" (Rom. 10:17). If they had dwelt on the Scripture as they ought, they would have had more faith. Faith is a gift of God, often given in answer to prayer as it was given evidently to this father who prayed, "Lord... help thou mine unbelief" (Mark 9:24). If these nine disciples had gone with Jesus and the other three up in the mountain to pray, they might have had faith enough for this blessing when they returned. Unbelief is a sin, a sin that can be avoided.

The proper study and meditating on the Word of God, praising God for past blessings, obedience to God's commands, earnest and constant submissive prayer will result in growing faith. Faith is a part of the fruit of the Spirit (Gal. 5:22). Those who are filled with the Spirit will have more faith. See how being filled with the Spirit and faith are connected in the case of Stephen (Acts 6:5, 8), and in the case of Barnabas (Acts 11:24). Notice particularly the connection of faith and prayer in verses 20 and 21, and in Mark 9:29. Most certainly persistent, unceasing, self-surrendered prayer results in faith that is pleasing to God. If these disciples had prayed as they ought, they would have had faith for the healing of the boy. See the author's book, *PRAYER – Asking and Receiving,* the chapter on "Have Faith in God," for how to grow faith.

Some ancient manuscripts of the Greek New Testament leave off verse 21 and the words "and fasting" from Mark 9:29. In the American Standard Version of the Bible these are therefore omitted. However, even if verse 21 be omitted, that does not change the fact that fasting is often commended with prayer in the Bible. The greatest Bible characters included fasting with praying (Matt. 9:15; Acts 13:2, 3; II Cor. 11:27). Nor does it change the plain, explicit teaching of Jesus that the disciples failed because of unbelief (vs. 20), that this unbelief was displeasing to Jesus (vs. 17), and that the unbelief was the result of prayerlessness (Mark 9:29).

Let us not doubt that this child was literally possessed of a devil. Evil spirits are about us, often causing diseases such as insanity (vs. 15; Matt. 8:28; Luke 8:27, 29, 35). Evil spirits were sometimes responsible also for blindness and dumbness (Matt. 12:22). These were cases that medical skill could not cure and there are many such cases today.

We ought to believe verse 20 literally. Jesus said the same thing again in Matthew 21:21, 22; Mark 9:23, and Mark 11:23, 24. Those promises expressly say that they are for "whosoever," that they involve any request, "What things soever ye desire" and "whatsoever." There is not a hint that they were meant only for the apostles or even for that age alone. God does not change His principles in regard to answered prayer. Faith is as precious to God in one dispensation as in another. For other such blessed promises of unlimited answers to the prayer of faith see Psalm 81:10, Jeremiah 33:3, John 14:13, 14; 16:23, 24, and I John 3:22, where again the blessed word "whatsoever" is used.

Verses 22,23 Jesus Again Foretells His Crucifixion

Here again the Saviour presses on His disciples' hearts the certainty of His betrayal, death, and resurrection. See also Mark 9:30-32 and Luke 9:43-45. Jesus was not surprised, but knew from the beginning what the end would be, and deliberately gave Himself up to die for sinners. This time still the disciples did not understand the necessity for His death (Mark 9:32), did not accept His statement as a literal fact, for they did not expect His resurrection from the dead even when He was crucified (Luke 24:11-24 and especially John 20:9). They did not understand and were afraid to ask Jesus what He meant (Mark 9:32; Luke 9:45). They were very sad (vs. 23). We suppose their timidity was caused by Jesus' rebuke of Peter in Matthew 16:22, 23, over the same question.

Jesus never forgot for one moment His coming death. The multitudes who followed Him around, wanting Jesus to heal their sick and feed their stomachs, did not fool Jesus and they ought not to fool preachers today. This wicked, unregenerate world is the enemy of Jesus Christ, and it is the enemy of every Christian who is faithful as he ought to be (John 15:18-24). Jesus knew the wicked heart of mankind, but that wickedness was not fully manifested to us until it crucified the dear Son of God Himself.

This passage suggests that Jesus denied Himself, crucified Himself daily as He commanded Christians to do (Luke 9:23). That is, He consented daily to the coming crucifixion and faced it joyfully and determinedly (Isa. 50:6, 7).

Verses 24-27 Jesus and Tribute Money; the Miracle of Money in a Fish's Mouth

"They that received tribute" (vs. 24) were publicans, tax collectors, in Capernaum. Publicans were a greedy bunch, greatly despised by the Jews, though Matthew or Levi, one of the twelve apostles, had himself been a publican (Matt. 9:9; 10:3). Remember that Matthew had come from this very town, Capernaum; and other unconverted publicans, possibly those who had eaten supper with Jesus after Matthew's call (Matt. 9:10) were the ones here who asked Peter for tax money. These publicans may have been relatives and were almost certainly acquaintances and friends of some of the apostles. It is possible that they had known Jesus from

His boyhood since He grew up in Nazareth, not far from Capernaum, and had now made Capernaum His home for some while and had preached there many times, working there some of His greatest miracles as you see from Matthew 4:13; 9:1; 11:23, 24. That helps to explain verse 25. It was not customary for publicans to collect revenue from their own loved ones for the Roman government, we suppose.

The question of tribute money or taxation was brought up later by the Pharisees and Sadducees (Matt. 22:15-21). There Jesus definitely committed Himself that one should "render therefore unto Caesar the things which are Caesar's," should support with taxes the government that protects us. This teaching is borne out further in Romans 13:1-7, especially verse 7. Notice in verse 27 Jesus' desire not to offend unsaved tax collectors. A Christian should be particularly careful not to offend in money matters. We should rather suffer ourselves to be defrauded and take wrong from others than to go to law with Christians or have unseemly controversy over money matters (I Cor. 6:1-8). In the Sermon on the Mount Jesus particularly warned that we should "agree with thine adversary quickly" (Matt. 5:25), and the teaching is that if a brother holds ought against us (that is, that we owe him any money) it will hinder our prayers (Matt. 5:23, 24). That Jesus spoke particularly of money is shown in the following verse (Matt. 5:26). Matthew 5:40-42 gives further instructions about how we should feel toward avoiding offense in what we owe people or in what they think we owe, giving more than they ask.

It becomes apparent that Jesus went to infinite pains in training these apostles. Notice that He allowed Peter here to participate in the miracle of the money in the fish's mouth and doubtless thereby Peter never forgot the blessed teaching of the Saviour concerning taxation, avoiding offense, and paying one's debts.

These verses also illustrate the poverty of Jesus. "For ye know the grace of our Lord Jesus Christ, that, though he was rich, yet for your sakes he became poor, that ye through his poverty might be rich" (II Cor. 8:9). No money, literally nowhere to lay His head (Matt. 8:20), Jesus was as poor as any man who ever lived. Preachers and Christian workers who must have regular salaries, nice homes, cars, money to educate their children, should be humbled by the poverty of Jesus. And all of us should love Him better for His infinite compassion since it was for our sakes He became poor.

MATTHEW XVIII

Verses 1-10 Jesus Teaches a Lesson From a Little Child

Mark 9:33-37 and Luke 9:46-48 should be read in connection with this passage for additional light. This occurred in Capernaum (Mark 9:33). The occasion of the question in verse 1 was that the disciples on the road had "disputed among themselves, who should be the greatest" (Mark 9:34). Jesus asked them what they had been discussing. They were ashamed. His probing finally brought out the question, "Who is the greatest in the kingdom of heaven?" The response of Jesus was most kind. Instead of sharply rebuking them for their pride and selfishness, He took time to teach them the lesson of true greatness shown here in verses 2 to 4.

Christians should be like little children in several respects. First, children are more innocent and guileless by nature than older people. The only way an elder person can become childlike in the true sense is to be converted; he must have a change of heart, that is, be born again. A newborn person is naturally childlike.

Second, Christian greatness depends upon humility (vs. 4). Those who seek greatness do not find it. "And whosoever of you will be the chiefest, shall be servant of all" (Mark 10:44; Matt. 20:27). "Whosoever exalteth himself shall be abased; and he that humbleth himself shall be exalted" (Luke 14:11; 18:14). "For whosoever will save his life shall lose it: but whosoever will lose his life for my sake, the same shall save it" (Luke 9:24). "If any man desire to be first, the same shall be last of all, and servant of all"; so said the Saviour at the same time, as mentioned in Mark 9:35. A Christian should be partaker of the humility of Christ (Phil. 2:3-9).

With great patience Jesus taught His disciples this lesson of humility. Its importance cannot be overestimated, and it is needed for preachers more than for most people. So many people love preachers; they have such a place of leadership that naturally they are tempted with pride. For this reason young preachers should not be advanced immediately to positions as pastors. A bishop should be "not a novice, lest being lifted up with pride he fall into the condemnation of the devil" (I Tim. 3:6). Peter, James, John, and other apostles were not fit to be leaders until they learned this secret of humility. Young preachers ought to listen to older preachers, ought to be willing to learn the lesson of humility. Elisha was a servant of Elijah even to pouring water for him to wash his hands (II Kings 3:11). Timothy, Titus, Epaphroditus, and many other preachers went with Paul to obey his orders, learn from him, do his writing, etc. (Acts 16:1-3; Titus 1:5; Phil. 2:25). Even Paul was first sponsored and guided by Barnabas (Acts 9:26, 27; 11:25, 26, 30). The great Stephen, who became a marvelous preacher and was the first Christian martyr (Acts, chap. 7), started out as a deacon, or servant, waiting on the widows in Jerusalem (Acts 6:1-6). Another of those same servants, or deacons, was Philip, who became a great evangelist (Acts 8:5-40). You see why Jesus took three and one-half years to train these apostles and why young preachers or Christian workers must take time to prepare themselves for their ministry.

Accountable Children Need to Be Saved

Child conversion is clearly taught by the Saviour in this passage. Jesus is speaking about conversion (vs. 3). Christians are to receive little children like the one Jesus was using as an example, as a Christian among them (vss. 4, 5). The little boy whom Jesus used (called "him" in vs. 2) was an example typical of other "little ones which believe in me." The lad had trusted in Christ as Saviour and so was a Christian. In the next chapter we find some, encouraged by this incident, who brought little children to Jesus, and Jesus gave that beautiful gem of Matthew 19:14, "Suffer little children..." We are to allow little children to come to Christ, not to forbid them. The kingdom of Heaven is made up of such as the little children who really came to Christ.

Do not misunderstand. Little children must be converted just as grown people, if they are to be Christians. An unaccountable baby who never consciously sinned is not a Christian; he is not saved, though he is kept safe by the blood of Christ until he reaches accountability. We believe that infants who die go to Heaven, and we base this hope on I Corinthians 15:22, II Samuel 12:23, and other Scriptures. All one lost in Adam is repurchased in Christ, so no one is lost because of inherited taint, but because of his own sin. Besides, the Scripture plainly teaches that the Lord is "not willing that any should perish" (II Pet. 3:9), that He takes "no pleasure in the death of him that dieth" (Ezek. 18:32), even that He atoned for the sins of the whole world (I John 2:2). Unaccountable infants are but not *saved.* When they come to the time of conscious sin against God, and to accountability, they become lost sinners and must be born again by faith in Christ, just as the most hardened sinner must be. God has only one plan of salvation, the same for a child of seven or a man of seventy, the same for the purest girl or the vilest criminal or infidel.

The Bible nowhere sets an age at which children become accountable. It varies with individual children, depending on what light, teaching, and experience they have had. Some claim to have been converted at four years of age. All this writer's six children professed to trust Christ when they were no more than five and six years old and have given abundant evidence of salvation. Prayerful teaching, discipline, church services, and the family altar may bring a child to see his need of a Saviour earlier than he otherwise would.

Remember that one does not need to know much in order to be saved. Notice the instant conversion of the thief on the cross (Luke 23:39-43), of the woman who was a sinner (Luke 7:36-50), of the jailor at Philippi with his entire household (Acts 16:25-34), of Cornelius and his household (Acts 10:34-48). Study Bible conversions in both the Old and New Testaments and you will realize that it does not take a great deal of knowledge to be saved. If one knows he is a sinner and trusts God to forgive and save through His mercy, that is enough to be saved. Any faith is saving faith when a penitent heart confesses its sins and depends on God for forgiveness. Remember that Old Testament saints were saved just as we are, though they had little Scripture and a very dim idea of the death of Christ. Children must repent and trust just like older people. But they may do that definitely while very young if they are clearly taught that they are sinners, that God loves them, that Christ died for them.

Many commit the great sin of discouraging child conversion (vs. 6). Notice the terrible warning Jesus gives in verses 6 to 8. If you cause a little child who has trusted in Christ to stumble and doubt, cause him to postpone baptism and church membership, then you have committed a terrible sin for which you will suffer. Parents should be particularly careful not to commit this sin. My dear father hindered me from joining a church when I was converted at about nine years of age. He rather lightly cast doubt on my conversion, supposing I was not really saved.

There is Bible evidence that the Prophet Samuel must have been converted very, very young (I Sam. 3:15). From a child Timothy knew the Scriptures which made him wise unto salvation (II Tim. 3:15). Remember that this little child here with Jesus was a Christian, having believed in Christ (vs. 6).

Physical Bodies to Go to Hell

Speaking of offenses or causing people to stumble or sin led Jesus to give verses 7 to 9. Older people may cause a child to stumble at the point of salvation and not to be saved. So sin may cause some reader to miss the way of salvation and go to a Hell of everlasting fire (vss. 8, 9). Men love sin and that is why they reject Christ (John 3:18-21). How desperately important it is that you lose any friend, any job, even a member of your body rather than lose your soul! If any unsaved person sees this lesson, I beg you, do not sell your soul to gratify the pleasure of eye, or hand, or foot, and so enter into everlasting fire.

Notice that Jesus teaches here that people with *physical bodies* will go to Hell. At present only the souls go to Hell while the bodies of unsaved people decay in the graves. Even now spirits in Hell have all the feeling and senses of the body, as you see in the case of the rich man who *thirsted, felt* the flames, *heard, remembered, spoke* (Luke 16:19-31). But at the resurrection of the unsaved dead, death and Hell will deliver up both dead bodies and spirits, and they will come forth to be judged (Rev. 20:12-15). With literal, physical bodies they will appear before Christ, when literal knees will bow and literal tongues will confess (Rom. 14:11; Phil. 2:10, 11); then both soul and body will descend into Hell. Jesus expressly warns us of this in Matthew 10:28. Before that judgment, two men, "the beast" or Antichrist, and his false prophet will be cast alive into Hell (Rev. 19:20). Any honest interpretation of Matthew 18:8, 9 must accept it that Jesus taught a Hell of literal, physical fire for literal, physical, human bodies. It is dangerous and wicked to explain away the plain words of the Saviour.

Guardian Angels

Guardian angels look after little children (vs. 10). Is that only taught of saved little children or is it also taught of unaccountable infants and unsaved children? We suppose it is taught of all, but we do not know. Thank God for this teaching of guardian angels. Every Christian is guarded by angels (Ps. 34:7). See especially how many angels guarded God's prophet, Elisha (II Kings 6:13-17). There are millions of angels (Rev. 5:11). Part of their business is caring for men, particularly ministering to the "heirs of salvation" (Heb. 1:14). We suppose that guardian angels are intended principally to care for saved people, though in His great mercy God may have them to protect unsaved people much of the time, just as His Spirit pleads long with unsaved people. The angels ascend and descend, evidently guarding and working on earth and reporting in Heaven (Gen. 28:12).

Verses 11-14 Parable of the Lost Sheep

Compare this with the story of the lost sheep in Luke 15:3-7. Jesus "is come to save that which was lost," *all* the lost people including little children. It is the "little ones" whom Jesus is speaking about in this passage (vs. 14) as well as others. This is a continuation of the discussion in the first part of the chapter.

Children do not give as much money to the church. Their influence is not as wide. One cannot certainly know whether any particular child will amount to much in this world. There are many reasons why children are neglected by those who give themselves to soul winning. It seems likely they will have more time and opportunity in which to be saved. Their hearts are not so hardened in sin. They are not so guilty. Hell and eternal punishment seem much nearer for an old sinner than for a young sinner. But Jesus teaches that each little one should be sought for Christ like one lost sheep on the mountains. In fact, the Saviour infers from verse 12 that one might well pay less attention to the ninety-nine settled Christians and more to winning the one unsaved child.

God is not satisfied with the ninety-nine. He wants the whole one hundred. Every person counts with God. A little child counts. A criminal counts. The poor, the dirty, the ignorant, the wicked count. God wants us to reach the outer fringe. In Luke 14:21-24 the servant was commanded to bring in not only those first invited but "the poor, and the maimed, and the halt, and the blind." He was to go not only into the streets but into the lanes or back alleys of the city. He was even to "go out into the highways and hedges [of the country] and compel them to come in." As long as there is one child unsaved, every Sunday School teacher and preacher has an important work to do.

Verses 15-20 How to Deal With a Trespassing Fellow Christian

The Saviour has said that we ought to be careful not to give offense to anyone or cause him to stumble (vss. 6, 7). Being in fellowship with other Christians is so important that to sin about this means that our prayers will be hindered (Matt. 5:23, 24; 6:14, 15; Mark 11:25, 26; Luke 6:35-38). Even the wrong attitude of heart which causes anger with a brother without cause, or which causes one to call him "dunce" (Raca), or "fool," may be as guilty as a murderer in God's sight (Matt. 5:21, 22). How important it is, then, for Christians to reconcile their differences.

"If thy brother shall trespass against thee" – and he certainly will! Thy brother is as human as thou art! Sooner or later any two human beings thrown much together will fail to agree perfectly about something. The very best Christians in the world are subject to mistakes, misunderstandings, even sin. James, John, and the other disciples were. The apostles disagreed and argued who should be the greatest (Mark 9:34). James and John sought what seemed to the other disciples an unfair advantage when their mother asked for them the first places in the kingdom (Matt. 20:20-24). Paul and Barnabas had sharp contention over whether they should take with them John Mark who had left them once before (Acts 15:36-40). Peter and Paul also had a sharp disagreement over a serious doctrinal matter, and that publicly (Gal. 2:11-14). Euodias and Syntyche, ladies at Philippi, evidently had misunderstandings arid differences that were known publicly and needed to be settled in Christian love (Phil. 4:2). Among the saints at Corinth, some Christians went to law with others which was a sin and brought the church into reproach (I Cor. 6:1-8). Abraham's herdsmen and Lot's herdsmen disagreed (Gen. 13:7). Jacob and

209

Esau had trouble; so did Jacob and Laban; so did Joseph and his brethren. Moses, Isaac, David, Nehemiah, and many other Old Testament saints had the problem of dealing with troublemakers and offenders. How important it is that a Christian should know how to treat those who wrong him.

What should a Christian do in case someone wrongs him? The first step is, "Go and tell him his fault between thee and him *alone*" (vs. 15). Give any man a chance to correct his wrongs or to tell his side of the case before you tell others. Nine-tenths of the gossip, ill-feeling, and broken fellowship among Christians would be avoided, I believe, if Christians resolved never to tell others about someone's sins until they first honestly and kindly approached the offender to hear his side of the question. Tell no one else until you tell the one who has wronged you or who *you think* has wronged you. Usually the offense was not as bad as you thought. Sometimes it never happened at all, but you only thought so. Sometimes there was an adequate reason to explain it. At other times the offender has cooled off and is sorry. Great good can be done by quiet, Christian *private* approach to another Christian. Even if no other good is done, you can find out the full truth, see the other man's viewpoint, and have the consciousness that you have honestly tried. If you do not do this, you offend God and sometimes make useless your prayers (Matt. 5:23, 24). In fact, the brother should be approached immediately, before sundown, if possible (Eph. 4:26), so that no bitterness will develop in your heart.

Notice the important aim of this private visit: "thou hast gained thy brother." If one wrongs you, your visit should not be primarily to get restitution but to gain your brother. If you gain your brother and lose a dollar or ten dollars or a hundred dollars, you have gained much. Forgive as quickly and as mercifully as you hope to be forgiven (Luke 6:36, 37). One of the first motives of every Christian should be to keep intact the brotherly love and fellowship of the body of Christ. It is a terrible sin to prolong or cause divisions and strife among Christians and in the churches of Christ.

Notice also who should make the visit – the one trespassed against (vs. 15). But Matthew 5:24 shows that the one who trespasses should also go seek the other. You should go to be reconciled with your brother, whether you or he did wrong. In fact, the teaching of the Scripture is that any Christian whose fellowship with another Christian has been broken for any reason should immediately do his best to have that fellowship restored, no matter who is guilty. The Bible says nothing about Christians' meeting each other halfway. Rather, each Christian should be eager to go the whole way if necessary to have agreement and to do more than is required or asked (Matt 5:39, 48). Do not go to law with a Christian brother even if he does owe you. Rather, suffer yourself to be defrauded. Do not fight your brother who thinks you should go with him a mile and you think not. Instead, go with him two miles. Gain your brother!

The second step, if the private interview is not effective, is to take "one or two more, that in the mouth of two or three witnesses every word may be established." Most brothers can be won to friendship if they are approached privately, with earnest desire to please Christ and have peace. Sometimes they cannot be won but persist in wrongdoing that harms others and becomes a public issue so that it must be dealt with. In such cases, the intreaty of other men may help to reclaim a sinning brother to his duty and fellowship. If not, then spiritually minded witnesses will hear every word so that there will be no misunderstandings of what has happened. The Bible requires two or three witnesses before anybody should be condemned (Deut. 17:6). It is particularly urged that no charges should be heard against a preacher except by the mouth of two or three witnesses (I Tim. 5:19). Thus it can be shown that the matter is not purely a personal quarrel. No person should be made an outcast among Christians without sufficient evidence.

The third step is this: if the brother could not possibly be won by the offended person nor by others who went to plead with him and hear his side of the question, then the matter should be told to the church. If that seems a long and hard way to show up a man as an offender, then remember God wanted us to be quick to forgive and slow to condemn and He did not want unnecessary divisions among Christians. According to this Scripture, for a church to withdraw fellowship from a Christian should be a very rare occurrence and only after very careful efforts have been made to win the offender back to fellowship and Christian duty. Jesus gave this plan for individuals and churches, and we should carefully follow it.

Remember that God does sometimes want people turned out of churches when they are guilty of gross and persistent sin and are impenitent. Paul's command about one individual is given in I

Corinthians, the fifth chapter, especially verses 3, 5, 7, and 13. Certainly God does not want His church endorsing wickedness. All over this land are churches which dishonor God by having deacons, stewards, elders, Sunday School teachers, finance committee members, and trustees who are unchristian in their daily lives and whose dishonesty or worldliness, drinking, gambling, profanity, and covetousness dishonor the name of Christ and harm the church. Many churches ought to clean house, but they are to do it in the Bible way and after the most heart-searching conviction, penitence, and prayer, and do it in the spirit commanded here, seeking to gain the brother and hoping not to expel him.

It should be noticed here also that the word "church" in this passage means a New Testament congregation of Christians able to receive members and to withdraw from members. For the reception of church members see the case of Cornelius and his household (Acts 10:47), where they were approved for baptism, whether by formal vote or common consent, and Acts 18:27, Romans 16:2, where letters were sent, asking congregations to receive Apollos and Phebe. Acts 9:26-28 tells how Paul tried to join the disciples at Jerusalem, was first refused, and then received on the testimony of Barnabas.

Verse 18 reminds us of the promise in Matthew 16:19. It was evidently given primarily to the apostles, the Holy Spirit revealing to them what was God's will to loose or bind, to permit or forbid.

Verse 19 is a blessed promise about prayer. Notice that in this case agreement among Christians is the only condition, not faith as in Mark 11:24, not persistence as in Luke 11:5-8 and Luke 18:7, 8, not asking in Jesus' name as in John 14:15, 14, not abiding in Him as in John 15:7, or doing His will as in I John 5:22. If God demanded that all these conditions be perfectly fulfilled in each case to get our prayers answered, then we would very rarely get anything from God. He knows our frailty and makes different conditions, usually requiring only that one condition be fulfilled in a given promise. If you meet any single promise of God's Word, you are safe in expecting God to answer. God is so anxious for us to pray that He offers us great blessings on very simple conditions. If we cannot meet one condition in one case, then perhaps we can meet another and so get the blessing. How anxious God is to have us pray!

Actually, if we set out to fulfill one requirement which God makes, we get nearer to Him and nearer right on all the other things that will please Him. Two Christians who get everything out of the way between them so that they can be perfectly agreed in heart, wanting certain things, will have dealt their selfishness such a blow that they are likely to be able to ask it for Jesus' sake, not their own. Then their hearts will not condemn them, and they will know that they are doing things according to God's will, at least in the matter of fellowship. Forgiving others, they will certainly have more faith to be forgiven. In fact, when Christian people are really agreed in heart, then they have fulfilled all the law, for love is the fulfillment of the law (Rom. 13:10; Gal. 5:14).

Verse 19 does not say that if two agree *to pray*, but rather if they agree *as touching the particular thing* that they ask. Two persons may agree to pray about something but in their hearts not be agreed upon it, that is, not want it just alike and for the same purpose. To agree with the lips does not always mean agreement in the heart.

Verse 20 is still dealing with the same question of brotherly love and agreement. What a comfort verse 20 is to little groups who meet for prayer meetings, to Bible classes, or to small churches that, though discouraged and feeble and without crowds and equipment and strong leadership, yet meet in Jesus' name. Let each discouraged Sunday School teacher who only has one or two pupils remember and claim this blessed promise. Jesus sits there beside you as you teach one or two. Jesus meets in that prayer meeting with only two or three! This verse shows that no limit on the size of a legitimate New Testament church is necessary. Christ can meet with two or three as well as He did with the thousands in the church at Jerusalem.

Verses 21-35 Jesus Teaches Forgiveness

Luke 17:3, 4 is similar to verses 21 and 22 here. The plain teaching of these two verses cannot be denied. Many people feel that if a brother repeat a sin against one three times, it should then not be forgiven. Peter was more liberal and willing to forgive seven times (vs. 21). But Jesus plainly said he should be forgiven at least "seventy times seven" or 490 times. Actually, that practically means an unlimited number of times. If you forgive your brother

213

490 times, you will probably be in the habit of forgiving and out of practice in carrying grudges. Remember that a. Christian should not be like the unsaved in this wicked world.

The remarkable parable of Jesus in verses 23 to 34 has a teaching we must not miss. The "king" (vs. 23) represents God. The one brought to Him owing ten thousand talents is any one of us. Ten thousand talents would be an enormous fortune. A talent of silver was worth about $1,940. A talent of gold was worth about $29,000. So ten thousand talents even of silver would equal at least 19 million dollars! That illustrates how God feels about our sins toward Him. We owe Him an enormous fortune, more than we can ever pay, more than anybody else can ever owe us. Verse 25 shows what is our just due. If God should take all that we have – our lives, our families, our possessions – and cast our souls into Hell, it would be no more than we richly deserve! Oh, the depth of our wickedness! How awful has been our sin against God!

Verse 26 shows the attitude which many of us had toward God when we came for forgiveness. I was conscious of how deep was my debt to God. Not knowing the wickedness of my heart I promised to please Him, promised to live right, never to dishonor Him again. I did not keep my promises. No one else, I suppose, ever has perfectly kept such promises.

Verse 27 shows how God feels toward our sins. Moved with compassion, the king "loosed him, and forgave him the debt." When we found peace with God, we found it, not on the basis that we would pay in due time, but rather on the basis of free forgiveness. The debt was wiped out by payment by another, Jesus Christ.

Now compare an offense of one man against another and how it looks in God's sight as pictured in verse 28. The size of the offense is pictured as "a hundred pence." Yet the vicious, vengeful spirit of unforgiveness on the part of one man for another is pictured in verses 28 and 29. After God's abounding mercy toward us, how little, how mean, how ungrateful we appear in the sight of God when we are angry and bitter toward a brother who wrongs us. Our sin toward God was like a debt of ten thousand talents (vs. 24). Other sins toward us are no more, comparatively, than one hundred pence.

The attitude of the outside world toward a Christian who will not forgive and cannot live at peace with others is shown in verse 31. Brotherly love is one Christian virtue that the most wicked man on earth recognizes and values as befitting a Christian (John 13:35). The world has little confidence in a Christian who cannot forgive.

The attitude of the king toward his servant in verse 34 represents the way God feels toward even His own children who will not forgive "from your hearts... every one his brother their trespasses." Any Christian who will not forgive is destined for certain punishment and the wrath of God. There is no way to measure the infinite harm and sin that follows in the wake of unforgiveness. Hindered prayers (I Pet. 3:1-7), the grieving of the Holy Spirit (Eph. 4:30-32), and countless other evils follow the unforgiving heart.

Suppose you this moment close the door to your room, get down on your knees and ask God to search your heart. If there be one shred of unforgiveness or grudge or bitterness toward any person on earth, you should here and now forgive it freely for Christ's sake and trust Him also to forgive you all your trespasses and let it be truly "from your hearts."

MATTHEW XIX

Verses 1,2 Jesus Goes From Galilee to Judea

This marks a turning point in the ministry of our Lord. Before this, Jesus as a boy had gone up to Jerusalem with His parents every year at the feast of the passover (Luke 2:41). Then later, being about thirty years old, Jesus went over the Jordan River to be baptized of John (Matt. 3:IB). After this, Jesus stayed for a time in Judea to preach and make converts who were baptized by His disciples (John 3:22, 23; 4:1-3). Then He went to Galilee, and practically all His ministry as recorded in the book of Matthew up to this time has been around the Sea of Galilee with headquarters at Capernaum. However, He had gone regularly to Jerusalem for certain feasts and was known to the whole nation for His teaching and miracles. In this chapter Jesus goes to the province of Judea and soon will be in Jerusalem offering Himself as King of the Jews (Matt. 21:1-11). Events rush headlong to the crucifixion.

From the above it should be easy for you to see that the earthly ministry of Jesus was not principally in and about Jerusalem, but in the province of Galilee. All the twelve apostles and His immediate followers were Galileans (Acts 2:7, 8; Mark 14:70).

It will be noticed by comparison of the four Gospels that Matthew and Mark give most of the attention to the ministry of Jesus in Galilee and little to His work in Judea and Jerusalem. Luke gives, I think, some more attention to the ministry in Jerusalem; John a good deal more. The feasts at Jerusalem are mentioned frequently in John (John 2:13; 5:1; 7:2, 8, 10; 13:1; etc.). What Jesus did and said, and the occurrences at these feasts are told in John's Gospel, but principally omitted in Matthew except for the events of the week preceding the crucifixion. Verse 2 mentions great multitudes following Jesus in the new region. Jesus was now known to the whole nation. Crowds would assemble quickly wherever He went. Perhaps many of these were en route to Jerusalem for the passover feast. The mercy of Jesus was shown again in healing many.

Verses 3-12 Jesus Answers Pharisees About Divorce

"The Pharisees" (vs. 3). This indicates that the Pharisees of the whole nation were united against Christ, and that these came representing the whole sect, still determined to trip Christ, to betray Him, to murder Him as they had planned all along (Matt. 12:14; John 5:16-18). The question was given insincerely, "tempting him." The question is, "Is divorce lawful 'for every cause'?" See the previous notes on Matthew 5:31, 32. Mark 10:1-12 is a parallel passage. See also Luke 16:18, I Corinthians 7:10-15.

Notice that Jesus accepted the Genesis account of creation and verified it (vss. 4-6). The condition in the Garden of Eden with one man and one woman indicates that God intended one man and one woman for each other – that He did not favor polygamy or divorce. Old Testament men were allowed to have more than one wife. God did not rebuke Abraham, Jacob, David, and others for having more than one wife, and there is no general command on the subject. In the New Testament, having only one wife was a condition of being a bishop or pastor of a church (I Tim. 3:2), but it is evident that a New Testament Christian, converted out of the pagan world, sometimes had more than one wife. Often it would not be advisable or even right for a man to abandon some of his wives with their children when he became a Christian, but such men could not become bishops of churches to set the example for others.

Old Testament Jewish men were encouraged to marry the wives of brothers who died (Deut. 25:5-10; Ruth 4:5-10). Specific instructions were given to govern cases where a man desired to take additional wives besides the first (Exod. 21:10). Remember that this was under the Mosaic Law. At the same time, God's perfect plan was for one man to love and marry one woman, and that these two should not be separated until death. The ideal arrangement which God Himself instituted in the Garden of Eden indicates that, as Jesus proves in these verses.

Verses 5 and 6 show that the closest human tie is between man and wife, that literally and really a proper marriage makes two people one; they are so united in heart and interests by the very hand of God that it would be a crime to separate them. In scriptural marriage a wife must be closer than father and mother (vs. 5, quoted from Gen. 2:24). Here is God's best reason against divorce. Men ought not to separate what God has joined together.

Polygamy was permitted in the Old Testament, and so was divorce, but this divorce was only "suffered" (vs. 8), never commanded, never approved. The Pharisees called it a "command... to put her away" (vs. 7), but they were wrong. Divorce was only "suffered" because of the hardness of Jewish hearts (vs. 8). The permission for divorce referred to here is given in Deuteronomy 24:1-4 – note this. The divorce permitted in the Old Testament was more or less unconditional, or "for every cause." Divorce always meant the right of remarriage to someone else.

Before you study verse 9, read carefully Luke 16:18 and Mark 10:11, 12, which say the same thing, but leave out "except it be for fornication." To the clause, "Whosoever shall put away his wife," Mark adds, *"marry another."* Divorce is not adultery, but when it gives excuse for another marriage, and when the divorce was not on Bible grounds, it *causes* adultery. When a man puts away his wife who is his own flesh and marries another woman, then the second marriage is adultery. Or if another man marries the woman who was put away, then that man, taking another man's wife, commits adultery. In other words, a true marriage is really not broken by a piece of paper saying that the woman and the man are legally free from each other. Unless the marriage is broken by fornication, God still counts them married when they separate; therefore when either remarries, that one commits adultery.

Note the single exception here: "Except it be for fornication." According to this Scripture, a man is permitted to divorce his wife for fornication. In that case, he is counted blameless. Doubtless the same instructions would fit for a woman's divorcing her husband. In Bible times, men were the ones who wanted divorces, since women were dependent and usually had no independent means of making a livelihood. In modern times, women are independent, and women sue for far more divorces than men. In any case, the Saviour says that, in case of fornication, divorce is permissible. And divorce, in Bible language and usage, involves the right to remarry. Where one's companion is clearly guilty of fornication, one has a right to divorce and to marry again. Divorce is *not commanded* in such cases, but *permitted.*

218

What is the difference between adultery and fornication? Do not be deceived by fancy definitions. Some people think fornication is a sin of unmarried people, adultery the sin of married people, but the Scripture does not say so, nor do die Greek words mean that. Fornication simply means harlotry. Evidently it is a stronger word than adultery. Adultery might involve only one act of sin, while the term fornication is used of a woman who is given over to a life of shame. It is the same sin, only the terms used indicate that a wife who was led into one act of adultery might probably be forgiven and taken back, but one who was past redemption in a life of sin might properly be divorced.

Notice that the term the Saviour uses about one who marries a second wife or husband after divorce (except for fornication) is that he *"commits adultery"* The idea is singular, I think, not plural. The modern term "living in adultery" is not what the Saviour said, nor what He meant. The improperly divorced man who marries again commits an act of adultery when he takes another wife. The new marriage at first is adultery, because the man was in truth already married. But it is a mistake to suppose that the former marriage still continues in force while one lives with a second wife, since fornication (continued adultery) breaks a marriage and gives a right for divorce. Then the adultery of the second marriage would certainly break the first marriage. Thereafter it would not be proper to speak of a man's having "two living wives" or of a woman's having "two living husbands," as we sometimes do. In such a case, the Bible speaks, not of the woman's two *husbands,* but of "her *former* husband" (Deut. 24:4). So in the scriptural language those who continue in the second marriage are not living in adultery. Divorce is a terrible thing, and when the marriage is not already broken by fornication, to break it for a second marriage on the part of either companion causes adultery. That is a terrible sin. But it is not an unpardonable sin, not a sin which has no forgiveness, or no remedy. It may be confessed to God and forgiven. After the second marriage is consummated and settled, the sin, grievous as it is, cannot be helped. It can be confessed and forgiven.. It cannot be undone.

Some preachers have insisted that all second marriages ought to be broken, and the parties should return to their former mates. In the first place, this is often impossible. The second marriages have often resulted in children, and a man cannot throw away his responsibility to the woman who has left all for him, nor his responsibility to his own children. Again, if one party were willing to leave the second marriage to return to the first, the former mate would often not be willing. I say, to break all the second marriages and to return to first marriages would be impossible. More important, according to God's Word, it would be a sin. Even under Mosaic Law, which was looser than New Testament righteousness, so that divorce was permitted because of the hardness of the people's hearts, a divorced wife was absolutely forbidden to return to her former husband after she had been married to another man and released from the second marriage either by a divorce or death! (Deut 24:3, 4).

That passage is very important. Remember that it would be a sin to break second marriages just as it was to break the first marriage. If any read this who have been guilty of the sin of improper divorce – not caused by fornication – and have married again, then, according to the Saviour, you were guilty of adultery in marrying the second time. But that act of adultery is in the past. The former marriage is broken. To break the present marriage and return to the first would be a sin. Your duty is to confess your past sin to the Lord and trust Him to forgive it, then take care that you safeguard the present marriage as holy and not to be broken.

Remember, marriage is sacred. What God has joined together, let not man put asunder. If you are married, then leave father and mother, and cleave to your mate as one flesh. First Corinthians 7:10-15 plainly teaches that marriage should not be broken because one party is a Christian and the other is not. That passage in I Corinthians refers to the teaching of Jesus here. First Corinthians 7:12 means that Paul had additional inspiration, giving more teaching beyond what Jesus gave. First Corinthians 7:15 shows that sometimes a Christian cannot prevent an unsaved companion's leaving, but need not get a divorce or marry again.

The disciples rebelled against the idea of marriage without freedom to divorce (vs. 10), saying that if that were the case, "it is not good to marry." Strict interpretation of the rule of Jesus about divorce is offensive to the carnal mind, even to modem preachers, as to these twelve. Modern, worldly preachers and leaders often advocate divorce for drunkenness, cruelty, desertion, or even for incompatability. They are wrong. Yet marriage is of God (Heb. 13:4). Marriage is not a sin (I Cor. 7:28). But some people would serve Christ better if they felt clearly led to forbear marriage in order to put the Lord first in everything. Paul did so (I Cor. 7:29-40). All men cannot receive this saying (vs. 11). It is better to marry than to burn (I Cor. 7:9). But God intended some men to be eunuchs. Some were born incapable of marriage or with no disposition to marriage (vs. 12). Some men are made incapable of the duties of marriage by a physical operation. That was true in ancient times of some male servants in the households of kings. There are indications that Daniel was a eunuch (Dan. 1:3, 9, 10). Some have made themselves eunuchs for the kingdom of Heaven's sake (vs. 12). This evidently means not physical, but refers to men who, like Paul, resolutely purposed in their hearts to put the service of God first and to forego the pleasure and responsibility of a home in order to please Christ only. Consider carefully the command of Jesus: "He that is able to receive it, let him receive it," and His saying in verse 11, "All men cannot receive this saying, save to whom it is given." God intended that most men and most women should marry.

Verses 13-15 Little Children Brought to Jesus

This incident occurred naturally, we suppose, as a result of the teaching of Jesus in the preceding chapter (Matt. 18:1-14). Learning that Jesus so loved little children and estimated their value so highly, people naturally wanted Jesus to touch their children, to mess them, or to pray for them (vs. 13). Please notice that nothing is said here about children's being baptized. Compare this passage with Mark 10:13-16, where we are told that Jesus took them up in His arms and blessed the children. The companion passage in Luke 18:15-17 calls the little ones brought to Jesus here infants. There is no case of infant baptism in the New Testament. (Of course, you know that Christian baptism was not taught or practiced in the Old Testament.) Bible preachers refused to baptize anybody except those who had sincerely repented of sin, trusting in Christ for salvation. So with John the Baptist (Matt. 3:7-9), with Philip (Acts 8:37), with Peter (Acts 10:47). Baptism pictures a change of heart, a burial to sin, a resurrection to a new life (Rom. 6:3*5; Col. 2:12).

Some say that infants must have been baptized where households were baptized in the New Testament, but this is not so. In the jailor's home, those who were baptized all heard the Word of God (Acts 16:32), and all rejoiced, believing in God (Acts 16:34). Lydia's household probably contained only servants. Not even a husband is mentioned, certainly no children. She was a business woman, a merchant (Acts 16:14, 15). For Jesus to bless little children, or for preachers to take children in their arms and pray for them is proper, but to count unaccountable infants as church members and let them grow up supposing that they are all right with God without a change of heart, without ever having trusted Christ for themselves, and to so pervert baptism, which should be the glad public profession of a believer in Christ, is a sin not excused by any Scripture.

Compare verse 14 with a similar statement in Mark 10:14 and Luke 18:16. By all means memorize one of the three, preferably verse 14 here, since you are studying Matthew, and use it in personal soul winning with children.

Verses 16-20 The Rich Young Ruler

This same incident is told in Mark 10:17-30, and Luke 18:18-30. The case in Luke 10:25-29 is not the same, but gives important light. Compare the three accounts of Matthew, Mark, and Luke. All three tell that the man was very rich, or had great possessions. Matthew only says that he was young (vss. 20, 22) and that he had great possessions (vs. 22). Luke only says that he was a ruler (Luke 18:18). Therefore, we call him "the rich young ruler." Mark 10:17 shows the anxiety and humility of this young man: "There came one running, and kneeled to him." When a rich man runs and kneels, you may be sure he is in earnest. However, a fatal, selfish pride is revealed in verse 16, which makes clear that the rich man did not ask, like the Philippian jailor, "What must I do to be saved?" but rather, "What GOOD THING shall I do, that I may have eternal life?" He wanted to be saved by his own goodness. He preferred salvation by works instead of salvation by grace. This was the sin of Cain who brought fruits of the ground, representing his own labor, instead of a bloody sacrifice, representing the atonement of Christ (Gen. 4:3-5). The human heart has a natural bent away from the humility, confession, repentance, and trust required in

222

accepting Christ as our Sin-Bearer. Men want to get to Heaven by good deeds of their own. This was the sin of the Pharisees so clearly pictured by Jesus in Luke 18:9-14. This conception of salvation is at the heart of all false religion. It honors man instead of God. It exalts good deeds instead of the blood. It makes man big, human works big. Those who believe one is saved, or partly saved by church membership, baptism, or a good life, are that much akin to this rich young ruler. Try to understand the attitude of this rich young ruler, for that is the reason for the answer Jesus gave him. Compare his question with that of the Jews at Pentecost (Acts 2:37), with that of the jailor at Philippi (Acts 16:30), and of the questioners in John 6:28. The Philippian jailor, deeply convicted, wanted to know simply and only what to do to be saved; so the answer of Paul there is the model and direct answer which always fits.

To believe on and rely upon the Lord Jesus Christ is God's only plan of salvation (Gen. 15:6; John 1:12; 3:14-18, 36; 5:24; 6:40, 47; Luke 7:50; Acts 10:43; 13:38, 39; Eph. 2:8, 9). Jesus gave the same answer to the inquirers in John 6:29. Believing on Christ is the true work that God requires. There is something one must *do* to be saved, but it is to believe.

In Acts 2:37 the inquirers wanted to know not only what to do to be saved, but what to do to have the power of the Holy Spirit which had fallen upon the Christians present and was being discussed in Peter's sermon. Therefore, Peter not only gave the plan of salvation, but the course of obedience after salvation (baptism) necessary if one was to have the gift of the Holy Ghost which is there promised (Acts 2:38, 39). Comparisons must show that repentance and faith each involve the other. They are not two plans of salvation, but the same plan. They are not even entirely separate steps in the plan of salvation. When the jailor believed in Christ for salvation, he had repented. When the inquirers at Pentecost repented, we know they had believed. Repentance and faith are different terms describing the penitent trust of one who accepts Christ.

But the rich young ruler was not willing to repent, was not seeking to trust in Christ. He did not address Jesus as Lord or Christ or Saviour or Son of David or Son of God. He only called Him "Good Master," which is simply the word for teacher, not more than rabbi. All this rich young ruler wanted was a good, wise, human teacher who could tell him good things to do so that he himself might earn

223

salvation. He wanted salvation by works, his own works, so he would get the credit, and so Jesus gave him the only possible answer.

One who wants to be saved by good works must keep every bit of the law. One who never sinned would need no Saviour. One who perfectly kept the law would be a perfect man. Remember that if one will not accept the atonement offered by Jesus Christ, then the only other alternative is absolute perfection in every thought, word, deed, and impulse every moment of a person's life. No person ever lived, save Jesus, who kept all this law. The Jews did not (Acts 15:10). No one else will ever be saved by keeping the law (Rom. 3:20; Gal. 3:11). All who look to human righteousness for salvation are certain of eternal doom if they fall short of absolute perfection from birth to death in every thought, word, and deed every moment of their lives.

Notice the rebuke of Jesus in the first part of verse 17, "Why callest thou me good? there is none good but one, that is, God." Jesus was good, but only because He was God. No sinful man is good. If Jesus were only a teacher, then it was foolish to call Him good. If He was good, then the rich young ruler ought to have called Him "Lord," and ought to have asked for a divine salvation instead of a human one.

'Which commandments must one keep in order to enter into life?' the young man asked. The answer of Jesus in verses 18 and 19 comprises the second table of the law, the last six of the Ten Commandments, omitting covetousness (Exod. 20:12-17). Jesus mentions only that part of the Ten Commandments having to do with one's neighbor, not one's direct obligation to God as in the first four commandments. Then He summed up these commands in the words, "Thou shalt love thy neighbour as thyself" (vs. 19, quoting from Lev. 19:18). In Matthew 22:37-40 Jesus summed up the first four commandments in one, the command to love God with all the heart, soul, and mind. He summed up the last six commandments in the command to love thy neighbor as thyself. There we are told that these sum up all the law and the prophets. In Luke 10:25-29 the same teaching is given to another lawyer who wanted to be saved by keeping the law.

Notice the subtlety of Jesus' answer. He is using the law for conviction to show the young man his need of Christ. That was exactly what the law was given for, and never to save men (Rom. 3:20). Again, notice that Jesus omitted the command, "Thou shalt not covet," which the young man had terribly broken in the sight of Jesus who knew his heart. Four of the Ten Commandments are given in order (vs. 18), but, "Honour thy father and thy mother" is given last. Jesus is going to call for a practical demonstration on the question of covetousness which was better than arguing with the man who would probably have said he was not covetous, just as he would have denied that he was an idolater, worshiping his wealth, and so had broken the first two commandments, and failed to love God with all his heart, mind, and soul.

The young ruler had earnestly tried to carry out the letter of the law, and as multitudes do, tried to convince himself that his life was above reproach and pleased God, yet a haunting, uneasy conscience made him ask, "What lack I yet?" That conscience had made him come running and kneeling to Jesus with a sense of his lack, and yet determined to earn salvation by his own good works. The answer of Jesus (vs. 21) was intended to reveal his sin, as it did. The word *perfect* means complete, adult. The proof of his loving God with all his heart and his neighbor as himself would be in selling what he had (Mark 10:21 says, "sell whatsoever thou hast," while Luke 18:22 says, "sell that thou hast"). Jesus does not give this as essential to salvation. Rather, it would be essential to proving one had kept all the law. No one can claim to love his neighbor as himself as long as one other person has less to eat than he has, and one cannot claim to love God with all his heart, mind, and soul as long as one possession is held dearer than the command of God.

The young man turned away sorrowful, sad over his sin of covetousness, but determined. He loved his possessions more than he loved God or man. Actually, he had not kept even the first commandment. Certainly in his heart he had not kept any of them completely, since hate is murder (I John 3:15; Matt. 5:18-21), lust is adultery (Matt. 5:27, 28), and all sin is in the heart (Matt. 15:19). One who breaks one point of the law is "guilty of all" (James 2:10). Riches are a definite hindrance to salvation (vs. 22). The love of money is the root of all kinds of evil (I Tim. 6:10), and no doubt thousands of others so love their possessions that they will not trust Christ, and turn away sorrowful.

People are not lost because they are covetous, but because of unbelief in Christ. Yet covetousness often hardens the heart of a man. And if he must choose between loving his money first or loving Christ first, he often rejects Christ. "The deceitfulness of riches" often chokes the Word (Matt. 13:22). The love of money and pursuit of money so hardens the heart that only the supernatural, miraculous power of the Holy Spirit can bring a rich man to conviction and repentance. For a camel to go through the eye of a needle would be a miracle which with God is not impossible (vs. 26). God must work a miracle in saving a rich man, even a greater miracle than when others are saved. Verse 25 shows the discernment of the disciples. They saw that a poor man may be as covetous as a rich man. If it takes a miracle to save a rich man, it takes a miracle to save anybody else.

Verses 27-30 Jesus Promises Eternal Rewards for Following Him

The apostles had not been rich men. Nevertheless, they had left their possessions for Jesus just as truly as He asked the rich young ruler to do. Matthew (or Levi) had left his good position as a publican or tax collector (Matt. 9:9). Peter, Andrew, James, and John had left their father, nets, and ships (Matt. 4:18-22). We may be sure that in their hearts each of them, except Judas, had made a full surrender. Jesus said that "whosoever he be of you that forsaketh not all that he hath, he cannot be my disciple" (Luke 14:33). The strictest test of discipleship had been given them when Jesus sent out the twelve (Matt., chap. 10, particularly vss. 22-42). See also Luke 9:23-26; 14:26-33. They were not trusting in their works for salvation, and doubtless they had understood the subtle exposure of the rich young ruler's covetousness. But what they asked now (vs. 27) is partly for an explanation of the promise of Jesus in verse 21. Since salvation cannot be earned by good works, then what will those receive who forsake all for Jesus?

The apostles themselves were assured that in the literal reign of Christ on earth they should sit upon twelve thrones judging the twelve tribes of Israel (vs. 28). This verse is to be taken literally. It will be fulfilled, with Isaiah 1:26, when Jesus, the great Seed of David, returns to sit on David's throne. That was promised in II Samuel 7:10-16, I Chronicles 17:9-14, and Psalm 89:3, 4, 36. The time 'when the Son of man shall sit in the throne of his glory' is clearly told in Matthew 25:31. After Christ comes into the air and calls out His saints, He will later return with us with clouds, and every eye shall see Him, and then He will sit upon the throne of His glory. Israel will be saved then (Rom. 11:26; Deut. 30:1-6). The nation Israel will be restored, and Christ will reign on David's throne (Isa., chap. 11; Jer. 23:3-8; Ezek. 36:24-28; Zech. 14:9). Other saints as well as these apostles will rule then with Christ on the earth (Dan. 7:13, 14, 18; Luke 19:17, 19; Rev. 5:10; 20:4, 6).

Notice the phrase, "in the regeneration." That does not have reference to the regeneration of an individual soul, but to the regeneration of the nation Israel and of the entire political and social order on earth in the personal reign of Christ. Compare this with the phrase, "the times of restitution of all things, which God hath spoken by the mouth of all his holy prophets since the world began" (Acts 3:21). That, too, is spoken of as occurring after the return of Christ. Compare this statement also with Acts 15:16. There will be a "regeneration," a "restitution" of the kingdom of David when Christ reigns over the Jews. That kingly line and house of David and the whole political and social order will be "built again," the Scriptures say. Then it is that the apostles will sit on twelve thrones judging the twelve tribes of Israel.

Note that this reigning with Christ is a reward. This must be the reward that Christ promised in Matthew 16:27 at His return to reign. It is not salvation. We know that salvation is settled when one trusts in Christ, as many Scriptures show. Verse 29 shows that all Christians will be repaid a hundredfold for all they give up for Jesus, and besides that, they will have everlasting life by trusting in Christ.

Let us not be afraid, then, to leave all and follow Jesus. No one ever lost by trusting Him or by giving to Him or suffering for Him. Since Christ is to reign, then we shall reign with Him, if we suffer with Him (II Tim. 2:12). Be bold to give up for Jesus, knowing the blessed reward which is promised! But verse 30 reminds us that the reward will not be according to human standards. Some who think themselves first may be last, and some who are last may first receive their reward. Praise God that the Lord Jesus, who knows every heart (John 2:24, 25) and knows our works (as He said to each of the seven churches of Asia, Rev., chaps. 2 and 3), will reward each one according to his deserts.

MATTHEW XX

Verses 1-16 Parable of the Laborers in the Vineyard

"For" connects chapter 20 with the closing verses of chapter 19. Matthew 19:27-30 speaks of the rewards of those who leave all and follow Christ or serve Him, and this parable is on the same subject, adding more light. Compare verse 16 with Matthew 19:30; it appears that Jesus is repeating the same teaching.

"The kingdom of heaven is like unto..." This is another of the "kingdom of heaven" parables. These parables of the kingdom of Heaven illustrate the course of the present age in relation to the future postponed kingdom. The immediate occasion here for a parable about the kingdom of Heaven is that Jesus has just been speaking to His disciples about that future kingdom and the rewards of the twelve apostles and others in that day (Matt. 19:28, 29). Remember that Jesus promised that He would sit "in the throne of his glory" and that the twelve apostles should "sit upon twelve thrones, judging the twelve tribes of Israel." Do not let preconceived opinion keep you from accepting the literal teaching of Jesus in that passage. That literal teaching is the background for this parable of the kingdom of Heaven and of the later requests of James and John for the first places in the kingdom (vs. 21).

We are told that the "householder" who owned the field in Matthew 13:27, 37 is "the Son of man." The "householder" owning a vineyard and sending servants and his son to collect the rent in Matthew 21:35 is evidently the Father. Here (vs. 1) it is the same thought and Christians who labor for the Father labor for the Son in the vineyard which belongs to both. The daytime was divided roughly into twelve hours, beginning at sunrise and ending at sunset. The third hour (vs. 3) would be approximately nine o'clock. The sixth hour would be noon, the ninth hour would be approximately three o'clock in the afternoon (vs. 5). The eleventh hour would be one hour before sunset. At all these times the householder hired laborers. With the first group who worked all day, He agreed "for a penny a day" (vs. 2). With the others He simply promised "whatsoever is right I will give you" (vss. 4, 5, 7).

In payment, the steward was instructed to call and pay the laborers "beginning from the last unto the first" (vs. 8). God often pays the last first and the first last (vs. 16; Matt. 19:30).

The word *penny* here means the Roman *denarius,* equal to fifteen or seventeen and a half cents, then a day's wages for a laborer or soldier. It was satisfactory pay, agreed upon by the laborers ahead of time (vs. 2). The householder, however, gave the last who had only worked one hour, the full day's wages (vs. 9). This was the householder's grace, not the laborer's merit. The first workers grumbled against the goodman of the house (vss. 11, 12). They were offended at His generosity toward others, and supposed that they should have had more.

Several lessons are intended here by the Saviour. May the Holy Spirit help us to learn these lessons. Some of them are these:

1. The rewards for serving Christ will be decided by Him and not by human wisdom. "Many that are first" in men's sight will not be first in God's sight. It is not wise for us to compare ministers or Christians, Apollos, Peter, Paul, etc., judging this one to be greatest and this one least, since none of us knows the heart or the outcome and relative value of their labors. First Corinthians 4:1-7 gives clear teaching. There we are told that faithfulness is the great virtue rewarded (I Cor. 4:2), that the Lord Himself is the One who judges (I Cor. 4:4), that we are not to judge until the Lord comes, bringing to light the hidden things, the counsels of the hearts (I Cor. 4:5), that, therefore, one should not be puffed up against another (I Cor. 4:6), that whatever good things we have we get from others and are given of God, so we should not boast (I Cor. 4:7).

Men often give us credit we do not deserve. In John 4 is recounted the marvelous revival in Sychar when the woman at the well and many others were saved. Yet the disciples were warned by the Saviour that the fields so "white to harvest" had been cultivated by others, and He said, "And herein is that saying true, One soweth, and another reapeth. I sent you to reap that whereon ye bestowed no labour: other men laboured, and ye are entered into their labours" (John 4:37, 38). In many a great revival one man or two gets most of the credit when his ministry was primarily reaping where others had sown, and entering into the labor of others. Thus only God is able to evaluate the rewards due each workman.

2. In point of time, the last often come first. We are promised to reap "in due season... if we faint not" (Gal. 6:9). But the exact time of our reaping is not told. Often bread cast on the water will return "after many days" (Eccles. 11:1). Sometimes it returns at once. The eleventh hour laborers were paid first.

3. Salvation and rewards are both of grace. It is clear in this case that the laborers who worked only one hour, others who worked only a quarter of a day, others a half day, and others three-quarters of the day, did not earn a full day's wages. Their reward, then, was of grace. But from Luke 17:7-10, another parable of the servants which Jesus gave about the same time as this parable, it is clear that we never deserve all the rewards that Christ gives. We are commanded after we "shall have done all those things which are commanded" us, to say, "We are unprofitable servants" (Luke 17:10). In the instruction of the twelve apostles about rewards in Matthew 19:28, 29, Jesus did not see fit to make a marked distinction between the blessings faithful workers will receive in the regenerated kingdom when He reigns on His throne, and everlasting life. Christians who have left all and followed Christ "shall receive an hundredfold, and shall inherit everlasting life" (Matt. 19:29). We know from many, many plain statements that salvation, everlasting life, is given freely, immediately, and eternally to those who simply believe (John 3:15, 16, 18, 36; 6:24; 6:40, 47; I John 5:11-15), that everlasting life is wholly of grace. Likewise, if a man gives one dollar and gets back one hundred dollars, or loses one friend and gains one hundred more, as is promised here, that is also grace.

To be sure, salvation and rewards are two entirely separate things. Salvation comes from believing, and rewards come from service, but both properly represent the mercy of God, not really our deserts. No wonder that we are told even if our bodies are literally every day living sacrifices, with no will and way of our own, yet it is only our "reasonable service" (Rom. 12:1, 2). It is true that "He hath not dealt with us after our sins; nor rewarded us according to our iniquities" (Ps. 103:10). Most of the workmen did not really deserve their wages, and none of us deserves all the good things God will give us. However, we must not forget that rewards will be proportionate to our labor and sacrifice as is clearly taught in Matthew 16:27, I Corinthians 3:12-15, and Revelation 22:12.

Christ will not only pay every Christian for his labor, but will *overpay* him.

4. As a fourth lesson, let us beware of jealousy of Christian workers. There is a semblance of justice in the cry of these "which have borne the burden and heat of the day" (vs. 12) and feel they should receive more than others who have done less. Workers who have kept the Sunday School or choir or other religious work going for years are often jealous of newcomers who get more attention, inject new life into the work and are given leadership. Older preachers are often jealous of successful young pastors or evangelists who have not spent the labor or study or sacrifice their elders have. But all such jealousy is a sin. We have no right to be thinking about our deservings. All of us have already received of the Lord manyfold more than we have ever deserved. If our hearts were really concerned about the carrying on of the work of Christ and His honor, then we should rejoice gladly when new workers come, even if at the eleventh hour of the day. "In honour preferring one another" (Rom. 12:10) is God's plan about Christian work. Here is a severe testing point. Here we need to manifest Christian grace. Here personal ambition and selfishness show themselves in most of us.

We think the immediate application of the parable was to the apostles. They must understand that many other workers would come after them who would have right to high places in the kingdom of Christ. Paul was not even converted then, yet he came to be behind these apostles in no gift, and was more abundant in labor than them all (I Cor. 15:9, 10; II Cor. 11:5, 23-28). God has a great place in the kingdom for Moody. The apostles must not think that because they would sit on twelve thrones in Israel, others coming later might not have and deserve as great honor from God when the rewards are given.

Another application given to these apostles now would involve the Gentiles. Jewish Christians, even the apostles, were very slow to accept Gentile Christians on the same basis as Jewish Christians (Acts 10; 11:1-3). Jewish converts later would jealously watch young Gentile Christians, feeling that they were newcomers, so did not have the proper background of the law which Israel had. Even Jewish Christian leaders would have a tendency later to insist on the Gentiles' being circumcised and really becoming Jews before they could be Christians (Acts 15:1, 2). The book of Galatians was written to answer these Judaizers. Jesus was here warning His disciples and succeeding generations not to be jealous of those who came later in the vineyard to labor. We need it now. There is a widespread distrust of Christians who profess to have been saved in old age, and many believe deathbed repentance impossible despite the case of the thief on the cross (Luke 23:39-43). Let us rejoice in God's mercy to others instead of having wickedness in our hearts to envy others their blessings.

On this point remember the sin of Jonah, angry because God forgave the Ninevites (Jonah, chap. 4). Some Israelites were jealous when seventy elders were filled with the Spirit and prophesied (Num. 11:16-29). Even John forbade others to cast out devils, though they were doing it in the name of Jesus and should have been praised (Mark 9:38-40; Luke 9:49, 50). This was the sin, too, of the elder brother who was not willing that the prodigal son should be forgiven, feasted and restored by the father (Luke 15:25-32). God forbid that our eye should be evil because God is good and deals in abundant mercy with others (vs. 15).

Compare verse 16 with Matthew 22:14. Many are invited to be saved, but only those who wholeheartedly turn to Christ in faith are chosen as children of God, chosen to be saved (Mark 13:20; Rom. 16:13; II Thess. 2:13).

In this parable of the vineyard, Jesus deals a blow at socialism. Here is vindicated private ownership of property, ownership of means of production, the hiring and firing of laborers. Jesus has the owner say with divine approval, "Is it not lawful for me to do what I will with mine own?" So for a Karl Marx, a Stalin, a Hughey Long, or a Roosevelt, or a socialist labor leader to advocate "redistribution of the wealth," whether by communist revolution or by New Deal law, taking away from an individual his right to own, to control, to give his children by inheritance, his property, is to violate a moral standard of God, and violate a precious human right.

Verses 17-19 Jesus Again Prophesies His Death by Crucifixion

The above parable of the laborers in the vineyard is given only by Matthew, but these verses have parallel passages in Mark 10:32-34 and Luke 18:31-34. Remember the setting: Jesus and the apostles were en route from Galilee to Jerusalem. Instead of coming through Samaria, they crossed the Jordan River and went down the plain on the eastern side (Matt. 19:1, 2). A great multitude followed Him. Such a crowd regularly went to Jerusalem for the passover season. In this case they followed along with Jesus to hear His preaching and teaching and to see His miracles. He was going to Jerusalem (vs. 17). They would go back across the Jordan and through the city of Jericho (vs. 29), thence mount steadily through Bethphage to Jerusalem (Matt. 21:1).

Mark 10:32 tells us that as Jesus went before them to Jerusalem "they were amazed; and as they followed, they were afraid." The time is at hand; Jesus is going to Jerusalem to be crucified 1 The disciples do not understand it, nor do the multitudes, yet they know the Pharisees plan to kill Jesus (Matt. 12:14). Jesus has repeatedly told them that He is to die (Matt. 12:40; 16:21; 17:22, 23). His coming death was the subject of conversation between Jesus, Moses, and Elijah on the Mount of Transfiguration (Luke 9:31). There must have been a holy light in the Saviour's eyes and an exultant, yet sad, determination in His face as He walked straight toward the cross. It amazed and frightened His followers. When you compare Matthew 16:21, Matthew 17:22, 23, with Matthew 20:18, 19, you see that each time Jesus foretold His death He was more explicit. This time He mentions that He will be betrayed to the Gentiles (vs. 19), and mentions the scourging; that His death shall be by crucifixion instead of the traditional stoning. Let these verses make it clear in your mind that no one took the life of Jesus from Him. He laid it down Himself and took it up again (John 10:17). He died when the work was finished and when He "gave up the ghost" (Mark 15:37). The crucifixion of Christ pictures not only the hate and wickedness of mankind, but the deliberate, loving surrender of Christ to the suffering which He could have avoided, but would not, because He planned to die for our sins.

As plain and repeated as these statements of Jesus were, not one of the disciples understood about His coming death. "This saying was hid from them, neither knew they the things which were spoken" (Luke 18:34). Jesus will stop at Bethany, near Jerusalem, six days before the passover (John 12:1). There Mary will anoint

Jesus for His burial (Matt. 26:12; John 12:7). So she, of all those who loved Jesus, may have been the only one who understood that Jesus was literally to die on the cross. These apostles later, after Judas betrayed Him and He was taken in the garden, all forsook Jesus and fled (Matt. 26:56), and when Jesus was crucified, they gave up all hope (Luke 24:21). The enemies of Jesus remembered that He had promised to rise from the dead the third day (Matt. 27:63, 64), but the disciples seemed to forget it and would only believe He was risen from the dead when they saw Him eat and drink, and when they felt His wounded hands (Luke 24:36-45).

The stubborn blindness of the apostles was because they had a preconceived idea of the kingdom without crucifixion. They did not know about Christ's second coming, so did not see how He could have a kingdom if He died. Beware, reader, lest preconceived opinion blinds you to the plain statements of the Bible. The highest and best truth, repeated again and again by the Saviour, cannot be comprehended by those who have their minds made up. So multitudes of good men are utterly ignorant about the second coming of Christ so plainly and literally foretold, of His reign on earth, and of kindred truths. So multitudes who think of salvation by works cannot conceive of the eternal security of a Christian and a salvation wholly of grace, though the Scriptures are full of statements that prove them.

But the blindness of the apostles beforehand is encouraging proof that Jesus did really rise from the dead. They were convinced of His resurrection (which they had not expected and did not believe) only by infallible proofs and a multitude of eyewitnesses (Acts 1:3; I Cor. 15:4-8).

It is important to notice that every detail about the crucifixion of Jesus was planned ahead of time. He was to go to Jerusalem at a certain time as the passover approached, was to be "betrayed unto the chief priests and unto the scribes" (vs. 18). He should be then condemned by the Sanhedrin, later by the Gentiles, after mocking and scourging, and be crucified. Then on the third day He should rise again (vs. 19). Every step in the redemption was planned before by God the Father and His Son, our Saviour.

Verses 20-28 Mother of James and John Seeks First Places for Them in the Kingdom

The same account is given in slightly different words in Mark 10:35-45. Notice one remarkable difference. Mark omits telling that the mother of James and John came to make a request of Jesus. Verse 20 shows that the three came together to Jesus. Not all the conversation is told here. Mark 10:35-37 shows that they, too, asked Jesus for the first and second places in the kingdom, probably after the mother broached the matter to Him. Mark 10:35 shows that they were timid and wished Him to commit Himself favorably before making known their request.

Commentators and Bible teachers have very generally accused these disciples of a false impression concerning the kingdom. Many such have insisted that Jesus will have no literal kingdom on earth, no literal throne. Such do not believe the promise to Abraham about his seed's inheriting forever the land of Palestine (Gen. 13:15-17; 17:8) is true. They ignore or disbelieve the promises to Israel to the same effect, that the nation will be regathered to Palestine, converted, and the kingdom restored (Deut. 30:1-6; Isa. 14:1; Ezek. 20:33-44; 37:11-23; Micah 4:1-7, and many other such passages). They ignore or disbelieve the promise of God that He would restore the kingdom of David, with Christ the Seed of David, seated on David's throne to reign literally at Jerusalem as recorded in II Samuel 7:10-16; Isaiah 9:7; 11:1-9; Jeremiah 23:3-8; Ezekiel 37:24, and many other places. The apostles were right about the coming literal reign of Christ on earth. They knew the Old Testament Scriptures and believed them.

Read the passages indicated above and notice that those promises are about literal Israel, about the literal land of Canaan and the literal throne of David; they were to be fulfilled in the future, and repeatedly the promised restoration is said to be "for ever." "Jerusalem," "Zion" (the hill on which part of the city was built), "the mountains of Israel," the twelve tribes, and the throne of David are all mentioned so carefully and literally that honest Bible believers must accept it as true that God has planned a kingdom on earth, when Jesus literally, physically of the seed of David, will reign at Jerusalem on David's throne. Just previous to this Jesus Himself had promised the apostles that they should "sit upon twelve thrones, judging the twelve tribes of Israel" and that that would be in the time of "the regeneration when the Son of man shall sit in the throne of his glory" (Matt. 19:28). It is foolish to accuse the apostles of being misled about the literal nature of Christ's kingdom. They were wrong in selfishly seeking preferment by bringing such influence to bear instead of by earning the place. They doubtless did not understand, as we often do not, the secret of real spiritual greatness. But they were right in expecting Jesus to have a literal kingdom on earth.

Jesus did not rebuke their idea of the kingdom here. He did not rebuke it later when He was risen from the dead and when He had opened their hearts to understand the Scriptures, and they still expected the kingdom to be restored to Israel (Acts 1:6 in the light of Acts 1:3; Luke 24:44, 45). Jesus explained that the time of the kingdom was not for them to know, that they must now be concerned about the power of the Holy Spirit upon their witnessing (Acts 1:7, 8). But Jesus did not indicate that they were mistaken in expecting a literal kingdom. James and John did not know what they were asking (vs. 22), did not know how much suffering would be necessary to earn the position they sought. They knew not how worthy some others might be for the places they sought. They did not realize fully how true greatness must come as a result of suffering and service (vss. 26-28). They had no real understanding that Jesus must be crucified before the kingdom could be set up (Luke 18:34).

Yet they were resolved to go anywhere with Jesus, suffer anything for Him. We must not forget that they had really left all to follow Him as they said in Matthew 19:27. See the earnest resolve of Peter and all the disciples never to be offended in Christ nor to deny Him, though all men might (Matt. 26:35). Doubtless, James and John were sincere in that earnest resolve and thought themselves able to drink the cup of suffering and be baptized (overwhelmed or buried) in the flood of sorrows that would overtake Him. Notice the promise of Jesus in verse 23, that these two should drink of His cup and be baptized with His baptism, referring to persecution and suffering. James was the first of these twelve to be killed for Christ's sake (Acts 12:1, 2). John, his brother, years later, when he was the only apostle left alive, was exiled to the Isle of Patmos because of his faith and testimony (Rev. 1:9), and there God gave him, by divine inspiration, the last book in the Bible. These two disciples were doubtless wrong in their personal ambition and seeking preferment over others in Christ's coming kingdom, but they were not at all insincere in their willingness to suffer for Christ and be true to Him.

Notice the figurative use of the word *baptized* in verses 22 and 23, meaning buried or overwhelmed with suffering. Literal baptism, of course, is immersion in water, so in the literal sense there is only "one baptism" (Eph. 4:5). Figuratively, one may be baptized or immersed in suffering, or in the body of Christ, as all are at salvation (I Cor. 12:13), or in the Holy Spirit (Acts 1:5).

We do not know what two people, if any, will sit on the right hand and left hand of Christ when He sits "in the throne of his glory" (Matt. 19:28; 25:31). That was not to be decided arbitrarily and simply given by the Saviour in answer to a request. Christ can *give* salvation free, and does (John 10:28; Rom. 6:23; I John 5:1), but to reign is a reward that is not *given* but is *earned* as a reward for serving, suffering, overcoming (II Tim. 2:12; Luke 19:16-19; Rev. 2:26, 27). The Father prepares those special places of honor (vs. 23) with the Son on the basis of what is proper and fittingly due.

Notice the indignation of the other apostles against James and John (vs. 24). Jealousy among Christian workers is a great sin but a most natural one. Let us take much to heart the warning of Jesus in verses 25 to 28. Real greatness must come from being a servant, even as Jesus Himself took the place of a servant. In this matter of humility, Jesus gave the example of humility, brotherly love, in honor preferring one another when He washed the disciples' feet (John 13:3-17). The humility of Jesus in denying Himself, taking the place and form of a servant, should be our constant pattern (Phil. 2:5-8). Likewise, the coming reward of Jesus should be our inspiration (Phil. 2:9-11). We do not get greatness by pulling strings, thinking highly of ourselves, seeking preferment above our brethren. Rather, God resists the proud but gives grace to the lowly, and those who humble themselves shall be exalted (Matt. 23:12; James 4:6, 10).

Verses 29-34 Jesus Heals Two Blind Men

With this passage study Mark 10:46-52 and Luke 18:35-43. Notice the differences in the account. Verse 29 here and Mark 10:46 tell of healings which happened as Jesus *departed* from Jericho. Luke 18:35 seems to tell of a different case, when Jesus *came nigh unto Jericho.* Mark tells of one man and gives his name, Bartimaeus, while Matthew (vs. 30) speaks of "two blind men sitting by the way side." But there were many other facts which were not recorded here. Neither of the Gospels professes to tell all that happened. The Holy Spirit selected the incidents and facts for a particular lesson in each case, and omitted others that did not need to be mentioned there. This principle of divine inspiration is stated in John 20:30, 31, and John 21:25.

No part of the Bible really contradicts any other part. There are no mistakes in the Word of God. If there seem to be, then the seeming so is only because of our ignorance or unbelief. In so many incidents in these thousands of years the Word of God has so proved Itself infallibly correct that it would be folly now to have a doubt because in some few cases our ignorance leaves us in the dark.

Jesus healed many blind men and probably worked hundreds of miracles of healing. Generally among the people who believed He was the Son of God, He was called "the son of David," because He is that, the promised Son of David who will reign. We believe Jesus healed one blind man on entering Jerusalem, then when He left the city other blind men had heard about it and asked for healing, calling Him by the same name and following the example of the first man healed. Mark was inspired by the Holy Spirit to give striking details about one man, Bartimaeus. Matthew was inspired to tell the general fact about both the blind men who were healed on this occasion. Neither one professes to tell all that happened. Each one of the four Gospels tells some events and sayings of Jesus omitted by the others, and that, we are sure, by the inspiration of God.

There is a great lesson from the healing of these blind men. One of them, at least, Bartimaeus, was a beggar (Mark 10:46). Blind people had little chance to make a living otherwise. Blind beggars in the Orient are usually pitiful creatures – dirty, discourteous, offensive. These may have been so. The multitude was offended because they interrupted Jesus (vs. 31). There were so many poor, so many in trouble, so many sick or blind or lepers, and they wanted to hear Jesus preach!

Take lesson from these *hinderers.* They meant well but they stood between the Saviour and sinners. Those who gather not together always scatter abroad (Matt. 12:30). If we are not helping win souls, we help to damn them. Some Christians discourage children from being saved. Many of us are stumblingblocks in the way of sinners by our worldly lives and our cold hearts. Most of that crowd were spectators, so most of those who attend our churches are only bench warmers, spectators who do not really lift a hand to keep people out of Hell. They do not want any excitement. They sometimes discourage revivals. Often they are fearful about fanaticism. They are shocked at the idea of shouting or weeping in services. They do not make strangers feel at home. Often they do not wish to see drunkards and harlots brought into the congregation. They feel that little children are safe enough as they are and should not be excited or "overpersuaded," as they say. In the average congregation, evidently most of the people are *hinderers,* as it was so here.

There were *helpers* here, too. Somebody told the blind men that Jesus was passing by (vs. 30). When Jesus wanted to heal them, He sent someone to call them (Mark 10:49). In the kindness of Jesus, He is willing to let us share His redemption work. How happy when He commands us to call someone for Him! Every Christian should be a helper, saying to sinners, "Come!" instead of saying, "Hold your peace!"

Notice the insistence of the poor blind men. They would not be stopped but "cried the more" (vs. 31). It sounded impolite and crude, but how sweet it was to the ears of Jesus! God honors insistent praying because it honors Him. He wants us to pray with that urgency that will not give up, will not take "no" for an answer, the urgency that must keep on crying. That was what pleased Him about the Canaanite woman (Matt. 15:21-28). That was what got Jacob the blessing when he must face his brother the next day (Gen. 32:24-29, especially vs. 26). This importunity is what Jesus especially commanded us to have in prayer in Luke 11:5-8 and in

239

Luke 18:1-8. Notice from the context of the first passage (Luke 11:6, 13) that we are invited so to pray for the Holy Spirit's power that we may be able to take the bread of life to those who have none. Persistent prayer pleases God and gets the blessing.

The blind beggars asked for mercy (vs. 30). Compare their prayer with that of the rich young ruler (Matt. 19:16). How different! These wanted salvation by grace, by God's mercy, while the other simply wanted instructions as to how to save himself by works. The rich young ruler called Jesus simply "Master" or "teacher," but these called Him "O Lord, thou son of David" (vss. 30, 31). These beggars believed in His deity, believed He was the promised Son of David who would reign on David's throne, the Messiah, the Lord. They admitted their need, their helplessness. All who come to Christ must come as helpless beggars, not as rich or wise or good.

There is evidence that these men were really converted. Jesus answered their prayers and opened their eyes (vs. 34). Doubtless, He also saved their souls. They seemed to have trusted Him fully and "they followed him" (vs. 34).

How grateful we should be that Jesus has an ear keenly atuned to hear those so far in sin that others care nothing about their salvation.

Jesus won the woman at the well while the disciples wondered why He talked with her (John 4, especially vs. 27). When they were absorbed in food, Jesus would not eat, but had His eyes upon the throng coming out from the city and begged them to lift up their eyes and look on the harvest (John 4:31-35). The disciples would have sent the Canaanite woman away with her poor helpless daughter still possessed with a devil (Matt. 15:23), but Jesus was better than the disciples. Today He is better than Christians. He is better than we preachers. Praise His name, He always cares for the troubled, the sinning, the beggars who want mercy! Hallelujah, what a Saviour!

MATTHEW XXI

Verses 1-11 The Triumphal Entry Into Jerusalem

The triumphal entry of Jesus into Jerusalem is of much importance. It is discussed by all four Gospels. See Mark 11:1-10, Luke 19:29-38, and John 12:12-19.

This triumphal entry was five days before the passover, as shown by John 12:1, 12. The same thing is evident when you count the days after the triumphal entry as mentioned by Mark (Mark 11:1, 20, 27; 14:1).

The previous night Jesus had spent at Bethany, we suppose in the home of Mary, Martha, and Lazarus (John 12:1, 2). If the supper given Jesus there is the same as that mentioned in Matthew 26:6-13, which we doubt, then the supper was in the house of Simon the leper. But probably Jesus was the guest of Mary, Martha, and Lazarus. Some of the nights that remained before His crucifixion Jesus spent at Bethany, going in the morning to Jerusalem and returning in the evening to Bethany (Mark 11:11, 12, 19, 20).

Remember that Jews throughout the whole nation came to Jerusalem for the combined feasts of the passover and of unleavened bread as they were commanded to do in Deuteronomy 16:5-8. Thus there would not be room in the city for all the people, so some slept in the villages around about as Jesus and His disciples did. And it probably seemed necessary for the people to come several days ahead of time because the passover lamb was to be selected on the tenth day of the month, kept until the fourteenth day of the month, then slain in the evening or afternoon (Exod. 12:3-6). Those who lived near would bring their own lambs for the passover and those who came from afar would buy the lambs at Jerusalem (Deut. 14:22-26). Picture in your mind the crowded condition of the city Jerusalem, with the whole nation there gathered for this great feast of the year, the passover time.

Coming from Bethany to Jerusalem, Jesus arrived at Bethphage (which is not found there now), at the Mount of Olives. Jesus planned the triumphal entry (vs. 4), planned to fulfill the Scriptures which foretold His entry into Jerusalem on a colt of an ass (Zech. 9:9). Jesus knew the hearts of all men and knew that He would be welcome to the use of the asses when its owner knew "the Lord hath need of them." See John 2:24, 25. He knew just where the ass was tied – does that seem strange when we remember He is the Creator of all things and that all things are made by Him? (Col. 1:16, 17). We do not suppose, as some do, that Jesus had privately made arrangements with the owner of the ass to leave it tied at a certain place. Jesus would not deceive about such a matter and He who worked so many miracles need not avoid one here. Men did make objection as Jesus said they would (Mark 11:5, 6; Luke 19:33, 34), but were satisfied when given the answer Jesus commanded. Compare this incident with the way Jesus secured a room for that part of the passover season before His death (Luke 22:7-13). Jesus knew there would be a man with a pitcher of water upon his head, knew that the master of the house would willingly have Jesus use the* room. Jesus here acted as one ought, offering Himself publicly as the King of Israel.

The ass and her colt were both brought (vs. 7), though it was the colt that Jesus sat upon (vs. 5; Mark 11:7). No one had ever ridden the colt before, but we may be sure there was no difficulty and that the colt went straight forward as he should. Consider how God directed the cows who left their calves and pulled the cart with the ark of God from the country of the Philistines straight into the land of Israel (I Sam. 6:7-12). Consider that during the personal reign of Christ on earth lions, leopards, wolves, and snakes will be perfectly tame so that a little child may lead them and play on the hole of the asp and lions shall eat straw like the ox (Isa. 11:6-8; 65:25). If the winds and waves obeyed the voice of Christ, the Creator (Matt. 8:26), if the fig tree withered at a word (vs. 19); if the fish with the coin in his mouth got on die hook as Jesus wished (Matt. 17:27), and if other fishes filled the nets at the word of Christ (Luke 5:6; John 21:6), we need not be surprised if an ass's colt was meekly subject to his Maker though he had never been ridden before!

Compare the entry of an ass's colt with the second coming of Christ when He comes in His glory, riding from Heaven upon a white horse and followed by armies of angels on white horses (Rev. 19:11-16). Both are kingly entrances of the same Jesus, the King of the Jews. But the first entrance to Jerusalem is in humility, while the second is in power. Christ came the first time in tender mercy, meek and lowly in heart. He will come the second time in wrath and judgment on His enemies and to smite them and slay the wicked with the breath of His lips (Isa. 11:4; II Thess. 2:8). Jesus came the first time as the Lamb of God. The next time He will come as the Lion of the tribe of Judah. Psalm 24, especially verses 7 to 10, foretells that entrance of Jesus into Jerusalem following His return to the earth to reign.

The disciples put their garments on the asses and Jesus sat on the colt, on their clothes (vs. 7). The great multitude spread garments in the way, cut down branches from the trees and put them in the road (vs. 8). Others came out from Jerusalem to meet Him with palm branches (John 12:12, 13). Notice the glorious cry of the multitudes, "Hosanna to the son of David: Blessed is he that cometh in the name of the Lord; Hosanna in the highest" (vs. 9). This was one of the cries. Compare this with that given in Mark 11:9, 10 where others added, "Blessed be the kingdom of our father David, that cometh in the name of the Lord." See also Luke 19:38. The multitude realized that this was the Messianic entry of Jesus, offering Himself as King to sit on David's throne as was foretold by many prophets (II Sam. 7:10-16; Isa. 9:6, 7; 11:1, 10; Dan. 9:25; Zech. 9:9). The multitude knew of Christ's miracles; they had seen His mighty works and rejoiced and praised God (Luke 19:37). They saw Him ride on the colt of an ass as prophesied, and greeted Him as King. Their praise was superficial. They did not understand the nature of the kingdom. They did not understand that Jesus had to die. They were not willing to repent. Yet the majesty of the occasion was overwhelming. Some of the Pharisees, and probably many others, did not join in the praises but rebuked the disciples (Luke 19:39).

Heretofore Jesus had not encouraged public praise nor tried to prove Himself the Messiah. He had tried to keep it a secret when He raised the twelve-year-old girl from the dead (Mark 5:41-43). He had warned the three disciples who saw Him transfigured to say nothing of it until He was risen from the dead (Mark 9:9). The blind man healed outside Bethsaida had been commanded not to go into the town (Mark 8:26). But now Jesus made much of His triumphal entry and evidently rejoiced in the praises. If the disciples had held their peace, He said that even the very stones should have cried out (Luke 19:40), giving Him the praise that was His due.

243

Dr. B. H. Carroll and many other scholars think that this triumphal entry is the appearance of the Messiah which was dated and prophesied in Daniel 9:25 and he says that it was 483 years (sixty-nine weeks of seven years each, as prophesied) to a day from the command which went forth (by King Cyrus, we suppose. II Chron. 36:22, 23; Ezra 1:1-4) to restore and rebuild Jerusalem. Certainly it was a prophesied date of great importance (Zech. 9:9). He knew that in a few days He would be crucified, slain at the passover time as God's passover Lamb (I Cor. 5:7). He knew, of course, that some of these same people perhaps would join in the cry, "Let him be crucified!" Yet He offered Himself as the prophesied Jewish King riding upon the colt of an ass. The next time Jesus comes to Jerusalem He will have a triumphal entry as glorious as this was humble, as victorious as this was a failure, accepted with sincere mourning, repentance, and turning to God (Zech., chap. 12, especially vss. 10 to 14, and Zech. 13:1). Then it will come to pass, "so all Israel shall be saved" (Rom. 11:26) and then people will say again, "Blessed is he that cometh in the name of the Lord" (Matt. 23:39). This entry of Jesus into Jerusalem was typical of His future inauguration as King.

Verses 12-17 Jesus Cleanses the Temple and Heals Therein

This purification of the temple is described in Mark 11:15-18, and in Luke 19:45, 46. It occurred the next day after the triumphal entry (Mark 11:11-15). Do not confuse this, however, with the cleansing of the temple described in John 2:14-16. That was in the very beginning of Christ's ministry, probably three years before this time, but likewise at a passover season. Just preceding the passover, the city was filled with people. People from various parts of the country would buy sheep, oxen, and doves for sacrifice in the temple (John 2:14), and so people had made it a market place. Comparing verse 12 with John 2:14, it seems that the reform Jesus had insisted upon some three years before had helped conditions. In the second case no sheep or oxen are mentioned, but there were tables for money-changers and seats for them that sold doves. Worldliness always creeps back in. Christians and churches must be constantly awake lest they be led astray by convenience, carelessness, and the constant pressure of greed and worldly things. Before Jesus had said, "make not my Father's house an house of merchandise" (John 2:16). However, this second time Jesus speaks more sharply, quotes the Scripture, Isaiah 56:7, "for mine house shall be called an house of prayer" and says, "but ye have made it a den of thieves." Notice that covetousness here is connected with stealing. Christ sees the heart. And these coveters were thieves in heart, if not openly, just as the lustful are adulterers (Matt. 5:27, 28) and those who hate are murderers (I John 3:15).

Jesus' bold attack against sin created a great sensation. Great crowds were at the temple. The blind and lame came and were healed (vs. 14). Children in the temple seeing His miracles cried, "Hosanna to the son of David" (vs. 15).

Little children soon learn to feel about Jesus as their elders do. They say the same things as they hear mothers and fathers say. These followed the example of those who hailed Jesus with the same words at the triumphal entry. See the anger of the chief priests and scribes in verses 15 and 16. They were not willing to acknowledge Jesus as the "son of David" who should reign. They hated Him for His attack on sin, His demand for repentance. These same scribes and chief priests planned to destroy Jesus (Mark 11:18) and sought constantly an opportunity. However, during this passover season the city was so full of people that they found it hard to catch Jesus alone without a multitude about Him, and for this reason paid Judas later to lead them to Him when He was in the secluded Garden of Gethsemane at night.

The praises of little children pleased Jesus (vs. 16). The Scripture He quoted is Psalm 8:2. Let that encourage every mother and father, every Sunday School teacher to train little children to sing praises to Christ, to drill them in memory verses of Scripture* and to teach them to pray. Christ is pleased with the praises of children.

Verses 18-22 The Barren Fig Tree Cursed and Withered: Blessed Promise Given

The incident of the barren fig tree cursed and the promises about the prayer of faith are also given in Mark 11:12-14, 19-26. Jesus clearly went to a good deal of trouble to teach His disciples the lesson of faith and prayer. Only a few days are left before His crucifixion, yet He gives Himself continually to the preparation of His disciples for the burdens and responsibilities that will be theirs. Teachers and preachers must have training. Jesus could have known whether the fig tree had figs, but He wanted the lesson to be obvious to His disciples. As far as we have record, the fig tree is the only thing that Jesus destroyed in His earthly ministry, though He pronounced a woe upon the Pharisees (Matt. 23), upon Bethsaida, Chorazin, and Capernaum (Matt 11:20-24), and prophesied Jerusalem's destruction (Luke 21:20-24). Millions have thanked God for the curse on the fig tree because of the exceeding precious promises given in connection therewith. The fig tree bore no fruit that we might bear much fruit!

In verse 21, Jesus plainly means that the apostles should have the same faith He had and the same miracles in response to faith. See also John 14:12. Do not make the mountain in verse 21 too figurative. There is no limit to the promise if the faith is not limited (Mark 11:24). But the promise is not only to the apostles. We, too, are commanded, "Have faith in God" (Mark 11:22). Mark says, "WHOSOEVER shall say unto this mountain" instead of "If YE shall say unto this mountain," as Matthew does. So the promise is for the apostles and all others who are saved – "whosoever." If the "whosoever" in John 3:16 is for this age, then so is the "whosoever" in Mark 11:23. There is unlimited power in the prayer of faith. God has changed His requirements and plans about some things in different dispensations. For instance, we now are not expected to observe circumcision, the Jewish dietary laws, the Jewish sabbaths, etc. (Col. 2:14-17). But a review of the heroes of faith given in Hebrews 11 shows that in every age those who please God are those who believe. Compare this promise with Luke 17:6. Verse 22 is a resum6 of verse 21. Thank God for a promise of "all things." "Faith will bring the blessing every time." See also Mark 9:23.

Verses 23-27 Chief Priests and Elders Challenge Jesus' Authority

Mark 11:27-33 and Luke 20:1-8 also give account of this incident.

"When he was come into the temple" – that is, on the second day after the triumphal entry, as you see from Mark 11:11, 12, 19, 20. "As he was teaching" – Jesus came each of these five days before His crucifixion to the temple and taught there (Luke 19:47; Matt. 26:55).

"Who gave thee this authority?" They meant, what authority had He for His bold authoritative teaching which differed from that of the scribes and Pharisees, the authority for His miracles, particularly His authority for taking charge and cleansing the temple. These scribes and Pharisees hated Jesus and planned to kill Him (Mark 11:18; Matt. 12:14; John 5:18; 7:19; 8:37, 40, 59; 11:47-53). They were not sincere. Their plan was to get Jesus to claim to be the Son of God openly and boldly, then accuse Him of blasphemy, and have Him killed. Mosaic Law provided the death penalty for blasphemy (Lev. 24:16). Before this, at a previous feast at Jerusalem, Jesus had claimed to be the Son of God, and for that the Jews sought to kill Him, as well as for breaking the Sabbath (John 5:17, 18). Later, when Jesus was arrested and carried before the Sanhedrin, it was on this point that He was condemned to die (Matt. 26:63-66).

The answer of Jesus was an honest answer. He had proved Himself approved of God by His miracles. John and the voice from Heaven had publicly proclaimed Him the Son of God, and He publicly entered into Jerusalem on the foal of an ass, as the prophesied Son of David would. There would be no profit in telling them again what was proved; so instead, He showed them their insincerity by the question in verse 25: "The baptism [and ministry] of John, whence was it? from heaven, or of men?" John had proclaimed himself the forerunner of the Saviour and announced Jesus as "the Lamb of God, which taketh away the sin of the world" (John 1:29). A mighty revival had shaken the whole nation (Matt. 3:5, 6). If John's ministry was from Heaven, Christ was the Son of God. If these scribes and Pharisees had dealt honestly in their own minds about John the Baptist, seeking the light, they would have long ago accepted Jesus as the Christ and Messiah. The evidence was overwhelming, the evidence of His birth and ministry, the voice from Heaven at His baptism, etc.

Notice the dilemma of the Pharisees in verses 25 and 26. They sought not to answer Jesus truthfully, but to answer craftily for their own benefit. If they said John's ministry was from Heaven, then they should have followed the preaching of John and repented. They dared not say his ministry was of men, for the entire nation held John as a prophet, as he was. So their mouths were closed and they dared not answer. Their insincerity was manifest to all.

Verses 28-32 Parable of the Two Sons

The outspoken boldness of Jesus was marvelous. He did not seek to make peace; He pressed the matter with these wicked Pharisees until they must either accept Him as Saviour or crucify Him! So with every sinner, Jesus will make no peace except in absolute surrender. One must be for Christ or against Him, must love Him or hate Him (Matt. 6:24; 12:30). Jesus would not take the place as a mere teacher. He is the very Son of God and demands to be worshiped as God and obeyed as Lord. Here is a brief parable which Jesus Himself explains. The two sons (vs. 28) represent the scribes and Pharisees on the one hand; the publicans and harlots, the vilest sinners, on the other. The Pharisees and scribes are like the son who said, "I go," but went not. The publicans and harlots, who were being converted under the loving, plain ministry of Jesus, and who were accepting Him as Lord and Christ, were like the son who said, "I will not," but afterward repented and went to serve his father. A publican or harlot who sincerely repents is better than the proudest, self-righteous, moral man who does not repent in his heart and is never born again. Compare the last part of verse 31 with "Except your righteousness shall exceed the righteousness of the scribes and Pharisees, ye shall in no case enter into the kingdom of heaven" (Matt. 5:20). This is the same teaching Jesus gave Nicodemus in John 3:1-7, and in the parable of the Pharisee and publican in Luke 18:9-14.

According to verse 32, a disbelieving and disobedient attitude toward the Gospel proves a wicked heart. Let every reader remember that to get drunk or to commit adultery or to steal or to murder are not as great sins as rejecting Jesus Christ.

Again Jesus connects the ministry of John the Baptist with His own ministry. Those who were against John would be against Jesus. So it ought to be about every good preacher and teacher of the Gospel. God help us to be in the will of Christ, endued with His power, true to His doctrine until He will identify Himself with us, and men who reject us will reject Christ, while those who receive us will receive Christ (Matt 10:14, 15, 40, 41).

Verses 33-46 The Parable of the Householder Demanding Fruit From His Vineyard

This parable of the householder's demanding fruit from the vineyard is also given in Mark 12:1-9 and Luke 20:9-19. Jewish leaders would know the meaning of it. The vineyard was Israel, as Isaiah 5:1-7 clearly pictures. All were familiar with that passage. The point of Isaiah's inspired parable was that the Jewish people themselves had not brought forth good fruit. Here the point is that the leaders have kept the people from God and prevented God from getting what was His due out of His own vineyard. The servants (vss. 34, 35, 36) represent the prophets whom God had sent to Israel, so many of whom had been abused, hated, disobeyed, and sometimes slain. See II Chronicles 24:20-22; Jeremiah 2:30; 20:2, 10; 38:6. If Jews had listened to the prophets, they would not have gone into captivity in Babylon (II Chron. 36:16). Jesus said, "it cannot be that a prophet perish out of Jerusalem" (Luke 13:33), and addressed Jerusalem, "O Jerusalem, Jerusalem, thou that killest the prophets, and stonest them which are sent unto thee" (Matt. 23:37; Luke 13:34). The son of the householder (vs. 37) represents Jesus Himself. Mark 12:6 says, "one son, his wellbeloved." Luke 20:13 says, "my beloved son." The Jewish rulers were determined to kill Jesus because they did not love God and wanted their rulership for their own selfish and covetous reasons. They were usurpers, unworthy to sit in Moses' seat. See Jesus' sharp denunciation of them in Matthew, chapter 23.

Jesus meant that God was calling the Jewish rulers to account just as John the Baptist preached, "the axe is laid unto the root of the trees" (Matt. 3:10-12). The judgment pictured in verse 41 was later fulfilled in the destruction of Jerusalem in A.D. 70 by Titus and the Roman army. This destruction was also foretold in Luke 19:41-44, Luke 21:20-24, and Matthew 23:29-39. Notice in the latter Scripture that other prophets and wise men were to be sent after Christ's crucifixion to fill up the iniquity of the Jews, so that the blood of all the righteous prophets killed by the Jews would come upon this generation of Jewish leaders who crucified Jesus (Matt. 23:31-35). When this vengeance came, the Jewish government and leadership were broken down entirely and Jews have never had a national home since and will have no such national home and government until they say, "Blessed is he that cometh in the name of the Lord" (Matt. 23:39), until they receive Jesus at His Second Coming.

Verse 42 quotes Psalm 118:22, 23. Christ is the stone which the builders rejected, and He has become the head of Israel as well as the head of all the Lord's building (Col. 1:18). Peter preached from the same Old Testament text to these same Jews after the resurrection of Christ (Acts 4:11, 12).

The kingdom of God in verse 43 is not quite the same as *the kingdom of heaven,* the literal future reign of Christ on earth. During the present church age, more Gentiles will enter the kingdom of God and, in that sense, the kingdom of God is taken from the Jews for the present. Christ is the Son in the parable, and Christ is the stone of stumbling (Isa. 8:14; Rom. 9:32, 33; I Cor. 1:23). Verse 44 seems to mean that whosoever fights against Christ shall be broken, but upon whomsoever Christ falls in judgment, he shall be ground to powder. Verse 44 also reminds us of the coming destruction of the Gentile world powers under the Antichrist at the second coming of Christ as foretold in Daniel 2:34, 35 (explained in Dan. 2:44, 45).

The chief priests and Pharisees understood that Jesus was talking about them (vs. 45) and wished to take Him, but did not because of the multitude that surrounded Him (vs. 46).

MATTHEW XXII

Verses 1,2 The Prince's Wedding Feast

This parable is similar to that given in Luke 14:16-24. Notice these differences. Here it is "a certain king, which made a marriage for his son," while in the parable in Luke it is "a certain man made a great supper." The king's son in Matthew is the "certain man" in Luke. The Gospel of Matthew more particularly pictures Jesus as the coming King of the Jews, and the kingdom idea is not stressed in Luke as in Matthew. Here the king is pictured as sending forth his armies to destroy the murderers of his servants (the prophets) and to bum up their city (vs. 7), while that is omitted by the parable in Luke 14:16-24. This was probably intended particularly for the city Jerusalem, while the Gospel of Luke has a wider application. The part of the parable about the wedding garment (vss. 11-13) is omitted in Luke. Parables are simply illustrations. Jesus originated His own. He probably told the same parable repeatedly to different crowds and on different occasions, varying it to suit the occasion, just as preachers today repeat sermons upon the same subjects and vary them as occasion requires. Jesus did so much teaching that not all of it could be given in any one of the Gospels nor in all of them (John 20:30, 31; 21:25).

"The kingdom of heaven is like unto..." This is a parable interpreting the course of events until Christ returns. The "certain king" is God the Father. "His son" is Jesus Christ. The "marriage" will occur following the rapture of the saints when Christ comes into the air to receive us. The church is likened unto a bride (II Cor. 11:2; Eph. 5:27). After the rapture, when we are caught up to meet Christ in the air, we will never leave Him any more (I Thess. 4:17). So that may be properly likened to a marriage. See Revelation 19:7-9, which indicates that the marriage is in Heaven during the time of the Great Tribulation on earth and before Christ returns with saints and angels. Do not confuse this with the same figure (marriage) used about the heavenly city Jerusalem when it comes down from Heaven to the new earth after the millennium is finished (Rev. 21:2). The figure of marriage is also used about Jehovah and Israel in the Old Testament (Isa. 54:5; Jer. 3:14; Hosea 2:19, 20).

251

Here is a repetition of the truth of a preceding parable of the householder's demanding fruit from his vineyard (Matt. 21:33-43). Again the servants represent the prophets who had been sent repeatedly to Israel. This parable, with its teaching about the King's Son and the wedding and wedding garment, clearly shows that all the prophets preached the same plan of salvation as given in the New Testament. See also Luke 24:25-27, 44; John 5:46; and especially Acts 10:43.

Verses 3-10 The Gospel Rejected

"They would not come" (vs. 3). It was the response of sinners to God's grace and it is the same today. Those who accept are the exceptions. "Many are called, but few are chosen" (vs. 14). See John 1:11 and John 5:40. Preachers and teachers should know ahead of time that this world will not all be saved. We can pluck some out of the fire (Jude 23), but we cannot put out the fire of sin in this world. When Christ returns at the end of the age, there will be tares among the wheat, bad fish in the net, leaven in the meal, evil birds in the trees of religious institutions (Matt., chap. 13). Those who were previously bidden (vs. 3) were called first. Christ came first to the Jews. He had selected Israel as a chosen nation through the centuries and had sent unto them His prophets. To them He gave the law and the prophets and the Old Testament Scriptures (Rom. 3:1, 2; 9:4, 5). Of them to whom so much had been given, much would be required (Luke 12:47, 48).

Notice how the Gospel was rejected (vs. 5).

1. "They made light of it." Men do not take seriously the question of sin or death and salvation. It is a fatal mistake (Heb. 2:1-3). The first attempt of Satan is to take the Gospel seed out of the heart (Matt. 13:4, 19).

2. They "went their ways." Man's own way is the way of sin (Isa. 53:6; 55:7, 8). One must forsake his own way in order to be saved. "There is a way which seemeth right unto a man, but the end thereof are the ways of death" (Prov. 14:12). Since Adam sinned, every child born has been tainted with sin so that the carnal mind is enmity against God and cannot please God (Rom. 8:7; I Cor. 15:21, 22). People who reject Christ are like these who "went their ways." To go your own way means death. Men love their own evil

ways and hold on to sin. That is why they are condemned (John 3:18-21).

3. One went "to his farm, and another to his merchandise." Is it a sin to farm or to work in a store? It is a sin for anyone who does that instead of trusting Christ. It is a sin to eat or sleep or give attention to anything else in the world before attending to the salvation of your soul. Jesus taught that any man was a fool to give attention to food and drink when he was not rich toward God (Luke 12:16-21). Even "the plowing of the wicked, is sin" (Prov. 21:4). And again, "whatsoever is not of faith is sin" (Rom. 14:23). According to these Scriptures every thought, word, and deed of the Christ-rejecting sinner is displeasing to God, for "without faith it is impossible to please him" (Heb. 11:6). If it comes in its proper place, attending to farms or merchandise may be a virtue second to salvation and subject to God's will. If it comes before pleasing God and is put in first place, good becomes evil. So, to love wife or children or parents or neighbors is good and commanded, but if that love comes before love for God, it is a sin (Luke 14:26). Remember it is a sin to go your own way and attend to your farm or merchandise unless first you are at peace with God and in His sweet will.

4. Verse 6 refers to the way the Jews mistreated God's prophets; they "entreated them spitefully, and slew them." It also shows us the heart of a Christ-rejector. Those who turn down Christ are murderers at heart and guilty of the death of Christ. A sinner who will not receive Christ as Saviour, if Jesus were with him in person and persistently pressed the matter, would hate Him and crucify Him just as did these Jewish leaders who were outwardly moral. We think of rejecting Christ as a very respectable sin, but it is worse than murder and is the very sin that led to the crucifixion of Christ.

Verse 7 is a prophecy of what would happen to Jerusalem. Compare with it Matthew 23:34-39; 24:1, 2; Luke 21:20-24. This prophesied destruction of Jerusalem did occur in A.D. 70, when the city rebelled and was besieged and taken by the Roman army under Titus. Multitudes of the Jews were slain and the rest were scattered to all the world.

However, verse 7 is typical of the wrath of God against all sinners who reject Christ.

After repeated invitation to those first bidden, symbolizing the Jews, (vss. 3, 4), the servants were commanded to invite all they found (vss. 9, 10). In the first part of the Gospel of Matthew the twelve were instructed first to go not to the Gentiles or Samaritans, but "rather to the lost sheep of the house of Israel" (Matt. 10:5, 6). This had seemed the policy of Jesus, too, while offering the kingdom to Israel (Matt. 15:24). But the Jewish nation would not have Christ as king, did not repent of their sins, and so He soon began to invite more specially all individuals to come unto Him who were burdened and weary (Matt. 11:28-30). Jesus Himself followed the plan which the servants were commanded to follow and did follow as told in verses 9 and 10. He received publicans and harlots, Gentiles and Samaritans, all who would repent. So it is to this day. This parable does not mean that God ever turned down any sincere, penitent heart, but is meant to show how many special mercies God showed the Jews. Those who do not hear the Gospel first may lose their opportunity. There are many others who are poor and sinful who will be reached by the Gospel. Thank God, the wedding will be furnished with guests. All are invited. God is not willing that any should perish (II Pet. 3:9). But not all invited will come (vs. 14).

Verses 11-14 The Wedding Garment

The wedding refers to the glorious meeting of Christ and His saints in the air at His Second Coming (I Thess. 4:13-18). The wedding garment is salvation. Every Christian is covered with the righteousness of Christ. He "is the end of the law for righteousness to every one that believeth" (Rom. 10:4). Every Christian has his own sinful nature covered up, hidden, and paid for, so that his sins are not imputed to him (Rom. 4:5-8). Our own righteousness is no more than filthy rags (Isa. 64:6). But since Christ has taken our place and died for us, His righteousness is charged to our account. This robe of righteousness is pictured by the new robe given by the father to the prodigal son (Luke 15:22). When blind Bartimaeus was healed, he cast away his beggar's garment (Mark 10:50), like a new convert who no longer depends upon his own life, but is safely resting in the finished work of Christ. The king of Babylon lifted up the head of Jehoiachin, set him on a throne, changed his prison garments and Jehoiachin "did eat bread continually before him all the days of his life" (II Kings 25:27-30). Surely that is typical of a child of God who is forgiven; his sins are covered with the righteousness of Christ and he is fed from God's table. We will reign with Him, too! The beautiful garments which Jerusalem, the holy city, is to put on when Christ comes to reign (Isa. 52:1) symbolize the righteousness which will be the garments of the saints at the wedding supper. In Isaiah 61:10 the prophet is rejoicing that "he hath clothed me with the garments of salvation, he hath covered me with the robe of righteousness." That means the same as the wedding garment of Matthew 22:11, 12.

Some will try to be saved by their own works and without blood, as did Cain (Gen. 4:3-5), and like the Pharisee who went to the temple to pray (Luke 18:10-12). But a poor, wicked sinner, when covered in the wedding garment of Christ's righteousness, looks much better in God's sight than the finest praying, tithing, fasting, church-going moral Pharisee in his own goodness.

Men boast loud now about their own goodness, and their alibis and excuses are many, but then all the self-righteous, so-called moral men will be "speechless" (vs. 12). There will be no excuses when the Christ-rejecting sinner meets God!

Verse 13 pictures a literal Hell, a place of "outer darkness" where there is weeping and gnashing of teeth. Hell is a place of darkness, as is also mentioned in Jude 13.

Compare verse 14 with Matthew 20:16. Hell is so terrible that there are many phases of its torments, "Many are called," that is, everybody is invited to the wedding supper. "Few are chosen"; no one can attend the wedding supper but those who are willing to take by faith the wedding garment ahead of time.

Verses 15-22 Jesus Asked, "Is It Lawful to Give Tribute to Caesar?"

Passages parallel to this are given in Mark 12:13-17 and Luke 20:20-26.

These Pharisees planned to "entangle him in his talk." Mark 12:13 says they intended "to catch him in his words." Luke 20:20 tells us that these wicked men sought to "take hold of his words, that so they might deliver him unto the power and authority of the governor." There were three questions propounded to Jesus in order. They were this one by the Pharisees and Herodians, the one by the Sadducees about the resurrection (vss. 23-33), and the question by the Pharisee who was a lawyer (vss. 35-40).

These Pharisees hated Christ and planned to have Him killed. The Herodians (vs. 16) were a political party among the Jews who favored the family of the Herods as governors or kings of Judea.

Notice the flattery in verse 16. They meant to please Jesus and to cause Him to talk freely so they could trap Him and get Him killed. Beware of flatterers! They usually mean evil and the Scripture warns often against them (Prov. 20:19; 26:28; 28:23; 29:5). The question of the tribute money was dangerous. Nearly all the Jews hated the Roman government and did not like to pay taxes or tribute. Therefore, the publicans or tax collectors were in disrepute in Bible times. If Jesus answered yes, that they should pay taxes, many Jews would be displeased. Some would not think Him the Messiah since the Messiah was expected to overthrow the Roman government. On the other hand, if He answered the Jews against paying taxes, then He would be a rebel against the Roman government. They hoped to have the governor, Pilate, against Jesus so that He would be condemned to death. In fact, later when Jesus was on trial before Pilate, they gave the false testimony that Jesus forbad to give tribute to Caesar (Luke 23:1, 2). But here "Jesus perceived their wickedness" (vs. 18), plainly called them "hypocrites," and answered them so wisely that they had not a word to complain. They could not "take hold of his words" as they planned to do (Luke 20:20-26), could not answer, could not accuse Him.

It is proper to support governments by paying taxes. Christians should "render therefore unto Caesar the things which are Caesar's." If a government furnishes money as a medium of exchange, furnishes police protection and such civil blessings, then it is worthy of support. The classic New Testament teaching on this subject is Romans 13:1-7, and verses 6 and 7 there clearly command us to pay taxes. Governments should punish crime, should execute those who deserve it, should maintain order, justice, and peace, and in these matters rulers are the ministers of God. Under the hateful Roman yoke, Jews were yet advised by Jesus, "Render therefore unto Caesar the things which are Caesar's." Duty to government does not conflict with duty to God.

256

Jews would sin if they went after Roman idolatry, but they would properly pay taxes to support the government then in power which furnished them so many of the protections and facilities of the nation. Jesus Himself and Peter paid taxes (Matt. 17:24-27). Christians are urged to pray for rulers (I Tim. 2:1, 2). It is proper for Christians to vote and to use their influence for good government.

Verses 23-33 Jesus Answers Sadducees About the Resurrection

Passages parallel to this are given in Mark 12:18-27 and Luke 20:27-38. Sadducees did not believe in the resurrection (vs. 23). Neither did they believe in angels or spirits (Acts 23:8). They were typical modernists. There was much dissension between the Pharisees and Sadducees on the question of the resurrection, as in the case of Paul (Acts 23:6-10). Here the Sadducees intended to prove that the resurrection of the dead was impossible. They argued that if people were raised from the dead it would result in an unbearable confusion as in the supposed case of seven brothers who had married the same wife one after the other. The quotation from Moses in verse 24 refers to Deuteronomy 25:5.

The Pharisees erred on two accounts. First, they did not know the Old Testament Scriptures which clearly teach a resurrection (Job 19:25-27; Ps. 16:9, 10). Joseph had believed in the resurrection and instructed that his body be carried out of Egypt (Gen. 50:25). Abraham had believed in the resurrection and that he would receive the promises after he was raised from the dead (Heb. 11:8-13). Jesus later told His disciples that the Old Testament Scriptures taught that He should rise from the dead (Luke 24:44-46). If the Sadducees had known and believed the Old Testament Scriptures, they would have believed in the resurrection. Their second mistake was in not knowing the power of God (vs. 29). Thus they could not imagine the resurrection life without marriage and the frailties of our poor human bodies.

In the resurrection people do not marry (vs. 30), but are as the angels of God. We do not know all that this means but we do know that there will not be marriage. We suppose there will not be reproduction. Evidently children will not be born to us in our

257

resurrection bodies. Marriage will not be necessary because there will be no sin among glorified saints. Then, too, we will all love perfectly and beautifully with a holy love. This teaching does not minimize the fact of an actual physical body in Heaven. Jesus had the very body that was put in Joseph's tomb when He was raised from the dead, except that it was glorified. He had the same hands with the nail prints, the same side where the spear pierced. He had a body that ate and drank before His disciples (Luke 24:39-43). It is with that same body that Jesus is coming again (Acts 1:11). When Jesus comes we will receive bodies like His (Phil 3:20, 21). Though there is no marrying in the resurrection yet people will have literal, human bodies of flesh and bone (and we suppose of blood since those bodies will contain liquid). We will eat and drink in the kingdom of Christ in our resurrection bodies (Matt. 26:29; Luke 14:12-15). After the resurrection we will have real bodies; we will recognize each other just as the disciples recognized Moses and Elijah on the Mount of Transfiguration (Matt. 17:3).

Notice the argument of Jesus for the resurrection (vss. 31-33). Jesus speaks of the words of God which came to Moses out of the burning bush, as Mark 12:26 tells us, referring to Exodus 3:1-6. The point is, if God is the God of Abraham and Isaac and Jacob, after they had died; then their spirits are still alive and if Abraham, Isaac, and Jacob are somewhere alive, then we may expect their bodies to rise from the dead.

This argument goes deeper than you might have thought. The salvation of the soul proves that we can one day have perfect bodies. The connection is expressed in Romans 8:19-23. If there is an eternal home for the soul, then there is an eternal home for the body, too. Thus there must be a resurrection of the bodies of the saved and the unsaved. There will be bodies in Heaven and in Hell (Matt. 10:28; 18:8, 9; Phil. 2:10, 11).

Verses 34-40 Jesus Answers Which Is the Great Commandment

This is also recorded in Mark 12:28-34. A similar passage is given in Luke 10:25-29, but the occasion is not the same, we think. Read carefully Mark's account of this lawyer's question, as it is more in detail. The scribe or lawyer, "perceiving that he had answered them well" (Mark 12:28), asked the question. This lawyer may have been sincere and earnest, for Jesus answered him frankly. And the lawyer, not an attorney, but a specialist in the Mosaic Law (scribe, Mark calls him), was pleased with Christ's answer, and understood it (Mark 12:28-33).

The greatest commandment is given in verse 37, quoted from Deuteronomy 6:5. Jesus also quoted Deuteronomy 6:4 as given in Mark 12:29. Remember, Jesus is quoting from the Hebrew Old Testament. After it has been translated into Greek, then into our English, we would expect to find some variation in the words. Besides, each one of the Gospels gives some things that the others omit. The first commandment is to love God and the second commandment is to "love thy neighbor as thyself" (vs. 59). That is quoted from Leviticus 19:18. These two sum up all the commandments of the law and prophets (vs. 40). The first one involves the first four of the Ten Commandments (Exod. 20:1-8). It covers the whole duty of one to God direct. The second covers all the last six commandments (Exod. 20:12-17) and covers the whole duty of man to his neighbor. God should come before others. Read the discreet answer of this scribe as given in Mark 12:32, 33 and how Jesus told him he was not far from the kingdom of God (Mark 12:34). Love is a fulfillment of all the law (Rom. 13:8-10; Gal. 5:14). After this answer of Jesus they dared not ask Him any more questions (Mark 12:34). Do not forget the definition of a *neighbor* in the parable of the good Samaritan (Luke 10:30-37).

See how the passage reveals the folly of those unbelievers who say that the Old Testament is not the revelation of the God of love, that the Old Testament is inadequate, not perfectly authoritative. The quotations summing up the great commandments are from the Old Testament. The God of the Old Testament is the God and Father of our Lord Jesus Christ.

Verses 41-46 Jesus Stops the Pharisees With a Question

Here the tables are turned. Jesus questions the Pharisees after they have been embarrassed into silence. It is told also in Mark 12:35-37 and Luke 20:41-44. Consider the question of Jesus in verse 42, "What think ye of Christ? whose son is he?" The word

Christ is the Greek translation of the Hebrew word *Messiah.* The word means *Anointed.* So in Psalm 2:2 the Scripture speaks of Christ as God's "anointed." The Jews knew that their Christ was promised in the Old Testament. Jesus was the promised Christ or Messiah and He here intended to prove that He, the Messiah, was more than a mere man.

The Pharisees answered that the Christ would be the Son of David (vs. 42). In this they were correct, for they understood from II Samuel 7:10-14 that the coming King would be the Son of David. Isaiah 9:6, 7 told them that the wonderful Prince or Messiah would sit on the throne of David. Isaiah 11:1 taught them that the coming ruler would be a Branch from the stem of Jesse (David's father), as many other Scriptures had so taught. Both the genealogies of Christ show Him to be the Son of David (Matt. 1:6, 16 and Luke 3:23, 31). The Pharisees realized that Jesus would come humanly of the seed of David. They did not understand about the virgin birth and how Christ would be conceived of the Holy Ghost in the virgin's womb. However, they should have known so from Isaiah 7:14. In verse 44 Jesus quoted Psalm 110:1.

How could David call the Messiah his Lord, his God, if the Messiah was to be descended from him? Since Christ is God in human form, He is both the Son of David and the Son of God, David's Son and David's Lord. The Pharisees and Jews had an inadequate conception of the Messiah. Yet Jesus was Himself the perfect fulfillment of the Old Testament promises concerning the Christ.

This put a stop to all the questions. They could not face Jesus. Note that here Jesus stopped His critics *with the Scriptures,* even as He vanquished Satan at His temptation by quoting Scripture (Matt. 4:4, 7, 10).

MATTHEW XXIII

Verses 1-7 Jesus Names the Marks of a Pharisee

Following the questions and answers of chapter 22, Jesus plainly "in the audience of all the people" warned His disciples against the scribes and Pharisees (Luke 20:45-47; Mark 12:38-40). From the way Jesus uses interchangeably the terms "scribes" (copyists, and therefore, teachers of the law and the prophets), and the "Pharisees" (a very strict sect, religiously), it is evident that most of the scribes belonged to the religious party called Pharisees. Jesus here speaks of Pharisees (vs. 2), but in Mark and Luke similar words are given about the scribes.

These words of Jesus are warnings to the disciples. Jesus said at this time, "Beware of the scribes" (Mark 12:38; Luke 20:46).

The scribes were bad men in good places. They sat "in Moses' seat," that is, they learned the law, copied it, and their business was to teach the Word of God. A scribe did not need to be bad. Ezra was a scribe (Ezra 7:6, 11, 12, 21). If the scribes in Jesus' day had followed Ezra's example, this warning would have been unnecessary. Scribes were needed. The people must look to them for the Word of God. No books were printed; copies, then, must be made by hand and by learned and careful men. The familiarity which these scribes had with the letter of the Scriptures made it proper for them to teach the people the facts about the law and the rest of the Old Testament. Therefore, the people must not turn against the office because the men who held it were unworthy. Even today there are some evil men in the ministry, but God wants people to respect the ministry. There are hypocrites in the churches, but that is no excuse for those who would scoff at Christianity and the churches. Likewise, officers of the law are sometimes corrupt, but we should maintain our respect for the law and institutions of government despite corrupt politicians.

Verse 3 reminds us how poor are leaders who say and do not, whether officers of the law who do not keep the law, or preachers who do not live according to their own preaching. Everyone in authority has a special obligation to set an example in his action

261

as well as in his precepts. What parents do influences their children as much as what they say. Sunday School teachers do as much good, or harm, by the way they live, as by the way they teach. Let the reader be careful that he is not one like the scribes who "say and do not."

See what strict standards God has for pastors (bishops) in I Timothy 3:2-7; "blameless... vigilant, sober, of good behaviour," hospitable, "not given to wine, no striker, not greedy of filthy lucre; but patient, not a brawler, not covetous... Moreover he must have a good report of them that are without." Deacons also are to be blameless (I Tim. 1:8-13). Even young Timothy was commanded, "...be thou an example of the believers, in word, in conversation" (manner of life), "in charity, in spirit, in faith, in purity" (I Tim. 4:12). Of Barnabas it is written, "For he was a good man, and full of the Holy Ghost and of faith: and much people was added unto the Lord" (Acts 11:24). "Good man" is the first requirement for service after one is born of God.

The scribes were professional religious leaders, in the work for what they could get out of it, not for love of God nor because of compassion toward men, as we see from verse 4. Any service for God which does not spring out of a tender, compassionate heart cannot be pleasing to Him. To bear one another's burdens is to fulfill the law of Christ (Gal. 6:2). One who sows the seed of the Word of God should go forth weeping (Ps. 126:5, 6). Such selfish leaders as these scribes and Pharisees lead people away from the truth. Paul called them "wolves" (Acts 20:29, 30). The Judaizers who misled the Galatian Christians were similar in spirit to these scribes. They insisted on circumcision, but only "to make a fair shew in the flesh" (Gal. 6:12). For their own glory they sought to make disciples as these scribes made proselytes (vs. 15). Sincere, unselfish love to God and man should be the motive behind all Christian work, and that motive will lift men's burdens instead of binding heavier burdens upon them (vs. 4).

"To be seen of men" – that was the motive of the scribes and Pharisees. Phylacteries were small cases containing Scriptures and tied upon the arm or forehead, used by these men to impress the world with their love of the Scriptures. Enlarged borders on their garments would mark them as rabbis or teachers. They loved "the uppermost rooms at feasts, and the chief seats in the synagogues" (vs. 6), because that would make them seem important to the world. They wanted everybody to greet them in the markets as important, learned, and well-known men; they loved to be called "Rabbi, Rabbi." In other words, they sought to please people and have the approval of people instead of having the approval of God.

How different were the disciples of Jesus after Pentecost (Acts 4:18-20). "The fear of man bringeth a snare" (Prov. 29:25). Anyone who will be used of God should first decide whether or not he is willing to displease men. It is impossible to please both God and man (John 12:43). To please the world after we claim to be married to Christ is spiritual adultery (James 4:4), and to be a friend of the world is enmity to Christ.

Thus the religion of the Pharisees was outward, professional, insincere. They gave money to the poor to have glory of men (Matt. 6:2). They prayed standing in the synagogues and on the street corners to be seen of men (Matt. 6:5). They fasted, then put on a sad countenance, disfiguring their faces to appear unto men to fast (Matt. 6:16). They were insincere, in other words, hypocrites, and Jesus used that term repeatedly to describe them (vss. 13, 14, 15, 23, 25, 27, 29).

Verses 8-12 Jesus Warns About Seeking Exalted Titles

The word *rabbi* means *a great man* or *teacher* and *master* means *teacher*. Christ was called *rabbi* by John's disciples (John 1:38), by Nathanael (John 1:49), by Nicodemus (John 3:2), by people at Capernaum (John 6:25). John the Baptist was called *rabbi* by some Jews (John 3:26). Mary Magdalene called Jesus *Rabbi*, or rather *My Rabbi* (*Rabboni*, John 20:16), after He was risen from the dead. There was nothing wrong with the term *rabbi*, except that Christians should not seek to appear greater than others, should not be thinking of self-preferment.

To be called *professor* (similar to *rabbi*) or *teacher* (similar to *master*) or *father* is not necessarily wrong. Some men are teachers and leaders, and it is not wrong to so regard them, provided God has made them so. Notice that Paul, by divine inspiration, calls Abraham *father* (Rom. 4:1, 11, 12, 16, 17, 18) and calls Isaac *father* (Rom. 9:10). Abraham is called a *father*, not only of the Jews, but of all believers (Rom. 4:11). Paul called Timothy his *son* (I Tim. 1:2; II Tim. 1:2). Timothy doubtless called him, since Timothy served with Paul "as a son with the father" (Phil. 2:22). Paul called himself a *father* to the Corinthian Christians (I Cor. 4:15). But Paul did not thus seek to dominate the spiritual life of these with his own plans and ideas. It was not self-seeking, but rather, seeking their own good in the will of God.

This should help us understand commands here. None of us should be overlords. None of us should seek preeminence. All should honor Christ as the Master, and our Father in Heaven as the Father of all Christians, and all Christians should regard one another as brethren.

This teaching should color the attitude of servants toward their masters and masters toward their servants. Servants should be all the more obedient to their masters, "with fear and trembling, in singleness of your heart, as unto Christ," and masters should deal with servants, forbearing threatening and remembering that their Master also is in Heaven (Eph. 6:5-9; Col. 3:22-25; 4:1). Remember how Jesus rebuked the ambition of James and John (Matt. 20:20-28), and New Testament churches were especially warned not to have respect of persons, honoring the rich and dishonoring the poor (James 2:1-9). Compare verses 11 and 12 with Matthew 20:26-28, with John 13:13-16 and with James 4:6-10. Let Christians beware that they do not love the uppermost rooms at feasts and the chief seats in the synagogues, and to be called great among men. If we exalt ourselves we shall be abased, "and he that shall humble himself shall be exalted."

Verse 13 First Woe Pronounced Against Pharisees

Jesus was first speaking to His disciples in the presence of the scribes and Pharisees and spoke of the latter in the third person (vs. 2). But here He turned, in burning denunciation, to the scribes and Pharisees themselves.

Let us here learn two severe lessons. First, the people must sometimes be warned about scribes and Pharisees and other false religious leaders. Paul warned the elders of Ephesus about "wolves" (Acts 20:29-31). The Colossian Christians were warned to beware of false teachers who taught salvation by works (Col. 2:8). Paul warned Timothy of Alexander the coppersmith (II Tim. 4:14, 15), and all Christians are repeatedly warned about the false teachers who will come in this age (I Tim. 4:1-3; II Pet. 2:1-3; Jude 18). Preachers and teachers, then, should speak out plainly and warn Christians against false leaders and false religions such as modernism, Christian Science, Jehovah's Witnesses, Unity, the "I Am" Presence, Spiritualism, Mormonism, and other like evils. We will not always please men, but we will please God if we be honest in such matters. Preachers are responsible for their flocks and for all the body of Christ, and should be faithful.

Second, we ought to warn those of false religions and of false hopes just as Jesus warned these Pharisees and scribes here. We ought to preach most plainly and tenderly to Jews that there is no salvation without Christ, and to other false and hypocritical religionists we should make plain just where their doctrines and practices lead them. We should be bold against modernism and against any doctrine that exalts human virtue and character without holding up Christ as the atonement and propitiation for man's sins. Jesus was plain and bold in His teaching in the presence of sinners. So was John the Baptist before Herod (Matt. 14:3, 4). So was Peter before the Jews who crucified Christ (Acts 2:36), particularly before the high priest and rulers and scribes (Acts 4:5-12). Paul was brave even in rebuking the Apostle Peter (Gal. 2:11-14). Those who would pattern after Jesus must be against sin and must say so openly and boldly as Jesus did.

Eight times in this chapter Jesus pronounced a woe or curse against the scribes and Pharisees: verses 13, 14, 15, 16, 23, 25, 27, 29; seven times the words are the same, "Woe unto you, scribes and Pharisees, hypocrites!" This chapter is the most terrible denunciation of hypocrisy ever uttered or ever written.

In verse 13 the first curse is pronounced because the Pharisees shut up the kingdom of Heaven; they prevented people from being saved. This was evidently literally true as you see from John 7:48. These Jewish leaders had agreed to put anybody out of the synagogue who confessed that Jesus was the Christ (John 9:22). The question they discussed in their councils was this: "If we let him thus alone, all men will believe on him" (John 11:48). Later, "the chief priests and elders persuaded the multitude that they should ask Barabbas, and destroy Jesus" (Matt. 27:20). The Pharisees particularly objected to Jesus' offer of salvation to publicans and sinners (Luke 7:39, 49; 15:1, 2). Besides, no one knows how many millions of people were led to Hell by these leaders and their emphasis on human righteousness instead of faith in Christ. In our own day secret orders and many religious leaders teach people to depend upon their own good works. In this way they shut up the kingdom of Heaven against people. What a terrible curse Jesus pronounced against those who prevent others from being saved.

Verse 14 Second Curse: Praying Pharisees Devour Widows' Houses

People who make loud pretentions of morality often do the most immoral things. The outwardly moral, self-religious Pharisees would stand high with the people. Widows would be easy prey for them. It is surprising what a large part of their support false teachers get today from women. Since these Pharisees and scribes set themselves up as interpreters of the law and sat in Moses' seat (vs. 2), they could and did take advantage of widows. Many even taught grown children that it was proper for them not to support their parents if the children dedicated the money that should have been so used to the service of God. The Pharisees called this tradition of theirs "Corban," and by it they often got money that should have gone for the support- and honor of parents (Matt. 15:1-14). Notice particularly Jesus' burning denunciation of the scribes and Pharisees in that passage, calling them hypocrites, blind leaders of the blind and plants which the Father had not planted (Mark 7:1-23). The Pharisees were covetous and guilty of extortion and excess (vs. 25).

Notice the long prayers the Pharisees offered in pretense. Prayer is often used by hypocrites (Matt. 6:5-7; Luke 18:9-14; Isa. 1:15). Long prayers in public are often insincere. The more eloquent they are with high-sounding language, the less likely they are to be sincere and pleasing to God. Preachers often sin in this matter, laymen just as often, and we have known women called "able in prayer" who offended. Preachers should teach their people to beware of this sin of hypocrisy in prayer and should insist on short, simple, sincere public prayers, prayers intended for God and not for men.

Verse 15 Third Woe on Proselyting Pharisees

The Pharisees were eager to make proselytes, that is, to get Gentiles to become Jews. We are accustomed to hearing people speak evil of proselyting. But it was proper to turn a Gentile to the true God and the worship of the temple. The Ethiopian eunuch was evidently a proselyte (Acts 8:27), and many such were at Jerusalem at Pentecost (Acts 2:10). It is not wrong to turn people from ignorance to knowledge of the true God, from darkness to light, from sin to righteousness, from error to truth. But the motives of the Pharisees were evil motives. They knew about the true God but did not love Him from the heart. They had the sacrifices, but never considered their spiritual meaning pointing to the coming Saviour. It would do a Gentile no good to become a Jew in name only, if in his heart he did not have faith in Israel's God and trust in the promised Messiah and Saviour of Israel. Many made proselytes to get credit for themselves and to gain the money and prestige that would be received with more followers. Such proselytes being blind and led by blind leaders would be enslaved by the forms of Jewish customs without any spiritual benefit.

Similarly, notice how secret orders that have stolen away good men from the church, on a pretense to be righteous, have grown a generation of lodge members openly antagonistic to churches, with unbelief in the Bible and with hardened hearts toward the Gospel. Having put their faith in morality led by church people, they see no need of Christ and are harder to reach than if they had never been taught the oaths and secrets and virtues of the lodges. So it was with the Pharisees who made their followers, Jesus told them, "twofold more the child of hell" (vs. 15).

Modern church leaders, with no teaching of the new birth, denying the fundamentals of the faith, are utter hypocrites to promote "evangelism" with a false Gospel, getting more unconverted people in churches. These are under Christ's curse on the Pharisees.

Verses 16-22 Pharisees Were Hypocrites About Oaths, Jesus Said

The Pharisees were "blind leaders." They had many oaths but no spiritual discernment about them. They held an oath by the temple not binding, but an oath by the gold of the temple was binding, and the one who swore was a debtor. Doubtless, the reason was that they would profit by gifts of gold. They held that an oath by the altar was nothing, but an oath by the gift on the altar they held binding, doubtless, because they received part of the sacrifices. Actually the temple was greater than the gold and the altar than the gifts upon it, and only their covetousness and blindness made them careless and irreverent with artificial distinction

that should not have existed. They cared more about rites and ceremonies than about God Himself or His temple. The Old Testament permitted oaths (Lev. 19:12) but Jesus commanded, "Swear not at all" (Matt. 5:34-37). The word of a Christian should be sufficient without an oath. Swearing is forbidden again (James 5:12).

"Swear not at all," said Jesus. Because many Quakers and others had conscientious scruples against taking even legal oaths in court or oaths of office, our American constitution, and most state constitutions, provide that those who wish may say, "I solemnly affirm" instead of saying "I solemnly swear." Many do not feel that the simple oath required of the law is hurtful or forbidden, but certainly it is not wrong to make affirmation.

How can any Christian be guiltless in the bloody and blasphemous oaths required in the lodges and secret orders? They are forbidden and sinful, measured by Matthew 5:34-37 and by James 5:12.

Verses 23,24 Tithing Pharisees Who Neglected Justice, Mercy, and Faith

The Pharisees gave tithes even down to each sprig of mint, anise, and cummin, spices and flavoring herbs that grew in their gardens. Luke 11:42 speaks of the same matter. "These ought ye to have done," Jesus said. It was proper to tithe. Tithes and offerings were commanded by the Old Testament law (Lev. 27:30). One who did not bring both tithes and offerings robbed God (Mai. 3:8, 9). But Abraham practiced tithing long before the law (Gen. 14:20). So did Jacob (Gen. 28:22). Perhaps even righteous Abel tithed for he "brought of the firstling of his flock" (Gen. 4:4),

We are not under law, but the principle followed by devout men before the law is still good for Christians. All property still belongs to God, and it is only proper that we should acknowledge His ownership by bringing some proportion of our income for His service. First Corinthians 16:1, 2 commands giving in proportion to one's income. Notice the promise of Malachi 3:10, 11 and compare it with Luke 6:38 and with II Corinthians 9:6-11, and you will see that the same blessing is promised for New Testament giving as for Old Testament giving.

If there be any difference, it is this: Old Testament Jews were commanded to give one tenth, and we New Testament Christians are commanded to put *ALL* on the altar for God, even our bodies (Rom. 12:1, 2; I Cor. 6:19, 20). If a Jew under the Old Testament law ought to love God enough to tithe, so ought a Christian under grace. If God would prosper a Jew and make it profitable for him to give tithes and offerings for the support of the temple, then will not the same God provide for His own dear children who through love give as much for the spread of the Gospel? There is no excuse for a Christian who pretends to love God and believe the Bible to give less than a tenth of his income for the Lord's work. Many reap sparingly because they sow sparingly and those who sow bountifully certainly reap bountifully today. Remember that Abraham and Jacob were no more under law than we are. Both were heroes of faith (Heb. 11:8, 9), both were abundantly prospered.

So the Pharisees were right to tithe. Their sin was in omitting "the weightier matters of the law, judgment, mercy, and faith." Remember there was no justice or righteous judgment in their charges against Christ (Matt. 12:24), in their bribing Judas (Matt. 26:15), in their suborning or bribing false witnesses to swear a lie about Jesus (Matt. 26:59-61). There was no mercy in their attitude toward the publicans, harlots, and Samaritans whom they were not willing to see saved. There was no faith at all in Christ though they saw fulfilled before their eyes many Scriptures with overwhelming proof of His deity. Tithing is proper but will not keep an unregenerate man from going to Hell. They were so careful not to do wrong about tithing that they 'strained at a gnat.' But they were so careless about justice, mercy, and faith that they 'swallowed a camel' of sin. How blind is a religion that makes much of little details and altogether leaves out regeneration and faith in Christ! So in the sight of God is all human righteousness which does not repent of sin and trust in Christ.

Verses 25,26 Pharisees Were Hypocrites in Insisting on Outward Religious Ceremonies With no Heart Cleansing

The trouble with the righteousness of the Pharisees was that it was all outside. Tithing can be seen; faith cannot be seen. Many religious people err here. Speaking in tongues is external; the fullness of the Holy Spirit is internal. Therefore, men are more anxious to speak in tongues than to have the soul-winning power and fullness of God. A lodge member's religion shows outside and in the sight of men is often as good as that of church members. Remember that Judas appeared to be such a good Christian that he deceived everybody but Jesus until the time of the betrayal. Baptism can be seen, but regeneration cannot be seen. Too many people make more ado about baptism than they do about repentance and a change of heart. Some are so anxious about a "social gospel" of doing good outwardly to others that they forget all about the Gospel of Christ which emphasizes that one must be born again, must have the individual regeneration which is as invisible and unexplainable as the wind (John 3:8). God help us to beware that our cleansing, our Christianity, be internal and not simply external; that we be right in the sight of God, not simply right in the sight of men, as were these wicked Pharisees.

This does not mean that individual regeneration minimizes righteous living. The cleansing of the heart will promote righteous living as you see from verse 26, "that the outside of them may be clean also." All sin begins in the heart, and cleansing of the heart is the only remedy for sin (Matt. 15:18-20). Real Christians should live uprightly, but remember that the outward appearance of upright living does not make a Christian nor even prove one.

Verses 27,28 Unconverted Pharisees Were as Hateful to Christ as Stinking Corpses in Whitewashed Tombs

Only God sees the heart, and the morality of modernists and of unconverted members of secret orders may "indeed appear beautiful." But you may be sure that however moral and beautiful the outward life, unregenerated hearts "are within full of dead men's bones, and of all uncleanness" like whited sepulchres, whitewashed graves. The Pharisees outwardly appeared "righteous unto men," but within they were "full of hypocrisy and iniquity." That is the reason the Pharisee, with such a fine moral life and such bold claims in public prayer (Luke 18:9-14), went down to his house not justified, while a penitent publican was forgiven. That explains also Matthew 5:20. No one can get to Heaven without better righteousness than the Pharisees had. Remember that Paul before his conversion was a vigorous Pharisee (Acts 26:4, 5; Phil. 3:4-6), yet was killing Christians, even as these Pharisees were guilty of the murder of Jesus Christ. Remember Judas Iscariot and these Pharisees, and never be deceived by the professed righteousness of any man who rejects Jesus Christ. There is always but one reason for any man's rejecting Christ, and that is sin, sometimes hidden, but always loved and clung to (John 3:19-21). That means that the pretention of any man to live righteously while he rejects Christ is simply hypocrisy, and this chapter perfectly fits any man who claims morality while rejecting Christ.

Verses 29-36 Unconverted Church Leaders – the Pharisees Brought Upon Themselves All the Blood of Prophets They Praised by Rejecting Christ

The last curse pronounced on these "scribes and Pharisees, hypocrites!" is because of their hypocrisy in pretending to be grieved about the death of prophets slain by their fathers, while they proceeded to crucify Jesus and later to kill Christians. This is a strong and remarkable Scripture that you need to study

271

carefully. These verses explain why Jerusalem later was destroyed in A.D. 70 by Titus and the Roman army and the Jews scattered to all the world as they are to this day. God did not take the land of Canaan away from the Amorites until the cup of their iniquity was full (Gen. 15:16; Lev. 18:24, 25; Judges 6:10). But those sins piled up high in the sight of God until they must meet judgment. The same thing happened in the sins of Israel and Judah. Awful sins brought the wrath of God with repeated warnings of captivity and then repeated promises of mercies. But eventually God brought the threatened captivity upon Judah and Israel and the land was laid waste (II Kings 17:5-23; 24:1-16, 20; 25:1-21). So now in the rejection of Christ the nation Israel inherited punishment due their fathers in the murder of all the prophets and righteous men that ever died in all the world from Abel on down. The reason is this: in Christ is all righteousness, and in rejecting Christ is all wickedness and sin. The Jews who rejected Christ were guilty of all the sins man could commit, and on the nation at that time came judgment for all the sins ever committed. One who rejects Christ has committed the greatest sin and has a heart wicked enough to be guilty of any other crime he might be tempted to do.

In verse 32 Jesus shows that these Jewish leaders in rejecting Him and crucifying Him simply sum up the wickedness of all the Jewish race and, of course, of all human beings.

Verse 33 shows that the race, in crucifying Jesus, is poisoned with all the sin of Satan. Notice the word "serpent" applying to Satan and sin in the Garden of Eden (Gen. 3:1, 2, 4, 13) and applying to Christ's bearing our sins on the cross, pictured by the brazen serpent (Num. 21:9), then that Satan is called "that old serpent, which is the Devil, and Satan" (Rev. 12:9; 20:2). Verse 33 "ye serpents..." means the same as John 8:44, "Ye are of your father the devil, and the lusts of your father ye will do." I cannot imagine more awe-inspiring preaching than this when Jesus faced those Pharisees with these words and gave them a solemn warning about eternal damnation and Hell.

Verse 34 shows that Jesus knew about His own crucifixion, about the persecution of the apostles and other Christians which should follow (Acts 4:1-7; 5:17-40; 7:54-60; 8:1; 12:1-3; etc).

Verses 37-39 Jesus Grieves Over Jerusalem; God Has Forsaken the Temple

A similar passage is given in Luke 13:34, 35. Luke 21:20-24 throws great light on this passage. How these words picture the tender heart of Jesus! Luke 19:41-44 tells us of other prophecies about the destruction of Jerusalem and how Jesus wept over the dear city. His tender, compassionate heart longed to see every person in the city saved. So He prayed, "Father, forgive them," when they crucified Him (Luke 23:34). Verse 38 refers to the temple. See Matthew 27:51. The death of Christ did not put an end to Jewish sacrifices in the temple.

In the book of Hebrews we see that high priests were still appointed when that epistle was written (Heb. 5:1). Sons of Levi were still in the office of the Jewish priesthood (Heb. 7:5). These priests still stood daily in Jerusalem, in the temple offering sacrifices (Heb. 10:11). But the Shekinah glory had left the temple. The house was no longer owned of God as His house. It was already condemned to destruction with the impenitent of Jerusalem.

Notice the significance of verse 39. "Ye shall not see me henceforth till..." Upon His resurrection Jesus went into Jerusalem secretly, only to appear to the twelve in the upper room with the doors shut (Luke 24:36; John 20:19). His public appearance to crowds of people was in Galilee, not Jerusalem (Matt. 28:7; John 21:1, ff.). Jesus ascended from Bethany on the Mount of Olives (Luke 24:50, 51; Acts 1:12), but as far as we know He had no general ministry during those forty days He was on earth after His resurrection. More than five hundred brethren saw Jesus at once after His resurrection (I Cor. 15:6). But Jerusalem as a whole did not see Him and will not see Him until His Second Coming to reign. Then they will see Him (Zech. 14:3, 4). Then they will see the wounds in His hands (Zech. 13:6), will be convinced of His deity and their sins, will mourn in deep penitence (Zech. 12:10-14), then the fountain for sin and uncleanness will be opened in Jerusalem (Zech. 13:1), and so shall all Israel be saved (Rom. 11:26). Then the revival at Pentecost will be multiplied a thousandfold and the prophecy of Joel concerning the pouring out of the Spirit on Israel in the last days will be completely fulfilled, as it was only partly fulfilled at Pentecost (Acts 2:16-21; Joel 2:28-32). Careful reading of those passages will show that they were primarily for the whole age, ending in the last great revival which will come for the Jews, and only incidentally picturing Pentecost. Pentecost was not just before the "great and terrible day of the Lord," And other signs mentioned in Acts 2:19, 20 were not fulfilled then perfectly, as they will be. Jesus is coming and will be received by penitent people of Israel as their Saviour and King. This will be at the close of the tribulation period when the saints return with Christ, when He smites the armies of the Antichrist or Man of Sin, and sets up the throne of His glory.

Of that coming and reign at Jerusalem, see the author's book, *The Coming Kingdom of Christy* same publishers.

MATTHEW XXIV

The 24th chapter of Matthew is paralleled by Mark 13 and Luke 21.

Verses 1,2 The Temple to Be Destroyed

Do not fail to connect these verses with the last part of chapter 23. Jesus had just pronounced a curse upon the scribes and Pharisees and upon Jerusalem (Matt. 23:29-39). He clearly had in mind the coming destruction of Jerusalem which occurred some forty years later, in A.D. 70. Verse 2 here refers to the same thing. The temple would be utterly destroyed. Coming out of the temple which Jesus has declared will be left desolate, the disciples call His attention to the wonderful adornment of that building, with its goodly stones and gifts (Luke 21:5). The disciples said, "Master, see what manner of stones and what buildings are here!" (Mark 13:1). The temple standing in the time of Christ was the third one built. The first was Solomon's temple, built in his reign (I Kings 6:1-38), and destroyed at the Babylonian captivity (II Chron. 36:18, 19). The second was the temple of Zerubbabel, built on the same spot by those who returned from the captivity after seventy years (Ezra 3:8-13; 6:15, 16). This temple of Zerubbabel was plundered by Antiochus Epiphanes, king of Syria, 168 B.C., was attacked by the Roman general Pompey, in 63 B.C., and stormed by Herod the Great in 37 B.C. So after standing nearly five hundred years, the temple of Zerubbabel was much decayed and Herod the Great rebuilt it at enormous expense. The whole of the building of the temple and its outbuildings, walls and gates, occupied forty-six years (John 2:20).

One authority says the outer wall of this temple standing in Christ's time was an eighth of a mile square. At one place the wall is said to have been 130 feet high. The stones were enormous and there were many pillars and cloisters and columns and gates. Josephus tells us of stones in the temple and walls about twenty-five cubits long, eight cubits high, twelve cubits wide, which, counting eighteen inches to a cubit, would be about 40 x 12 x 20 feet. Some gates were covered with solid brass; the courts were paved with marble. The sanctuary itself was nearly 180 feet high. The temple was one of the most magnificent buildings in the whole world. It is described by Josephus and other authorities. See

Smith's Bible Dictionary or others on the temple. How startling was Jesus' pronouncement that not one stone should be left upon another that was not thrown down! This was fulfilled literally by the Roman army when the temple was destroyed.

It is particularly mentioned that Jesus "departed from the temple." He left it for good, never to return to this temple. In fact, He was never to return to Jerusalem publicly and openly until His Second Coming when He will have a second triumphal entry and the people shall say, "Blessed is he that cometh in the name of the Lord" (Matt. 23:39; Ps. 24). He appeared secretly after His resurrection to His disciples in the upper room, with the door shut (John 20:19, 26). But His public appearances after His resurrection were in Galilee. There, by appointment, He met His disciples and His brethren after His resurrection (Matt. 28:7, 10, 16; John 21:4-25). The ascension, after forty days, was from this same Mount of Olives, just outside Jerusalem, on the east, in the neighborhood of Bethany (Luke 24:50; Acts 1:9-12). Jesus departed from the temple for good and this temple was to be utterly destroyed before Jesus ever set foot there again.

Matthew Henry says on Matthew 23:38:

Note, That house is left desolate indeed, which Christ leaves. Woe unto them when I depart, Hos. 9:12; Jer. 6:8. It was now time to groan out their Ichabod, The glory is departed, their defence is departed. Three days after this, the veil of the temple was rent; when Christ left it, all became common and unclean; but Christ departed not till they drove him away; did not reject them, till they first rejected him.

Notice also that Jesus has finished His last *public* discourse. Hereafter His speech will be with His disciples. All the teaching and events of Matthew, chapters 24, 25, and 26, as well as the discourses in John, chapters 14, 15, 16, and 17, follow this, but those discourses were all to His disciples, not to the people.

Verse When Would Jerusalem Be Destroyed?

Leaving the temple itself, Jesus went outside the temple wall and sat down upon the Mount of Olives nearby. Notice the question in verse 3 divides into two parts. (1) When will come this destruction of Jerusalem and of the temple? (2) What shall be the sign of Jesus' Second Coming and of the end of the world, or more correctly, end of this age? They are two separate questions.

However, you will note that Jesus did not give a full answer to the question as to when would come the destruction of Jerusalem and of the temple. The more we read the Olivet discourse as given here in Matthew 24, in Luke 21, and in Mark 13, the more clearly we see that while Jesus mentioned the destruction of Jerusalem which would take place in A.D. 70 by the Roman army under Titus, that destruction did not end the matter discussed, but only began it. A little fuller statement on the destruction of Jerusalem is given in the midst of the Olivet discourse as recorded in Luke 21:20-24 which reads:

"And when ye shall see Jerusalem compassed with armies, then know that the desolation thereof is nigh. Then let them which are in Judea flee to the mountains; and let them which are in the midst of it depart out; and let not them that are in the countries enter thereinto. For these be the days of vengeance, that all things which are written may be fulfilled. But woe unto them that are with child, and to them that give suck, in those days! for there shall be great distress in the land, and wrath upon this people. And they shall fall by the edge? of the sword, and shall be led away captive into all nations: and Jerusalem shall be trodden down of the Gentiles, until the times of the Gentiles be fulfilled."

The destruction of Jerusalem was simply the first drastic, public punishment of Jews for their rejection of Christ. But the punishment did not end there. It was not simply a punishment of the Jews of that generation, but of the whole nation of Israel. And so as a clear picture of God's disapproval throughout this whole age: "Jerusalem shall be trodden down of the Gentiles, until the times of the Gentiles be fulfilled." Thus the trouble in Jerusalem, and the dispersion of Jews among all the nations of Jerusalem throughout this whole age, is simply a continuation of the punishment of God upon the whole race of Jews.

That leads us to say that the apostles were right to join the two questions in Matthew 24:3: "Tell us, when shall these things be? [the destruction of Jerusalem and of the temple] and what shall be the sign of thy coming, and of the end of the world?" later at the end of this age. The dispersion of Jews is simply a type of the age-long trouble of the poor Jews, "people of the restless feet," scattered among the nations until Christ shall return and restore Israel. The destruction of Jerusalem by Titus symbolizes that the nation is to be trodden down of the Gentiles all through these years until Christ returns to reign, and just before Christ comes, another tremendous destruction of the city is to take place. In a measure, the two questions are one, and they are answered together. Jesus, in the Olivet discourse, looks far beyond the destruction of A.D. 70, till the time when the Man of Sin himself will harass Jews and murder them, will commit the abomination of desolation in the temple, and pillage the city again, just before Christ shall defeat the Man of Sin in the battle of Armageddon, then triumphantly take Jerusalem and regather the Jews.

That future desolation of Jerusalem is often referred to in the Bible. For example, Zechariah 14:2 says, "For I will gather all nations against Jerusalem to battle; and the city shall be taken, and the houses rifled, and the, women ravished; and half of the city shall go forth into captivity, and the residue of the people shall not be cut off from the city." Then follows the clear statement of the literal return of Christ and His reign over the whole earth. So it is a still future destruction of Jerusalem here described. Revelation 11:2 says, "But the court which is without the temple leave out, and measure it not; for it is given unto the Gentiles: and the holy city shall they tread under foot forty and two months." It is significant that the book of Revelation was written nearly thirty years after that destruction of Jerusalem in A.D. 70, so a later occupation of Jerusalem by the Man of Sin is there foretold.

The Apostles' Question Did Not Concern the Rapture hut the Later Revelation of Christ to Reign

"And what shall be the sign of thy coming, and of the end of the world?" Again we say, here the disciples very properly put two events together – the future coming of Christ and the end of this age. We should note that the apostles are not asking about the time of the rapture when Christ will come into the air above the earth, when the Christian dead will be raised and we that remain will be changed, and all will be caught up together in the air to meet Him (I Cor. 15:51, 52; I Thess. 4:13-18). They did not have in mind this rapture when they asked, "What shall be the sign of thy coming?" For one thing, that rapture only begins and does not consummate His Second Coming. It is only one phase of a series of events which will culminate in Christ's literal, physical return to set foot on the Mount of Olives (Zech. 14:4), to sit on the throne of His glorious reign in Jerusalem (Matt. 25:31).

Remember that the Old Testament says very little about the rapture when Christ will come into the air and catch away His own. But the Old Testament is full of promises about His later literal, bodily return to the earth to restore David's throne, to regather and save Israel. (On this subject, see the author's book, *The Kingdom of Christ,* fifteen chapters, 208 pages, same publisher.) Hence, these Jewish apostles would naturally tend to speak of Christ's coming as being the final phase of His coming and His restoration of the Jewish kingdom.

It was this return in glory with saints and the angels to reign that the disciples discussed in Acts 1:6 when they asked Jesus, "Lord, wilt thou at this time restore again the kingdom to Israel?"

These same apostles throughout the book of Acts referred repeatedly to this literal return of Christ to reign. Peter said in Acts 2:30 that David, "being a prophet, and knowing that God had sworn with an oath to him, that of the fruit of his loins, according to the flesh, he would raise up Christ to sit on his throne..." And again Peter quotes from the second Psalm to prove that the Lord Jesus is to sit on the right hand of the Father "until I make thy foes thy footstool" (Acts 2:34, 35).

Again in Acts 3:20, 21 Peter preaches about Christ's personal return "whom the heaven must receive until the times of restitution of all things, which God hath spoken by the mouth of all his holy prophets since the world began." Surely He spoke of the restitution of the throne of David and of the nation Israel. So he did not have in mind the first phase of Christ's coming, our rapture, when we are caught out to meet Him in the air, but His personal, bodily, and literal return to the earth to reign.

Yet again, the Apostle James, at the great council in Jerusalem, said, "And to this agree the words of the prophets; as it is written,

After this I will return, and will build again the tabernacle of David, which is fallen down; and I will build again the ruins thereof, and I will set it up" (Acts 15:15, 16). Certainly these references are enough to show that the apostles, thinking in terms of the Old Testament prophecies, had in mind Christ's literal return with saints and angels to sit on His throne at Jerusalem, when they asked, "What shall be the sign of thy coming, and of the end of the world?" That coming of Christ to renew the throne of David and set up his kingdom on earth will be the end of the times of the Gentiles, therefore the consummation of the age. So the two statements are properly one. The times of the Gentiles will be fulfilled (Luke 21:24) and the present age will come to a close with the beginning of the personal reign of Christ (Zech. 14:9; Mic. 4:1-8; Dan. 2:44, 45; Rev. 19:11-16).

Remember that Jesus was speaking to Jewish apostles and that this record is given us in Matthew specially for the Jews and about Jesus as "King of the Jews." When the apostles spoke of "the sign of thy coming" (vs. 3), they did not mean what many Gentile Christians in these days mean by such language. These Jewish apostles were looking forward to Christ's visible, personal, glorious return to establish His kingdom on David's throne when they should reign with Him on twelve thrones judging the twelve tribes of Israel (Matt. 19:28; 25:31; etc.). That was the Jewish national viewpoint and naturally so, since promises to the Jews as a nation will not be fulfilled until Christ's bodily return to the earth to reign. But we Gentile Christians in this church age are taught to look forward to the time when Christ will come, at any moment, to catch us up in the air with Him for the wedding supper in Heaven with all the saved of all ages, which must come before He returns with us to reign on the earth. Christ must come FOR His saints before He returns WITH His saints.

Thus you will find in the epistles to the churches of the New Testament constant references to Christ's coming into the air (not down to the earth) to receive His saints (I Cor. 15:51, 52; Phil. 3:20, 21; I Thess. 1:10; 2:19; 3:13; 4:14-17; 5:23; Heb. 12:22, 23; James 5:7-9. Note that each chapter of I Thessalonians closes with warnings about the Second Coming!). On the other hand, the references to the Second Coming found in the Old Testament practically always refer to Christ's return to the earth to reign (Deut. 50:3-6; Ps. 2:6-9; Isa. 4:2-6; 11:1-6; 63:1-6; Jer. 23:5, 6;

Dan. 2:34; 7:13, 14; Zech. 12:10; 13:6; 14:3, 5, 9). To Jews Christ at His Second Coming is "the Sun of righteousness" (Mal. 4:2), the beginning of the glorious millennial day. But to New Testament saints He is to be "the bright and morning star" (Rev. 22:16) who will come at midnight (Matt. 25:6), in the darkest and most sinful period of the world's history. The Bright and Morning Star will appear, then, before the Sun of Righteousness. That is, Jesus will come for us, to raise the Christian dead and transform the Christian living before He returns as the Sun of Righteousness to establish the Jewish kingdom on David's throne. With the above in mind you will see why the rapture of the saints is not discussed more in this chapter. But verses 27 to 30, in this chapter, clearly describe His return in glory with the angels and saints to reign.

The sign the disciples asked for here is not to be a sign of the rapture, not to be a sign of Christ's coming into the air to receive His saints. It is to be a sign of the return of Christ to reign, and we will find later in this same chapter that the sign will occur after the rapture of the saints and will indicate to those enduring the tribulation time when that terrible tragic time will end, when Christ will return to set up His kingdom. There are no signs now by which one can tell when Jesus will come.

Verses 4-8 The Course of the Age

This is a picture of the course of the whole age. Some have supposed that these are signs by which we may know approximately when Christ will return for His saints. We think they are mistaken. Here false christs will arise to deceive many. But this has been true down through the centuries since Christ went away. "Wars and rumours of wars" have plagued the world throughout these nineteen centuries and more. Jesus plainly says, "For all these things must come to pass, BUT THE END IS NOT YET." Wars and rumours of wars are not signs of the end. "For nation shall rise against nation, and kingdom against kingdom." This is a picture of one war and then another, in various parts of the earth, a necessary and inevitable feature of the human governments of weak and sinful men. There can be no world-wide peace because man himself is wicked. The race is fallen.

Other marks of the whole age are famines, pestilences, and earthquakes. This earth has been under a curse since God said to

281

Adam, "Cursed is the ground for thy sake" (Gen. 3:17). The earthquake which occurred when Jesus was on the cross so that certain graves were opened (Matt. 27:51, 52), the earthquakes which are prophesied to occur in the future Great Tribulation (Rev. 16:18), and the earthquake which will occur when Christ returns and His feet stand on the Mount of Olives (Zech. 14:4), are simply manifestations of a troubled nature during the course of this whole age from its beginning till its end.

These events are to be accepted as the ordinary events in the course of this age. They are not signs. Jesus said, "Take heed that no man deceive you... for all these things must come to pass, but the end is not yet" (vss, 4-6). Neither wars, famines, pestilences, nor earthquakes are signs at all of Christ's coming. They simply mark the natural course of this age.

"All these are the beginning of sorrows." Perhaps this means that all the plagues on the earth during the whole age simply point to a greater time of sorrows in the period called the "great tribulation" (vs. 21).

Briefly, the great destruction of Jerusalem in A.D. 70 climaxed the judgment of God on the city and the nation Israel. Smaller and individual griefs, troubles before that time were simply a beginning of sorrows on wicked men, and point toward that destruction. So the wars, pestilences, famines, and earthquakes of this age simply point toward a great time of the wrath of God poured out on the earth in the future tribulation time.

Verses 9-14 Persecutions and False Prophets Mark the Fall of Jerusalem and the Age Culminating in the Great Tribulation

These verses seem to have a particular reference to Jews. Doubtless they were applicable in part to the Jewish apostles to whom they were spoken. Note the statement in verse 9, "...and ye shall be hated of all nations [Gentile] for my name's sake." The apostles were hated, hounded, and persecuted in their effort to carry the Gospel to all the world. But in a much stronger way, we believe these verses will fit a Jewish remnant in the future tribulation time. Certainly some saints and martyrs have died for Christ down through these centuries – from Stephen, stoned to death outside Jerusalem, on down to many, many Christians murdered by communists in Korea and China in recent years.

"And then shall many be offended" – or caused to stumble. Many people who profess faith in Christ will fall into sin, will lose courage. Some professing Christians will betray others to persecution. We may be sure that this would apply to the Spanish Inquisition and to the tremendous persecutions of the Catholic church through the Middle Ages and on into modem times. Now Protestants are killed in Mexico, in Bolivia, and in other Latin American countries.

"And many false prophets shall rise, and shall deceive many" (vs. 11). Think of all the cults and isms. These false prophets would include Mary Baker Eddy, "Pastor" Russell and Judge Rutherford, the Fox sisters (spiritists), Joseph Smith, the founder of Mormonism, and many such. But during the Great Tribulation there will be false prophets even more. It seems to me that the course of the age as pictured in verses 4 to 14 simply leads up to the intensified persecution and plagues of the tribulation time itself.

Jews Enduring to End of Great Tribulation to Be Rescued

"But he that shall endure unto the end, the same shall be saved" (vs. 13). What does it mean? Arminians have often insisted that it meant people would be saved or kept saved by their own enduring, by their holy living. But that interpretation would contradict some of the plainest statements in the Bible like, "For by grace are ye saved through faith; and that not of yourselves: it is the gift of God: Not of works, lest any man should boast" (Eph. 2:8, 9); Again it is promsied, "Verily, verily, I say unto you, He that heareth my word, and believeth on him that sent me, hath everlasting life, and shall not come into condemnation; but is passed from death unto life" (John 5:24). Clearly one who trusts in Jesus Christ is saved, not by works, but by God's grace.

The Scripture makes clear that our salvation is solely on the merits of Jesus Christ and His atonement. "Forasmuch as ye know that ye were riot redeemed with corruptible things, as silver and gold, from 'your vain conversation received by tradition from your fathers; But with the precious blood of Christ, as of a lamb without blemish and without spot" (I Pet. 1:18, 19). How could I be saved by enduring to the end, and at the same time be saved by the precious blood of Christ? How could I be saved by enduring, yet be saved by grace and without Works?

No, the word *saved* here has a different context. Here in Matthew 24:13 Jesus is not speaking of the redemption of a soul. He speaks rather of the rescue of Jews in the midst of the tribulation. That tribulation is plainly described in verses 15 to 21, and verse 22 says, "And except those days should be shortened, there should no flesh be saved." So the word "saved" in verse 13 and the word "saved" in verse 22 refer to the same thing: the salvation or rescue of the flesh of Jewish people during the tribulation time. In mercy God will cut short the tribulation time and will rescue Jews out* of the tribulation. Surely some Jew, greatly tempted and threatened with death in the tribulation time, will read this promise of Jesus with joy and faith. He will hold on to his faith, will not renounce the Saviour, and the time will be cut short and he will be rescued.

It would be a serious mistake to make verse 13 refer to the great plan of salvation for the soul, for thus it would contradict many other plain statements in the Bible showing that salvation is not by works, not by man's goodness or faithfulness or endurance, but by virtue of the blood of Jesus Christ. That salvation is received by penitent faith.

Converted Jews Will Again Preach the Gospel in the Light of the Coming Kingdom

"And this gospel of the kingdom shall be preached in all the world for a witness unto all nations; and then shall the end come." The end of what? The end of the Great Tribulation.

"The gospel of the kingdom"? The same Gospel, of course, the Gospel Paul defined in I Corinthians 15:3, 4, the one Gospel (there is no other – see Gal. 1:6-9). But in the tribulation time just before Christ returns to set up His kingdom, that blessed Gospel of salvation will be colored by and accompanied by the promise of Christ's kingdom. It will be the Gospel preached in the light of the great event about to transpire, the coming of the King.

Who will preach the Gospel after the rapture of the saints when every Christian then in the world will be taken out? "We shall not all sleep, but we shall all be changed, In a moment, in the twinkling of an eye" (I Cor. 15:51, 52). "Then we which are alive and remain shall be caught up together with them in the clouds, to meet the Lord in the air..." (I Thess. 4:17). Who will preach the Gospel after all the living saints will be taken out at the rapture to meet the Lord in the air, before the Great Tribulation?

Part of the answer is given in Revelation 11:3-6. God will have two witnesses whom He will raise up to prophesy, that is, to preach, in the power of the Holy Spirit, for "a thousand two hundred and threescore days," or the period of the Great Tribulation time.

Also, God will have 144,000 of all the tribes of Israel, described in Revelation 7. These are "the servants of our God" (vs. 3). We are told of them in Revelation 12:11 that it will be announced, "And they overcame him by the blood of the Lamb, and by the word of their testimony; and they loved not their lives unto the death." God will have many Jewish converts in the tribulation time, winning souls and giving their testimonies.

And the results of this preaching and testimony? Revelation 7:9 and 14 tell us of "a great multitude, which no man could number, of all nations, and kindreds, and people, and tongues..." and we are told, "These are they which came out of great tribulation, and have washed their robes, and made them white in the blood of the Lamb."

"And this gospel of the kingdom shall be preached in all the world... and then shall the end come." Some people suppose that now the return of Christ for His saints is delayed until we can take the Gospel to every tribe of people in the earth. But this passage does not refer to the present day, but to a future date in the Great Tribulation time, as the context indicates.

Besides, it is clear from many Scriptures that the Gospel has already been preached in every nation. At the first Pentecost after

Christ's ascension, we are told, "And there were dwelling at Jerusalem Jews, devout men, out of every nation under heaven" (Acts 2:5). To the Colossian Christians, Paul wrote of the "gospel; Which is come unto you, as it is in all the world..." (Col. 1:5, 6). Paul wrote to the saints at Rome that "your faith is spoken of throughout the whole world" (Rom. 1:8). Then if the faith of the Christians at Rome was spoken of throughout the whole world, then the whole world had heard the Gospel. So the preaching of the Gospel to all the world for a witness, mentioned in Matthew 24:14, is to occur during the tribulation time. And "the end," which will come soon, will be thereafter, but it will be the personal, bodily return of Christ at the close of the tribulation time.

Certainly now Christ's coming for His saints does not wait for any predicted event. Nothing is clearer than the oft-repeated teachings of Jesus that He may come at any moment, that Christians are constantly to watch, expecting His coming to catch us away with Him (Matt. 24:44; 25:13; Mark 13:32-37).

Verses 15-26 The Great Tribulation for Jews Foretold

Here we have a more definite picture of the Great Tribulation. Verse 21 plainly says, "For then shall be great tribulation." Not an ordinary time of trouble, but the one specially prophesied event "such as was not since the beginning of the world to this time, no, nor ever shall be." To understand this "great tribulation," one should study Daniel 9:24-27, which describes seventy weeks of years which God determined for Daniel's people, Israel. These seventy weeks of years are divided into two periods. The first period, "seven weeks, and threescore and two weeks" (Dan. 9:25), or the period from the command to restore and build Jerusalem in the days of Nehemiah down to the coming of the Saviour, "the Messiah the Prince."

But after that above period, we are told "shall Messiah be cut off." Jesus died, and the Romans under Titus destroyed Jerusalem. Then there is a long period of timeout, when the game does not continue. Israel is dispersed, scattered through the world, not in her own land. The seventieth week of years still waits.

But in the future, there will be another week of seven years. Daniel 9:26 tells us that a prince will come, of the same people who destroyed Jerusalem before, and Daniel 9:27 says, "And he shall confirm the covenant with many [Jews] for one week [of years]: and in the midst of the week he shall cause the sacrifice and the oblation to cease, and for the overspreading of abominations he shall make it desolate, even until the consummation, and that determined shall be poured upon the desolate."

I understand that Scripture to teach that there will rise a prince, a dictator, Antichrist, Man of Sin, who will have a treaty purporting to be for seven years with the Jews, and a remnant of Jews in Jerusalem will again have their sacrifices in some kind of temple at Jerusalem. This will obviously be after the rapture of the saints, that is, after Jesus catches up all the saved into the air to meet Him.

But those sacrifices, that present treaty relationship between the dictator and the Jews, will not long continue. "In the midst of the week," that is, after the first three and a half years of the seven are past, the Man of Sin will commit the "abomination of desolation" which Jesus mentions here in Matthew 24:15, the very thing foretold by Daniel the prophet in Daniel 9:27.

Second Thessalonians 2:3, 4 tells us about this. That dictator called "that man of sin," "the son of perdition" will be one "Who opposeth and exalteth himself above all that is called God, or that is worshipped; so that he as God sitteth in the temple of God, shewing himself that he is God." This wicked man will demand that the Jews stop their worship, will defile the temple, will command that they worship him as God. And this "abomination of desolation" will start 'the Great Tribulation.'

That Great Tribulation time will continue for the last half of Daniel's seventieth week of years. That is, it will be a period of three and a half years, or forty-two months, or 1,260 days. It is often named; and the figures, when all Scriptures are compared, must be taken literally. The Jews will be given into die hand of the Antichrist "until a time and times and the dividing of time," that is, three and a half years (Dan. 7:25). The period is called "a time, and times, and half a time" (Rev. 12:14), It is called "forty and two months" (Rev. 11:2). It is called "a thousand two hundred and threescore days" (Rev. 11:3; 12:6). For further study of this tribulation, see the author's pamphlet, *The Second Coming of Christ in Daniel,* the pamphlet, *Bible Lessons on Revelation,* and the book, *The Coming Kingdom of Christ.*

This period of Great Tribulation and trouble called "the time of Jacob's trouble" (Jer. 30:7) will be God's dealing especially with Israel, allowing persecution and trouble. There will be many plagues on the earth. It will be after all the saved people are taken out. However, many others will be saved during that tribulation time, as we indicated above.

From verse 15 it is clear that Jews would need to run for their lives from Jerusalem. The Man of Sin, or Antichrist, as a second and greater Hitler, will hate Jews like Hitler, and will set out to exterminate them, because they will not agree to worship him as God. A hidden and secret sanctuary will be found by Israelites who flee for their lives from Jerusalem (Rev. 12:14). The woman in Revelation 12 is Israel. We should take these verses as picturing literal persecution of literal Jews, and a literal fleeing for their lives.

Verse 19 does not mean that there is any plague upon childbearing, but only that the woman heavy with child or a woman carrying a baby would be handicapped in fleeing for her life.

Likewise, Jews are to pray "that your flight be not in winter" because of the extra suffering entailed.

"Neither on the sabbath day." It appears that the remnant of Jews in Palestine will form a treaty with the Man of Sin and restore their temple worship and sacrifices. No doubt they will also observe again the Jewish Sabbath, even the Talmudic requirement that one must travel not more than two thousand paces on a Sabbath. Thus orthodox Jews, trying to observe their rules, would, on the Sabbath day, be caught and slaughtered by the raging persecution of the Man of Sin.

"Except those days should be shortened" (vs. 22). I do not think that the tribulation will be less than the prophesied period, but that it will be suddenly, miraculously ended. Otherwise, "there should be no flesh saved," that is, Jews would all be literally killed.

"But for the elect's sake those days shall be shortened." The elect are Israel. This does not refer to salvation, but to the nation of Jews as a chosen people. Nationally, Jews are still near to God and He still has plans for the nation. "Hath God cast away his people? God forbid... God hath not cast away his people which he foreknew" (Rom. 11:1, 2). The nation Israel is still chosen of God, and He will fulfill His plan with her. Remember that the Angel Gabriel promised Mary about Jesus that "the Lord God shall give unto him the throne of his father David: And he shall reign over the house of Jacob" (Luke 1:32, 33). Not just a spiritual Israel, but literal sons of Jacob are included in God's plan for the millennial reign of Christ on earth. Note that term *the elect.* It is the same group as "his elect" in verse 31.

Read carefully verses 23 to 26. They indicate that the Jews, in the midst of the Great Tribulation, will be looking for Jesus Christ, longing for Him. Zechariah 12:10 tells how Jews will receive Jesus when He does appear: "and they shall look upon me whom they have pierced and they shall mourn for him..." When Jesus comes again then "one shall say unto him, What are these wounds in thine hand? Then he shall answer, Those with which I was wounded in the house of my friends" (Zech. 13:6). It is not surprising that, even in the tribulation, Jews will begin to know that they have turned down their own Messiah, and multitudes of Jews will at last begin to get their hearts prepared to receive Jesus, because of the heartless persecution of the Antichrist and the incessant danger and trouble. False prophets will arise in those days to deceive the people (vs. 24). Some will urge Jews to go to this place in the desert or to visit secret chambers where cults worship, hoping to find Christ. But they are not to believe it. For when Jesus comes to end the tribulation, to put down the Antichrist, He will come boldly, visibly from Heaven, with the saints and with clouds of angels. We are told, "Behold, he cometh with clouds; and every eye shall see him..." (Rev. 1:7). Read the description of His descent from Heaven with the armies of Heaven following Him. He will ride upon a white horse, and will come as "KING OF RINGS, AND LORD OF LORDS" (Rev. 19:11-16). So when Christ returns to defeat the armies of the Antichrist as described in Revelation 19:17-21, He will come visibly, boldly, in catastrophic judgment upon His enemies.

All are warned that the coming of Christ in His glory will not be secret (vs. 26). Rather, it will be like a flash of lightning shining from the east to the west (vs. 27). Verse 28 has reference evidently to the battle of Armageddon following which the fowls of the air will all be called together to "the supper of the great God," that is, to feast on the bodies of the men in the army of the Antichrist who will be killed by the sword from the mouth of Christ when He returns (Rev. 19:7-21). The whole world will know when Jesus returns with the armies of Heaven following Him on white horses (Rev. 19:11-16). He will come with clouds (Rev. 1:7), accompanied by angels (Matt. 25:31), by ten thousands of saints (Jude 14). His feet shall stand on the Mount of Olives and cause an earthquake, the mountain dividing in two with a great valley between (Zech. 14:4). He will utterly ruin the armies attacking Jerusalem at that time and take the reign over the whole earth (Zech. 14:9). Mark carefully the teaching of verse 29. The return of Christ will bring to an end the Great Tribulation. The terrible signs in nature of verse 29, sun darkened, stars falling, etc., are mentioned a number of times in the Bible (Isa. 13:9, 10; 24:23; Ezek. 32:7; Joel 2:31; Zech. 14:6, 7; Mark 13:24-26; Luke 21:25; Acts 2:19, 20; Rev. 16:10).

When Jesus so returns to the earth He will come as the Smiting Stone cut out of a mountain without hands; He will smite the great empires and governments of the world, and grind them to powder; and He will set up His kingdom filling the whole earth (Dan. 2:31-45).

Note a distinction: when Jesus comes to take away us who are Christians (the rapture), we will be caught out of this world to meet Jesus in the air. We will "be caught up together with them [the Christian dead] in the clouds, to meet the Lord in the air" (I Thess. 4:17). Of course, that rapture of saints cannot be secret. It will be "with a shout, with the voice of the archangel, and with the trump of God." The resurrection of the Christian dead, the sudden changing of all living Christians, and the miraculous transporting of all of us into the air to meet Christ, could not be a secret. But at least we are not told that the unsaved world will see Jesus at that time. But later, (at the revelation) after the tribulation time, when Christ returns with the saints and angels, He will come so boldly, so visibly, so publicly, that everybody will know it. So Jews in that day need not expect to find Him in some secret hideout "in the desert" or "in the secret chambers" (vs. 26).

Verses 27-31 Christ's Visible, Physical, Literal Return to Reign

Here we have more detailed discussion of the return of Christ, the King, in glory. It is discussed also in Mark 13:24-37 and in Luke 21:25-36.

"As the lightning..." so sudden will Christ's coming be, and as brilliant in His blazing personality.

"For wheresoever the carcase is, there will the eagles be gathered together." This seems to mean simply that wherever Jesus comes on the earth, there will all the people be assembled, or certainly all the saints of God will be gathered together.

"Immediately after the tribulation of those days..." shows that all these things are to come after the tribulation. See the marvelous physical manifestations: the sun darkened, the moon failing, stars falling, and evidently the movement of the heavenly bodies disrupted. Such a mighty impact on the physical universe will be caused by Christ's coming to take over His reign on the earth.

"Then shall appear the sign of the Son of man..." Here, at last, is the direct answer to the question in Matthew 24:3. The disciples said, "Tell us... what shall be the sign of thy coming, and of the end of the world?" or more properly, the consummation of the age. The disciples did not have in mind a series of signs that would appear before the rapture, to warn us of Christ's coming. No, they had in mind one sign, and Jesus had in mind one sign, long after the rapture, even after the tribulation time, when He Himself should appear in the heavens, and return. "All the tribes of the earth... shall see the Son of man coming in the clouds of heaven with power and great glory." What heavenly brightness, what signs in the heavenly universe when Jesus Himself with saints and angels begins His triumphant descent to the earth!

Again let me insist that this Olivet discourse has nothing to do with signs whereby Christians may know when Jesus will come for His own. The Lord Jesus purposely left that time of His coming for the rapture to call out His saints a secret. It is always imminent; that event might occur at any moment. There are no prophesied events that must precede it. There are no signs by which anyone can tell it approaches. It is an event concerning which we are repeatedly told that no one knows the day or the hour.

But after a remnant of Jews enters into a measured period of time called the Great Tribulation, which is plainly described as three and a half years, or forty-two months, or twelve hundred and sixty days in duration, naturally signs would be in order about the return of Christ with saints and angels after the rapture, and after the tribulation. It is then that the sign of Christ's coming will appear in the heavens. But there are no signs now and can be none until the Great Tribulation time.

Christ's Angels to Regather Every Living Jew to Palestine

The miraculous regathering of living Israel to Palestine is told ill verse 31, "he shall send his angels." That is, Zionism will not bring the whole nation of Jews back to Palestine; the angels of God will gather these "elect," chosen people, and bring them back to their own land.

That regathering of Israel is often foretold in the Old Testament. See particularly Deuteronomy 30:1-6, where we are clearly told of the repentance of Israel, the miraculous regathering of the people, including every living Jew, and their conversion.

That regathering is described also in Jeremiah 23:3-8. Jesus Christ there is described as "a righteous Branch" unto David. He as "a King shall reign and prosper, and shall execute judgment and justice in the earth."

That regathering of Israel is also clearly told in Ezekiel 36:24-28, also in Ezekiel 37:21-28. And the marvelous reign of Jesus Christ over His people, Israel, is described in Isaiah, chapter 11.

How this prophesied regathering of Israel contrasts with the present literal nation Israel constituted in 1948! This handful is coming back now, but in the future, God's angels will bring back every living Jew! These came in unbelief. But God will bring back Israel and her people shall be converted, a nation in a day. "And so all Israel shall be saved" (Rom. 11:26). The present relatively small group of Jews in Palestine is not the fulfillment of this prophecy.

This handful of Jews, coming back naturally, in unbelief, could not possibly be the fulfillment of the promised regathering of every Jew, brought back by angels to Palestine, there to know Christ and love Him, and to dwell in perfect peace in Palestine.

When we speak of the regathering of the Jews, we do not refer to dead Jews. Both Jew and Gentile alike, who die without Christ, are eternally lost and will get no second chance. But living Jews will be brought back to Palestine and converted.

Verses 32-35 The Parable of the Fig Tree: The Race of Jews Cannot Be Destroyed

"Now learn a parable of the fig tree..." Some say that the fig tree always pictures Israel; therefore, to see a remnant of Israelites back in Palestine is a sign. Not so. What do verses 32 and S3 mean? They mean that when Jews then living in the tribulation and at the close of the tribulation "shall see all these things," that is, the appearance of Christ and angels and the saints all coming from Heaven, and shall see the angels regathering every Jew out of every nation under Heaven to bring them back to Palestine, then one may know that Christ's kingdom "is near, even at the doors." The events which will close the tribulation are positive signs that Christ will immediately appear and set up His kingdom. That is all the parable means. Certainly none of us now Christians on earth, before the rapture, can see any of these signs, because they will not occur until "immediately after the tribulation of those days" (vs. 29).

Verse 34 is difficult. "...This generation shall not pass, till all these things be fulfilled." What does "this generation" mean? A note in the Scofield Bible comments:

Gr. *genea,* the primary definition of which is, "race, kind, family, stock, breed." (So all lexicons.) That the word is used in this sense here is sure because none of "these things," i.e. the worldwide preaching of the kingdom, the great tribulation, the return of the Lord in risible glory, and the «gathering of the elect, occurred at the destruction of Jerusalem by Titus, A.D. 70. The promise is, therefore, that the generation – nation, or family of Israel – will be

293

preserved unto "these things"; a promise wonderfully fulfilled to this day.

I agree.

Certainly Jesus did not mean that the people then living would not pass away "till all these things be fulfilled," except in type. In a sense, all these things were fulfilled in the destruction of Jerusalem. Jews then entered into a time of great tribulation and trouble, as Jews will again in the Great Tribulation. Jews then ran for their lives, as Jews will do again in the Great Tribulation. In one sense, the destruction of Jerusalem fulfilled all these prophecies about the Great Tribulation. But they did not perfectly fulfill the promise. However, this race of people, the Jews, will not pass away. The Jews cannot be destroyed. Hitler and many other enemies have tried it. So will the Antichrist try it, but he will not succeed. This race of people will not be destroyed, even up till the time Christ comes. I The Jew is indestructible because he is chosen of God for a future purpose.

"Heaven and earth shall pass away, but my words shall not pass away." Thus Jesus seems to close the somewhat consecutive and orderly prophecy about the course of the age (vss. 4-14), about the Great Tribulation (vss. 15-26), about Christ's personal return in glory (vss. 27-31), then the exhortation that Jews in the tribulation time seeing these things which will occur at the close of the tribulation may know that Christ is near. Now Jesus says concerning the whole passage that His words are to be taken with deadly seriousness. They are infallible and perfect words. Heaven and earth shall pass away, but the words of Jesus Christ shall never pass away. In a sense this closes the progressive order of the prophecy. Now will come some comments and exhortations regarding the whole passage.

Verses 36-41 Christ's Coming to Receive Us to Be Sudden, Unexpected, Without Signs to Presage It

"But of that day and hour knoweth no man, no, not the angels of heaven, but my Father only." The apostles then alive could not know when Christ would return. They could not know about that particular day of His coming to reign, and of course they could not know when the rapture or the whole group of events of the Second Coming would occur. No man then living could know. The angels of Heaven did not know. In Mark 13:32 Jesus included Himself in the statement: "neither the Son." Jesus Himself, in His body of humiliation, having emptied Himself of some of the outward manifestations of His deity and having taken on Himself the form of a servant, did not then know when He would return to the earth. So we understand the Scriptures to say.

And how could we possibly know when Christ will return? The one clearest matter in all Christ's teaching about His Second Coming is that no one can know when it will occur. This matter is so important that it is reiterated again and again in Matthew. See in this chapter verses 34, 42, and 44. See Matthew 25:13; Mark 13:32, 33, and 35 to 37. It is part of the perversity of the carnal human nature that we seek to learn what God has chosen to keep secret. But the angels in Heaven do not know, and Christ in the flesh did not know when He would return.

Jesus perfectly knew the Old Testament and so, we suppose, do the angels. Therefore there is nothing in the Old Testament Scriptures from which anyone can find any signs that will indicate when Jesus will return. It is folly, then, to count dates in Daniel, or to make a day mean a year, as many heretics have done. What angels do not know and what Christ Himself did not know when in the flesh, surely we are not intended to know.

In Acts 1:6 and 7 we learn that, after the resurrection of Christ, the apostles asked Him, "Lord, wilt thou at this time restore again the kingdom to Israel?" He answered, "It is not for you to know the times or the seasons, which the Father hath put in his own power." Here we are clearly told that it is plainly not intended for Christians to know the future, particularly about Christ's return and the setting up of His kingdom. Those things are secret. God has planned it that way. Christians are not to know them. There are no Scriptures, no signs, no methods of computation by which a Christian can know when Christ will return.

On this matter see my book, *The Coming Kingdom of Christ*, chapter 14, "No Signs of Christ's Coming."

"But as the days of Noe were, so shall also the coming of the Son of man be" (vs. 37). It is a mistake to use this passage as if it gave some signs or marks to distinguish the closing days of the age. Not so. What Jesus is saying is simply that in the days of Noah the flood came so suddenly and unexpectedly that people went on with the normal routine of life, "eating and drinking, marrying and giving in marriage, until the day that Noe entered into the ark, And knew not until the flood came, and took them all away." There is nothing wrong in eating and drinking, in marrying and giving in marriage. Not a word here is said about the sinfulness in the days of Noah, but only that the flood came so suddenly and unexpectedly. It could not be foreseen. "So shall also the coming of the Son of man be."

Consider verses 40 and 41. Does this refer to the rapture, or later to Christ's physical return in glory to reign? I think that verses 36 to 51 speak of the whole event of Christ's coming, and so verses 41 and 42 would refer to the rapture. At that time two people will be in the field, unsuspecting, till suddenly one is snatched away. Two women will be grinding at the mill. Suddenly one will be taken away and the other left. Christians will be taken; unconverted sinners will be left.

This is a picture of a great separation. Some Bible teachers think it is a picture of the separation at the close of the tribulation time when the wicked are all gathered out by the angels like the tares, as taught by Jesus in Matthew 13:36 to 43, and like the bad fish, as taught by Jesus in Matthew 13:47-50. That separation will take place and this passage could refer to either that occasion or the separation which occurs at the rapture. However, for many reasons it appears that Jesus here speaks of the rapture which will come so suddenly. In the tribulation time there will be no mystery about when Jesus will return. It will be three and one half years or 1,260 days after the "abomination of desolation" when the Man of Sin appears in the temple and claims to be God. That is a definite event and time could be counted. The time for the Saviour to return in glory with His saints and angels will not be a mystery then, as it is now a mystery just when He will return into the air to call away His saints for the wedding in Heaven. It is His coming as a thief in the night which is uncertain as to time. His open, bold coming as a King will not be so uncertain.

The passage which follows this in verses 45 to 51 speaks, I think, of the coming of Christ for His saints. It seems quite certain that the parable of the ten virgins, following this (Matt. 25:1-13), speaks of the coming of Christ and the rapture of His saints. The wedding cannot take place before the rapture. With these things in mind, I believe that the separation mentioned here (vss. 40, 41) is that which will occur among the living when Jesus comes for His saints.

"One shall be taken, and the other left" (vss. 40, 41). Those taken certainly include all the saved alive in the world. The Bible does not teach "the split rapture," so called. Instead, the Scripture plainly says, "We shall not all sleep, but we shall *all* be changed, In a moment, in the twinkling of an eye, at the last trump" (I Cor. 15:51, 52). Again Paul, divinely inspired, said, "Then we which are alive and remain shall be caught up..." (I Thess. 4:17). When Christ comes He will get all that are His own. Those left are the unsaved. In the parable of the ten virgins, the virgins which have no oil picture the unsaved. The coming of the Saviour will be so sudden no one will have a chance to get ready. Fathers will leave sons; wives will leave husbands. What a tragic separation of loved ones! But those who are not ready should be warned and get ready in time.

A similar passage in Luke 17:34 to 36 mentions night with two in bed, early morning with two women grinding together, and midday with two men in the field together. Now see how this fits with Matthew 24:27 and with Jesus' coming as sudden as the lightning from the east to the west! At one moment when Christ Comes, it will be night on parts of the earth; it will be nearly morning on other parts of the earth; it will be in the midst of the workday on other parts of the earth. Thus, long before Galileo or Columbus or Magellan, Jesus knew that the world was round and that it is night on one part of the earth while it is day on another part. How meticulously accurate is this inspired and infallible Word of God!

In the parable note verse 43, "But know this, that if the goodman of the house had known *what watch* the thief would come, he would have watched, and would not have suffered his house to be broken up..." The night was divided into four watches according to the custom of the Roman army, which then ruled the world and occupied Palestine. This division of the night into watches is more expressly stated in Mark 13:35, 36 which say, "Watch ye therefore: for ye know not when the master of the house cometh, at even, or at midnight, or at the cockcrowing, or in the morning: Lest coming suddenly he find you sleeping."

Note that the watches were the evening watch, from sundown to approximately nine o'clock; the midnight watch, from nine till midnight; the cockcrowing watch, from midnight to approximately three o'clock; and the morning watch, from three o'clock till sunup. Consider the implication. Jesus warned that His coming could be anytime after He went away. At least we may say that from Pentecost on, the return of Christ has been a constant possibility. New Testament Christians openly expected the return of Christ. Paul, writing by divine inspiration, expressed this legitimate and proper hope: "for the trumpet shall sound, and the dead shall be raised incorruptible, and WE shall be changed" (I Cor. 15:52). Note the pronoun "we." He expected to be among the living when Christ returned. And he was obeying the plain command of Jesus Christ in so expecting. Again in I Thessalonians 4:17 he was moved to write, "Then WE which are alive and remain shall be caught up together with them [the Christian dead] in the clouds, to meet the Lord in the air..." So we can say that for more than nineteen hundred years there has been a possibility of Christ's coming.

All this period of time until Christ does actually come to take away His saints could be divided into four watches in this parable of Jesus. If Christ should come after two thousand years, for example, then each watch would be a period of five hundred years. At any rate, Jesus clearly says that no one could tell then whether He would come in the first five hundred years, or the second five hundred years, or the third five hundred years, or the fourth five hundred years. In other words, though we do not know how long are the watches of this long night until Jesus comes, .yet we are certainly told emphatically that no one knows even in what watch Jesus will come. We may now be in the last watch, or we may be in the second or third – no one knows I You see, no one knows the day, nor the hour, nor the times, nor seasons (Acts 1:7), nor even in what century Jesus will come. That is hidden and Jesus plainly expected it to stay hidden.

Those who try to pry out signs of Christ's coming, whether they adduce their signs from falling meteors as did the Millerites, or from some manipulation of the figures in the book of Daniel, as have Seventh-Day Adventists and others sometimes, or from measurements of the Great Pyramid as have the British Israelites, or from wars, apostasy, and sin, are all mistaken. Jesus Christ plainly taught us that no one is to know the times nor the seasons. No one is to know the day nor the hour. People who look for such signs violate the plain intent of Deuteronomy 29:29. "The secret things belong unto the Lord our God: but those things which are revealed belong unto us and to our children for ever, that we may do all the words of this law."

Verses 42-51 Looking for Christ's Coming Greatest Incentive for Godly Living and Soul Winning

Compare this parable with that Jesus gave in Luke 19:11-27 where more details are given. Certainly the general teaching is the same. Christ has gone away to receive from His father the kingdom. When His enemies are made His footstool Jesus will return to reign. His coming will be sudden, unexpected. Notice the reward in verse 47. Compare it with that mentioned in Matthew 25:21, 25, and Luke 19:17-19.

What a solemn exhortation is given in verses 42 and 46. A Christian is to "watch therefore: for ye know not what hour your Lord doth come." Jesus may come today! We are told, "Therefore be ye also ready: for in such an hour as ye think not the Son of man cometh." If we have any work to do, any loved one to win to Christ, any neighbor to solemnly warn, then in Jesus' name let us do it now! In some hour when we think not, the Son of man will come.

The solemn warning in verse 44 was repeated by the Saviour many times. See Matthew 25:13, Mark 13:35, 37, and Luke 21:34, 36. With verses 40 and 41 compare Luke 17:34-36. The best Christians in the world are not expecting the coming of the Saviour as they ought. "In such an hour as ye think not" (vs. 44), the Saviour said, He will come. Remember that of the ten virgins, the five who were really wise and had oil in their lamps, yet slumbered and slept (Matt. 25:5). We cannot know when the Saviour is coming. If we make any plans at all for tomorrow we are likely to be surprised, so let us make only such plans as we will be glad to have broken when He comes. Let us watch and pray and beware lest His coming find us unaware.

The duties of faithful and wise Christians are indicated in verses 45 to 51. How sad it will be for one who is a servant of God but is worldly and ambitious and occupied with the things of this world and not looking for his Master from Heaven! Those who honestly work for Jesus and occupy till He comes may expect Him to make them "ruler over all his goods" (vs. 47). I take it to mean that those who are faithful now in carrying out the will of God will reign with Jesus when He returns.

But some are "evil servants" (vs. 48). Does this refer to saved people? I do not know. Certainly the implication is that even a Christian who goes into worldliness and sin, neglecting to do Christ's work, will be wholly unprepared to face Jesus, and will be ashamed before Him and will be punished by Him.

Consider I John 2:28: "And now, little children, abide in him; that, when he shall appear, we may have confidence, and not be ashamed before him at his coming." Oh, may we abide in Him and be unashamed when He comes.

This intimates a great spiritual truth: those who really look for Jesus' coming will tend to purify their lives. "And every man that hath this hope in him purifieth himself, even as he is pure" (I John 3:3). Certainly those who look for Christ's coming at any moment know that the time is short in which we may win souls, and those who are really in their hearts looking for Christ's coming (not simply arguing about it, but looking for His coming and expecting it) will be more urgent about soul winning.

It is certainly suggestive that the greatest soul winners this world has ever seen have been premillennial. It was so about Spurgeon, Moody, R. A. Torrey, J. Wilbur Chapman, Billy Sunday. It is so about Billy Graham today. I know the pastors of what I believe to be the ten or twelve greatest soul-winning churches in the world, and they are all premillennial and teach and preach that Jesus may come at any moment. I have known most of the great evangelists in thirty years in America and England, and almost without exception they preached and believed that Jesus may come at any moment. So an honest and earnest looking for Jesus tends to help Christians be about the business committed to us by the dear

Saviour whom we shall soon see and to whom we must report. Oh, may it be not in shame, but with His blessed approval over souls won!

I cannot refrain from saying here that the date-setters often miss the blessed impact of this premillennial truth. Those who spend all their time trying to prove from news reports and otherwise that they know just when Christ will come often use their statistics and reports as an excuse for their defeat and powerlessness and for the few souls they win! The way to have the blessed purifying and inspiring effect of the blessed hope of Christ's coming in one's life is to look for Jesus' coming daily, just because He said He might come, and He commanded us to watch! Then, Christian, watch! In a day that you think not, the Son of man will come.

MATTHEW XXV

Verses 1-13 Parable of the Ten Bridesmaids

This is another of "the kingdom of heaven" parables, parables explaining the future kingdom of Christ on earth, either the mystery form of the kingdom at present (Matt. IS: 11) or, as I prefer to think of it, showing the course of this age and events that come before the kingdom.

Our Lord here illustrates the state of affairs at one point before the kingdom of Heaven is to be set up. That point is the time of the rapture when Christ will come into the air to receive His saints (I Thess. 4:16, 17). This is plainly told in verse 13. The illustration is that of bridesmaids (virgins) going out to meet the bridegroom. Jesus Himself is the Bridegroom according to His own words in Matthew 9:15. All the saints are to be presented to Christ "as a chaste virgin" (II Cor. 11:2). With our resurrection bodies and glorified spirits we are to meet Him "not having spot, or wrinkle, or any such thing" (Eph. 5:27).

It is important to notice that in this parable nobody is mentioned but the ten virgins. The bride is not mentioned; the guests at the wedding are not mentioned. All the people who will be concerned about the rapture of the saints are represented by these ten virgins, five wise and five foolish. Let us learn a lesson by what Jesus omits as well as by what He mentions.

Elsewhere, husbands are commanded to love their wives, "even as Christ also loved the church, and gave himself for it" (Eph. 5:25). Thus the church, including all the saved, is pictured as the bride of Christ. But in that passage nothing is said about bridesmaids or guests. Again, in the parable of the wedding feast, when the king made a marriage for his son (Matt. 22:1-14), the king represents the Father; the son represents Jesus Christ; and those who came were called "guests." There no bride is mentioned, no bridesmaids. It must be clear that Christians are pictured in one passage as the bride of Christ, in another as the guests at the wedding, and in this one here as wise bridesmaids. It takes many illustrations to make clear the truths concerning the rapture. On the same principle

302

Christ is called by many terms: The Lion of the Tribe of Judah, the Lamb of God, Immanuel, Christ, Lord, Jesus, the Son of Man, the Son of God. All these are the same holy Person. So the wise virgins, the guests having on the wedding garments, and the bride all picture the same group, the saved.

"Ten *virgins*" Do not make the word *virgin* figurative. Bridesmaids are virgins. The word *virgin* here has no symbolical significance. Some think all represent the saved because the term *virgin* was used, but that is not true. The Bible nowhere makes *virgin* mean a saved person. Be careful about adding figurative and spiritual meanings to the Word of God where the context does not clearly authorize it. God reserved the word *virgin* for a literal use, concerning the mother of His Son when He said, "Behold, a virgin shall conceive, and bear a son, and shall call his name Immanuel" (Isa. 7:14). The five wise virgins represent saved people. The foolish virgins represent unsaved people. The difference was that the wise "took oil in their vessels with their lamps," while the foolish "took no oil with them."

Virgins With Oil Represent Christians: Those Without Oil Represent Lost People

The oil used for lights in the time of Christ was olive oil. The Greek word used here for is in the Greek literally *torches*. The foolish virgins simply took a twisted or plaited wick or torch, possibly of flax, for a temporary light which would soon go out. The wise virgins inserted this torch, as the custom was, in a small vessel of olive oil. The oil was not explosive but being absorbed into the wick would burn with a steady glow. This oil is a symbol of the Holy Spirit and is so used many times in the Bible. The priests were anointed with oil to indicate that they were chosen of God and anointed with, the Holy Spirit for their tasks (Lev. 8:12; I Sam. 10:1; Ps. 89:20; 133:2). Likewise, in Isaiah 61:1, where it was prophesied that Jesus should be endued with Holy Spirit power, the word *anointed* is used (see also Luke 4:18-21). The oil is a type of the Holy Spirit.

303

In this case it refers not to the baptism with the Holy Spirit or being filled with the Spirit as in Acts 1:5; 2:4; 4:31; etc., but to the saving work of the Holy Spirit. All who are regenerated are changed by the Spirit of God, "born of... the Spirit" (John 3:5; see also Titus 3:5). Every saved person has the Holy Spirit in him (Rom. 5:5; 8:9; I Cor. 6:19, 20; II Cor. 6:16). The wise virgins are those who have been born again, regenerated by the Holy Spirit, with the Holy Spirit living in them. They had oil in their vessels. The foolish virgins "took no oil with them," that is, they were never born again; the Holy Spirit did not live in them.

Take care that you be not deceived by those who would make this passage picture the *rupture* of the body of Christ instead of the *rapture*. They sometimes say that the foolish virgins picture converted people who are not spiritual, not filled with the Holy Spirit nor "baptized with the Spirit," and say that all such saved people will be left behind. Sometimes it is even taught that unless one has been sinless and perfect, Christ will leave him behind when He comes for His saints, even though he has been truly converted. Such teaching is altogether contrary to God's Word. God will make us perfect when Jesus comes for us (Phil. 3:20, 21). When Christ comes for His bride, He will not be content to tear off an arm and a leg and leave the body of His beloved. No, all the body of Christ will be taken with Christ.

In fact, the rapture of the saints is a part of the salvation that is purchased for us on the cross. Our bodies earnestly wait "for the manifestation of the sons of God... Because the creature itself [the body] also shall be delivered from the bondage of corruption into the glorious liberty of the children of God." All creation groans, "waiting for the adoption, to wit, the redemption of our body" (Rom. 8:19-23). Our redemption is secured by the death of Christ, and our redemption will not be complete until the body is redeemed. In that sense, bodily healing is in the atonement and perfect health is bought for us all, but we cannot claim it fully until Jesus raises the Christian dead and changes the Christian living. The same Holy Spirit who changes the heart in regeneration raised Christ from the dead and shall "also quicken your mortal bodies" (Rom. 8:11). Not a saved person will be left behind when Jesus comes for His saints; not a single body of the Christian dead will be left behind. "We shall not *all* sleep, but we shall *all* be changed, In a moment, in the twinkling of an eye, at the last trump: for the trumpet shall sound, and the dead shall be raised incorruptible, and we shall be changed" (I Cor. 15:51, 52). The wise virgins with oil picture people saved by the Holy Spirit and indwelt by the Holy Spirit. All such will be caught away with Jesus and taken into the marriage supper when He comes.

"They *all* slumbered and slept" (vs. 5). Here is a strange fact. Wise virgins and foolish virgins alike were found sleeping. Both were guilty. Perhaps in the outward appearance there was little difference. So will it be when Jesus comes. Jesus said, "In such an hour as ye think not the Son of man cometh" (Matt. 24:44). It is probable that the best Christians in the world will be somewhat surprised at the sudden coming of Christ to call away His saints to meet Him in the air, even though they have prayerfully looked forward to that event for years. It is a sad fact, here foretold in the Scriptures, that the churches and Christians in general will not be faithful as they should be when Jesus comes. Countless Christians will be in places they should not be, following sinful occupations, enjoying questionable amusements, keeping company that dishonors Christ, and so will be found 'slumbering and sleeping' at His coming. Many, many warnings are given in the Bible for Christians to beware lest we be ashamed before Him at His coming (I John 2:28), or, to watch and pray lest we enter into temptation (Mark 14:38), or to "take heed to yourselves, lest at any time your hearts be overcharged with surfeiting, and drunkenness, and cares of this life, and so that day come upon you unawares" (Luke 21:34), and similar warnings.

But praise God, these wise virgins with oil in their vessels were not left behind. They had neglected their duty and were doubtless embarrassed. Their lamps were smoky as ours often are. But they arose and trimmed their lamps (vs. 7) and went into the marriage (vs. 10). Saved people, imperfect in character and life, unworthy as we are, will be caught up at the rapture and will go with Christ to the wedding. The deciding feature is fully and solely the oil in the vessels, that is, the Holy Spirit within, as He is within every saved person, coming in at regeneration.

"At *midnight* there was a cry made, Behold, the bridegroom cometh" (vs. 6). The word is weighty for so it will be when Jesus comes. Postmillennialists have taught that after *we* bring in a millennium of righteousness, peace, prosperity, and godliness in the whole world, then Jesus will return, but the Scriptures do not so teach. Jesus will return at midnight, a midnight when the world has war instead of peace, sin instead of righteousness, modernism and worldliness in the churches instead of revivals and the fullness of the Spirit, infidelity instead of faith. When Jesus comes this world is to be at the midnight hour of spiritual darkness. So it is taught elsewhere. When Jesus comes, the field will have many, many tares as well as the wheat (Matt. 13:24-30, 36-43). In the net there will be good fish as well as bad (Matt. 13:47-50). Leaven, that is, wickedness, unbelief, and sin will be in the Lord's meal (Matt. 13:33). Instead of the simple sowing of the seed of the Gospel, the world will be growing trees of denominationalism and the foul birds that take away the seed from the hearts of men will make their homes in the branches (Matt. 13:31, 32). See "every unclean and hateful bird" (Rev. 18:2). See a tree as a willful human dominion ignoring God's rule, in Daniel, chapter 4. Christ's coming into the air to receive His saints is like "the bright and morning star" (Rev. 22:16) which arises in the night.

The Unconverted All Left Behind When Jesus Comes

"*All* those virgins arose, and trimmed their lamps" (vs. 7). The foolish expected to go. One of the saddest truths taught in the Bible is that multitudes expect to go to Heaven who will be disappointed. They depend on their wick of human profession and human righteousness instead of upon the oil of the Holy Spirit, the supernatural birth from above. Relatively, there are few who enter in at the strait gate and many enter into the broad way (Matt. 7:13, 14). Many will recount to the Lord their good works, pleading to enter in (Matt. 7:22, 23), but Jesus will answer back, "I never knew you." The new birth, a supernatural change of heart, is indispensable to a place at the wedding supper. It is pictured here by the oil in the vessels. It is pictured in Matthew 22:11, 12 as the wedding garment. Some try to come in without the wedding garment, but will be cast into outer darkness with weeping and gnashing of teeth (Matt. 22:13). Some will wish to attend the wedding without the oil of salvation but will be left outside.

Proxy religion will not help at that day. Mother's prayers, the absolution offered by priests, the ritual of christening or baptism all Will be unavailing then. The wise virgins had not enough oil for others; the foolish virgins could not borrow.

"They that were ready went in with him to the marriage: and the door was shut" (vs. 10). Christ's coming into the air to receive His saints will be sudden. There will not be time to repent, no time to be saved then and go away with loved ones. This does not mean that those left behind at the rapture can never be saved. According to verse 10, the foolish virgins "went to buy." Afterwards they came again, calling for admittance and presumably they had bought the oil, but the door was shut – not the door of *salvation,* but the door to the *marriage.* The door to the marriage will be shut instantly when Christ receives His saints. Thereafter, those who are saved must stay on the earth in the Great Tribulation time. Those who have rejected Christ and are yet alive when Jesus comes will be left behind. Those yet alive who have not committed the unpardonable sin may be saved if they will. Some such will be saved and some will not, but certainly those yet alive who trust Christ for salvation will be saved. Then those who get the oil of salvation after the Bridegroom comes will be left out of the wedding and remain here on the earth in a terrible time of persecution and darkness until they die naturally, or are killed for their faith in Christ, or until Jesus returns with saints and angels at the end of the Great Tribulation.

Be careful to notice that no Scripture promises a second chance to be saved *after anybody dies without Christ.* The opportunity to be saved during the tribulation time is only to the living. The unscriptural doctrine of one general resurrection and general judgment at the return of Christ is so widespread that it is hard for people to accept the plain, simple teaching of Jesus that the saved will be caught away before the end of this age, and that the world will go on without them for a time before Christ returns to reign, and long before the last judgment of the unsaved dead.

"I know you not" (vs. 12) is simply what a bridegroom would naturally say in an oriental city when, past the midnight hour, unexpected strangers knock at the door for entrance. Without street lights, without modern police protection, in the wee hours of the morning the doors would not be open to unknown and unexpected strangers. The Saviour merely used this to illustrate that the rapture of the saints will be a sudden event and only those who are previously saved will be taken away. Multitudes of others, finding loved ones gone and themselves left behind, will frantically desire to be taken but will be left behind. "The one shall be taken, and the other left." This is the separation pictured in Matthew 24:40, 41.

Therefore, let us heed the solemn application given by the Saviour Himself in verse 13. That verse means we should be ready. Surely its plain implication is that at any moment the Saviour will come to take His own. Only those who have oil in their vessels, the oil of salvation, the abiding Holy Spirit who regenerates and dwells within the believer; only such will be taken away at the rapture and all the unsaved will be left behind.

Verse 13 again reminds us to watch, since we know not when Jesus will come. That clearly means that Jesus may come at any moment, and that no one can, *any sign,* know even approximately when Jesus will come.

Verses 14-30 The Parable of the Talents

This passage should properly be considered along with Luke 19:11-27, where Jesus gives a similar parable. That parable was spoken first on the road approaching Jerusalem (Luke 19:28), a few days before. This parable of the talents is spoken later in Jerusalem. In the Luke parable, we find *pounds* mentioned instead of *talents.* Ten pounds were given to ten servants, one each. There, however, only three are mentioned in particular; two are promised a good reward, with commendation, as here, and one unfaithful servant is condemned.

For Christians, Degrees of Reward at Christ's Coming

This, too, is a "kingdom of heaven" parable. Although those words (vs. 14) are not in the original, yet following the parable of the ten virgins, it is on a like prophetic theme. The parable of the ten virgins pictures the rapture of the saints, the coming of Christ into the air receiving away His loved ones, while this parable pictures His accounting when He returns.

For Christians, does not this represent the same "judgment seat of Christ" before which all of us Christians must appear, "that every one may receive the things done in his body, according to that he hath done, whether it be good or bad" (II Cor. 5:10)? Thus it is clear that God's born-again saints, caught up into Heaven in glorified bodies, already saved, must still be judged, our works made manifest. That judging, not for salvation but for rewards, is clearly pictured also in I Corinthians 3:11-15. There we learn that after the foundation, which is Christ, we should all take care how we build the daily life. All deeds of the Christian will be tried by fire and shown to be "wood, hay, stubble," or "gold, silver, precious stones." If one's work be burned, he shall even in Heaven suffer loss, but "he himself shall be saved; yet so as by fire." But one whose work abides the fire "shall receive a reward." Make sure you see that the two faithful servants represent Christians, already saved, being rewarded for faithfulness.

We do not need to read into every parable many details which are not pictured there. This parable is clearly teaching a truth, that Christians will be judged for their works and rewarded for good works. For most Christians the judging time will be the judgment seat of Christ, after the rapture of saints when we are caught up to meet the Lord in Heaven. I suppose that we will enter into the rewards there assigned us, more definitely when we return with Christ to reign with Him on this earth.

However, in much of the Gospel of Matthew there is a special Jewish emphasis. So Certainly this parable of the talents pictures the judgment of those who live through the tribulation time, and will face Christ after His return.

This is especially clear in the companion parable in Luke 19:11-27. There the returning man, "having received the kingdom" (Luke 19:15), instantly awards positions to faithful servants to rule over five cities, over ten cities, etc., enters into His reign and slays the enemies who would not have Him reign over them (Luke 19:17, 19, 27). Then this parable is a picture of the accounting Jesus will have with those who live through the Great Tribulation time.

If we remember that this parable had special application to the Jews and that most Jews will not be saved until the tribulation time, it seems more understandable that this parable of the talents should discuss rewards for the saved as well as judgment for the unsaved, all in the same passage and parable.

In this same chapter, the parable of the talents is immediately followed by the story of Christ's return in glory, to sit on His throne and judge the living people on the earth.

However, the lesson must not be lost upon us. We, too, must face judgment for our works, and at the judgment seat of Christ when we are already in Heaven with glorified bodies we will see false works burned up and will be approved and receive a reward for good works that abide.

The Special Application to Israel

In this parable of the talents, both the faithful servant and the wicked servant are called servants in Matthew 25:14. The man travelling into a far country "called his *own* servants." As you will see later, the word *servants* here does not necessarily mean saved persons only. Rather, the word *own* is used just as it is in John 1:11, referring to, I think, the Jews, and to others over whom Christ has authority by virtue of His creation of all things. The sinner belongs to Christ, owes allegiance to Christ, even though he does not give it. But in a special way Christ's *own* are the Jews. Jews are the chosen people (Rom. 9:4, 5; 11:1, 2, 28, 29). They were entrusted with the oracles of God. To them were given the law, the rites and ceremonies of the Old Testament, the priesthood, tabernacle, and promises of the coming Messiah. From the Jews, according to the flesh, Christ came. Therefore, this parable seems to be especially for the Jews.

Remember that the Jews as a nation looked forward, not to the return of Christ for His saints and the rapture, but rather for His return to reign, setting up His throne in Jerusalem where David ruled, and the regathering and restoration of Israel. Most Jews will not be saved till after the rapture. It is not strange that in this chapter both viewpoints are given. Saints awaiting the rapture are given the parable of the ten virgins (vss. 1-13), while Jews looking specially for the kingdom are given this parable of the man and his servants and the talents (vss. 14-30).

Israel was accustomed to being spoken of as servants of God, the vineyard of God, sons of God, etc. Note how Christ spoke of two *sons* in Matthew 21:28-32. The one son pictured the harlots and publicans returning and being saved; the other son pictured the Pharisees and scribes who did not repent and would miss the kingdom of God. In Matthew 21:33-45 Jesus gave the parable picturing the Pharisees and scribes, Jewish rulers, as God's husbandmen put over His vineyard. Yet those husbandmen were pictured as being turned out and in the same parable scribes and Pharisees saw themselves pictured as being unsaved. The Old Testament declared, "The vineyard of the Lord of hosts is the house of Israel" (Isa. 5:7). Israel is particularly said to be the servant of God in Isaiah 41:8, 9; 44:1, 2, 21; 45:4; 49:3, and other Scriptures. Speaking to the Syrophenician woman, or Canaanite woman, Jesus called the Jews the *children,* while Gentiles were pictured as *dogs* (Matt. 15:26). Therefore, it seems that in this parable Jesus referred especially to the Jews, and the time of its fufillment will be at the return of Christ to reign.

"And delivered unto them his goods" (vs. 14). God has delivered His goods into the hands of the Jews, in some sense. The Old Testament was written by Jews; the New Testament was written by Jews. The throne which Christ will occupy on His return was the throne of David, a Jewish king. Christ's mother was a Jewess. Apostles who will reign with Christ sitting on twelve thrones judging the twelve tribes of Israel were all Jews. So we need not be surprised to learn that the Jews will be the messengers of the Gospel in the Great Tribulation time. The twelve apostles sent out over Israel to preach the Gospel of the kingdom (Matt. 10:6, 7) were typical of the Jews who will preach the Gospel in the Great Tribulation time. Compare Matthew 10 with Matthew 24 and this becomes evident, particularly Matthew 10:16-23 compared with Matthew 24:9-14. Revelation 12:17 tells how Satan will hate the remnant of the seed of the woman, Israel, "which keep the commandments of God, and have the testimony of Jesus Christ." Jews will have in the tribulation time "the testimony of Jesus." Also the two witnesses of Revelation 11:3,4 will probably be Jews and they will give their testimony: "They shall prophesy a thousand two hundred and threescore days, clothed in sackcloth." You see that this parable has a special application to the Jews. However, the lessons herein are good for all of us. Christ deals with Jews and Gentiles alike on the plan of salvation and in the matter of rewards.

Notice "to every man according to his several ability" (vs. 15). Men are not equal in abilities. God does not expect the same of all men. God expects faithfulness in all, but He gives to some five talents, to some two talents, and to some, one. Of those to whom He gives more, God expects more (Luke 12:47; Matt. 10:15; 11:22, 24; Mark 6:11; Luke 10:12, 14).

Both Saved and Lost Warned of Accountability to God

It is noticeable here that in this particular case Jesus does not make a distinction between salvation and rewards. We know that salvation is wholly of grace, "Not of works, lest any man should boast" (Eph. 2:9), and "that whosoever believeth in him should not perish, but have everlasting life" (John 3:16). But that is not the special truth that Jesus is teaching here. He is teaching accountability to God. However, it is obvious that the men who received the five talents and the two talents, and by loving industry doubled them, represent saved men who work for Christ. The fact that they appropriated the gifts of God, claimed Him as Lord willingly, tried to do His will, brought their fruits back to Him with rejoicing, indicates that they represent saved people. On the other hand, the man who had one talent "went and digged in the earth, and hid his Lord's money" (vs. 18). Verse 24 shows that the one-talent man in this case had no love for his master, no confidence in him, no surrender to his will. This is not a picture of a saved man.

Here is a strange truth about the tribulation time. Those who serve God in that time of great trouble, heartache and persecution will do so from the heart. Today there may be many hypocrites in the churches, professing publicly and openly to be better Christians than they really are, or claiming, like Judas Iscariot, to be children of God when they are children of the Devil. Today men are praised by many when they are thought to be good Christians. In the Great Tribulation time it will be sadly different. The better Christian one is, the better prospect he will have of dying for his faith. Then the Antichrist "shall wear out the saints of the most High" (Dan. 7:25), shall 'make war with the saints and prevail against them' (Dan. 7:21; Rev. 13:7). Multitudes will be slain for their faith (Zech. 14:1, 2; Matt. 24:9, 22; Rev. 11:7; 13:15; 20:4). It will be counted an honor, then, to wear the mark of the Antichrist in the hand or forehead (Rev. 13:16). Atheism will be popular. Jews will be despised as will all Christians, and there will be no reason for anybody to claim to be a Christian unless really in his heart he is.

Thus, in the Great Tribulation time, as in other times of martyrdom and persecution, those who claim to be Christians will be much truer than they are in these easy and prosperous times when it is popular to be called a Christian. Hypocrisy is the sin of popular religion, not the sin of persecuted Christianity, not a sin of martyrs. For that reason, during the tribulation time, when those pictured here are destroyed, those who are openly and publicly out and out for God, will be really so in their hearts. The one who is pictured by the slothful servant, despising his lord and not serving him, will be the unsaved man.

The Faithful Will Be Rewarded By Ruling With Christ

Note the commendation which the Master gave to the two servants, one who had five talents and added five more and the man who had two talents, increased to two more. Both are commended alike, word for word, for faithfulness (vss. 21 and 23), and promised a similar reward. In God's sight the great virtue is faithfulness. For this reason we will find many of the last will be first and the first, last (Matt. 19:30; 20:16). Those who appear to be great now will be excelled by many others who do not appear great in the eyes of men. God knows all them who are His and He will give honor where honor is due, to the faithful who have done their part with what God gave them. Blessed is the man who has been faithful in a few things; he will be ruler over many things.

Notice the reward given, "I will make thee ruler over many things." Remember, this parable pictures Jesus returning to reign on the earth. Christians will reign with Christ on the earth (II Tim. 2:12; Rev. 2:26, 27; 5:10; 20:4). "We shall reign with him on the earth." This is specially true about the Jews (Isa. 14:1, 2). The twelve apostles will sit on thrones (Matt. 19:28) and others, doubtless, will rule as princes with Christ (Isa. 1:26; 32:1). The blessings which will belong to the saints of the tribulation time are described in Revelation 7:14-17. That reward will be on the earth during the personal reign of Christ, when the tribulation is over. It is clear that those saved during the tribulation time will miss the rapture in Heaven, but there will be no distinction later between them and the saints who were ready at the rapture, no distinction after Christ returns and all the saints are together in His kingdom on the earth. Each shall then be rewarded according to his due and reign with Christ.

The Wicked and Slothful Servant

Consider the judgment of the unfaithful servant. His charges against the master in verses 24 and 25 show his wicked heart. This represents the attitude of unsaved people toward Christ. Hating Him, they accuse Him. Satan always teaches man that God is unjust, that God requires more than is right, that it does not pay to serve the Lord. He deceived the first man and woman in the Garden of Eden, indicating that God was withholding good things from them (Gen. 3:1-6). Backslidden Jews sinned in believing the slander, "It is vain to serve God" (Mai. 3:14). Wicked people do not like to believe in a Hell, do not like to admit the fact of sin, particularly hate the doctrine of human depravity. They do not like the teaching that men must be born again. Men like to claim themselves good. So this man claimed himself honest and despised his master. Sinners even deny God's right as Creator and try to rule God out of His own universe. This is really the secret background of those who believe in evolution and on one excuse or another try to do away with a personal God and a personal creation of man by direct act of God, likewise those who want to do away with the doctrine of a literal Hell of fire and eternal torment. Men would make the God of the Bible "...an hard man, reaping where thou hast not sown, and gathering where thou hast not strawed." That is a slander against a good God and shows the perversity of a human heart

The answer of Jesus teaches that slothfulness and wickedness are one. It is a sin to be lazy. Not to serve God with all your heart, mind, soul, and strength is a sin. Consider verses 26 and 27, One who is not willing to acknowledge Christ as Lord should not breathe God's air, should not eat the food God provides, should not enjoy the blessings God pours out. It is foolishness and wickedness

314

to try to escape responsibility to God after He has created us, provided for us, and given all things that we need day by day. The man did not acknowledge his master as being just nor acknowledge his duty to him. This shows that the man pictured here is unsaved. Incidentally, it shows the importance of the great fundamental doctrines of direct creation, responsibility to God, judgment, and eternity. Men who do not believe these fundamental doctrines are not ready to be approached on the plan of salvation.

No man need think he can properly win souls unless he preaches those truths which bring about conviction, a sense of responsibility to God, and repentance for sin. Therefore preachers should be bold, direct, plain, and emphatic in Bible teaching and condemnation of sin, warning sinners of judgment. It is not enough to preach the love of God. We must also preach that "our God is a consuming fire" (Heb. 12:29); that "it is a fearful thing to fall into the hands of the living God" (Heb. 10:31); that "it is appointed unto men once to die, but after this the judgment" (Heb. 9:27). In the Scripture, law comes before grace, conviction before repentance, condemnation before reconciliation. Let no one minimize the importance of the great fundamental truths of Christianity, the deity of Christ, His claim on all men, the certainty of judgment on sin, the universal depravity of mankind, the need of being born again. Then one can preach the love of God, too, and it will bring results. One can preach Christ's sacrifice and offer of mercy after preaching judgment, and find many who feel their need.

Jesus Opposed Socialism and Marxist Ideology

The foolish idea which communists and socialists have, that it is wrong for one man to have more than another, is certainly exploded by the words of Jesus in verses 28 and 29. Some people have more because they can be trusted with more, because they work harder. God intended that the thrifty, the hard-working, the intelligent, the energetic, should have more than the lazy, shiftless, the immoral, and the unreliable. Money and other property is a trust from God and should be so used. The whole socialistic philosophy is contrary to Scripture. The very genius of it is against God. For this reason communism generally ends up in atheism, as has been so terribly the case in Russia. The communist is not only against man, seeking to destroy governments that are, to seize property unlawfully, to violate human rights, but he is against God, against the Bible, and against those virtues which build and maintain society. God never intended that the arrogant, the lazy, the rebellious, like this one-talent man, should have rule along with the thrifty, the hard-working, the loyal citizen. The whole trend of the radical labor union movement, to destroy faith in the capitalistic system, to deride the rights of executives, to make light of the value of brains and energy and initiative, is foolish and unscriptural. God does not intend that the lazy laborer, demanding a thirty-hour week and increased wages, begrudging every bit of toil, seeking to slow down production, deriding authority, sometimes seizing or destroying property, should have the same responsibility and authority as the man who has prepared himself, paid the price in toil, energy, planning, and thrift. Those ought to rule who have proved themselves worthy to rule.

Compare verse 30 with Matthew 22:13, II Peter 2:17 and Jude 13. There are plenty of Scriptures which plainly foretell the awful torment of the unsaved and the eternal separation from God.

If the parable of the talents has any special application to Jews during the tribulation time, then the one-talent man must picture rebellious Jews, and verse 30 must indicate that some of the living Jews will not be saved at the return of Christ. This is true. Romans 11:26 says that "all Israel shall be saved," that is, every living Jew who will be left alive on the earth. But Ezekiel 20:33-38 shows that upon Christ's return He will meet Israel out in the wilderness and there He will "purge out from among you the rebels, and them that transgress against me: I will bring them forth out of the country where they sojourn, and they shall not enter into the land of Israel." So rebels will first be purged out and then "all Israel," those left alive, will be saved.

Verses 31-46 Christ to Sit on Throne at Jerusalem Judging Living Gentiles After Return to Reign

This is still the discourse on Mount Olivet (Matt. 24:3) which fills chapters 24 and 25 of Matthew.

Notice that this passage is not a parable but plain and exact prophecy, foretelling in the words of the Saviour what will actually occur on His return to the earth. The time discussed is the same as that pictured in the last parable, "When the Son of man shall come in his glory, and all the holy angels with him."

Verse 31 settles beyond any doubt just when Christ will sit on the throne of His glory. It is at His coming in glory. The throne of Christ will be at Jerusalem (Mic. 4:7, 8), David's throne, (II Sam. 7:16; Isa. 9:7; Luke 1:32, 33).

Verse 32 begins the story of a great judgment. However, this is not the last great judgment. It is not "the general judgment." A little comparison shows that it is not the same judgment as that discussed in Revelation 20:11-15. This judgment in Matthew 25 is at the return of Christ to reign. The judgment in Revelation 20 is *after the close* of the thousand years' reign. This judgment is of the people of all nations alive on the earth when Christ returns. Nothing is said here about the raising of the dead. But the judgment in Revelation 20 is of the unsaved dead. Here three classes are mentioned, "sheep," saved Gentiles, "goats," unsaved Gentiles, and "brethren," the Jews. The judgment in Revelation 20 is only of lost people, and all are condemned, judged "according to their works." The resurrection of the Christians will have taken place a thousand years before (Rev. 20:5, 6). This judgment in Matthew 25 will take place on the earth, evidently with Jesus sitting on the throne of His glory at Jerusalem. The judgment in Revelation 20 will take place somewhere out in space with Jesus on a Great White Throne "from whose face the earth and the heaven fled away" (Rev. 20:11). Certainly the two judgments are not the same. Those cast into Hell here will later be raised ("death and hell delivered up the dead which were in them" – Rev. 20:13), and be condemned publicly at the Great White Throne judgment.

"All nations" (vs. 32) does not indicate a judgment of nations as separate entities. It does not mean that one nation will be saved entirely and another entire nation be condemned. Rather it means a judgment of people, individuals of all nations. Nations cannot be condemned to depart into fire (vs. 41). Nations do not visit the sick, give people water or food, etc., and are not rewarded with everlasting blessings. No other government will stand after Christ comes to set up His kingdom, as the Scripture explicitly says (Dan. 2:35, 45). The government of Christ excludes and must destroy every other government. No, this judgment is of individuals, of all nations, living people who will come through the Great Tribulation.

Note that at this time the battle of Armageddon will just have been completed and all the armies of the Antichrist will have been destroyed (Rev. 19:20, 21). Here the civil population of the earth will be judged, saved Gentiles (sheep), unsaved Gentiles (goats), and "brethren" of Christ (Jews). Notice again that what people do in the Great Tribulation time for Christ and for His people will truly represent their hearts. It will not be a time where people could hope to gain anything by deceit and hypocrisy. Men will suffer for taking the part of the Jews, suffer for witnessing for Christ. Those who hate the Antichrist, who defy him and risk his wrath, those who take up for God's chosen people, the Jews, will do so because of truly Christian hearts. Men could not be judged now by their religious acts, since it is popular to appear good, to appear Christian, and it is unpopular to appear an atheist, to appear immoral. The contrary will be true during the Great Tribulation time. Those who take the part of God's people Israel will do so because they are led of God and do it from sincere hearts.

Revelation 12:6 tells how the woman representing Israel will flee into the wilderness and how God will have prepared her a place "that they should feed her there a thousand two hundred and threescore days," and Revelation 12:14 and 16 refer to the same thing. God will prepare a place for fleeing Jews, running for their lives from the Antichrist. Those fleeing from Jerusalem as they are commanded to do when the abomination of desolation takes place (Matt. 24:15-21) will find Gentile friends whose hearts God has opened to receive them and protect them. Verses 34 to 40 show how these Christian Gentiles will be received and rewarded on His return for taking the part of his beloved "brethren," the Jews, so dear to God, so wonderfully chosen, and never cast away.

On the other hand, Gentiles who take the mark of the Antichrist and help follow his policies of destroying the Jews will be against God. Their lives will reflect the state of their hearts. Revelation 13:8 indicates that everybody on earth will worship the Antichrist except those 'whose names are written in the book of life.' The plain inference of that verse is that to be for the Antichrist is to be forever lost, and to be openly against the Antichrist and taking part with God's people will be positive proof of salvation. The Man of Sin will be Satan incarnate. Those who rebel against him and protect the

Jews from his fury will be for Christ. That must be why Christ here so addresses those who will have befriended the Jews at that time, and those who will have refused to do so.

It must be kept clear in studying these Scriptures that God has no change in the plan of salvation. People are not really saved by visiting those in prison. *Good deeds do not save.* Nothing is clearer from the Word of God than that. Again and again we are told, "By the deeds of the law there shall no flesh be justified" (Rom. 3:20; Gal. 2:16), that it is "not by works of righteousness which we have done, but according to his mercy he saved us" (Titus 3:5), and "not of works, lest any man should boast" (Eph. 2:9). People are not saved by good works. Nor is it safe to judge people in this generation by good works. Only God sees the heart, and we are commanded, "Judge not, that ye be not judged" (Matt. 7:1). Only Jesus Himself knows all about people and can properly judge those who are saved and unsaved, and He will do so in die judgment pictured here. Besides, the stand of people for or against God will be much clearer in those tribulation times than now, and will more truly picture the heart.

It is true that everything one does even now, in Jesus' name, for His disciples, will receive a reward as if it were done for Christ (Matt. 10:40-42). But not all good deeds are now done in die name of Christ. Many benevolent acts are done in the name of Masonry or false religion or self- righteousness. For such no one gets a reward from God. The Pharisees did all their good deeds "to be seen of men" (Matt. 23:5).

Verse 34 is clear evidence that when Jesus judges the living of all nations on His return to the earth the saved will enter immediately into the joy of their Lord (vss. 21, 23) and into "the kingdom prepared for you from the foundation of the world." Just as certainly verses 41 and 46 show that living Gentiles who will reject Christ in the tribulation time, and come to face Him unsaved, will be immediately cast into Hell-fire. Notice the literal word in verse 41 and the word *everlasting* in verses 41 and 46. That is a clear picture of Hell. We ought to take it at face value. Hell is everlasting torment in literal fire for those who reject Christ.

Even before the millennium, before the last judgment, Hell is now a lake of fire, as we see here.

319

MATTHEW XXVI

Verses 1-5 The Passover of Christ's Death Draws Near

Mark 14:1, 2 and Luke 22:1-6 are parallel passages.

"...after two days is the feast of the passover" (vs. 2). Mark says the same. Luke says the passover "drew nigh." Jesus stressed that there was a connection between the passover and His coming crucifixion. The crucifixion had been foretold in the passages beginning in Matthew 16:21; 17:22; 20:18. The connection here is important. The only reason for the passover these fifteen hundred years past was to foretell the crucifixion of Christ. "Christ our passover is sacrificed for us" (I Cor. 5:7).

A careful study of the detailed instructions about the passover feast and the feast of unleavened bread following (Exod. 12:1-11) shows that every detail is full of meaning concerning the death of Christ and the blessings we have therefrom. The lamb without blemish (Exod. 12:5) could represent no one but the sinless Christ. That not a bone was broken (Exod. 12:46; Num. 9:12; Ps. 34:20; John 19:36) pictured that Christ would not be stoned, but must be crucified, and that Jesus' legs should not be broken on the cross as were those of the thieves. The roasting of the lamb with fire, without water, meant that Jesus suffered judgment without mercy, the wrath of God on sin, which judgment should have properly been ours. The bitter herbs (Num. 9:11) pictures His suffering as a Man of sorrows. The blood on the door (Exod. 12:7) pictures salvation by the atoning blood. The unleavened bread for seven days following the passover supper pictures Christ as the Heavenly Manna who wants to be the daily bread of a Christian all his life after salvation.

There would have been no reason for a passover lamb and the feast of unleavened bread except to picture the coming crucifixion of Jesus Christ. Therefore His disciples should have expected His crucifixion, which had been so dearly foretold before, to occur *at the time of the Passover* – in fact, at the very hour when the passover lamb was being slain, on the day of the preparation (John 19:14, 31).

"After two days" (vs. 2). This could mean that the passover was more than two days away, that is, two full days and parts of two other days. Compare Matthew 17:1, Mark 9:2, and Luke 9:28. Was it six days or eight days from the promise of Jesus of the transfiguration until the transfiguration took place? It was evidently on the eighth day. The time included six full days and parts of two others, that is, it was one week, and in the Greek idiom it was called "about an eight days" (Luke 9:28). Yet it was literally true that it was only after six full days. With that Bible usage for an example, then Matthew 26:2 may mean that two full days intervened before the passover time and parts of two other days. This, I think, is correct.

Also, we should note that "the feast of the passover" was a very general term. First, the word *passover* referred to the one day when the passover lamb was eaten in the evening, the night that Israel came out of Egypt. The meal itself "is the Lord's passover" (Exod. 12:11), as originally given. But common usage linked the seven-day feast of unleavened bread and the passover meal together, so that Luke 22:1 says, "Now the feast of unleavened bread drew nigh, which is called the Passover." That is much more general than when the word *passover* referred to one day.

But the term was more general than that even, for Jews, required not to have leavened bread or any leaven in their homes during the passover time, had added a day of preparation, and the meals of this day of preparation, before the passover, were included under the term *Passover*. See Matthew 26:17 and 18. That passage speaks as if they were already beginning the passover week and as if Jesus would eat the passover lamb with His disciples. But John 19:14 and 31 show that when Jesus went to the cross the next day, it was still the day of "the preparation of the passover"! So by common custom this preparation day had been added to the passover season. Just as we speak of "going home for Christmas" when we may mean a week's holiday or several days, and not simply Christmas Day, so the Jews had begun to speak of the passover, including not only the passover feast itself, but also the seven-days' feast of unleavened bread, and even the preceding day when they put all leaven out of their houses, killed the passover lamb, and prepared for it. So when verse 2 says that "after two days is the feast of the passover," Jesus probably meant that 'after two days is the day of the preparation of the feast of the passover.'

Possibly the reason this period of time is specifically mentioned (vs. 2) is that the passover lamb was to be taken up four days before he was killed, taken up the tenth day of the month, and killed the fourteenth day of the month (Exod. 12:3, 6). The passover lamb's being set aside for the days of observation and so dedicated to death must have pictured the fact that the Pharisees and scribes would ahead of time plot to take Jesus and set Him aside for death. Certainly here Jesus makes some connection between the fact that it is a certain length of time to the passover and that He is (in the minds of the Pharisees and rulers) already betrayed to be crucified. The assembly of the chief priests and scribes at the palace of the high priest (vs. 3), planning to take Jesus and kill Him, was the official setting aside of Jesus as the nation's Passover Lamb to die for their sins. Doubtless, these wicked men did not understand the prophetic significance of that act, just as Caiaphas the high priest prophesied by divine inspiration that Christ should die for the whole nation, though he did not know it (John 11:49, 52). That occurred at this same time, though omitted by Matthew. Notice that that prophecy is connected with the taking of counsel to put Jesus to death (John 11:53, 54). Consider also that in these three days before His crucifixion Jesus did no public ministry, did not enter into the temple (Matt. 23:39; 24:1; John 11:54). He was put up for crucifixion. Every detail of the instructions about the passover lamb must be fulfilled in Jesus, for all of it was a prophecy of His death as our Passover, our Atonement.

Remember that an enormous multitude, most of the whole nation, was now at Jerusalem or would be there for the passover feast. These hypocritical Pharisees did not want the feast disturbed by an uproar, so hastened to have Jesus betrayed and crucified before the passover feast was eaten. They seemed not to realize that they thus helped fulfill the Scriptures by having Jesus killed exactly on time.

Verses 6-13 Mary of Bethany Anoints Jesus at a Feast

Compare this passage with parallel Scriptures in Mark 14:3-9 and in John 12:1-8. See also Luke 7:36-50, a similar case, but not the same. The case in John seems to be the same as this. John 12:1 says that "Jesus six days before the passover came to Bethany," but the supper might properly have been some days later. It would take some time to prepare the kind of feast made here. Jesus spent His nights in Bethany (Matt. 21:17), we suppose in the home of Mary, Martha, and Lazarus. Mornings He would go to Jerusalem and in the evenings return to Bethany to lodge (Matt. 21:18; Mark 11:11, 12, 15, 19, 20, 27), This feast was "in the house of Simon the leper" (vs, 6) but Mary and Martha helped serve and Lazarus was also at the table (John 12:2). John 12:3 tells us that it was Mary who brought the precious ointment and adds that it was ^ointment of spikenard, very costly." Mary anointed both His head and His feet as you see by comparing verse 7 with John 12:3. It was customary to anoint both head and feet of honored guests (Luke 7:46). To keep such ointment (really perfume) in fine alabaster boxes was not unusual, we suppose. The odor filled the house (John 12:3).

The word SAT (vs. 7) should be really RECLINED. The oriental custom was not to sit upright at tables as we do now, but to lie on couches with the head toward the low table. The U-shaped fable was served from inside. The couches surrounded the outside of the U. Thus Jesus, outstretched upon the couch, had His feet accessible to be anointed with oil, as was His head. Verse 12 indicates that Mary probably poured the ointment or perfume on other parts of His body as well. Remember that no one of the Gospels tells the whole story, yet they do not contradict each other.

The disciples "had indignation, saying, to what purpose is this waste?" They thought the expensive ointment might properly have been "sold for much, and given to the poor" (vss. 8, 9). We learn from John 12:4-6 that it was Judas Iscariot who spoke up to this effect and that "this he said, not that he cared for the poor; but because he was a thief, and had the bag, and bare what was put therein." Doubtless other disciples at first agreed with the plausible reasoning of Judas.

Truly waste is a sin and giving to the poor is a virtue greatly honored in the Scriptures (Ps. 41:1; Prov. 19:17; 21:13; Gal. 2:10; etc.). But duties never conflict. It is good to give to the poor, but far better to give to Christ. It is good to be thrifty instead of wasteful, but the complete abandonment of all for Christ which may seem like waste and shiftlessness is the highest virtue in His sight! To the unspiritual mind it may appear contradictory that Jews were commanded, "Go to the ant, thou sluggard; consider her ways, and be wise" (Prov. 6:6), that the thrift of the ant was commended (Prov. 30:25), and that Jesus commanded that not a fragment should be wasted after feeding the five thousand (John 6:12); while on the other hand He commanded, "Lay not up for yourselves treasures upon earth" (Matt. 6:19), even that Christians were to "take therefore no thought for the morrow" (Matt. 6:34). But the spiritual mind will understand that giving to Christ is better than thrift and better than giving to the poor.

A special importance was attached to this anointing of the body of Jesus in that it was done for His burial (vs. 12). This verse indicates that possibly Mary was the only one of all those who loved Jesus who believed and understood what He had said about His crucifixion. It was 'for His burial.' "Without faith it is impossible to please him" (Heb. 11:6), so it was this faith which so pleased the Saviour as well as her love. How great the act was in the sight of Jesus is indicated from verse 13. That promise has been fulfilled in the Bible accounts of this act of Mary who did what she could in loving anticipation of and gratitude for His death for our sins.

Verses 14-16 Judas Covenants to Betray Jesus

Compare with Mark 14:10, 11 and Luke 22:3-6, parallel passages.

At this supper in Bethany (vss. 6-13) Lazarus, whom Jesus had just raised from the dead, ate at the table with Jesus (John 12:1, 2, 9-11) and many, seeing Lazarus, believed that Jesus was the Messiah and trusted in Him. Therefore the chief priests hated Him and planned to kill Him. At the same supper Judas Iscariot had been greatly angered at the rebuke given him by Jesus when he objected to Mary's anointing Jesus with ointment. Satan entered into him. Thus Judas went to the chief priests and offered to betray Jesus for money.

Judas was never a saved man, as you see from John 6:64, 70, 71. Judas had not believed in Christ; he was a devil. Jesus knew ahead of time Judas would betray Him. This betrayal is foretold in the Old Testament (Ps. 41:9). Even the price – the thirty pieces of silver – was foretold (Zech. 11:12, 13). When the eleven elected another apostle to take Judas' place, they prayed for divine guidance for one, "That he may take part of this ministry and apostleship, from which Judas by transgression fell, that he might go to his own place" (Acts 1:25). Judas fell from the ministry and apostleship, not from salvation. He was a minister but not a Christian. There have been and will be many others who prophesy without being saved (Matt. 7:22, 23). "His own place" must have been Hell. Jesus said it would have been better for Judas if he had never been born (vs. 24).

We are told that at this time Satan entered into Judas (Luke 22:3) and put the betrayal into his heart (John 13:2).

He already belonged to Satan and this case simply fulfills the parable of Jesus in Matthew 12:43-45, where the unclean spirit returned to his reformed but empty house with seven other devils. Judas was a self-righteous, outwardly moral man heretofore, but was never regenerated. Satan may leave such men to their morality temporarily, but "the last state of that man is worse than the first." No man who rejects Christ can know to what awful depth of sin he will be led by Satan.

Verses 17-25 A Preliminary Meal of the Passover Season; Jesus Eats With the Disciples

Compare this passage with Mark 14:12-21 and with Luke 22:7-30.

In verse 17 note that the words *day* and *feast of* are in italics, which means they were not in the original Greek. It was not yet the feast of unleavened bread. The real feast of unleavened bread did not begin until the passover lamb was slain. However, because Jews were so strictly charged not to have any leaven even in their houses during the seven-days' feast of the unleavened bread (Exod. 12:15) they grew accustomed to putting away the leaven a day early. So the time was simply when Jews began to eat unleavened bread, but a day before the first day of the *commanded* "feast of unleavened bread."

Be careful to note the usage of the word *passover* in verses 2, 19, etc. In the Old Testament the word *passover* referred particularly to the one meal with the roasted lamb (Exod. 12:11, 27, 43 ff; Lev.

23:5; Num. 9:5), and the feast of unleavened bread, beginning at the same time, was spoken of separately and called "the feast of unleavened bread" (Lev. 23:6). However, in New Testament times the Jews had become accustomed to speaking of both the feasts as one, as you see from Luke 22:1, and that combined feast was preceded by a day of purification when all leaven and leavened bread was put out of the houses and they began ahead of time to eat only unleavened bread. It was evidently such a meal here that Jesus ate. It was one of the meals of the passover season, characterized by unleavened bread (vs. 17). But the supper which Jesus ate then was evidently not the passover meal. No mention is made of a lamb, but only of bread and wine (vss. 26, 27). Besides, from John 19:14 and 31 it was the day of the preparation of the passover lamb when Jesus was crucified. Jesus died the next afternoon, perfectly fulfilling the type and prophecy, just when passover lambs were being killed for the entire nation gathered in Jerusalem for that holy ceremony. So Jesus Himself did not eat the passover lamb on this occasion.

This evening meal was the day before the day when the passover lamb would be killed. As we would count, it would be the next day. Actually, since the meal was past sundown it was already the next day, the day of the preparation, as you see from Luke 22:7. Jews counted days from sunset to sunset. This night Jesus was to go to the Garden of Gethsemane and the next morning He was to be brought before Pilate, condemned, crucified, and in the afternoon was to die.

Not given here in Matthew, but recorded in Mark 14:13-16 and Luke 22:8-13, is the incident in which Peter and John were sent into the city where they were to meet a man bearing a pitcher of water. Following this man, they should ask the master of the house to which he went where the guest chamber was in which Jesus and the disciples should eat this passover meal. It occurred just as Jesus said: they were led to the friendly upper room; they ate this evening meal; the disciples later gathered there in despair, then happily, still later, after Christ's ascension, to pray for the power of Pentecost.

In connection with this passage read John 13:2-30 where we are told that Jesus washed die disciples' feet, dipped a sop of bread, possibly into wine, (grape juice) and gave it to Judas Iscariot as a sign that he would betray Him.

Verses 26-29 The Lord's Supper Instituted

The institution of the Lord's Supper is told also in Mark 14:22-25, Luke 22:17-20, and by Paul in I Corinthians 11:23-25. Paul received the account of it by direct inspiration from God, not from the lips of any who were present (I Cor. 11:23). Of course all the accounts were given by divine inspiration and the writers did not depend on their memory. The meaning of the Lord's Supper is very simple. The broken bread pictures the body of Jesus broken for us. The grape juice ("fruit of the vine") pictures the blood of Jesus "shed for many for the remission of sins." Christ died, not as our example, but as our Saviour. The blood of this righteous and holy Son of God in human form really paid for man's sins. "The Lord hath laid on him the iniquity of us all" (Isa. 53:6). See also I Peter 1:18, 19; 2:24; I John 2:2. This is the Gospel we are to preach – "Christ died for our sins according to the scriptures; And that he was buried, and that he rose again the third day according to the scriptures" (I Cor. 15:3, 4). This blessed Supper is meant to picture to every Christian the death of Christ, as a holy reminder. It is to be continued by Christians to "shew the Lord's death till he come" (I Cor. 11:26). Our hearts need the remembrance that Christ died for our sins.

It must be understood that no one is saved by taking the Lord's Supper. All the power is in the Saviour Himself, not in the bread nor grape juice which picture Him. God does not put it in the hands of priests or churches to pass out salvation through bread and wine. This is a holy rite, to be done in remembrance and showing forth Christ's death. We become real partakers of the body and blood of Christ through faith (John 6:27 58, noticing particularly verses 29, 35, 40, and 47). "This is my body" and "this is my blood" are intended to be figurative, as the context clearly shows. The passover lamb was not Christ's flesh but *pictured* His flesh. The blood on the doorpost was not the blood of Christ but *pictured* Christ's blood. All Jews were accustomed to this symbolism and would understand what Jesus said and meant.

The Scripture does not here nor anywhere else say how often the Lord's Supper should be observed. Acts 20:7 indicates that the church at Troas may have met for the Lord's Supper every Sunday.

If they did, other churches may not have observed the Supper so frequently. We are nowhere commanded to do so. Likely Christians ought to observe the Lord's Supper more frequently than is usual. It should be observed often enough to keep fresh in our mind the death of Christ for our sins and not so often as to become meaningless and a matter of ritual only, as it often does with Catholic and ritualistic churches.

The attitude of heart is most important. Before taking the Lord's Supper Christians should examine their hearts (I Cor. 11:28). To eat the Supper unworthily, not observing the Lord's body and blood, brings condemnation and trouble (I Cor. 11:29). Divisions and worldliness are hindrances to the proper observance of the Lord's Supper (I Cor. 11:17-21). Spiritual Christians should not eat with fornicators, nor with the covetous, nor railers, nor drunkards, nor extortioners, nor with idolaters (I Cor. 5:11). By the Bible example it appears that New Testament Christians were baptized before taking the Lord's Supper. Certainly each Christian, before taking the Lord's Supper, should examine his heart and try to be in the will of God, an obedient Christian, right with his neighbor.

The Lord's Supper is not called an *ordinance* in the Bible. The word *ordinances* refers usually to the Mosaic Law (Col. 2:14; Heb. 9:1). The Lord's Supper is not law in the sense of the Mosaic Law but is a command for New Testament Christians and churches. Incidentally, there is no record in the New Testament of individual's or families' taking the Lord's Supper alone. It was observed in public congregations.

God has often made use of rites and ceremonies as object lessons, teaching spiritual truths. All the sacrifices of the Old Testament were such object lessons, picturing the death of Christ for us. The feasts had special meanings. In the New Testament present-day Christians are taught to observe the following meaningful rites or object lessons: (1) The Lord's Supper. (2) Baptism, picturing the burial and resurrection of Christ, the new birth of the Christian, and the resurrection of the body. (3) The anointing with oil for the sick under certain circumstances, picturing the faith in the Holy Spirit's power to heal when it is according to God's will, in answer to prayer (James 5:14-16). (4) Long hair for women as a sign of their dependence and obedience to husbands or fathers, and short hair for men as a sign of their independence and responsibility before God for their families (I Cor. 11:1-16). (5) The laying on of hands in ordination services.

Verse 29 teaches that, in the coming kingdom on earth, Christ, in a physical body, will drink grape juice with His saints. This is clear evidence that we will have physical bodies and will eat and drink. Other Scriptures teach that Christians in resurrection bodies will eat fruit and fish, will need salt, etc. (Ezek. 47:9-12; Rev. 22:2). Our physical bodies will be as real and literal as those of Adam and Eve in the Garden of Eden, like the body of Jesus after He rose from the dead with flesh and bones and ate and drank before the disciples (Luke 24:39-43).

The cup the disciples drank at the Lord's Supper is nowhere called wine but "the fruit of the vine." We believe it was simply grape juice. Even if the word wine had been used, wine in the Bible means grape juice, whether fermented or unfermented. Fermented Wine, with microbes of decay, would not picture the perfect blood of a sinless Christ.

Verses 30-35 Jesus Warns All Will Be Offended; Peter Will Deny Him

Compare verse 30 with the last part of John 14:31 and it becomes evident that Jesus here gave the 14th chapter of John before going out to the Mount of Olives. Then between the upper room and the Garden of Gethsemane, the discourses of Jesus in John, chapters 15 and 16 and His prayer in chapter 17 all occurred following verse 30 and before verse 36 here. This should help us to remember that the Gospel of John gives many discourses of Jesus not mentioned in the other Gospels, but does not give as many of the events in order as the synoptic Gospels – Matthew, Mark, and Luke.

In verse 31 Jesus quoted Zechariah 13:7. Every detail of this holy time when the sins of the world were to be paid for by our Saviour was planned before the beginning of the world and most of it was foretold in prophecy. Notice the "all" in verse 31 and "all the disciples" in verse 35. Do hot blame Peter alone for being offended in Christ. Others fled when Peter denied Him.

Every one of us should take solemn warning from this incident. After repeated warnings by Jesus, these disciples did not believe

329

they would deny Him nor forsake Him. We never know how great the pressure will be. Therefore we ought to watch and pray that we enter not into temptation (vs. 41). If such good Christians as the apostles were, who had sincerely left all to follow Jesus and later proved their loyalty even unto death, could be so surprised and deceived by Satan, so attacked in their weakness as to be offended in Christ and leave Him, then we ought to be very careful about criticizing others and take heed lest we fall (I Cor. 10:12). The best men who have ever lived on this earth – Noah, Abraham, Lot, Isaac, David, Peter, Paul, and Barnabas – have been tempted by Satan and have been guilty of terrible sins, either drunkenness or lying or murder or adultery or dissension or going against the plain leading of the Spirit. This passage and such examples ought to greatly humble our hearts. Let us earnestly resolve never to deny Jesus, but let us make sure that we do not boast of our strength, for "whosoever shall exalt himself shall be abased; and he that shall humble himself shall be exalted" (Matt. 23:12).

Verses 36-46 Jesus in Gethsemane

The Garden of Gethsemane experience of Jesus is discussed in Mark 14:32-42 and in Luke 22:39-46. John 18:1 only mentions it.

The time is far into the night. In the evening Jesus met with His disciples in the upper room for the preliminary meal of the general passover season. There He washed the disciples' feet and taught them the lesson on humility (John 13:4-17). There He instituted the Lord's Supper (vss. 26-29). He also comforted their hearts with the marvelous teaching of the 14th chapter of John. Then Jesus and the disciples departed from the upper room (vs. 30; John 14:31) and leisurely walked in the night through the streets of Jerusalem, through the city gate, across the brook Cedron or Kidron (John 18:1), into the Garden of Gethsemane on the edge of the Mount of Olives (Luke 22:39). During the walk Jesus gave the teachings of John, chapters 15 and 16, and stopped for the prayer in John, chapter 17. Therefore it was late, possibly past midnight, when the Gethsemane experience began.

Judas alone was absent. The other eleven disciples were with Jesus. To eight of them Jesus said, "Sit ye here" (vs. 36). He took the other three, Peter, James, and John, with Him a little farther to one side. All the disciples were tired and sleepy (vss. 40, 43, 45).

They were depressed and sad (John 16:6, 22). The disciples were in no condition of heart to pray. Even Peter, and we suppose James and John, also of the chosen three (vs. 40), went to sleep. Jesus Himself "went a little farther" (vs. 39) than any of the others and eventually did His praying alone. No one else can go as far as Jesus. Though His soul hungered for companionship, comfort and help in prayer, Jesus prayed alone.

Let us learn here a serious lesson. The price for the sins of the world must be paid by Jesus alone. He died alone. No other person could pay for man's sins. No other blood shed could purchase our redemption. In the Garden of Gethsemane no room is left for any to believe that the prayers of any saint would avail in the same sense that Christ's prayer would avail. In fact, Jesus did not even ask them to join Him in prayer *in this matter* – doubtless they did not know enough about it to pray intelligently. Rather, He asked them to "tarry" and "watch" (vs. 38), and rebuked them because they went to sleep instead of watching (vs. 40). The disciples were commanded, "Watch and pray, *that ye enter not into temptation*" (vs. 41). They needed to pray for *themselves.* They were not able to join in intercessory prayer for Christ, but were in great need to pray for themselves. Because they did not watch and pray they did enter into temptation, Peter denied Christ and all deserted Him and fled (vss. 56, 69-75).

Yet it is significant that Jesus wanted the comfort of having the disciples near. It is rare that more than a very few people can pray together for long periods of time. All night prayer meetings, days of fasting and prayer are usually attended by relatively few people if the time is really spent in prayer. Many times people under great burden and grief must pray alone since they have no one who can perfectly join in their petitions. So it was with Jesus here. He went where no one else could go. Those who can perfectly agree in some definite prayer ought to do so and they have a sweet promise of God's answer (Matt. 18:20). But where others cannot join in the prayer they can at least stand by and watch. On this last night before His cruel torture on the cross, Jesus longed for the companionship of His disciples. He wanted them near while He prayed. He loved His own even -unto the end" (John 13:1). He had earnestly commended them all to the Father in prayer (John 17:9 ff). We know His breaking heart had been comforted by the beloved John's leaning on His bosom (John 13:23, 25) but pained by the hatred and betrayal of Judas. He wanted His beloved ones near, wanted them to watch!

We cannot die for sinners. We cannot even know the awful wickedness of this world as Jesus knows it. But at least we can and we ought to watch with Him. I believe that God wants us to have fellowship with Christ in meditating on His Gethsemane experience and His death on the cross and try to enter into the understanding of His grief. Paul earnestly sought "That I may know him, and the power of his resurrection, and the fellowship of sufferings..." (Phil. 3:10). If we cannot die with Christ we can at least suffer with Him (II Tim. 2:12). We can be hated by the enemies of Christ (John 15:18, 19). We can go with Him outside the camp, bearing His reproach (Heb. 13:13). In some sense, we can fill up what is behind of the afflictions of Christ (Col. 1:24). Let us learn to watch with Jesus and watching, let us learn the secret of intercessory prayer.

If you do not notice verses 37 and 38, the meaning of the Gethsemane prayer will be missed. Jesus was sorrowful and heavy and His soul "sorrowful, even unto death," that is, was literally dying of grief. It had been Satan's plan all along to prevent the crucifixion. He had offered Jesus the kingdoms of the world without a cross (Matt. 4:8, 9). Satan had used Peter to tempt Jesus and to try to discourage Him from going to the cross (Matt. 16:22, 23). Even on the cross Satan did not let up with his temptation but put it in the heart of men that passed by (Matt. 27:39, 40), of the chief priests and elders (Matt. 27:41, 42), of the thieves beside Him (Matt, 27:44) to suggest that Jesus come down from the cross! Jesus was about to die in the Garden.

The cup mentioned in verses 39 and 42 was the cup of death, death that night in the Garden of Gethsemane. This is made clear especially by Hebrews 5:7 where we are told that Jesus "offered up prayers and supplications with strong crying and tears unto him that was *to save him from death,* and was heard in that he feared." About to die in the Garden of Gethsemane, Jesus prayed that the cup of death would pass from Him that night so He could live to die on the cross the next day. The Scripture says that "He was heard"! God answered His prayer.

So many have thought that in the Gethsemane prayer Jesus was pleading to escape the cross. No, no! He was not praying *against* the will of God, but praying *with* the will of God and He got His prayers answered.

How thankful we ought to be that Jesus "prayed through" that night and got the answer to His prayer. If Jesus had died in the Garden of Gethsemane, then we would have no saving Gospel, for the Gospel is "that Christ died for our sins ACCORDING TO THE SCRIPTURES: And that he was buried, and that he rose again the third day ACCORDING TO THE SCRIPTURES" (I Cor. 15:3, 4). No ordinary death would do; the death of Christ must be according to the Scriptures. It must fulfill all the type of the passover lamb. Jesus must have His beard plucked out (Isa. 50:6). He must be beaten with many stripes (Isa. 53:5). He must make His grave with the wicked and the rich in His death (Isa. 53:9), that is, He must die between thieves on the cross and be buried in a rich man's grave. They must pierce His hands and His feet (Ps. 22:16). He must hang on the cross naked so that "I may tell all my bones" (Ps. 22:17). Even the very cry, "My God, my God, why hast thou forsaken me?" that the Saviour must utter on the cross was foretold in the Scriptures (Ps. 22:1). The mocking of the chief priests and the people must be fulfilled to the letter as it was foretold (Ps. 22:7, 8). They must cast lots for His vesture (Ps. 22:18).

If Jesus did not die literally "according to the scriptures," then He could not be our Saviour. Thank God, His prayers in the Garden of Gethsemane were answered! The cup of death which Satan offered Him that night did pass from Him and He was saved for the cross so that we could be saved for Heaven and everlasting life. The answer to the prayer is not mentioned in Matthew, but Luke 22:43 tells us "there appeared an angel unto him from heaven, strengthening him." Without this supernatural strengthening of His body, Christ would surely have died in the Garden that night.

The sorrows of Jesus in the Garden of Gethsemane can never be known by us until we meet Him in Glory. He was "sorrowful, even unto death" (vs; 38). He was "in an agony" and "his sweat was as it were great drops of blood falling down to the ground" (Luke 22:44). We are told that "he hath poured out his soul unto death" (Isa. 53:12). His sorrow was called "the travail of his soul" (Isa. 53:11). His prayer was "strong crying and tears" (Heb. 5:7). We do not know how long Jesus spent in the Garden of Gethsemane. The first period of prayer may have lasted about one hour (vs. 40); the entire time may have been several hours. No one can know now the infinite sufferings of Christ in the Garden of Gethsemane and on the cross. He suffered the judgment and wrath of God due the sinners of the whole world.

The Saviour continued in importunate prayer. He repeated the same words three times (vss. 39, 42, 44). He did not let go. Let us learn here the solemn lesson of being faithful and not being discouraged in prayer. Jesus was praying in the will of God, praying for the things that He knew were right; yet the Father did not immediately give Him the answer. He begged that the cup of death might pass from Him in order that He might fulfill the Scriptures, that He might save sinners, that all the plan of God should be fulfilled. There is nothing good that we can think of that was not in some way involved in the things for which Jesus prayed. He Himself was holy and good and sinless. There was no fault that even the Father in Heaven could find in His own dear Son. Jesus had every reason to expect the answer; yet it was delayed. The pleading, persistent prayers of Jesus, with strong crying and tears, were continued until the answer came. In fact, from Luke 22:43 and 44 it appears that after His prayer was partly answered, His concern and fervency increased. Jesus did not stop praying until He received the perfect answer to His prayers. Verses 45 and 46 picture our Saviour with peaceful heart, with strength to go through the torture of the day approaching and confidence that the will of God would be carried out. Jesus "prayed through."

This was not the first time Jesus had engaged in prolonged seasons of prayer. He had fasted forty days and nights at the temptation in the wilderness (Matt. 4:2). Fasting goes logically with prayer and our Saviour must have spent most of that time in prayer. At other times Jesus spent whole nights in prayer or arose a good while before day to go into a mount to pray (Matt. 14:23; Mark 1:35; etc.). He prayed so much that His disciples begged Him, "Lord, teach us to pray" (Luke 11:1). Jesus prayed before every great crisis in His life. He is the best Example for Christians in the matter of prayer. When He was filled with the Holy Ghost He prayed (Luke 3: 21, 22). Before calling the twelve disciples He spent the night in prayed (Luke 6: 12, 13). Jesus slept none at all this night before His crucifixion, but in holy conversation and in prayer He found preparation and strength and thwarted Satan's plan to prevent the promised death on the cross.

At this point it is well to remember prolonged seasons of prayer which God blessed in the cases of others. Consider Jacob (Gen. 32:24), the Jews who followed Esther and Mordecai (Esther, chap. 4), the Ninevites whose city was spared because of their fasting and praying (Jonah 3:5-10), and other cases (Ezra 8:21-23; Neh. 1:4; Dan. 9:3, 4; etc.). Perhaps the best known case of Christians' continuing in prayer is that of the disciples before Pentecost (Acts 1:14). Later, at Jerusalem the disciples had a prolonged prayer meeting until Peter's life was saved and he was delivered from jail (Acts 12:5-12). Preachers, prophets, and teachers fasted and prayed before sending out Paul and Barnabas on the first missionary journey (Acts 13:1-5).

Verses 47-56 Betrayal and Arrest of Jesus in Gethsemane

The betrayal and arrest of Jesus is told also in Mark 14:43-50, Luke 22:47-54, and in John 18:3-11. The great multitude that came to arrest Jesus (vs. 47) included Judas the traitor, a "band" of soldiers (John 18:3), at least one servant of the high priest (slave, Mark 14:47; Luke 22:50). The servant's name was Malchus (John 18:10). In the group also were chief priests, captains of the temple, and elders (Luke 22:52). The soldiers were armed with swords; others had staves or clubs. An irregular mob had come with the soldiers and Jewish leaders. The large number they brought to arrest Jesus indicates how Jewish leaders feared Him. In Galilee when His townsmen had attempted to kill Jesus, He had miraculously passed through them and escaped (Luke 4:29, 30). For long the Jews had sought to kill Jesus (John 7:1, 19, 25), but in some way no man could lay hands on Jesus before His hour was come (John 7:30). The Pharisees and chief priests sent officers to arrest Him (John 7:32). They tried to do so but could not (John 7:44-46). That was a few months before this time, and knowing the miraculous power of Jesus, these scribes, Pharisees, and elders secured a large band of soldiers armed with swords, and armed the mob with clubs and came to arrest Jesus.

When they approached Him in the Garden and Jesus spoke to them, "they went backward, and fell to the ground" (John 18:6). It is certain that Jesus allowed them to take Him only because He chose to do so. Every step of the way He had been in the will of the Father; now He submits to arrest because His hour is come.

Consider Jesus' treatment of Judas. He received his kiss (vs. 49) and called him "Friend" or comrade (vs. 50). Matthew Henry notes that Jesus called Judas "friend," betraying Him, and called Peter, loving Him truly, "Satan" (Matt. 16:23), since Judas unconsciously aided in fulfilling the long foretold crucifixion, while Peter tempted Jesus to avoid the cross. Jesus knew from the beginning that Judas was a hypocrite, was unsaved, did not believe in Him, and would betray Him (John 6:64, 70, 71). Yet He had never exposed Judas to the other disciples nor spoken harshly to him. Surely this is indication that Jesus loves the vilest sinner on earth and will forgive him gladly if he will but repent. The attitude of Christ toward Judas was the same as His attitude toward the chief priests and soldiers, "Father, forgive them; for they know not what they do" (Luke 23:34). The martyr Stephen had the same attitude (Acts 7:60).

Two of Christ's disciples had swords (Luke 22:38). They asked Jesus, "Lord, shall we smite with the sword?" (Luke 22:49), but one of them, Peter (John 18:10), waited for no answer, but drew his sword when he saw what was about to occur and attacked the high priest's servant, cutting off his ear (vs. 51). Notice that neither Matthew, Mark, nor Luke tells that it was Peter who struck the high priest's servant or that it was Malchus whose ear he cut off, but John's Gospel, written much later, after Peter was dead and no longer in danger of persecution, tells more about the incident and names both Peter and Malchus. The Lord had some reason for giving these details in only the Gospel of John and this may be the reason. Luke 22:51 tells that Jesus touched the ear and healed Malchus. What tender love for others was in the heart of the betrayed Saviour!

The warning of Jesus in Luke 22:36, "he that hath no sword, let him sell his garment, and buy one," was probably not intended to be taken literally, certainly not in this particular case, since Jesus here forbids the use of the sword. The warning, "all they that take the sword shall perish with the sword" (vs. 52) should be sufficient for Christians. Compare it with Matthew 5:39 and 44. Christians are to "be not overcome of evil, but overcome evil with good" (Rom. 12:21). See also I Thessalonians 5:15. We should remember that "the weapons of our warfare are not carnal, but mighty through

God to the pulling down of strong holds" (II Cor. 10:4). Christians do not need arms for self-protection.

Officers of the law on official business, representing the government, have authority from God to bear arms. Concerning a governor, king; or such ruler, the Scripture says, "he beareth not the sword in vain" (Rom. 13:4). Thus it is proper for soldiers to be armed and for Christians to serve the government.

Christians who keep a pistol in the house for protection from burglars are too likely to learn that "all they that take the sword shall perish with the sword." It is safer for a private Christian to trust in God and in spiritual weapons than to trust in physical weapons. It is significant that, of all the heroes in New Testament times, not one offered physical resistance to the persecution, beatings, or even death that threatened him. Stephen offered no resistance when stoned (Acts 7:54-60). Paul, stoned and left for dead at Lystra (Acts 14:19), left the city to avoid further trouble. At Damascus Paul was let down in a basket over the wall to escape with his life (Acts 9:22-25; II Cor. 11:32, 33). Christians ought to depend on spiritual weapons of faith and prayer, on the angels of God and the power of the Holy Spirit to protect them.

The Scripture indicates that officers of the government should enforce order with physical weapons, and in this wicked world it is proper for governments to arm soldiers. The Scripture nowhere condemns it. Wicked, rapacious, cruel outlaw nations must be held in check, just as individual outlaws must be held in check, by human government, but individual Christians do not need carnal weapons for their warfare.

Jesus and the eleven disciples would be foolish to depend upon human arms for protection in that hour, because Jesus could have had, if He had prayed for them, "twelve legions of angels" for protection (vs. 53). A legion was about six thousand soldiers. Multiplied thousands of angels of unlimited power were available had Jesus asked for them. But He did not ask for them. His time was at hand and He went "as a lamb to the slaughter, and as a sheep before her shearers is dumb..." (Isa. 53:7).

Though Jesus willingly surrendered and gave Himself to the shame that awaited Him and for which He came into the world, yet the people must be reproved for their sin (vs. 55). Not a semblance of blame could be left on Jesus, our sinless Saviour. None could convince Him of sin (John 8:46).

Is the first sentence in verse 56 the words of Jesus or the inspired words of Matthew writing the story? Perhaps either, but Mark 14:49 indicates that the words are those of Christ. It is true that every detail of the Scriptures was being fulfilled in the life, death, and resurrection of Christ.

Note (vs. 56) that all the disciples forsook Christ and fled. Frightened, unable to protect themselves or Christ, they ran away. In John 18:8 we are told that Jesus interceded for His disciples. Jesus answered, "I have told you that I am he: if therefore ye seek me, let these go their way." None of the disciples was arrested. While Jesus did not protect Himself, He doubtless did protect His own so that none would be lost (compare John 18:9 with John 17:12). Blessed thought, "He saved others; himself he cannot save" (Matt. 27:42). Jesus permitted the disciples to flee and went on to His sufferings. We, too, may flee from the wrath to come, since our Saviour has already suffered wrath for us all and tasted death for every man (Heb. 2:9).

Verses 57-68 Jesus Before the Sanhedrin Condemned to Death

They did not at first lead Jesus to Caiaphas the high priest (vs. 57). Matthew does not tell all the story here. They "led him away to Annas first; for he was father in law to Caiaphas, which was the high priest that same year" (John 18:13). Annas was a former high priest and was still counted a high priest by the people. Several of his sons followed him in the high priestly office besides this son-in-law, Caiaphas. Caiaphas was recognized by the Roman government, but the elder man, Annas, was probably the most influential. Annas questioned Jesus, then bound Him and sent Him to Caiaphas (John 18:24). Both probably lived in the palace of the high priest (Mark 14:54; John 18:15), but had separate quarters.

"Where the scribes and the elders were assembled" (vs. 57). Part of the Sanhedrin was assembled at the high priest's palace waiting for the Jewish leaders, soldiers, and mob to return with Jesus.

Compare this with Matthew 27:1, Mark 15:1, and Luke 22:66. That assembly in verse 57 was an informal meeting of the Jewish Sanhedrin, the ruling body of the Jews. However, they were not allowed to pass the death penalty in night sessions, so the formal and official meeting came the next morning, when all, or approximately all, the Sanhedrin could be present. Joseph of Arimathaea was a "counsellor" (a member of the Sanhedrin), and he had not consented to the death of Christ (Luke 23:50, 51). From John 19:38, 39 it seems that Nicodemus was agreed with Joseph in this matter. He also was "a ruler of the Jews" (John Sri), a member of the Sanhedrin. Whether these two were present and objected to the condemnation, or whether they were not notified of the meeting, we cannot say.

We learn that Peter and one other disciple (probably John, since he tells it modestly, as he refers to himself elsewhere) followed to the palace of the high priest (vs. 58; John 18:15, 16). The building was probably a large rectangle. In such buildings there was usually a courtyard in the center, paved with stone. Peter probably loitered here with the servants (vs. 58) and officers (John 18:18). Peter sat with them and stood with them to warm by the fire. He put himself in the presence of temptation and in bad company.

The trial of Jesus was a fake trial. The chief priests did not impartially seek to find the truth. Rather they "sought false witness against Jesus, to put him to death" (vs. 59).

Malice and hate were their motives. Let this remind us that there can be no such thing as an honest rejection of Jesus Christ. The only reason anybody ever rejects Christ is from a wicked heart, loving sin and so hating Christ. See Matthew 6:24 and Luke 11:23. John 3:18-21 plainly shows there can be no such thing as innocent unbelief.

Behind all unbelief is love for sin and deliberate rejection of Christ, the Light of the world, because men love darkness. Thus God calls the man who says "no God," a "fool" (Ps. 53:1), and the man who is even "slow of heart to believe all that the prophets have spoken," a "fool" (Luke 24:25). The evidence that there is a God, that the Bible is His holy, inspired, and infallible Word, that Jesus Christ is His Son, is so overwhelming to any honest mind that only wicked malice could keep one from gladly accepting it.

These wicked rulers of the Sanhedrin would not be convinced of the deity of Christ now because already they hated Him and had chosen to have Him murdered. Since they could find no true witnesses against Jesus, they deliberately sought false witnesses. Anyone who rejects Christ may be expected to have false reasons. There are no good reasons for rejecting Christ nor for not believing the Bible. Insincere hearts are behind all infidelity and all Christ-rejection.

Note how malice twisted the words of Jesus (vs. 61). Evidently the witness referred to the words of Jesus in John 2:19 where He says, "Destroy this temple, and in three days I will raise it up." Jesus had never indicated that He would destroy the temple of God. Rather, He had prophesied that when they would kill Him, His body, a temple, would rise the third day (Matt. 16:21; 17:22, 23; 20:18, 19). Elsewhere, also, Jesus had forewarned His disciples that for the sins of the city Jerusalem would be destroyed (Luke 21:20-24), that even the temple itself should be completely destroyed (Matt. 24:1, 2), but this was in the Olivet discourse to His disciples alone and was not known to the Sanhedrin nor the public.

Verse 60 shows that though they found many false witnesses, they could not find two or three to agree to the same charge as was required by the Mosaic Law (Num. 35:30; Deut. 17:6; 19:15). Even if Jesus had threatened to destroy the temple and to rebuild it, that was not an offense worthy of death. The high priest, vexed, sought to get Jesus to commit Himself and so put Him on oath to answer the question in verse 63, "I adjure thee by the living God, that thou tell us whether thou be the Christ, the Son of God." Christ, before the Sanhedrin and the high priest, ought to answer such a question asked in the name of God. The high priest would have a right to ask such a question and when asked in God's name, it ought to be answered. The high priest had no right to hate Jesus, and his motives were evil, but Christ had taught that Jewish leaders ought to be respected and obeyed wherever possible (Matt. 23:1-3). So Jesus answered plainly, "Thou hast said" (vs. 64). Mark 14:62 gives an addition, "And Jesus said, I am." In effect Jesus said, "What you have asked is true. I am the Son of God." Heretofore Jesus had often avoided saying publicly that He was the Son of God and asked His disciples not to declare it (Matt. 16:20). He had repeatedly urged that those healed not tell it abroad (Matt.

8:4; Mark 8:26, 29, 30, etc.), and commanded the disciples not to discuss His transfiguration glory until after He should be raised from die dead (Matt. 17:9).

Let us add that Jesus nowhere denied being the Son of God. His birth and ministry fulfilled overwhelmingly the Scriptures prophesying His coming and any willing mind should have been convinced. Jesus allowed Himself to be called "the son of David," a term indicating that He was the promised Messiah who should reign on David's throne, and He continually called Himself "the Son of man," a term used of the prophesied Messiah in Daniel 7:13. Jesus had made the triumphal entry into Jerusalem (Matt. 21:1-11) just as it was foretold that the Kingdom of Israel would do (Zech. 9:9). Jesus wanted to be accepted as the Son of God, but the final evidence that He was the Son of God would not be given until Christ rose from the dead (Matt. 12:38-40; 16:4). The resurrection itself is part of the Gospel (I Cor. 15:3, 4). The apostles were to be witnesses of the resurrection (Acts 1:22; 4:33). Now that Jesus faces His death and resurrection, He boldly declares Himself to be the Son of God. Perhaps one reason He did not press His claim to be the Son of God more boldly before was that it was not time for Him to die.

"Hereafter shall ye see the Son of man sitting on the right hand of power" (vs. 64) refers to the fact that after His resurrection Jesus would sit down with the Father in His throne (Rev. 3:21), sitting at the Father's right hand in Heaven until it should come time for His enemies to be destroyed and Christ to take up His earthly reign (Ps. 110:1). The Jews were familiar with the promise of Psalm 110:1. How could these Pharisees see Jesus sitting on the right hand of God? Some commentators think it is meant they would see the evidence of His earthly ministry in the work of His disciples following His resurrection. More likely it is meant that in Hell they would know what is going on in Heaven. The rich man in Hell saw Lazarus and Abraham in paradise (Luke 16:23). Those in Hell are tormented "in the presence of the holy angels, and in the presence of the Lamb" (Rev. 14:10). So people in Hell see Jesus sitting at the right hand of the Father! If any of these were saved before they died, then of course in Heaven they would see the Saviour seated with the Father in His throne. Likewise, then, these wicked Pharisees, even those who never repented and who went to Hell, will see Jesus "coming in the clouds of heaven" (vs. 64) when He returns to reign as King. Compare "coming in the clouds" with Matthew 24:30, Revelation 1:7, etc. Jesus went away with clouds (Acts 1:9); the same Jesus will return in like manner (Acts 1:11).

The profession of Jesus to be the Messiah, the very Son of God, was so bold that the Jewish rulers were now enabled to accuse Him of blasphemy and agreed by acclamation, "He is guilty of death," or worthy to die (vs. 66). Then followed the shameful abuse of verse 67. It was to be repeated later by the soldiers (Matt. 27:29, 30). The horror of this abuse was much worse than is generally supposed. The details were foretold in the Scriptures (Isa. 50:6; 52:14). When it became apparent that Christ would not use His miracle-working power against them, even the servants slapped His face (Mark 14:65), blindfolded Him (Luke 22:64), struck Him, and asked Him to prophesy or tell by divine inspiration who it was.

Remember that the trial in verses 57 to 68 was in the nighttime. When the whole Sanhedrin was called together in the morning (Matt. 27:1), they went through the form of a trial again and immediately asked Him the question, "Art thou the Christ?" (Luke 22:66-71). Jesus answered them immediately that He was, though He charged they would not believe nor let Him go, and so the farcial trial was soon over.

Verses 69-75 Peter Denies Christ

Peter's denial is told also in Mark 14:66-72, Luke 22:54-62 and in John 18:15-18, 25-27. After fleeing when Jesus was arrested (vs. 56) Simon Peter later followed Him afar off unto the high priest's palace and sat with the servants (vs. 58). Another disciple (we think John), known to the high priest and the servants, vouched for Peter and got him inside (John 18:15, 16). At first Peter was "without in the palace" (vs. 69), that is, not in the room where Jesus was held before the Sanhedrin. Possibly he was in the servants' quarters (vs. 58). Here he was accosted by a damsel and made his first denial (vss. 69, 70). Then Peter went "out into the porch" (vs. 71), probably nearer where Jesus was. There he was questioned by another maid and denied again, this time "with an oath" (vs. 72). Others also spoke to him on the question, probably more than one (vs. 73), and this time "began he to curse and to swear, saying, I know not the man" (vs. 74). Jesus had previously, the same night, told Peter that "even in this night, before the cock crow twice, thou shalt deny me thrice" (Mark 14:30). The other Gospels do not mention, as Mark does, that the cock was to crow twice and did (Mark 14:68, 72), but only mention that the cock crew at the last. Jesus was nearby, and Peter was looking on the scene, probably through a doorway. When Peter denied the third time, and the cock crew, "The Lord turned, and looked upon Peter" (Luke 22:61), then Peter remembered the Saviour's words and went out and wept bitterly (vs. 75).

How we ought to thank God that He has a cock to crow when we deny Him! Peter had the conscience of a saved man; he had been born again. For such people God repeatedly has warnings. How many a saved man, backslidden, worldly and covetous, has come back to God by his mother's casket! How many mothers and fathers who have drifted away from the path of right have been moved by a baby's fever as Peter was by the crowing of the cock! Reverses in business, accidents, poverty, human troubles, uneasiness of conscience – how we ought to thank God for these things which call us back to Him. It was a part of Christ's love for Peter that He had the cock crow. Tradition says that the rest of his life Peter could never hear a cock crow without weeping. If so, his tears for his own weakness and sin ought to be mingled with rejoicing for the unfailing love of God who called him, sought him still when he was backslidden and disobedient.

Peter denied three times, but he may have been questioned by more than three people as you see by comparison of verses 69-75 with Luke 22:56-60 and John 18:15-18, 25-27. Two girls questioned Peter (vss. 69, 71; Mark 14:66, 69). At least two men seemed to have accused him also (Luke 22:58-60). However, these two men may be included in "they that stood by" (vs. 73). There is no contradiction in these Scriptures.

Peter's sin was great. (1) He denied Christ. (2) He lied, even saying, "I do not know the man" (vs. 72). (3) He cursed and swore. It would be hard to imagine more dreadful sins committed at one time by a professed disciple of Christ, a preacher, yea, an apostle!

Sin is never excusable, but there were extenuating circumstances. (1) Peter sincerely loved Jesus and it took some courage to come into the very house of the high priest to see the trial. Doubtless, Peter was heartbroken and anxious about the result. (2) It was a cold, spring night, now near morning and that gave Peter seemingly a good reason to be by the fire with the officers and enemies of

Christ (John 18:18). (3) Remember that Peter's life would have been really in danger but for the protection that the Saviour gave. Peter was the most prominent disciple of Jesus; he had struck the servant of the high priest with his sword. He had openly declared that he would die with Jesus if necessary (vss. 33, 35). Later, Stephen and James were killed (Acts 7:54-60; 12:1, 2) by the Jewish rulers, and others were beaten. Peter had good reason to be afraid. (4) Two things made him conspicuous. One was his speech – that of a Galilean fisherman. The Galilean dialect differed enough from that of Judea to be noticeable, and Peter had a tendency to talk too quickly. Besides, the man who had his ear cut off by Peter (John 18:10) had a kinsman also in the court (John 18:26) who had seen Peter and remembered him carefully. Altogether, Peter found himself in a very difficult place. He had not taken time to pray as he ought (vss. 40, 41). His life seemed in danger; the Saviour's cause seemed hopeless, and Peter found himself in the midst of the enemies of Christ.

The things that led to Peter's denial of Christ were probably these; (1) his self-confidence. He would not be warned (vss. S3, 35). (2) He was sleepy and did not take time to pray (vss. 40, 41). (3) He depended on human strength instead of divine power, using the sword (vs. 51; John 18:10). (4) He got in bad company, mixing with the servants and officers.

The cursing and swearing that came from Peter's mouth must have been a throwback to his old wicked days. No man can ever sin with impunity. Any man who ever drank liquor is in danger of taking it up again, so he ought to be desperately afraid. I have known of two or three preachers, earnest, good men, who fell into temptation and became drunkards again after they had been gloriously saved from the life of drink and had entered the ministry. A man who quits tobacco should be constantly on his guard lest he fall into the same temptation; so, one who has cursed in the old wicked days will find himself tempted to think the same thoughts in his heart, and even in time of great stress to say the same things. Sin is such a frightful thing because it leaves the tracks and marks of habit. Sin so easily becomes a habit and habits are so hard to erase!

No man is safe from temptation except he who flees from temptation. Peter, having been warned about the temptation to deny Christ, should have avoided temptation altogether, but he did not take the warning. Consider how Joseph fled when he was

344

tempted to sin with Potiphar's wife (Gen. 39:7-12), how Abraham avoided a quarrel with Lot (Gen. 13:8, 9), how Isaac gave up the wells he had digged to keep out of temptation and trouble (Gen. 26:17-22). On the contrary, notice how good men – Samson, David, and Solomon – sinned when they did not avoid bad company (Judg. 16:1-21; II Sam. 11:1-5; I Kings 11:1-8; Neh. 13:26). Lot lost everything but his soul by pitching his tent in Sodom (Gen. 13:12; 19th chapter). The strongest men in the Bible fell into sin because of bad company. No Christian in the world is safe except as he avoids bad company. Anyone with whom you associate will influence you. One of the first requirements of success in the Christian life and spiritual prosperity is that a man "walketh not in the counsel of the ungodly, nor standeth in the way of sinners, nor sitteth in the seat of the scornful" (Ps. 1:1). You are no stronger than Peter, Samson, Lot, and David, and I beg you to take to heart this warning.

The events surrounding the death of Christ on the cross are world events, the most momentous that have ever occurred on this planet and to the human race. I believe that the action of unregenerate men in hating Jesus, plotting against Him, abusing Him and murdering Him is a condemnation of the whole race, showing the awful wickedness and depravity of human nature. When Christ was condemned to die on the cross it proved nothing against Christ, but it did prove much against the race of men for whom He died. The fact of the crucifixion proves the fact of sin, the fact of Hell, and the fact of judgment. A race who would crucify Christ must be dealt with in judgment. In the same way we learn much from the actions of redeemed people, the born-again disciples of Jesus in their actions surrounding the betrayal and death of Christ. Long before the last week many of the disciples had left Jesus to follow Him no more (John 6:66).

This last week in Jerusalem, the public is interested, but of true friends, Jesus has very few. Where are the throngs He fed with the five loaves and two fishes? (Matt. 14:15-21). Where are the multitudes He taught in the Sermon on the Mount? (Matt., chaps. 5, 6, 7). Those he had healed of terrible sicknesses, blindness, leprosy, palsy, and demon possession would have made an army – where are they? Where are the seventy whom Jesus sent out to preach His Gospel over Judea? (Luke 10:1, 2).

345

Remember that nearly all Israel is gathered at this pass-over season in Jerusalem, yet many of those formerly near to Jesus are not seen nor heard of as His friends in this time of testing when Jewish leaders plan to kill Christ. Joseph of Arimathea, a member of the Sanhedrin, is a believer in Jesus but keeps it secret (John 19:38). Some of the dear women – His mother, Mary of Bethany, and others – would doubtless have died for Him but they are not here in His testing!

Finally of the twelve chosen apostles, those who declared they would willingly die for Him (vs. 35), we find they all fail. First Judas, unsaved, betrays the Saviour. The eight disciples in the Garden went to sleep; even Peter, James, and John could not watch with Him one hour (vss. 37, 40). Then when He was arrested "all the disciples forsook him, and fled" (vs. 56). Now Simon Peter has denied Christ, cursing and swearing like any wicked, drunken, unbelieving fool. Not a single Christian in the world stood faultless and without blame in relation to the betrayal, sufferings and death of Jesus. This surely is a fair indictment of the best of men and women. None of us is perfect. If we claim so, it only means that, like the disciples, we do not know what temptation we will meet and how sorely we will be tried. We are all unprofitable servants (Luke 17:10). When we would do good evil is present with us, so that with the mind we serve the law of God but with the flesh the law of sin (Rom. 7:21, 25). Like Paul, we are not perfect and have not yet attained (Phil. 3:12), so must cry, "For I know that in me (that is, in my flesh) dwelleth no good thing" (Rom. 7:18). No living saint has yet reached the point of sinless perfection (Rom. 3:9-20; I John 1:8, 10). So then let us on the one hand deal charitably with Christians who sin and on the other hand let us take heed lest we ourselves, being tempted, fall into the same sins. Above all, let us thank God that He loves us and keeps us even in our temptings and testings. He prayed for Peter that his faith would fail not (Luke 22:32). Satan sifted Peter as wheat, but God did not let him go.

Verses 1,2 Sanhedrin in Daytime Meeting Makes Condemnation of Jesus Official

Let it be remembered that there was a dual government in Judea. The first element was the Jewish government, based upon the Mosaic Law and the Talmud, writings or traditions of Jewish leaders interpreting and adding to the law. The chief legislative body was the Sanhedrin or council, composed of about seventy chief priests and elders. The high priest was the most influential single person among the Jews even in secular matters and in civil law. But Judea was not an independent state; rather, it was a conquered territory of the Roman Empire, and the final say in government was exercised by Rome. Pilate was the Roman governor. The Jewish Sanhedrin could punish small crimes but was not allowed at this time to execute the death penalty. So after agreeing to condemn Jesus to death, the Sanhedrin took Him to the Roman governor, Pilate, to persuade him to execute the sentence.

The unofficial trial of Jesus took place in the night before those of the scribes and elders who were assembled (Matt. 26:57; Mark 14:53). However, by their rules the conviction of any man must take place in the daytime, so when the morning was come (vs. 1) the whole council came together (Mark 15:1; Luke 22:66) to go quickly through the form of trial. Jesus was again asked the question if He were the Christ, and, on His saying so, they immediately condemned Him (Luke 22:66-71) and led Him away to Pilate.

Verses 3-10 Judas Being Conscience-Stricken Returns Bribe Money and Hangs Self

None of the Gospels discusses the end of Judas but Matthew. In Acts 1:16-25 we have an inspired record of the words of Simon

Peter concerning Judas, when another apostle was elected to take his place as a witness of the resurrection of Christ.

Make a careful distinction in your mind between Peter and Judas in their sins. (1) Peter had a divinely given faith in Christ as the Saviour and Son of God (Matt. 16:16, 17; John 1:40-42), while Judas "believed not" and was a devil (John 6:64, 70, 71). (2) Christ, foretelling Peter's denial, had prayed for him so that his faith would not fail (Luke 22:32), sent a special message to Peter after His resurrection (Mark 16:7), and took particular pains to call Peter back into the work (John 21:15-17). Of Judas, on the contrary, Jesus said, "it had been good for that man if he had not been born" (Matt. 26:24). Jesus said, "those that thou gavest me I have kept, and none of them is lost, but the son of perdition" (John 17:12). Judas was never saved, After Peter was converted, he was never lost. Christians commit terrible sins, sometimes outwardly as bad as those committed by unconverted people, but their hearts are not the same as the hearts of unsaved people and they are not judged the same. Peter suffered for his sin of denying Christ, but he suffered as a born-again Christian whose heart had been truly changed and whose sins were all under the blood of Christ. Peter at heart was God's man and Judas at heart was Satan's man (Luke 22:3; John 13:2).

The word *repented* in verse 3 is not the Greek *metanoeo,* meaning change of mind or heart, used repeatedly in the New Testament for the repentance which brings salvation. It is a different word, *metamelomai,* meaning "to feel regret, to repent of, to alter one's purpose (Donnegan, Lexicon); "to be careful or concerned with" (Young's Analytical Concordance). Judas was remorseful, just as any man who has in the past lived a fine, moral life might be remorseful over shameful sin. He did not turn to God with true repentance to receive salvation. We may say he repented about the act of taking money for betraying Jesus but did not repent and turn from his rejection of Christ as Saviour. The repentance and confession of Judas (vss. 3, 4) did not mean that he was saved. He went "to his own place" (Acts 1:25), evidently to Hell. It were better for him if he had never been born (Matt. 26:24), and that could not be true if he were forgiven all his sins and went to Heaven. Besides, Judas went and hanged himself, which is no evidence of a new heart or of the peace of salvation.

The attitude of the chief priests, "What is that to us? see thou to that" (vs. 4) should be a tragic warning to all who let others lead them into sin. It is no true friend who leads one into sin. The prodigal son had plenty of friends while his money lasted, but when it was gone, "no man gave unto him" (Luke 15:16). Every sinner who follows his friends away from Christ will find that such friends forsake him when his sins find him out. Brewers and bartenders never support the widows and children of drunkards. Whoremongers never open homes for fallen girls. Satan has no comfort for those who reach the dregs in the cup of sin. Sinners help one into sin but do not help him out.

How did Judas die? He "hanged himself," then "falling headlong, he burst asunder in the midst, and all his bowels gushed out" (Acts 1:18). These Scriptures supplement but do not contradict each other.

Strange how religious were these chief priests! Their religion led them to keep petty details of the law while they bribed Judas, suborned witnesses and murdered Jesus, the Son of God! Compare verse 6 with what Jesus said of them in Matthew 23:23-28. Beware of any religious profession which does not place a love for and trust in Jesus Christ as Saviour and Lord as the foundation. There can be no sincere morality without trusting Christ for salvation and regeneration. In their dilemma the Jewish rulers unconsciously fulfilled the Scriptures in Zechariah 11:12, 13. It is remarkable that so many details concerning the death of Jesus were foretold in the Scriptures.

The Scripture may have some reference also to Jeremiah 18:1-4 and 19:1-3. However, it seems likely that the minor prophets were usually copied in the same roll with Jeremiah and so the term *Jeremiah* (vs. 9) would refer to the whole roll. So Ephraim, the principal tribe of the Northern kingdom, was sometimes used as a name for all the Northern kingdom, and Judah was continually used as the name for the Southern kingdom, though it also included the tribe of Benjamin and the Levites (Isa. 7:2, 5, 8, 9, 17; Ezek. 37:16). The first five books of the Bible written by Moses were very generally copied in the same roll and called "the law" (Luke 24:44; Acts 24:14; I Cor. 14:34 referring to Gen. 3:16), though Genesis really had none of the Mosaic Law.

Verses 11-14 Jesus, Brought Before Pilate, Answers Nothing

Read here Mark 15:1-5, Luke 23:1-5, and John 18:28-38. John's Gospel gives more details.

The chief priests took Jesus to Pilate's judgment hall and Jesus was taken in, probably by the soldiers, to the judgment hall, but they themselves stayed outside, "lest they should be defiled; but that they might eat the passover" (John 18:28). Pilate went outside the judgment hall for conference with the chief priests who would not come inside. Pilate urged the Jews to take Jesus and judge Him according to their law, but the Jews complained they could not put anybody to death (John 18:31). The conversation of Pilate and Jesus (John 18:33-38) is given only in John. Compare verses 12 to 14 with Isaiah 53:7. Jesus was the Passover Lamb and it was time for the slaughter, so He made no resistance.

The accusation of the chief priests (vs. 12) is not given in detail here. Mark 15:3 says, "The chief priests accused him of many things." In John 18:30 we are told they accused Him as a "malefactor," and in Luke 23:2 we are told that they accused Jesus of "perverting the nation, and forbidding to give tribute to Caesar, saying that he himself is Christ a King." They hoped to arouse Pilate against Jesus by accusing Jesus of sedition and resistance against Rome. Jesus had claimed to be the Christ, but the charge against Him of forbidding to give tribute was deliberate falsehood. They had hoped Jesus would forbid paying tribute to Caesar (Matt. 22:15-21), but He had stopped their mouths by commanding, "Render therefore unto Caesar the things which are Caesar's; and unto God the things that are God's." In fact, Jesus Himself had paid taxes (Matt. 17:24-27).

Another accusation they made was, "He stirreth up the people, teaching throughout all Jewry, beginning from Galilee to this place" (Luke 23:5). The reference to Galilee caused Pilate to learn that Jesus was a Galilean, so he sent Jesus before Herod for trial (Luke 23:6-12). Thus the prophecy of Psalm 2:1, 2, "the rulers take counsel..." was fulfilled (Acts 4:25-28). However, when Jesus worked no miracles, Herod returned Him to Pilate for judgment.

Verses 15-26 Barabbas Chosen for Release Instead of Jesus

Similar passages are in Mark 15:6-15, Luke 23:13-25, and John 18:38-40.

Note the contrast between the sinless Saviour, Christ, and Barabbas. Barabbas was a "notable prisoner" (vs. 16) guilty of insurrection and murder (Mark 15:7; Luke 23:25). He was also a robber or bandit (John 18:40). This contrast was mentioned by Peter in his sermon before the people of wicked Jerusalem in Acts 3:14, 15. God planned this contrast and put it into Pilate's heart so that they must choose between Christ and Barabbas (vs. 17). It was a custom to release one such prisoner at the passover time each year (vs. 15). Pilate probably selected Barabbas as an outstanding example of wickedness. He was as "notable" (vs. 16) a sinner as Jesus was "notable" for purity and holiness. Perhaps Pilate thought these all would prefer that Jesus be released instead of such a notorious murderer and robber, and hoped that thus he would be delivered from the responsibility of condemning Christ.

In choosing Barabbas the people chose wickedness in preference to goodness, sin in preference to holiness. Barabbas represented each one's own wicked nature. They were condemned because they "loved darkness rather than light, because their deeds were evil" (John 3:19). No one ever turns down Jesus without a cause, and the cause is always wicked. However hidden that real motive is, every Christ-rejector has his Barabbas of sin that he chooses in preference to Jesus.

Incidentally, Barabbas experienced substitution. Jesus literally died in his place. But He died in my place, too, and just as literally. I go free from the wrath of God and the just penalty of sin because Christ died in my place!

Consider the case of Pilate. He was thoroughly convinced that Jesus was innocent (vss. 23, 24; Mark 15:10; Luke 23:14, 15, 22; John 18:38; 19:4). In fact, the evidence is that Pilate really believed that Jesus was what He claimed to be – the Son of God and the coming King of the Jews. Notice how reverently he seems to have listened to Jesus in John 18:36-39. Pilate was afraid when he heard that Jesus claimed to be the Son of God (John 19:7, 8). Pilate

351

presented Jesus to the Jews as their King (John 19:14). Pilate, in the accusation over the cross, called Jesus "THE KING OF THE JEWS" (vs. 37) and refused to change the title when the Jewish leaders protested (John 19:19-22). Pilate tried to evade responsibility for the death of Christ without displeasing the Jews. He tried to avoid a decision. Notice: (1) He told the Jews, "Take ye him, and judge him according to your law" (John 18:31). (2) He sent Him to Herod for judgment, hoping to escape responsibility (Luke 23:6-12). (3) He selected Barabbas, the robber and murderer, and offered to release either Jesus or Barabbas, hoping they would ask for Jesus. (4) He desperately pleaded the innocency of Jesus (Luke 23:14, 15; John 18:38; 19:4). (5) He scourged Jesus, hoping thus to appease their hate without killing the Saviour (Luke 23:16; John 19:1). (6) Finally, he washed his hands, saying, "I am innocent of the blood of this just person: see ye to it" (vs. 24). Yet all the waters of the seas could not wash away the guilt of Pilate for not trusting Jesus as his Saviour and claiming Him openly. All those who had part in the death of Christ were used to carry out God's plan, yet that does not minimize their sin (Matt. 18:7).

Notice the terrible curse which the Jews brought upon themselves (vs. 25). I have no doubt that the present blindness of Israel (Rom. 11:25), the persecution of Jews everywhere, their scattering to the whole world, is because of the national rejection of the Saviour. Compare this with Luke 21:20-24 and Matthew 23:31-39.

After the scourging of Jesus (vs. 26) Pilate again intervened, pleading to the people to spare Jesus (John 19:1-15).

Verses 27-32 Soldiers Mock and Abuse Jesus

Similar passages are given in Mark 15:16-21, Luke 23:26-32, and John 19:16, 17.

This abuse is by the soldiers. "The common hall" (vs. 27) was called "Praetorium" (Mark 15:16). There the whole band of soldiers was called together to be amused in abusing our Lord. The Roman government has taken charge of Jesus to crucify Him. Compare this with the abuse by the high priest and his officers and servants and members of the Sanhedrin (Matt. 26:66, 67; Mark 14:65; Luke

22:63-65; John 18:22). They stripped Him and put on Him a scarlet robe, a king's garment (vs. 28), as Herod and his men of war had also done in mockery (Luke 23:11). His crown was of thorns; His sceptre was a reed; His tribute was spittle! (vss. 29, 30).

Every reader ought to have a chastened and reverent heart as he thinks of the shame our Saviour endured for us. And it is not all told here for they also plucked out His beard (Isa. 50:6). What was in the heart and mind of our Saviour during this shameful treatment? That is given us in the 69th Psalm. Psalm 69:5 would apply to Christ only in that He had our sins and foolishness upon Him. But in that chapter notice that the following verses are clearly about Jesus: (1) verse 9, "the zeal of thine house hath eaten me up," etc. (plainly quoted in the New Testament as a prophecy of Jesus, John 2:17). (2) Verse 8 pictures Jesus not believed in by His mother's children (John 7:5) until after His resurrection (Acts 1:14). (3) Verse 20 of Psalm 69 pictures the broken heart of Christ, with no comforters. (4) Verse 21, "They gave me also gall for my meat; and in my thirst they gave me vinegar to drink," was clearly about Christ (vs. 34). So the 69th Psalm reveals the thoughts of Jesus at this time just as the 22nd Psalm pictures the crucifixion and the thoughts of Christ as He hung on the cross.

The reverent heart will see in this passage a logical need for the glorious return and literal reign of Christ on earth. He who was mocked as a false King will in truth come to reign as pictured in Isaiah 11:1-12, Micah 4:1-8, Zechariah 14:9, Matthew 25:31-46, and Revelation 19:11-16. In the 2nd Psalm God connects this time of Christ's abasement with the coming time of His reign. They mocked His Kingship, yet Psalm 2:6 declares that Christ will sit on the holy hill of Zion, that the uttermost parts of the earth will be His possession (Ps. 2:8), that He will break the heathen with a rod of iron (Ps. 2:9). He who suffered as the Lamb of God must reign as the Lion of the tribe of Judah. It could never fit in with the plan of God that the only crown Jesus should wear on this earth should be a crown of thorns and that the only homage He would ever have would be mockery and spittle. It is only proper that Christ should wrest the kingdoms of this world from Satan and rule them Himself and that the wicked who will not have Him to reign over them should be destroyed before Him (Luke 19:14, 27).

Some have thought that Simon in verse 32 may have been a colored man. It is possible but not necessary. Cyrene was in Africa, but many Jews dwelt there. This Simon and his family were well known. His sons were Alexander and Rufus (Mark 15:21), and the Rufus may be the same as that mentioned in Romans 16:13. First, the cross was laid on Jesus to carry to the place of the crucifixion as the custom was (John 19:17). Then, "as they came out" (vs. 32), possibly as they came out of the city, they found Simon "who passed by, coming out of the country" (Mark 15:21) and made Simon bear the cross. It is thought that Jesus may have fallen under the cross, unable to bear it after His fasting, sleepless nights, suffering in the Garden, and the abuse of the mob, priests, soldiers. Possibly Simon of Cyrene offered some word of comfort to Jesus and so was seized by the soldiers. Or possibly he was simply seized because he was a Negro, since he came from Africa, or because he was a stranger. At any rate, that which was intended for shame and abuse on this stranger passing by lifted him to an immortal peak of fame through the centuries! What honor was his to bear the cross of the Lord Jesus and suffer some of the indignities of our Saviour as He went to the crucifixion! That is high honor indeed and we should, like the apostles, rejoice to suffer shame for His name (Acts 5:41). Persecution for Jesus' sake should cause us to rejoice and leap for joy (Matt. 5:10-12; Luke 6:23). In fact, we are told that all of us ought gladly to go with Jesus outside the camp, bearing His reproach (Heb. 13:13). Blessed Simon of Cyrene! Perhaps many times what we may count as shame will turn out to our eternal happiness and glory.

Verses 33, 34 At the "Place of a Skull" Jesus Was Offered Vinegar and Gall

The place where Jesus was crucified was called "Golgotha," meaning "a place of a skull" (vs. 33). Probably it looked like a skull. At least such a place has been selected which looks somewhat like a skull. We cannot certainly identify the place where Jesus was crucified. Luke 23:33 calls the place "Calvary" in our King James Version and the term has become very popular, but Calvary is not a proper name – it is simply a Latin word for *skull* and the Greek word used here in the Greek New Testament means literally *skull*. People usually speak of "mount Calvary," but the place usually thought to be where our Saviour was crucified is not a mount but only a small hill some few feet high. Jesus was crucified outside the city of Jerusalem. "They came out" (vs. 32); they "led him out to crucify him" (Mark 15:20). Jesus "suffered without the gate" (Heb. 13:12). However, the place was near Jerusalem (John 19:20). Doubtless all of us have longed to see the place where our Saviour died, but many of us cannot. However, we can enter into His experience, having "the fellowship of his sufferings" (Phil. 3:10). We can help to "fill up that which is behind of the afflictions of Christ" (Col. 1:24). We can spiritually go with Jesus outside the camp, bearing His reproach (Heb. 13:13). We can take up our cross daily and crucify self and so follow Jesus (Luke 9:23; Gal. 2:20; Col. 3:3).

I beg you to meditate on these things and let the Holy Spirit teach you the meaning of the crucifixion for us who are saved.

The vinegar and gall (vs. 34) were foretold in Psalm 69:21. Usually it is explained that this was a stupefying drink to lessen the suffering, but there is no indication in the Scriptures that any of these wicked men wanted to lessen the sufferings of Christ. Rather, from Psalm 69:21 it becomes apparent that this was a part of their wickedness. He was thirsty for water and they gave Him vinegar; in His hunger for meat they gave Him gall. There is nothing in all the Scriptures that lessens the guilt of those who crucified the Saviour and therefore the guilt of sinners everywhere! Let us not here, then, suppose them better and ourselves better (for those wicked men are *our* representatives) than the Scriptures declare them to be.

The gall might stand for anything terribly bitter. Mark 15:23 says "wine mingled with myrrh." It was doubtless pictured prophetically when the passover lamb was eaten with "bitter herbs" (Exod. 12:8; Num. 9:11). The wine, very sour, would be vinegar. Notice that they offered Him vinegar again later (vs. 48), near the time of His death. The vinegar and gall which Jesus drank picture the torment that was properly mine. Sin always turns to gall and bitterness and the way of the transgressor is hard. However, Jesus drank my cup for me, and instead, I am given the water of everlasting life, and all who believe in Him will never thirst again (John 4:14; 6:35).

Verses 35-44 Jesus Crucified With Two Thieves, Mocked by Chief Priests, Scribes, and Elders

Very carefully study the parallel passages, Mark 15:24-32, Luke 23:33-43, and John 19:17-24. For instance, you note that Luke tells how good women of Jerusalem followed Jesus weeping, and His answer to them (Luke 23:27-31). You will note that only John gives the words of Jesus on the cross committing His mother to John (John 19:26, 27). The death of our Saviour is of such importance that any earnest Christian should read over and over, with meditation, self-examination, prayer, faith, and praise, the accounts of our Lord's sufferings for us.

The hundreds of details concerning the sufferings and death of Christ foretold and typified in the Old Testament are amazing. The constant thought of Jesus was that "the scriptures must be fulfilled" (Matt. 26:54, 56; Mark 14:49). In the scriptural definition of the Gospel it is twice specified that the death, burial, and resurrection of Christ must be "according to the scriptures" (I Cor. 15:3, 4). If you study carefully the divine instructions concerning the pass- over lamb (Exod. 12:1-11), then read Psalms 22 and 69; Isaiah 50:6, 7; 52:14; 53; Zechariah 12:10; 13:6, many, many details of the sufferings and death of Christ will be found foretold there. So the four soldiers parted His garments .among them (John 19:23), but for a better seamless garment they parted lots, that Psalm 22:18 might be fulfilled. Two "thieves" (vs. 44) also called "malefactors" (Luke 23:33) were crucified also, one on either side of Him, that the Scripture might be fulfilled, "he was numbered with the transgressors" (Mark 15:28; Isa. 53:9, 12), as even Jesus foretold (Luke 22:37).

"They" in verse 36 included the chief priests and the soldiers, with many, many others. Many thousands of Jews were present at the crucifixion. It was the passover time and practically the entire nation was gathered in Jerusalem. Doubtless a continual stream passed by through the day (vs. 39), besides the "great company" that followed Him to the crucifixion (Luke 23:27). The chief priests, scribes, and elders were present (vs. 41). So were the Roman centurion (vs. 54), Pilate (John 19:19), the three Marys (John

19:25), and John (John 19:26). It was about the third hour, about nine o'clock, when Jesus was crucified (Mark 15:25). Jesus was on the cross until "about the ninth hour" (vs. 46), until about three o'clock in the afternoon or past. See my sermons on "Watching Jesus Die," in the book *When Skeletons Come Out of Their Closets*.

The love of Jesus for these sinners never wavered when they nailed Him to the cross, and it seems that His first words after the crucifixion, as He hung there, were, "Father, forgive them; for they know not what they do" (Luke 23:34). That prayer was for us, too, since all of us had a part in the death He suffered. Every sin falls on Jesus. But He longs to have us forgiven, and is "not willing that any should perish, but that all should come to repentance" (II Pet. 3:9). See also Isaiah 55:1, Ezekiel 33:11, I John 2:1, 2; Revelation 21:6 and 22:17.

What accusation was written over the head of Jesus? The four Gospels do not give it exactly the same. Compare verse 37 with Mark 15:26, Luke 23:38 and John 19:19. Remember that each one of the Gospels is verbally inspired and infallibly correct in what it tells but that none professes to give all the facts. The whole inscription was "THIS IS JESUS OF NAZARETH THE KING OF THE JEWS" as you will see by putting the verses together. However, since the inscription was written in three languages (Luke 23:38), Greek for the learned, Latin for Romans, and Hebrew for the Jews, the inscription could vary slightly in the different languages.

The mockery of those who watched Jesus on the cross was terrible. It reveals the wicked hearts of the whole race. Compare verses 41 to 43 with Psalm 22:6-8. Then read on in Psalm 22:9-20 and see revealed the heart of our Saviour and what were His thoughts and emotions as He hung on the cross.

Notice the threefold temptation of Jesus to come down from the cross: (1) the mob that passed by (vs. 40), (2) the chief priests and scribes (vss. 41, 42), and (3) the thieves also (vs. 44). Satan had tempted Jesus to reign without suffering (Matt. 4:9); had tempted Jesus to avoid the cross, speaking through the Apostle Peter (Matt. 16:22-25); had tried to kill Jesus in Gethsemane with the sorrows of the world (Matt. 26:37, 38). Jesus had prayed through and the cup of death passed by until the morrow (Matt. 26:39-44; Heb. 5:7). Even until He "gave up the ghost" on the cross, however, Satan continued his temptation.

Both thieves first railed at Jesus (vs. 44) and one of them continued until they killed Him, but the other repented and was saved (Luke 23:39-43). Thank God, at least one soul believed that Jesus was King of the Jews, perceived that He died like a God and not only like a man, and loved Him and trusted Him for salvation! "When thou comest into thy kingdom" – the thief properly understood the fact of the second coming of Christ and His millennial reign as foretold in the Old Testament. One thief was saved that the vilest sinner may not despair if he sincerely repents even upon his deathbed. The other thief died unsaved that no one might presume on the mercy of God and delay until the approach of death! Thank God for unbounded mercy, but let us take care, lest presuming, we lose taste for mercy and die unsaved.

Verses 45-50 Jesus Dies on the Cross

For three hours Jesus hung on the cross in the burning heat of the spring sun, very warm in Palestine. The spring nights were cool (John 18:18), but the days warm. Then from the sixth hour (noon) until the ninth hour (three in the afternoon) there was darkness over all the land.

> Well might the sun in darkness hide,
> And shut his glories in,
> When Christ, the mighty Maker, died
> For man the creature's sin.

In those three hours Jesus must have tasted all the pangs of Hell, the torments of a lost soul. Note the cry of Jesus in verse 46, "My God, my God, why hast thou forsaken me?" the cry long foretold in Psalm 22:1. During the darkness and agony on the cross God the Father seems to have forsaken Jesus. He was forsaken that we might not be forsaken. He suffered judgment for sin that we might be set free from judgment for sin. Speaking as a lost soul would speak, Jesus cried, "My God," not "My Father," but when He came to the point of death when He could say about the atonement for the sins of the world, "It is finished" (John 19:30), He addressed God not as "My God," but as "Father" and said, "into thy hands I commend my spirit" (Luke 23:46), and gave up the ghost. No lost sinner in Hell will have a right to call God "Father." This indicates that the torments of Jesus ended on the cross; the atonement was finished, and Jesus did not go to further torment after death.

358

Rather, He went immediately to His Father in Paradise as did the dying penitent thief (Luke 23:43). The so-called Apostles' Creed as used by Catholics affirms that "He descended into Hell" and that is based upon Psalm 16:10, "For thou wilt not leave my soul in hell." But the word there translated *hell* is *sheol*, meaning in the Old Testament, the place of the dead. To be sure those in Hell and torment are in sheol, the place of the dead, but so are those in Heaven in sheol, the place of the dead. The Greek word *Hades*, translated also *hell* (Acts 2:27) means the same. Jesus did not go to a place of torment when He died. His atonement was finished completely on the cross and He committed His spirit to His Father and went immediately to Paradise at death. When Jesus said after His resurrection, "I am not yet ascended to my Father" (John 20:17), He referred to His resurrection body, not to His spirit. It seems clear that Jesus on the cross suffered all the torments of Hell. Dr. B. H. Carroll thought that the words "I thirst" (John 19:28) picture the torment of lost souls in Hell like that of the rich man who pleaded for water (Luke 16:24).

Jews generally did not speak Hebrew in the time of Christ, but Aramaic. Hebrew was already becoming a dead language. Jesus quoted "Eli, Eli, lama sabachthani" (vs. 46) from Psalm 22:1. Not understanding Hebrew, when Jesus said, "Eli" (the Hebrew word for God), the Jews supposed that He called for Elias (the New Testament form of Elijah, vss. 47, 49). Remember Elijah's prominence in the Old Testament. Jews regarded him much, particularly because of the promised return of Elijah (Mal. 4:5, 6). Many had asked if John the Baptist were Elijah (John 1:21). Others had thought that Jesus was Elijah (Matt. 16:14).

When Jesus died, He "yielded up the ghost." Dr. Scofield says, "Literally, 'dismissed His spirit.' The Gr. implies an act of the will." See also Mark 15:37, Luke 23:46 where Jesus said, "Father, into thy hands I commend my spirit," and John 19:30 where we are told that Jesus said, "It is finished" and gave up the ghost. Jesus said of His life in John 10:18, "No man taketh it from me, but I lay it down of myself." The death of Christ was a willing death, a deliberately accepted death. He died according to the Scriptures and of His own choice, at the time appointed, and when the price for man's redemption was completed, altogether finished. Now we may properly say, "Who shall lay anything to the charge of God's elect? It is God that justifieth. Who is he that condemneth? It is

Christ that died…" (Rom. 8:33, 34). The Gospel says that "Christ died *for our sins*" and there is no other explanation for His death except our sins. The measure, time, and kind of His sufferings completely satisfied the requirements of our sins and then Jesus gave up the ghost. Praise God for redemption through His blood!

Notice the seven cries of Jesus on the cross:

1. *"Father, forgive them; for they know not what they do."* – Luke 23:34.
2. *"To day shalt thou be with me in paradise"* – Luke 23:43.
3. *"Woman, behold thy son!"* and *"Behold thy mother!"* – John 19:26, 27.
4. *"My God, my God, why hast thou forsaken me?"* – Matt. 27:46; Mark 15:34.
5. *"I thirst"* – John 19:28.
6. *"It is finished."* – John 19:30.
7. *"Father, into thy hands I commend my spirit."* – Luke 23:46.

Besides these, there was the loud cry of Jesus with no words (vs. 50).

Verses 51-56 Manifestations in Nature When Jesus Died

We cannot here go into a detailed discussion of the temple at Jerusalem. The part we are here concerned about (vs. 51) is the sanctuary itself, not the courts or porches about it, which were rich, large, and beautiful. We are told that the sanctuary, or temple proper, was about ninety feet long, thirty feet wide and ninety feet high and that a three-story structure was built about it. The sanctuary was divided into two parts. The first sixty feet was the Holy Place where were the altar of incense, the golden candlesticks, and the table of shewbread. A great veil separated the Holy Place from the other one-third of the building, the Holy of Holies or the Most Holy Place. Originally the Holy of Holies had contained the ark of the covenant (a box plated with gold in which were two tables of stone on which the Ten Commandments had been written by God on Mount Sinai), Aaron's rod which budded, and a part of the manna which fell in the wilderness, miraculously preserved. The lid of the ark was called the Mercy Seat and overshadowing it were two figures of cherubim (Heb. 9:1-5). However, these things had been lost and some authorities say that at the time Christ died the ark of the covenant was gone as well as the two figures of cherubim whose wings had overspread the golden Mercy Seat.

The symbolism of these two places, the Holy Place and the Holy of Holies, is the same as those of the tabernacle in the wilderness which preceded Solomon's temple. Those with their furniture are described in Hebrews 9:1-7, and the rest of the chapter makes clear the symbolic meaning. They picture the temple in Heaven. The high priest was a type of Christ, and the blood carried into the Most Holy Place by the high priest was a type of the blood of Christ. The Holy of Holies represents a sanctuary in Heaven where Jesus entered with His own blood to make atonement for the sins of the world. The fact that the high priest went once a year alone with blood into the Holy of Holies, under the separating veil, was meant to signify that the way into the true Holy of Holies was not yet made known. When Christ died on the cross, therefore, "the veil of the temple was rent in twain from the top to the bottom" (vs. 51). Being torn, beginning at the top, was an indication that God Himself rent the veil. When Christ died, the way into the Holiest of All was made manifest (Heb. 9:7-12). With the death of Christ and the tearing of the veil, the dispensation of the law came to an end. The ceremonies and ordinances of the law pointing forward to the coming of the Saviour were fulfilled and nailed to the cross with Christ (Col. 2:14-17). That is the reason that now no Christian needs to be judged concerning the ceremonial laws of diet, holy days, the Sabbath, etc., which are a "shadow of things to come." Hebrews 10:19, 20 says, "Having therefore, brethren, boldness to enter into the holiest by the blood of Jesus, By a new and living way, which he hath consecrated for us, through the veil, that is to say, his flesh."

Compare verse 51 with Ephesians 2:11-18. "The middle wall of partition"* (Eph. 2:14) was the wall that separated the Court of the Gentiles from the Court of Israel and the indication is that when Christ died that partition wall was broken down at the same time the veil in the temple was rent in twain. Certainly that was true symbolically and likely it was true physically. When the veil was torn down, then every barrier between God and man was removed for those who are willing to come through the torn veil (the crucified Saviour).

361

1. The *priesthood* was dismissed, since Christ is our High Priest.

2. *Peacemaking sacrifices* are all over; "there remaineth no more sacrifice for sins" (Heb. 10:26). The blood of bulls and goats throughout all the centuries only pictured the blood of Christ which would finally settle the matter of sin for those who trust in Him. When Christ came, all the other ceremonies pointing toward His coming were fulfilled and we need no more to kill lambs or bullocks.

3. The barrier of a particular place is no more. Jesus had cried out to Jerusalem a few days before, "Behold, your house is left unto you desolate" (Matt. 23:38). That referred partly to the coming destruction of Jerusalem, but more, surely, to the fact that from this time forth people could approach God anywhere boldly, without animal sacrifices, without human priesthood, and without an earthly temple or tabernacle. Jesus had this in mind when He said to the woman at the well, "The hour cometh, when ye shall neither in this mountain, nor yet at Jerusalem, worship the Father... But the hour cometh, and now is, when the true worshippers shall worship the Father in spirit and in truth" (John 4:21, 23). Jews had been required for centuries to bring all their sacrifices to Jerusalem (Lev. 17:1-9). They had been commanded, "Bring ye all the tithes INTO THE STOREHOUSE, that there may be meat in mine house," that is, to the temple at Jerusalem (Mai. 3:10). After the death of Christ, after the veil was tom down, men were free to approach God anywhere and worship in the Spirit and not necessarily through types and shadows, priests and sacrifices and ceremonial laws.

4. The barrier of a chosen people is broken down, too. The particular meaning of Ephesians 2:11-18 is that now Jews and Gentiles alike may approach God and those who trust in Christ are in one body. Gentiles who trust in God are not now far off, but nigh. To be sure, God's promises to Israel as a nation will be fulfilled. There are some promises to the nation as a whole which will be certainly carried out at the second coming of Christ. But any individual Gentile is as free as any Jew to approach God for forgiveness and to have his prayers answered and to partake of the riches purchased for us by the Lord Jesus Christ. Meditate prayerfully on the entrance that is ours because the veil is tom in

two from the top to the bottom. It should give us boldness to walk in spirit into the Holy of Holies in Heaven where our perfect High Priest has entered before us and there makes our wants known (Heb. 4:14-16).

Compare verses 52 and 53 with I Corinthians 15:21 and 23 which indicates that no one was ever resurrected from the dead before Jesus came out of the tomb. Remember that Lazarus (John 11:43, 44), the widow's son of Nain (Luke 7:14, 15), Jairus' daughter (Matt. 9:24, 25) and a good many others (I Kings 17:20-23; II Kings 4:33-37; etc.) were brought back to life, but they did not receive resurrection bodies nor immortality but had the same kind of bodies they had had before death, and later died again. There is some difficulty about the case of Moses on the Mount of Transfiguration – we do not know whether he had temporarily a borrowed body or whether a physical body at all, but the Scripture indicates that no one was resurrected from the dead before the resurrection of Christ. Verse 53 here carefully specifies that some of the saints "came out of the graves *after his resurrection.*"

The reference of I Corinthians 15:23 to Christ as "the firstfruits" points back to the typical feast of the firstfruits in the Mosaic Law which the Jews had long observed (Lev. 23:10-12). That sheaf of grain, the firstfruits of the harvest, pictured the resurrection of Christ and doubtless of other saints who arose immediately "after his resurrection." Christ alone pictured the grain of wheat falling into the ground to die (John 12:24), "but if it die, it bringeth forth *much* fruit" and these saints evidently are a part of the fruit, the first sheaf of the harvest. The sheaf is plural, not singular, as Dr. Scofield points out. The rest of the harvest will be at the rapture, "Afterward they that are Christ's at his coming." These saints "appeared unto many" to prove that the Scripture was fulfilled, doubtless an added proof of the resurrection and therefore of the deity of Christ.

Ephesians 4:8, 9, quoting Psalm 68:18, seems to some students to refer to these saints who went to Heaven with Christ, when He ascended the day of His resurrection (John 20:17) – not the final ascension forty days later – to fulfill the type of the high priest carrying the blood of the lamb into the Holy of Holies.

The Roman centurion in charge of the crucifixion "and they that were with him" (vs. 54), evidently Roman soldiers or other Gentile officials, "feared greatly, saying, Truly this was the Son of God." Matthew Henry remarks how strange it is that hardened soldiers should be afraid when Jewish citizens were not and should be convinced though "they were Romans, Gentiles who knew not the Scriptures which were now fulfilled," when Jewish rabbis and leaders were not convinced. Already here, "blindness in part is happened to Israel" (Rom. 11:25) and from that time on Gentiles have received the Gospel more easily than Jews! It will be a glorious day when "the fulness of the Gentiles be come in. And so all Israel shall be saved" (Rom. 11:25, 26).

Surely every preacher has often thanked God for godly women, women who were quicker to hear the Gospel than their husbands, women whose gentle hands prepared the preachers' food, women who from slender purses ministered to them as these women did to Jesus. So the Shunammite woman took the part of Elisha and provided for him a little chamber on the wall, a bed, a table, a stool, and a candlestick (II Kings 4:10). Elisha was supported by the widow whose oil and meal did not fail until the famine was passed (II Kings 4:1-7). Abigail ministered to David of her substance, perceiving he was God's anointed, when her churlish husband Nabal refused (I Sam. 25:2-38). Paul remembered gratefully "those women which laboured with me in the gospel" (Rom. 16:1, 2; Phil. 4:3), and the aged John must have had a deep personal gratitude for the saintly woman, "the elect lady and her children, whom I love in the truth" (II John 1). Surely he had been entertained in their home, and his warning was that she not let modernists abuse her great hospitality (II John 10). Thus Jesus was comforted and ministered to and blessed by good women. These women (vss. 55, 56) had been prominent in His ministry, following Him from Galilee. Compare with Luke 8:2, 3 which show that the ministering included providing for His needs from their substance. How touching it is that Galilean women followed Jesus and that the gifts of faithful women provided His food even until the day He died!

Mary of Bethany had delighted to hear Him preach and He delighted to teach her (Luke 10:38-42). She alone, by faith, anointed Jesus for His burial (Matt. 26:12). These two Marys (vs. 56) watched where Jesus was buried (vs. 61) and came early three days later to the tomb (Matt. 28:1). It was principally women who followed Jesus to the cross weeping (Luke 23:27-29). While Jesus selected no women to be apostles or preachers, and plain

364

commands are given forbidding them to take the place of Christian leadership assigned to men (I Cor. 14:34, 35; I Tim. 2:11, 12), yet the Scriptures teach us that holy women loved Jesus and ministered to Him even when they did not understand His preaching. They wept at His cross even when they did not believe He would arise from the dead! How blessed when women lay at the feet of Jesus all the love and self- sacrifice and faith of which they are capable! And how miserably sad when women do not love womanhood's best Friend.

Verses 57-61 Joseph of Arimathaea, the Secret Disciple, Buries the Body of Jesus

Compare with parallel passages in Mark 15:42-47, Luke 23:50-56, and John 19:38-42. Joseph of Arimathaea was a counsellor (Mark 15:43; Luke 23:50), that is, a member of the council or Sanhedrin which had condemned Jesus to die, but Joseph had not consented to it (Luke 23:51). He was Jesus' disciple (vs. 57), "a good man, and a just" (Luke 23:50), but up to this time he was a disciple "secretly for fear of the Jews" (John 19:38). Imagine the agony in Joseph's mind during the crucifixion. It was ordered by the Sanhedrin of which he was a member. He had been earnestly looking for the kingdom of God (Mark 15:43; Luke 23:51). He was a good man and so had trusted Christ for salvation upon hearing Him. But his position in the Sanhedrin was at stake. The other Pharisees and Jewish leaders except only Nicodemus, who was also a secret disciple (John 19:39), hated Jesus. Joseph had kept his discipleship secret until with breaking heart he saw Jesus die on the cross. Then he went to Pilate and there for the first time confessed his discipleship. He "begged the body of Jesus" (vs. 58), "besought" (John 19:38), "craved" (Mark 15:43). With him went Nicodemus. Over against "secretly for fear of the Jews" (John 19:38), be sure to remember he "went in boldly unto Pilate, and craved the body of Jesus" (Mark 15:43). Pilate inquired of the centurion if Jesus had been a sufficient time dead (Mark 15:44) and gave the body to Joseph. It is rather remarkable that the things attending the death of Christ made Peter, the brave man, a coward, and made Joseph of Arimathaea, the coward, a brave man! In all the shameful record of the failure and sins of men in connection with the death of Christ, how sweet it is that Joseph finally came out boldly for Him.

Joseph had already hewn out his own tomb in the rock (vs. 60). This was in a garden near where Jesus was crucified (John 19:41) and they lay Jesus there nearby instead of making other plans, "because of the Jews' preparation day" (John 19:42). That is, it was the day when passover lambs for the nation were being slain, and at sunset would begin the annual high Sabbath (John 19:31; Exod. 12:14, 16) which began the seven days of unleavened bread.

Do not confuse this annual Sabbath, however, with the regular weekly Sabbath. We believe Jesus was crucified on Wednesday and the annual Sabbath was Thursday, beginning at sundown Wednesday, while the weekly Sabbath was on Saturday.

Notice that Joseph was a rich man (vs. 57). Compare this with "he made his grave with the wicked, and *with the rich in his death"* (Isa. 53:9). Perhaps in the same garden were the graves of many aristocratic, rich, and ruling Jews, very possibly other members of Joseph's family.

Verses 62-66 The Sepulchre Sealed, and Guard Set

Notice the contrast here: the wicked chief priests and Pharisees remembered the saying of Jesus, "After three days I will rise again" (vss. 62, 63), which prophecy Jesus had repeated in Matthew 12:40; 16:21, and 17:22, 23, but His own disciples seemed never to have thought of the promise until after Jesus was risen, then they would scarcely believe it. Doubtless the disciples had interpreted these promises of Jesus spiritually and symbolically instead of literally. Let this be a lesson as to how dangerous and wicked is the practice of explaining away Scriptures which conflict with our prejudices or previous opinions. To explain Scriptures by spiritualizing them instead of taking them at literal face value is a form of unbelief of which the disciples surely were guilty. Many today commit the same sin concerning the Scriptures which plainly promise the literal second coming of Christ, the rapture of the saints, the Great Tribulation, Christ's return in glory to reign, the regathering and conversion of Israel and His millennial kingdom.

Fear gripped the heart of the Pharisees. Their explanation in verse 64 must have been partly an excuse. Did they not fear that really He might rise? They had seen many miracles which He did. Yet how foolish to believe that the Roman seal and the Roman soldiers could prevent His resurrection!

But thanks be to God that all the precautions wicked men could take to prevent the resurrection of Christ only make us the more sure that He did rise.. The palsied soldiers, the broken seal, the stone rolled away are but the glad symbols of our Saviour's resurrection.

MATTHEW XXVIII

Verse 1 At Dawn Sunday the Two Marys Come to the Tomb

"In the end of the sabbath" – the American Standard Version says, "late on the sabbath day." However, Mark 16:1 says, "And when the sabbath was past"; Luke 24:1 plainly says, "Now upon the first day of the week," that is certainly after the Sabbath was past, and John's Gospel says the same thing, "The first day of the week" (John 20:1). The positive statements of Mark, Luke, and John show that it was really after the Sabbath was over when these women came to the sepulcher. The Sabbath ended at sundown Saturday evening, and the first day of the week began at that time. The next morning the women came to the sepulcher "as it began to dawn," "when it was yet dark" (John 20:1).

The term "the end of the sabbath" could be translated, we learn, "after the sabbath," and possibly that is the way it ought to be translated. However, since Matthew is written more especially for the Jews, it has more dispensational teaching than any of the other Gospels. The Scripture often has far deeper meaning than appears at once. So "in the end of the sabbath" may mean *the end of all the Jewish Sabbaths* and the end of the ceremonial law. Christ now arises from the dead. After this time no Christian is under obligation to keep the ceremonial law, including the Sabbath (Col. 2:14-17). Certainly the resurrection of Christ from the dead meant the end of all the Sabbaths, the end of the ceremonial law, since it was all nailed to His cross. He is the fulfillment of all the types and shadows. Jewish Christians later many times sought to hold on to the ceremonial law (Acts 15:1, 5). The whole matter was discussed by the apostles and elders at Jerusalem (Acts 15:6-22). There the apostles agreed that circumcision and the law of Moses, that is, the ceremonial laws, were not required of Gentile converts. The book of Galatians reveals that in the churches of the province of Galatia, Judaising teachers, converted Jews who clung to the old ceremonies, had mistaught the people, laying stress again on the ceremonial law, and the entire book is written to show that one who trusts in the resurrected Christ has no need for the ceremonial law.

Note that this is not the changing of the Sabbath from the seventh day to the first day of the week. *Sunday is not a Sabbath.* Sunday is the Lord's day, an entirely different day from the Sabbath. There is no Scripture anywhere commanding us to observe Sunday as Jews observed the Old Testament Sabbath. Our observing the Lord's day is a matter of grace and not of law, a matter of worship and not primarily of rest. We believe the day should be observed reverently as a day set apart, not like other days, yet we must be careful not to make it a matter of law as was the ceremonial Sabbath of the Jews. Jesus rose "in the end of the sabbath." Dr. Scofield's Reference Bible says on this verse, "Lit. *end of the sabbaths.* The sabbaths end, the first day comes" (margin).

If Jesus rose "in the end of the sabbaths" (plural), the Scripture may refer to two different Sabbaths on Thursday and Saturday. Of the Sabbath which began at sundown after Jesus died, we read, "that sabbath day was an high day." It was the annual Sabbath, the first day of the feast of unleavened bread, on which Jews were commanded "no manner of work shall be done in them..." a day of "an holy convocation" (Exod. 12:16). If that came on Thursday that year, as we believe, then a regular weekly Sabbath occurred on Saturday. So it was "in the end of the sabbaths," or after both sabbaths, which occurred, we believe, while Jesus was in the grave three days and three nights.

Only two women are mentioned in verse 1, but there were three present – Mary Magdalene, Mary the mother of James, and Salome (Mark 16:1). They are named in Matthew 27:56. The second Mary is Mary the mother of James the less and Joses, evidently the wife of Alphaeus (Matt. 10:3). The third woman, Salome, was "the mother of Zebedee's children" (Matt. 27:56), that is, the mother of the other James, and of John. There may have been others besides these three (Luke 23:55 with Luke 24:1). They came "bringing the spices which they had prepared" (Luke 24:1).

The order of events may seem confusing when you compare Matthew, chapter 28, with Mark, chapter 16, Luke, chapter 24, and the 20th chapter of John. If so, read carefully the following from the Scofield Reference Bible on this point:

The order of events, combining the four narratives, is as follows: Three women, Mary Magdalene, and Mary the mother of James, and Salome, start for the sepulchre, followed by other women bearing spices. The three find the stone rolled away, and Mary Magdalene goes to tell the disciples (Lk. 23:55— 24:9; John 20:1, 2). Mary, the mother of James and Joses, draws nearer the tomb and sees the angel of the Lord (Mt. 28:2). She goes back to meet the other women following with the spices. Meanwhile Peter and John, warned by Mary Magdalene, arrive, look in, and go away (John 20:3-10). Mary Magdalene returns weeping, sees the two angels and then Jesus (John 20:11-18), and goes as He bade her to tell the disciples. Mary (mother of James and Joses), meanwhile, has met the women with the spices and, returning with them, they see the two angels (Lk. 24:4, 5; Mk. 16:5). They also receive the angelic message, and, going to seek the disciples, are met by Jesus (Mt. 28:8-10).

Verses 2-4 The Resurrection of Christ

The earthquake and the resurrection occurred before the women approached the sepulcher, possibly had occurred some time before.

Matthew does not make it clear, but Mark 16:4, Luke 24:2, and John 20:1, 2 all state that the women found the tomb already open, with Jesus' body risen and gone.

We know certainly that Jesus was in the grave "three days and three nights" as He plainly promised that He would be (Matt. 12:40). We believe Jesus had died and had been taken down from the cross Wednesday night before sundown. He was buried sometime that night, wrapped in spices. On Thursday of that week, that is, at Wednesday night at sundown, the annual high Sabbath began (John 19:31), the special day of convocation and rest, beginning the seven days' feast of unleavened bread (Exod. 12:16). Christ our Passover (I Cor. 5:7) had been sacrificed for us at exactly the appointed time for the slaying of the pass-over lamb. Do not confuse that high Sabbath, an annual affair (which we believe came on Thursday that year) with the regular weekly Sabbath, Saturday. Christ was in the grave, evidently, Wednesday night and Thursday, Thursday night and Friday, Friday night and Saturday, and then sometime during the night Saturday, He came out of the grave. Christ had to fulfill the three days and three nights. He could be in the grave longer, but could not be less, we believe, to fulfill literally His promise of Matthew 12:40.

"And, behold, there was a great earthquake" (vs. 2). Compare this with the earthquake when Christ died (Matt. 27:51). Surely a connection is intended. The resurrection of Christ is as important as His death. A dead Christ could not save anybody. The resurrection is a part of the Gospel. "Christ died for our sins according to the scriptures" and also "rose again the third day according to the scriptures" (I Cor. 15:3, 4), and this constitutes the Gospel, God's plan of salvation, so Paul declares (I Cor. 15:1, 2).

Notice how the angel's face and garments shined (vs. 3). It was shining time! If ever an angel shined gloriously, it was this angel! Compare his glory with that of the transfigured Christ, however (Matt. 17:2), when "his face did shine as the sun, and his raiment was white as the light," and you will see that the glory of Christ far exceeds that of the angels. See also Revelation 1:13-17 and note how John fell as dead when he saw on the Isle of Patmos the ascended Christ in His glory. No wonder "the keepers did shake, and became as dead men" (vs. 4), when Christ arose from the dead!

Note how powerless were these men, Roman soldiers, set to guard the sealed tomb. Compare with John 18:6 where the mob and soldiers fell to the ground before Jesus when they came to take Him in the Garden of Gethsemane. They of Nazareth had been powerless to touch Jesus when they wished to kill Him (Luke 4:29, 30). The power of Jesus also explains John 7:32, 44, 46. Thus the resurrection of Christ proves that He did not have to die. No man took away His life, but He laid it down of Himself (John 10:18). Jesus told Pilate, "Thou couldest have no power at all against me, except it were given thee from above" (John 19:11).

Verses 5-7 The Angel Announces the Resurrection

The first words of the angel were, "Fear not ye." As one reads the appearances of angels to individuals in the Bible, one must be struck with the fact that repeatedly angels, when they approached men, must still their fears! Men are afraid of heavenly beings. Nothing could show better our natural depravity, our guilty distance from God than this truth, that we do not feel at home in the presence of heavenly angels. How well the natural heart knows that none of us could ever stand before God but for His mercy! When angels appeared to Jacob, he was afraid (Gen. 28:17). Gideon was afraid he would die when he learned that he had seen an angel (Judg. 6:22). Manoah, the father of Samson, expected to die when he had seen an angel, and was afraid (Judg. 13:21, 22). The sons of Oman feared when they saw an angel and hid themselves (I Chron. 21:20). Even David likewise was afraid of the sword of the angel (I Chron. 21:30). Zacharias was frightened when the angel appeared to him (Luke 1:11, 12). Mary was troubled at the sayings of the angel who appeared to her (Luke 1:29). The shepherds, keeping watch over their flocks by night, "were sore afraid" when the angel of the Lord came to them, and the glory of the Lord shone round about them (Luke 2:9). Besides this occasion at the tomb of the resurrected Saviour, angels spoke to men, saying, "Fear not" in Judges 6:23; Luke 1:13, 30 and Acts 27:24.

Angels are perfect heavenly beings whose task is to be loving servants of Christians. They are "ministering spirits, sent forth to minister for them who shall be heirs of salvation" (Heb. 1:14). They are invisible to us, possibly partly because of our worldliness and sin. They appeared to some Bible characters and perhaps they now appear to some lowly-in-heart Christians. Little children have guardian angels (Matt. 18:10). Angels love us and surround us and camp around us to keep us from danger (II Kings 6:15-17; Ps. 34:7). They must feel some grief that we think so little about them, do not believe in their presence, or if men see them, are always afraid! It seems as though the constant message of angels to us who are the children of God is, "Fear not!" So this heavenly being, sitting on the stone which was taken away from the door of the tomb, said to those who came to see Jesus, "Fear not."

Notice the message of the angel in verses 5, 6, and 7. First, there is comfort, "Fear not." Second, there is understanding, "I know that ye seek Jesus, which was crucified." Third, there is explanation, "He is not here: for he is risen." Fourth, there is rebuke, "He is risen, as *he said!*" Fifth, there is the same tender compassion and willingness to prove Himself that God always has for troubled, inquiring, doubting hearts, "Come, see the place where the Lord lay." Sixth, there is urgent command, "Go quickly," etc. Seventh, there is a glorious promise, "Behold, he goeth before you into Galilee; *there shall ye see him*"!

Notice that the same Jesus "which was crucified" (vs. 5) is the one whom the angel declared "is risen" (vs. 6). It was a literal, bodily resurrection of the dead. There was no body left in the tomb of Joseph! There is no resurrection unless the body of Christ literally came out of the grave. The same body had the scars of the nails in His hands and feet and the wound of the spear in the side when Jesus appeared to His disciples (John 20:20, 27; Luke 24:40).

People who prattle about "a spiritual resurrection" talk willful or ignorant folly. Only the body was buried in Joseph's tomb and only the body could be resurrected. The spirit of Jesus He commended to the Father, "into thy hands I commend my spirit" (Luke 23:46). To the penitent thief Jesus said, "To day shalt thou be with me in paradise" (Luke 23:43). So the spirit was not buried. Only the body was buried, and only a bodily resurrection would be a resurrection at all.

"Come, see the place where the Lord lay." God deliberately prevented the scribes and Pharisees from seeing the resurrection of the Saviour. Wicked-hearted rebels against God who were not willing to do the will of God, He turned over to a reprobate mind that they might believe a lie and be damned (Rom. 1:28; II Thess. 2:11, 12). When people harden their hearts, God hardens the heart further. When people are not willing to do the will of God, God does not care to show them His will. But thank God for the teaching which abounds in the Bible, that honest hearts, however doubting and fearful, may put God to a test and learn what they need to know. To die two disciples of John who followed Him, Jesus said, "Come and see" (John 1:39). Philip could not win the brilliant-minded, unbelieving Nathanael, but he said, "Come and see" (John 1:46), and Nathanael came and Jesus proved Himself more than Nathanael had hoped to find! Often the best work new converts can do is to say like Philip, "Come and see," and like the woman in Samaria who said to her companions, "Come, see a man, which told me all things that ever I did: is not this the Christ" (John 4:29). They that are willing to do His will shall know the truth (John 7:17). So here the angel said, "Come and see." Later, doubting Thomas did not believe that the Saviour was resurrected, so Jesus offered the evidence of His wounded hands, feet, and side.

Thus, one may read this who has doubts about some great matter taught in the Bible. You can know for a certainty whether the Bible is the Word of God, whether Christ is the Son of God, whether God's promises are true. Only accept the blessed invitation of the angel to "come and see." The Bible will stand the test of investigation. God's promises will prove themselves when you meet them. We may be sure that the only people in the world who doubt the resurrection of Jesus Christ are those who do not accept the invitation to "come and see." God will reveal Himself to all who seek Him with the whole heart.

These women who went to tell the disciples that Jesus was risen from the dead must be able to say, "We saw the place where the Lord lay!" Likewise, the twelve apostles were to give constant, personal witness of their knowledge of the resurrection of Jesus Christ (Acts 1:22). These apostles knew the importance of firsthand, eyewitness testimony as to the fact of the Gospel. And repeatedly through the book of Acts they were to give their witness to the resurrection of the Saviour. In fact, hardly a sermon was ever preached, it seems, without a reference to the resurrection of Christ. See for instance Acts 2:24-36; 3:15, 26; 4:2-10, 33; 5:30-33; 10:40, 41; 13:30, 31, 33, 34, 37; 17:3, 18, 31, 32; 23:6; 26:8, 23. It appears that the resurrected Christ was the constant theme of those who had seen the empty tomb or had seen Christ.

Notice particularly that Paul often gave his experience of meeting the resurrected Christ on the road to Damascus. That was evidence to Paul that He was literally risen from the dead and so was the Son of God. Remember that Jesus Himself gave His resurrection from the dead as the positive proof of His deity (Matt. 12:39, 40; 16:4; Rev. 1:18). So, Romans 1:4 says, Jesus was "declared to be the Son of God with power... by the resurrection from the dead." The importance of the resurrection is indicated, too, in that it was as much a part of the Gospel as the death of Christ, as mentioned by Paul in I Corinthians 1:1-4. The eyewitnesses of the resurrection are counted very important as you see from Paul's argument (I Cor. 15:5-8).

"He goeth before you into Galilee." Why into Galilee? Why did not Jesus appear to all the disciples in Jerusalem? Because His public ministry in Jerusalem was now finished and He will not come to Jerusalem publicly any more to appear to the multitudes until His Second Coming to the earth when they shall say, "Blessed is he

374

that cometh in the name of the Lord." See particularly Matthew 23:37-39. Then Matthew 24:1 tells how Jesus went out and departed from the temple, and that was the end of His public ministry before His crucifixion. Thereafter He walked with His disciples and taught them and comforted them, but had no public meetings with the multitude.

All the twelve apostles were Galileans (Acts 2:7). Jesus appeared to His disciples in the upper room (John 20:19) in Jerusalem, and it was outside Jerusalem that forty days later from the Mount of Olives He ascended to Heaven (Acts 1:9). But here in Jerusalem He was seen, we suppose, by only a few. The "above five hundred brethren" (I Cor. 15:6) were those assembled in Galilee. It seems likely that a larger proportion of those in Galilee, where Jesus had had an extended ministry, believed on Him, than was the case elsewhere.

Verses 8-10 The Two Marys Meet Jesus Himself

Note the awe, the tremulous joy in verse 8. These good women "departed quickly" and "did run" to tell the disciples. There was good news indeed! They were convinced and yet frightened. Praise the Lord, some things almost too good to be true *are* true!

I believe there is a connection between this glad, swift obedience of these women and the fact that Jesus Himself met them. When they obeyed what light they had, Jesus gave them further evidence. He appeared to them Himself. And we may be sure that our doubts will disappear if we stay steadfastly in the road of obedience. I have found it sadly true that unbelief lives in an atmosphere of disobedience. If you begin to have doubts about the Bible, about God, you may be sure that sin has entered into your life. You are displeasing God. The obedient heart that runs quickly to do the command of God will meet Jesus in person and have the full, glad assurance that he needs!

I once was led to doubt whether the Bible was all true. Science, so-called, contradicted the Bible. The late William Jennings Bryan led me to make a new and bold investigation of the Bible to see if its claims were so. Thank God, I found that it is true. Since then, many times I have put God to the test and He has proved Himself. Dear troubled, doubting Christian, run quickly to do the least command of the Lord, and He will settle all your fears and doubts with the blessed assurance of His presence.

What a glad meeting in verse 9. Dear, good women, they held Him by the feet and worshiped Him! I am sure they felt they could hardly let Him go! And it was a joyful occasion for Jesus, too. The greeting of Jesus, "All hail" as given in the King James Version (vs. 9), is literally in the Greek, "O joy!" Can you imagine the triumphant, glorious joy in the heart of our Saviour as He defeated death, Hell, and the grave and came forth? The suffering was past, the triumph had come! Now to see His beloved disciples again! We are accustomed to thinking of God's mercy and God's grace toward us in that He provides for us. We ought also to remember that He delights in us. Strange as it may seem, we are lovely and attractive, we who have trusted Christ, in the eyes of our dear Saviour. If we ever long to see the Saviour's face, then let us remember that He longs, much more, to see ours! We talk about the joy of Heaven, but we ought to remember that Christ will have great joy there, too. It was that joy that He set before His face when He went to the crucifixion, "who for the joy that was set before him endured the cross, despising the shame" (Heb. 12:2). Isaiah 53:11 says, "He shall see of the travail of his soul, and shall be satisfied."

So Jesus was delighted here and shouted, "O joy!" when He saw these women who were dear to Him. The love that Christ has for us is not merely that pitying compassion we bestow upon the poor and the filthy and the unlovely. Rather, Jesus exalts us to be His friends, His brothers, and children of God. We are heirs of God and joint heirs with Christ. He delights in us!

There is a sweet touch here, too, in that Jesus sent a special message to His brethren (vs. 10), His half brothers, born of Mary and Joseph after Jesus was born. These brothers had not before believed in Christ (John 7:5). Jesus loved these brothers. They were probably saved at the crucifixion, for in the first chapter of Acts we find that they are in the small company with the disciples and their mother, waiting and praying for the Holy Spirit to come upon them in power (Acts 1:14). Mark 16:7 also reports that Jesus said, "Go tell my disciples and Peter..." Poor, backslidden Peter may no longer have felt that he was a disciple, so the compassionate Saviour mentioned him by name.

376

Verses 11-15 The Chief Priests Bribe the Soldiers to Say Christ's Body Was Stolen

The watch of Roman soldiers had been so frightened they "became as dead men" (vs. 4). That watch had been set and the tomb had been sealed with a Roman seal, because the chief priests had feared, and now their worst fears were realized. The chief priests had claimed to Pilate that they feared the disciples would steal away the body of Jesus. Doubtless, they had also a secret fear that Jesus would rise from the dead. They knew His plain promises about that (Matt. 27:62-66). Therefore, when the startling news came that the Saviour had literally risen from the dead, they at once called a meeting of the Sanhedrin (vs. 12). They had already confessed that if Jesus should rise from the dead, "the last error shall be worse than the first" (Matt. 27:64). Their fears for their wicked, hypocritical system and for their leadership over the people were well grounded. They could not keep the resurrection a secret.

Notice how the soldiers were bribed (vs. 12) to say that the disciples stole away the body of Jesus. They spread that lie and it was commonly reported among the Jews long years and today some believe it.

We may be sure that those who want to believe a lie will be allowed to do so. God hides Himself in the thick darkness from wicked, rebellious hearts. To those hungry to see Him, the Lord Jesus appeared in person. To those who wished He had remained in the grave, Jesus did not show Himself.

The evidence of the resurrection of Christ is overwhelming. The fact that the doubting disciples themselves were convinced, that above five hundred brethren saw Jesus at one time (I Cor. 15:6), the transformation in the life of Paul, the rapid growth of Christianity among those who had the evidence before them, the transforming power of faith in Christ today – all these things prove that Jesus did literally rise from the dead as the Scriptures say.

Verses 16-20 Jesus Meets the Disciples in Galilee, Gives the Great Commission

The Gospel of Matthew does not give the story of the ascension of Jesus which was from the Mount of Olives. This meeting was in Galilee (vs. 16) in a mountain where Jesus had appointed them. We suppose that only saved disciples of Jesus saw Him after His resurrection. There is no record of His speaking to or appearing to unsaved people. It is likely that His brothers were converted at the crucifixion or on hearing of His resurrection, and that when Jesus saw them, they were already Christians.

"Some doubted", (vs. 17). Surely none of the eleven. Others must have been present. Jesus had revealed Himself to the apostles in the upper room the same day He rose from the dead (John 20:19-23). Thomas alone evidently had not been present, and Jesus saw him a week later (John 20:24-29). All the eleven had seen Jesus. Therefore, these doubters must have been other Christians who had been notified to come and yet who could hardly believe that Jesus was risen from the dead. That is not surprising as it was true of all the disciples at first.

Verses 18 to 20 are properly called "The Great Commission." Compare this with Mark 16:15-18, Luke 24:46-48, and Acts 1:8.

Verse 18 shows the great central fact behind all proper Christian activities. All power (literally, all authority) is given to Jesus Christ, both in Heaven and in earth. He is Lord of all. Every true Christian must acknowledge Jesus as Lord. All Christian work to please God must be subject to the will of Christ and under His direction. One can not be a Christian believing that Jesus is only a man. He is the Son of God, the Lord of Heaven and earth. We are not to choose our own message but take what is given us. We are not to choose where we go or what we do. We are not to set our own rewards. All those are in the hands of our dear Saviour, the Lord Jesus Christ.

Notice the three parts in the Great Commission. First, we are to make disciples. The word "teach" in verse 19 is literally "to make disciples," to get people saved. Second, new converts are to be baptized. Third, new converts are to be taught to observe all the commands which Christ had given the apostles (vs. 20). So every convert has this same Great Commission.

378

These words, which Jesus commanded in verses 19 and 20, are among the most far-reaching in the Bible. Every Christian, every preacher, every church should follow this plan, getting people saved, getting them baptized, teaching them to get people saved and baptized and sent to win souls. God's plan can never be improved upon.

Note the extent of this Great Commission. It is literally for "all nations" (vs. 19). There will never be any change in dispensations, no difference in the plan of salvation nor Christian duty between one nation and another. The Gospel is the same to all nations. Notice again it is to continue to "the end of the world," literally to the consummation of this age. Do not listen to anybody who would tell you that since Christ gave this commission there has been a change in His plans, either in the plan of salvation, the duty of new converts to be baptized, the mode of baptism, or the soul-winning duty of Christians.

Baptism is to be for converts all through the ages. There are those who teach that baptism was for Jews only. Others teach that baptism was to last only during a "transition period." There is nothing in the Bible to indicate anything of the kind. In fact, the Saviour here plainly commands that as long as people are to be converted, they are to be baptized.

There is to be no change in Christian duty. Notice that every new convert is to be taught "to observe all things whatsoever I have commanded *you,*" that is, the commands that Jesus gave for the apostles to observe. The same commands are to be observed by every new convert and they are to be so taught. People today should pray like those in Bible times. They should have the same kind of answers to prayer. We should preach the same Gospel; we should have the same kind of conversion; we should baptize people the same way; we should teach them to live the same kind of lives. There has been no dispensational change since Jesus gave the Great Commission, and there will be no change at all until He comes again, until the consummation of the age. Soul winning will always be the first duty.

If we adhere with all our hearts to Matthew 28, verses 18 to 20, we have the antidote to modernism. There can be no modernism that acknowledges the deity and Lordship of Jesus Christ, and which sincerely attempts to follow out His Great Commission, His plan Id all the nations to the end of the world.

Notice that people are to be baptized "in the name of the Father, and of the Son, and of the Holy Ghost." The word "name" is singular. That is an indication that the three are one. Here the doctrine of the Trinity is clearly taught. Be sure to note that there is no difference between being baptized in the name of the Father, and of the Son, and of the Holy Ghost as commanded here, and being baptized "in the name of the Lord Jesus" (Acts 19:5). God did not change His plan. One who is baptized in the name of Jesus is baptized in the name of the Father, and of the Son, and of the Holy Ghost.

Christian, do you yourself try to follow the New Testament standard of observing all things whatever Christ commanded His apostles? Let us be satisfied with nothing less than an earnest attempt to follow the pattern given the apostles and really be New Testament Christians.

Note the duty of Christians and churches to train young converts. It is our duty to teach them the Bible. It is our duty to teach them to live right, to pray, to win souls, to study the Bible, to be filled with the Spirit. It is sinful to drop new converts after they are converted without having them baptized, and it is still short of the will of God, when they are baptized, not to teach them further duties of the Christian life. Particularly converts are to be taught to win souls. That is one reason Christians should band themselves together in churches, local congregations, for every new convert needs to be cared for, baptized, and taught to serve God according to the New Testament standard.

Blessed promise of Jesus, "...lo, I am with you alway, even unto the end of the world." Dear friend, if you are wholeheartedly surrendered to the will of Christ in this Great Commission work, getting souls saved, getting them baptized, teaching them to observe all that Christ has commanded, then you may be sure that the Lord Jesus Christ is with you, very near at hand! The joy of a wholehearted surrender to Christ and in His will is that He Himself will be your constant Companion. Jesus promised His disciples, "If a man love me, he will keep my words: and my Father will love him, and we will come unto him, and make our abode with him" (John 14:23).

Every student of the book of Matthew will see its dispensational character. There are certain things taught about the coming kingdom of Heaven, and the reign of Christ on earth is perhaps made clearer in this than in the other Gospels. In some sense this Gospel was directed especially to Jews. But it is important that no one be guilty of overemphasizing the dispensational teaching in Matthew. The book of Matthew is written for us today. It is for Gentiles as well as Jews; it is for this age as well as apostolic times. The Great Commission is in force until the Saviour comes again. Let us take the blessed promises of this Book as ours and the blessed commands as they were intended to be taken.

May I suggest that the study of Matthew will have been helpful if it results in Christians' winning souls in the power of the Holy Spirit, carrying out the Great Commission and getting souls won to God. If your study of this book makes you a soul winner, makes you a missionary, then your study shall not have been in vain. Now may the grace of our Lord Jesus Christ be with you always. Amen.

Made in the USA
Lexington, KY
22 April 2018